Why Bitmapped Graphics? Why The Revolutionary Guide?

Everywhere you look, computers are springing up, taking over the accounts department, monopolizing the secretary's day, controlling the look of the revolutionary new car design. Each of these computers must have an interface with the outside world, which is where The Revolutionary Guide to Bitmapped Graphics comes in.

With this book, you will learn how to control that interface, covering text, stills and moving images as well as the hardware that enables these interesting and often amazing sights to appear. This book is not designed for the computer novice. A grasp of C/C++ is essential. Knowledge of Assembly Language will also come in handy, though the tutorial chapter will provide you with a quick reminder of everything you need to know.

Bitmapped Graphics and the control of the user/computer interface have become essential components of all software/hardware packages on the market today. Stop being tied to what someone else wants you to see, go on, set your VDU free!

What is Wrox Press?

Wrox Press is a computer book publisher which promotes a brand new concept - clear, jargon-free programming and database titles that fulfill your real demands. We publish for everyone, from the novice through to the experienced programmer. To ensure our books meet your needs, we carry out continuous research on all our titles. Through our dialog with you we can craft the book you really need.

We welcome suggestions and take all of them to heart - your input is paramount in creating the next great Wrox title. Use the reply card inside this book or mail us at:

feedback@wrox.demon.co.uk
or
Compuserve 100063, 2152

Wrox Press Ltd.   Tel: (312) 465 3559
2710 W. Touhy   Fax: (312) 465 4063
Chicago
IL 60645
USA

The Revolutionary Guide to Bitmapped Graphics

Control-Zed

Wrox Press Ltd.®

The Revolutionary Guide to Bitmapped Graphics

© 1994 Control-Zed

Published by Wrox Press Ltd. 1334 Warwick Road, Birmingham, B27 6PR UK
Library of Congress Catalog No: 94-78389
ISBN 1-874416-31-1

Trademark Acknowledgements

Wrox has endeavored to provide trademark information about all the companies and products mentioned in this book by the appropriate use of capitals. However, Wrox cannot guarantee the accuracy of this information.

Credits

Author
Control-Zed

Technical Editor
Julian Dobson

Series Editor
Gordon Rogers

Technical Reviewers
Matt Nottingham
Jim Pratt
Dave Bolton
David Judge
Dave Stone
John Mclernon

Additional Material
Rosemary Lockie

Managing Editor
John Franklin

Language Editor
Deb Somers

Production Manager
Gina Mance

Book Layout
Ewart Liburd
Eddie Fisher
Greg Powell

CD Authoring
James Hare
Darren Gill

Proof Readers
Pam Brand
Graham McLaughlin

Cover Design
Third Wave

For more information on Third Wave, contact Ross Alderson on 44-21 456 1400
Cover photo supplied by Pictor International

Control-Zed Acknowledgements

Pete:
Months ago, when the book was still in progress, I started dreaming of the blessed moment to come when I would sit and type up my acknowledgments. Now, in a couple of days time, Rev BMG is to go to the printers, and the only thing left to do is thank various people and God.

As I am not the only (or even the main) author of this book, I'd like to first of all mention the guys from Control-Zed who I worked with. Was it the team spirit that glimmered in their eyes when I used to come in late to work? I acknowledge my wife's repulsion to me working hard. It stimulated me to work harder to get it done quicker. I'm also thankful to Dr. M for pulling me off the computer in the evenings - in his admirable fashion!

Yuri:
I want to thank the other Control-Zed guys for doing all the wording and writing and leaving me the time to code things up. If there are bugs, I'm happy: it means I'm still human.

Kilothanks to my family, who missed me for days and still fed me. Thanks to my best friend Sergey Shkredov who kept my mind in order and fought my brain-draining.

Igor:
I'm very grateful to my wife for supporting my life and work, and to my kids for not playing football on my desktop. Thanks also to the other Control-Zed guys for putting up with my idea of work.

Efim:
I'm thankful to my wife and daughter for their patience, and to the Control-Zed fellows for getting me into this business. Also to my brother Pavel for translating some of my programs into C++, a powerful language indeed!

Sergey:
I'd like to thank my wife, for understanding that writing this book would point me in a more valuable direction.

Theodor:
Thanks to all who have been by my side for the last 26 years.

****

We are all grateful to the respectable Graphics Guru for his guidance and to Deb Somers for her careful copy-editing and for looking after our various interests.

The Authors

Control -Zed

Peter Kalatchin	:	^Z special agent out there
Igor Chebotko	:	general systemizer
Efim Podvoiski	:	system fractalizer
Sergey Velikevich	:	mathematical upper
Yuri Kiselev	:	insider
Theodor Ryabov	:	^Z special side viewer

SUMMARY OF CONTENTS

CONTENTS

CONTENTS

Introduction

Welcome to 'The Revolutionary Guide to Bitmapped Graphics'. In this book, we have tried to illustrate all the techniques that you may find useful when playing around with your graphics card's capabilities. We cover both hardware and software elements of the subject area, and provide sample code to add some flesh to the points that we make. However, before we get into the thick of things, let's look at the foundations this book is based on.

Who Should Read On?

This book is designed primarily for those programmers who have a working knowledge of the C and C++ languages. Some knowledge of Assembly language may also be useful, but it's not essential, as we've include an Assembly language refresher in Chapter 2.

However, if you don't know any of these languages, then don't get disheartened. This book is written for all programmers, to explain morphing, merges and manipulations, with all the explanations, diagrams, source code and equations to make the ideas crystal clear.

Conventions Used in this Book

This book frequently 'quotes' from actual programs in order to help you follow the overall structures and the processes they deal with. The complete program source code appears on the CD-ROM. Other conventions for the information in the text include:

Any code that appears in the book is presented as follows:

```
float spherical_texture(float phi, float theta)
{
   int x,y;
   x = round(theta/pi* (real_picture_pointer->column_number-1)+1);
   y = round(phi/pi*(real_picture_pointer->row_number-1)+1);
   return 0.99*(real_picture_pointer->pict[0][y][x] /255.0)+ 0.01;
}
```

Any important words that are particularly relevant to the section in which they appear are like this:

These **words** are **important.**

Any additional information is separated from the text, in one of two ways, depending on the information's importance:

> Text like this is very important to the section.

> While text like this, is additional information for your interest and enjoyment.

We have attempted to break up the text with appropriate headings

▲ and with the judicious bulleting of lists

Any references to **code** in the text appear like this, and if the name of a file is mentioned, it will appear as **WROX.CPP.**

All the tables and figures have an appropriate descriptive title, and last, but not least, the book comes with comments from the Graphics Guru. The

Graphics Guru is our mentor, the oracle that we turn to in times of crisis, for timely advice and a word of encouragement. These comments have been included in the text, along with an image of the Great One, in the hope that they help you as much as they helped us.

 Welcome to my world of color and movement!

Programmers stop typing, start designing!

What's on the CD-ROM?

On the accompanying CD-ROM, we have included all the source code that is contained in the book... plus a lot, lot more. In fact, in the book we have attempted to keep the code down to a minimum. If we had included it all in the text, we would have had a 5,000 page book rather than a 500 page one!

We have also included executables of the examples, so even if you don't have a compiler you can still have some fun. For those of you with older video cards that are not VESA compliant, we've included a selection of TSR's to correct this shortcoming. As an added bonus, for those of you with Windows 3.1 and above, we have included the complete book as a multimedia file. Multimedia Viewer is also included if you don't have this already on your system (see below for installation).

There are several **.AVI** files that you can play for your entertainment, that illustrate the complete packages that you can put together..

Installing Multimedia Viewer

This is how to install the source code:

▲ Start Microsoft Windows

▲ Insert the Source Disk into your CD drive, (say d).

▲ From the File menu, choose Run

▲ Type **d:\cd_book\setup** and press *Enter*

▲ Then follow the on-screen prompts

Using The Multimedia Viewer

When you run the Multimedia Viewer, you will get the opening sequence, courtesy of Wrox Press. This sequence is produced using the effects mentioned throughout the book, and leads on to the first opening screen of the viewer as shown overleaf:

Behold the power of Bitmapped Graphics

However, as a more descriptive comment on how to use the viewer, see the screenshot shown below:

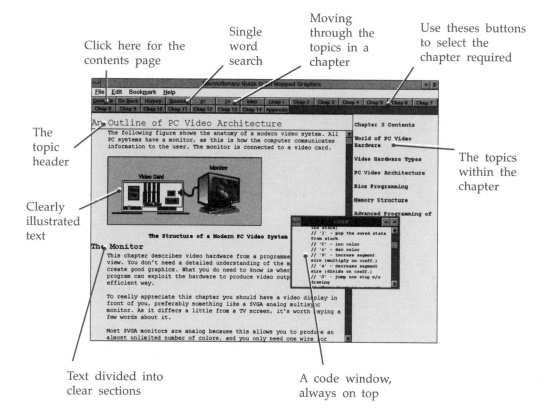

Click here for the contents page

Single word search

Moving through the topics in a chapter

Use theses buttons to select the chapter required

The topic header

The topics within the chapter

Clearly illustrated text

Text divided into clear sections

A code window, always on top

So Let's Go...

So without more ado, let's enter this fascinating world of computer graphics, storm the bastion of graphics card hardware, and plunge into the pool of animation, morphing and 3D images. Graphics revolution, here we come...

Bitmapped Graphics
An Overview

In this chapter, we'll cover the basics of the world of Computer Graphics, introducing you to the jargon, the history and the stimulus for this book. We cover all the major aspects of Computer Graphics that will appear throughout the book, together with some examples to whet your appetite.

Chapter Contents

In this chapter, we will cover the following:

▲ The differences between raster and vector images

▲ An historical overview of bitmapped graphics

▲ A look into the world of three dimensional graphics

▲ A few notes on how to create realistic images

▲ Some interesting words on the subject of animation

Who is this book for?

'Everything that is visible is seen somewhere, sometimes,
Everything that is invisible will also become visible
somehow, somewhere.'

A thought provoking saying from the Graphics Guru.

A long time ago, computers were just used to calculate things. Now we usually use them to show us information in different and varied ways, on a variety of subjects, some of which include:

 texts and graphs

 science and art

the past and the future

from macro environments to atomic structures.

Although many of these methods of viewing the information were available long before the idea of computers, Computer Graphics (CG), together with the speed that computers can handle instructions, means that seeing your information in any format is now not such a headache. How many of you have used the graph facility included with most spreadsheets? In just a few seconds, you can change the type of graph, its orientation, or even the data that is displayed - all with just a click of a button. With pen and paper, any of these a tasks would have taken anything from a few minutes to several hours!

The world is an exciting place because people are constantly looking for new ways to reveal the invisible. Maybe you don't realize just how exciting this can be, but keep reading and find out!

CG is now the most expressive and simple computer 'language'. By language we mean not the way the user programs a computer, but how the computer conveys information to the user. But, if it is that simple, why do we need to write a book about it? The results of CG magic are plain for all to see, but they are only the tip of the iceberg; mathematicians, software and hardware developers, and even the occasional philosopher, are all working together to create the perfect end result.

CG is a sophisticated technology supported by many applications such as PhotoStyler and PhotoFinish, CorelDraw, AnimatorPro and 3D Studio to name but a few. Some aren't so powerful, some aren't as substantial as others, and some are quickly superseded. New approaches and ideas arise from time to time but it should be remembered that the basic ideas and methods remain the same.

We decided that an appropriate subtitle for this book should be 'The *Summa* of Computer Graphics Technologies'. This is obviously quite a difficult task because each chapter is a book in its own right, which is why we decided to give you a wide variety of routines, algorithms and ideas. First we'll deal with hardware before moving on to the software issues. We'll be looking at some of the methods used to solve the complex problems involved in showing the real and imaginary parts of the CG world.

The Miracle Graphics Machine

But we still haven't answered the question, "Who is this book for?" It is for those people who have looked at the picture above and would like to know what is going on inside. Just turn the page and see!

Have you looked? It's only a joke but many complex CG miracles are really based on ideas that are as simple as this.

What will you learn from this book? Well, possibly you'll become more self-confident using CG, or perhaps you'll acquire a 'spell book' to guide you into that magic world of Computer Graphics. You may even get some ideas that could further your career. After all, the subject of CG itself is exciting, and wouldn't it be wonderful to learn how to make interesting and funny things appear on a PC's screen?

So, shall we begin? Whenever we need to think something over, we'll remember the CG Guru's advice:

'Everything that is visible is seen somewhere, sometimes,
Everything that is invisible will also become visible
somehow, somewhere.'

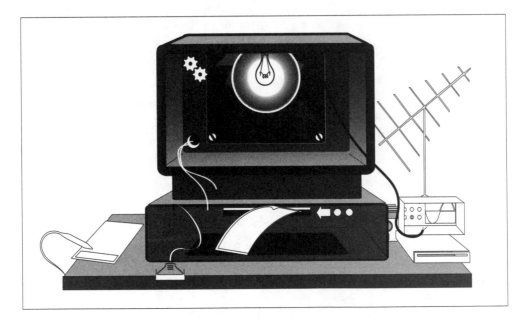

The Miracle Graphics Machine - The Inside Story

Some Tips on How the Book is Arranged

This book is divided into two parts; the first deals mostly with hardware and hardware-level routines. We will use Assembly language as the basis for these chapters as it is more efficient than C (even if C is double crossed), Pascal or FORTRAN and we want to show you how to get the most out of your hardware.

The second part introduces you to some abstract and some practical ideas. Sophisticated and detailed algorithms, which are given both in pseudo code and in C, are used to express these ideas. We'll try to avoid long listings in C as nobody finds them light reading, and you can find the entire code for all the examples on the companion disk.

Taking all this into account, we have decided not to include a C or C++ language tutorial in this book. Most programmers know C or C++, and if not, there are plenty of books on the subject. If your Assembler is a little rusty or non-existent, we have provided an Assembly language run down in Chapter 2, not as a comprehensive tutorial for the language, but as a stop gap to get you through the code that appears in this book. If you want more than just a stop gap, or Chapter 2 inspires you to learn more, then we would highly recommend 'The Revolutionary Guide to Assembly Language' as the book to read.

We've also decided to offer you some of our SI_LI_CON (SI(mple), LI(ttle) and CON(venient) by nature) PRIBOMBAS (Russian programmer's slang for demos). Some of the programs on offer are more than that, and these living applications, with their DOS Graphical User Interface (GUI), are based on the routines and ideas described in this book. We will be putting theory into practice, when for example, we look at:

- ▲ Loading and storing images to and from the most popular formats, as well as images manipulating, editing and printing

- ▲ Generating fractal landscapes, while making them come alive with grass, flowers and trees, or in other words, just about everything under the fractal sky

- ▲ And the means of morphing one image into another.

Raster Verses Vector

Over the course of CG history, little has changed, with vector and raster (read bitmap) technologies taking up opposite corners of the graphics squared circle. Their differences need to be explained and we must underline the key advantages of both approaches. Most of the topics covered in this book are simply ways to overcome the limitations of bitmap techniques, some of which vector graphics never had.

Internal Image Representation

The vector and bitmap graphic systems use completely different internal representations. A vector drawing system stores a graphic object as a set of primitives. For a line, the vector systems primitives are the two pairs of coordinates, a color, style and possibly thickness. The primitives that make up the object are arranged in a user-defined order, so that when they are output in that order, the correct image is displayed.

Correct Verses Incorrect Ordering of Primitives

The raster drawing system represents an image as a 2 dimensional (2D) array, where the values contained in the array identify the color, or gray scale, for the corresponding areas in the image. The small rectangular area of the image, called a pixel (Picture Element) was, until recently, the only primitive element of the raster system.

A complete 2D memory array is called a bitmap.

So with raster systems, you simply have an addressable 2D array rather than a complicated hierarchy of primitives. The Central Processing Unit (CPU) handles the bitmap in the same way as other addressable memory. The video hardware itself refreshes the screen by re-displaying the visible portion of the bitmap.

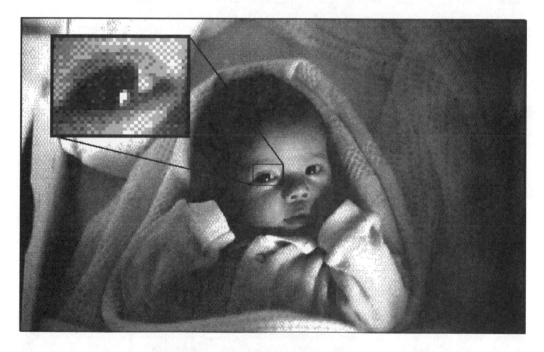

Bitmap Representation of an Image

Image Entry Methods

There are two different sources of computer images. Images are either generated within the machine or they are imported by some means.

Vector systems use some kind of data entry (either from the keyboard or the mouse) for the graphics primitives. You can 'easily' define and enter complex curves, text, and so on, so it relies mostly on image generation. Each method you use to import an image into the vector system, except those of compatible vector representation, contains a stage of raster-to-vector conversion. Sometimes you will do this conversion physically, with the help of a digitizer, and sometimes you will need to apply sophisticated algorithms; whichever way you use, it is a long and boring procedure.

Raster based systems use the same methods of image generation, and sometimes have even more flexible methods. Put this together with a wide scanning range and you will never get any problems, at least for black and white images.

Image Manipulation

The internal computational models of vector and raster technologies are completely different. The vector system relies on a quick transformation and fast drawing of the primitives.

> Note that the vector representation is converted into a bitmap for the computer to display it.

For the raster system, it's simply a question of addressing memory, together with an image independent method of display and large numbers of possible raster operations.

> **The costs of vector operations are roughly proportional to the number of primitives involved, whereas the costs of raster operations are roughly proportional to the area changed.**

The methods for spatial transformations involved in translations, rotations, and scaling are clearly distinguishable between the two systems. Both technologies provide such transformations, but each with differing effects. The vector system applies representation scaling, rotation and translation with almost arbitrary precision.

The raster system translates quickly and simply and it costs next to nothing. However, rotating raster images, by anything other than a multiple of 90 degrees, is a problem, as is image scaling. If you don't use special algorithms, errors can become a problem. Sometimes the image looks nothing like the original once it has been rotated several times, especially if the image includes thin lines. Even when you compensate for these errors, it still means that you will have some 'color interpolation', which in turn could mean that you lose some information. We'll go into this in greater detail in Chapter 3.

Screen Redraw

When you want to edit an image, naturally you will also want to redisplay the image on the screen. Vector systems have an advantage here because it is the redrawing method that is changed. Raster systems either have to preserve blocks of the bitmap for faster redrawing, taking a lot of memory, or they have to recreate a portion of the screen from scratch. Raster systems redraw the whole of the 'window' even after the slightest change in the image.

The long undo/redo list is another convenience of vector representation. It is a list of all manipulations made on the primitives and requires very little memory to store. As you can roll it back as often as you like, it gives you fine control over the editing of the image.

You can also use the undo list for bitmap representation, but you have to save the 'master' copy of the image, and even then some stages may be lost because of the accumulation of error.

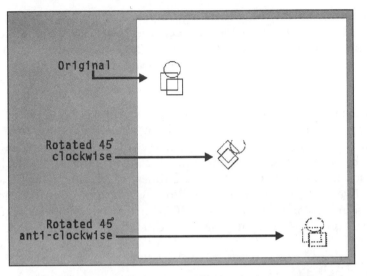

Accumulation of Errors in Manipulating a Bitmap

Image Storage and Translation

The two systems have different ways of storing and translating images. The vector system stores images in the following way:

Assuming you have a system which has an image description like 'the lake shimmering under the light of the moon', how do you think that vector technology stores the image? The vector system stores an image as a linked list of primitives, each of which has properties such as its color, size and position. In other words, the image is stored as a series of instructions that describe the image. This is the most compact way of storing images, as it shares primitives and structure definitions, so allowing you to store complex drawings using just a few parameters.

Raster systems simply store bitmaps as a series of numbers, one number for each pixel, and therefore require a greater amount of space. For example an image of 800 by 600 pixels, with each pixel being one of 256 colors, requires 468.75 Kbytes, excluding all the other bits of information needed to display the image correctly. However, there are powerful compression techniques which can attain a compression ratio of up to 200:1. In most cases, the size of a compressed bitmap is comparable to the equivalent vector definition.

The problems with data conversion between different vector drawing systems are like those of translating from one human language to another, negligible if the languages are similar. However, conversion from one binary raster format to another is quite simple. Some compressed bitmap formats are directly translatable but, if not, all you have to do is decompress it from the original format, and then recompress it into the new one.

You can easily convert vector Computer Aided Design (CAD) data to a raster representation but not vice versa. Complicated operations such as tracing are used to convert automatic bitmaps to vector representations. The quality of such conversions is often very poor and manual correction is usually needed.

Vector	Raster
Arbitrary precision of geometrical image manipulations.	Unique representation for natural, real images. No conversion is needed when scanning.
Compact image representation.	A bitmap is easily used as a generic drawing format.
Fast redisplay, almost unlimited undo/redo list almost at no expense.	Display speed doesn't depend on image complexity.

Summary of the Relative Advantages of Both Types of Graphics Systems

Looking from the PC platform you may think vector graphic technology is nothing but a dead end. However, most of the "miracle examples of computer graphics" which you will see below can hardly be imagined without vector representation. We'll make up for the lack of compact and precise ('vector') description when, as you will see, we rotate, shrink and zoom bitmap images.

 Surely one of the most tempting raster operations, from the vector point of view, is to fill an area (called flood filling). Let's imagine something more complicated than a solid color or pattern flood fill, something like gradient filling (i.e. starting with one color and as you fill the shape, slow change to another color). If you can divide any image into areas colored just like the gradient filling "paints", then you can combine raster and vector to produce one of the most compact and easy ways to manipulate image representation.

The next few pages guide you through the greatest ideas and achievements of today's Computer Graphics, which are mostly of a bitmapped origin.

An Historical Overview Of Bitmapped Graphics

There was a time when computers could neither `DrawLine` nor `PutPixel`, as they were only used to calculate. The only way to communicate with them was "to write them letters" by some strange, "perforated" means, now almost forgotten. This huge electronic, or in some cases electrical, apparatus usually involved some oscilloscopes. It should be of no surprise that one day a programmer, bored with ballistics, tried to draw something using this 'screen'. It may have even been a jumping ball, which is still one of the most expressive and impressive graphics examples today. The fact is that the first drawing hardware was analog and thus **vector** by nature, by which we mean it drew lines.

By the early sixties, computers could `DrawLine` but still couldn't `PutPixel` and the first graphical terminals were already being used for the computer aided design of cars. Graphics systems then became cheaper while the performance increased. As more people were introduced to computer graphics, it had to meet more demands. A lot of questions needed to be answered.

The first ten years of computer aided design led to a specially defined set of 'primitives'. This was a result of developers together with the users of drawing systems sharing certain assumptions concerning the nature of computer graphics, most of these assumptions coming from the world of engineering.

Assuming you define any lines, whether straight or curved, by parameters which have been obtained from the appropriate line equation, specified by the line, then you must consider the text to be parameterized as well, in terms of location, direction, font tag, and ASCII code. Add polygons, which may or may not be filled and you'll obtain a 'language' developed enough to describe almost any kind of engineering drawing. Now you only need some ways to create drawing tasks, to support the hierarchical structures of primitives and to formulate image transformation.

Various types of display hardware were invented which were able to display images directly from their description in this 'vector primitives language'. This came to be known as vector display technology. During this period, graphics software based on the vector drawing paradigm developed parallel to hardware technology. Software had solved many problems of computer aided drafting, such as grouping lines into symbols or other higher level structures, but specialized hardware helped to complete the picture.

However, alternatives to this vector style of computer graphics did exist. Raster representation of images had been around a lot longer than vector generated computer graphics, but raster representation needed a lot of fast memory for use as a frame buffer, a great disadvantage when memory was expensive (about one dollar per bit for RAM) as only government establishments with astronomical budgets (like NASA) could afford raster color graphic systems.

Rapid progress in television technology and cheaper computer memory made raster graphic technology accessible for everyday use, but how does the internal arrangement of a raster graphic differ from its vector counterpart? Raster represents a graphic image as an array of elements (dots) on a grid. The image is stored in the computer's memory as a 2D array (bitmap) whose values identify the color, or intensity of gray, for the corresponding grid location. The hardware directly reads the values from the bitmap row by row and displays the colored dots every time you want to see the new image on the screen.

This new representation and display method, called bitmap graphics technology, was first used by Xerox in the early 1970s. Aren't all new technological advances from Palo-Alto? Then Apple developed it further on its Macintosh line, and now it's the best technology. Even CAD workstations have it. Raster technology's hardware architecture continues to evolve rapidly and many powerful algorithms have been created.

Until recently it was assumed that vector systems were the best for engineering drawings but raster systems were better for colorful 'real' images. However, the advantages of vector technology aren't linked to that of the display hardware, many of them concerning the logical structure of data representation, a problem solved at the software level. It should be noticed that some modern bitmap oriented graphic systems provide vector-like primitives as well.

The World Of 3D Graphics

It takes you a few seconds and even fewer lines (two squares and four extra lines) to draw something that everyone calls a cube. Visualizing 3D objects in such a primitive way is known as 'wireframe' graphics. This drawing method takes its origin from vector graphics. As 'wireframe' graphics are quite simple to modify, change the projections of and even produce animations with, it is still a popular method for some purposes, for example when creating engineering and architectural drafts of 3D bodies. Wireframe 'landscapes' remain the usual way to represent two dimensional data in disciplines such as science and education. The values are organized in a regular gridlike fashion, and the actual value itself is used as the third dimension, thus producing a landscape.

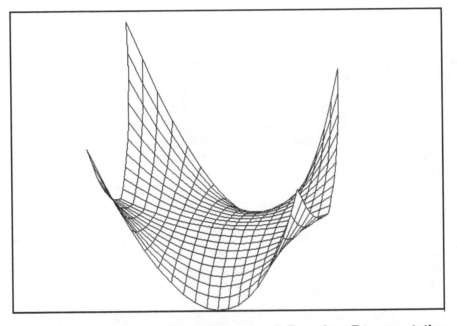

Wire 'Landscape' for Two Dimensional Function Representation

Surface modeling systems are much more precise. You need to define the ribs of the body and its surfaces to produce an image with these programs. They are the same as 'wireframe' graphics programs, but are also able to recognize surfaces, automatically erase invisible lines like cube ribs, and color the resulting 'mesh'. There are other models which color the surface's rectangular (or polygonal) grids to make it look like the real surface. We'll look at this in Chapter 13.

The image is made even more realistic if you use projections, light reflections and scattering accurately. You can also use many different textures and a well developed set of techniques for precise rendering which is called 'ray tracing'. This is a 'straight' method, and a huge number of calculations are needed to execute it. The general idea is that you compute all the reflections of each 'ray'. This is illustrated by the example of polished gold and silver balls on the black and white background of a chessboard mirroring each other. Although this is very impressive, it is rather 'cold' and perhaps too accurate.

'Solid' body constructive geometry (BCG) works in a completely different way. BCG systems are provided with a number of 3D 'building block' sets, which are also called primitives. Creating complicated objects using this method looks like a construction process rather than a drawing one. The image is compiled from a plurality of separate primitives. A 3D image of DNA molecules, which you may have seen in schoolbooks, is one of the best examples of how this method works. All you need to do is take several types of different colored and various sized spheres and combine them on top of one another in the proper configuration. Then you need to add some shades to the whole thing to make it look like a real 3D object. If you take other basic primitives, which may be of any imaginable form, you will be able to build a great variety of 'solid' structure images.

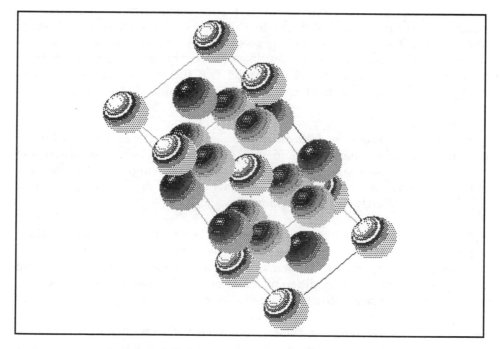

A Crystal Structured From Shaded Spheres

This technique has become so common that most people always imagine molecule or crystal structures in terms of colored spheres. This is obviously not a good thing, but it does prove that presentation influences the human mind.

Creating Realistic Images

Computers deal with two major types of image: those real in origin, which have been scanned in by some means, and those the computer 'imagines' for you. The problem of creating an artificial object that looks similar to the natural one remains rather difficult. There is something in nature, in trees, grass, mountains or the human body movement that distinguishes it from anything man or computer-made, a kind of intricacy which is characteristic of everything natural.

Nature Imitating Systems

The imitation of the random nature of real phenomena, such as dancing tongues of flame in a fire, interlaced tree branches, mountain cliffs and cracks, is impossible with 'straight' modeling programs. A painter, as well as a computer, would need too much time to depict every oak leaf, every pebble and stone crack. Also one should not forget that the sharply outlined contours created by such programs don't correspond to the vague forms of grass or clouds.

To get over this, various modeling methods are widely used. You can input tree or flame drawing programs into the computer, then point out where the computer should begin, and the electronics does everything else. You can use various models which may be quite close to the 'real' physics of phenomena or you can use completely different approaches.

The corpuscular program system is a modeling method which is by far the best for creating images of natural objects. The corpuscular system builds images by registering tracks of microscopic light particles. These particles are randomly scattered, move in different directions and explode every now and then making complicated structures on the display screen.

If you choose a wide range of colors, determine the restrictions on particle speed and brightness, set limits on how the particles respond to gravity and other conditions which influence their movements, you will obtain an enchanting sea of flame, refined still life or just beautiful bushes of exotic plants on a background of green grass. Computer graphics takes ideas from various fields including physics, philosophy and mathematics.

Fractals opened the world of irregular geometry. Usually we consider objects we draw on paper as one or two dimensional objects (think of a line and a plane figure on a sheet of paper). But almost a hundred years ago a new type of dimensioning was proposed, in which a curve could have a fractional dimension, not just an integer one. For instance, a circle is two dimensional, but if you look at a circle from a great distance, then the circle appears as a dot, or a zero dimensional object. Conversely, if you look really close at the line which makes a circle, then it appears to be a straight line (one dimensional). By 1977, Dr Benoit Mandelbrot invented a new type of dimensioning, in which a curve could have a fractional dimension, and published his theories in "The Fractal Geometry of Nature". He was the first person to use a computer to investigate fractal worlds.

Looking at fractals as geometrical objects, they have many marvelous features; for example, some of them are self-similar. This means that each part of such a fractal, when magnified by a certain amount, will look similar to the whole one. This is how natural objects are ordered. Natural fractals don't work in such a precise manner but a pile of rocks still looks like a mountain, while from a distance, a river looks like a tiny brook.

One more useful thing about fractals. Fractals are defined by simple mathematical formulas, which are applied to the same object over and over again, a process called recursion. These recursions aren't deep enough to generate fractals in their mathematical sense, but they are sufficient to produce images that resemble nature. This makes a fractal representation of an image very compact, and there are compression methods based on this principle. Such images also possess a rare and unusual beauty and it is no wonder that they are used to depict natural objects.

The simplest procedures to create fractal landscapes simply reproduce initial forms which can be repeated hundreds and thousands of times, each a different size to the previous one. A little randomness in the equations makes the results unpredictable but also creates real and credible nature scenes and fantastic geometrical constructions.

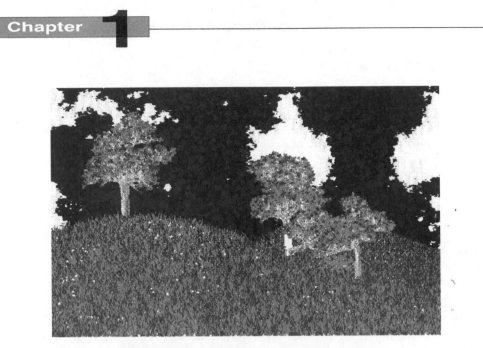

FractArt. A Sunny Summer Afternoon

Each part of the landscape from the figure above, except the landscape mesh itself, is generated by a special, recursive procedure.

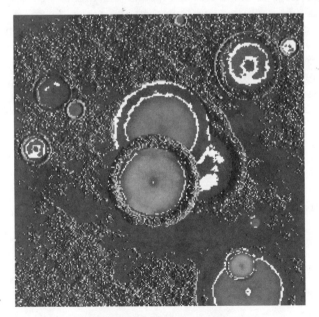

FractArt. Moonscape

This figure shows a fractal moonscape generated by the computer, which then added some projective shadows. We will explain all these techniques later.

You can create unreal and fantastic landscapes as well as 'real', natural ones. With some 'magic' parameters, creative coloring, a little abstract fractal mathematics plus some creative programming, you will be able to create something like the following:

The Dark Star Of Liapunov's Cosmos

Animation

Animation is the presentation of successive images, 25 or more per second, causing the brain to perceive the movement as fluid and smooth. Until recently, the only medium for animation was film. Firstly, key images were made by drawing on paper or creating special puppets. The animators then made successive frames of the films by changing the images as they went along. However, the technology was slow and it required special skills to draw the animated world.

It was obvious that animation could greatly benefit from computer graphics and thus computer animation was born. Now an artist need only draw the key frames himself and the computer, using a special program, will draw and paint the intermediate frames. The formulas governing simple motion, projections, light and color are quite simple, so it is possible to draw the real world accurately and create more realistic animations than ever before.

Now computer animation is more realistic than any model and is more controllable than drawn animation. It also makes such tricks as 2D and 3D morphing possible, but we'll give more details on this in Chapter 13.

Using various types of bitmap graphics and a developed model of reality, it's possible to visualize almost everything from elementary particle collisions, to blood circulation, to the births and deaths of galaxies.

Once computer animators perfect the 'physics' implemented into their model, it will be possible to achieve any kind of imaginable reality. But this really only concerns modeling, as used in physics, cinematography or maybe even history, rather than computer graphics. However we can easily imagine a not-too-distant future when creating a movie (by means of a 'movie processor') will be no more expensive than writing a novel. Anyone will be able to play at being Steven Spielberg himself and engage Dustin Hoffman or Marilyn Monroe to star in the sequel to 'Jurassic Park', (we've already had Marilyn Monroe and Humphrey Bogart starring together in a computer animation). But maybe there'll be a question of ethics.

The most challenging idea and the ultimate goal is Virtual Reality. This combines all the above mentioned techniques and a new generation of user interface technology which will enable you to create your own world in which to live. Unfortunately the virtual realm in which you can raise your 'Camanche', 'Alone in the Dark' to see your 'Doom' in the 'Eye of the Beholder' is beyond the scope of our book.

Summary

The bitmap graphics paradigm is about 25 years old. Now it's much more popular than the vector system and it has benefited from the fast progress of TV and silicon technologies. Nevertheless, most of the challenges we'll face in the first part of the book come from the main advantages and shortcomings of bitmaps. Everything began from vector graphics and we should return to it, combining other methods such as using graphic accelerators with MS Windows to make it more efficient.

However, before we get into the guts of the video architecture, let's have a quick tour of Assembly language. The next chapter will give enough information for you to get through the next few chapters and the Assembly language contained therein.

8086 Assembler for C Programmers

This chapter is intended as a quick tutorial of Assembly language for C and C++ programmers. Here, you will learn the basics about your computer's memory, the main instructions, about data and its structure, program flow, using BIOS and DOS interrupts, and the requirements for interfacing your Assembly language programs with C programs.

Chapter Contents

In this chapter, we will cover:

- ▲ Why Use Assembler?
- ▲ Memory - Structure, Map and Addressing Modes
- ▲ Using BIOS and Interrupts
- ▲ The Stack
- ▲ Data and Its Structure
- ▲ Program Flow Control
- ▲ The Basic Instruction Set
- ▲ Indexed Memory - Using The Index Registers
- ▲ Macros
- ▲ Floating Point
- ▲ Interfacing with the C language

Why Use Assembler?

Consider the following statement:

    a = b*c;

This, as you know, performs the operation of multiplying the contents of variable **b** by the contents of variable **c**, and storing the result in the variable **a**. Taking this simple statement, your compiler may generate several instructions in machine code, the binary form which your processor (CPU) understands, to perform your wishes. The instructions will vary, depending on whether your variables are integer, long or short, or floating point, the compiler making these decisions for you based on the type of variable you have defined. However, apart from that, you have little control over, or indeed knowledge of what these instructions are. Different compilers will implement the statement in different ways, some more and some less efficiently than others. However, it is almost certain that your compiler will generate more machine instructions than a program written in Assembly language, to produce the same result.

Programming in Assembly language gives you direct control over what instructions your processor performs. Apart from macros, there is a one-to-one correspondence between each Assembly language statement and the machine code instruction to be executed in response.

The result is that you can produce instructions to use your machine with greater efficiency. Your program will consume fewer CPU resources and probably much less memory. In fact, most programs written in Assembly language will fit into 64K of program space. In addition, there are some things which can be done only by using Assembly language, because a high level compiler does not provide the means. For instance, direct control of the video hardware, as described in Chapter 3, would be very problematic, if not impossible, using only a high level language.

Memory - Structure, Map and Addressing Modes

The IBM PC, including PC, XT and AT, and compatible non-IBM computers are based on a design produced originally by IBM in 1981. The most usual modern configuration has 1MB (1024KB, or 1,048,576 bytes) of addressable memory, of which 640K consists of random-access memory (RAM), and 384K normally reserved for system usage. The latter is the so-called 'upper memory area' (UMA), originally reserved by IBM for system use, including read-only memory (ROM), but which became available for the first time for program use with the advent of memory management utilities, such as QEMM. However, UMA is now accessible with the advent of DOS 5.0 as part of the standard operating system. Nevertheless, up to 256KB of UMA may be reserved for ROM, and other sections of it are still allocated for specific purposes. In particular, and relevant to other chapters of this book, the memory from 640K to 767K (A0000h-BFFFFh) is allocated for use by the Video Graphics Adaptor (VGA), and Monochrome Display Adaptor (MDA).

Both ROM and RAM capacities can be augmented by installing additional memory in the form of extra chips, either in empty sockets on the motherboard, or by means of an expansion board with a memory adapter. Indeed, most PCs these days often have a minimum of 4MB or more - extra memory chips are available in units of up to 4MB each called SIMM (Serial Inline Memory Module), and a motherboard usually has 2 memory banks with space for 4 SIMM in each, so a PC may have as much as 32MB memory.

However, this doesn't become available immediately for program use. The early 8086 architecture was designed to address, or access, just 1MB of memory and indeed, back in 1981 no one could foresee needing more, and compared with existing personal computers which had just 64K, it seemed an enormous amount. The limitation is in fact hardware dependent; the address bus - the part of the machine used to address memory - is just 20 bits wide on an IBM XT-compatible (8086).

The next generation of machines, the 80286 family, has a 24-bit addressing scheme which allows access to 2^{24} or 16MB of memory, and the 80386 family can directly address up to four gigabytes (GB) of memory, but a lot of software still lags behind these hardware advances, remaining compatible with the 8086 only, and so executing within the 1MB range available to the 8086.

Additional memory may be managed using several techniques. One way to work around the 1MB limit is with the LIM (Lotus-Intel-Microsoft) Expanded Memory Specification (EMS). Don't confuse EMS 'expanded' memory with XMS 'extended memory', which is located logically above the first megabyte of 80286 and above. Access to both EMS and XMS requires a memory management utility. For instance, DOS 5.0 (and later) provides EMM386.EXE

for EMS, and **HIMEM.SYS** for XMS. EMS is provided by mapping one or more 16K blocks into the 8086 upper memory address space (into what's known as the **page frame**), and swapping them in and out; XMS is located logically above the first 1MB of memory.

However, don't be surprised if you rush out to buy 16MB of memory and after you've installed it, you still get the message "Too little memory"! Applications may use one, the other, both or neither additional memory addressing standards.

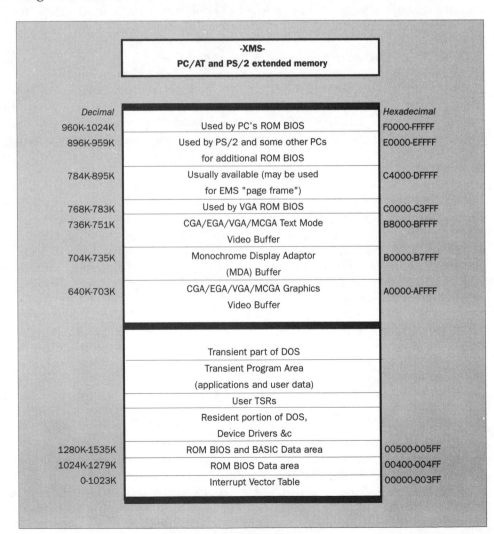

	-XMS- PC/AT and PS/2 extended memory	
Decimal		*Hexadecimal*
960K-1024K	Used by PC's ROM BIOS	F0000-FFFFF
896K-959K	Used by PS/2 and some other PCs for additional ROM BIOS	E0000-EFFFF
784K-895K	Usually available (may be used for EMS "page frame")	C4000-DFFFF
768K-783K	Used by VGA ROM BIOS	C0000-C3FFF
736K-751K	CGA/EGA/VGA/MCGA Text Mode Video Buffer	B8000-BFFFF
704K-735K	Monochrome Display Adaptor (MDA) Buffer	B0000-B7FFF
640K-703K	CGA/EGA/VGA/MCGA Graphics Video Buffer	A0000-AFFFF
	Transient part of DOS	
	Transient Program Area (applications and user data)	
	User TSRs	
	Resident portion of DOS, Device Drivers &c	
1280K-1535K	ROM BIOS and BASIC Data area	00500-005FF
1024K-1279K	ROM BIOS Data area	00400-004FF
0-1023K	Interrupt Vector Table	00000-003FF

The System Memory Map

> Please note the standard notation used by assemblers for hexadecimal values differs from C. Hexadecimal values are denoted by appending a letter h at the end; binary values have a letter b, for example, 0110b (binary 4+2 = 6), 0110Bh (hex 4096+256+11 = 4363). Octal notation may also be used, in which case, numbers end in letter o.

Memory Access - Addressing Conventions

As you have already learnt, the basic XT (8086) architecture provides for addressing a total of 1MB of memory. However, the 8086 is a 16-bit processor using only 16-bit arithmetic and addressing and so can't work directly with addresses larger than 16 bits. This means that theoretically only 64K (2^{16}) of memory can be accessed, but we already know the processor can access 16 times that.

How is this done?

The answer is that when the processor needs to calculate the address of a byte of memory, it uses two words (16 + 16 bits) to access both a segment of memory and an offset within that segment. The largest size of a segment is 64K, and theoretically 16 of these can be addressed.

You might expect these to be numbered from 0 to 15, with segment 1 following neatly on from segment 0, and so on, and that would be the end of that, but in fact things are never that simple. Any physical address in memory may be chosen as the starting position for accessing a segment, provided it is on a paragraph boundary. A paragraph is the term used to describe 16 bytes, the smallest amount of memory which can be allocated. This means that every byte in memory may have several different forms of address and in fact any address may be represented in up to 2^{12} different ways!

An address of this type may be written in the form *segment:offset*. To calculate an absolute address, shift the segment 4 bits left (multiplying by 16) and add the offset address. For instance take the address 0123:0321h, which is in fact, the address of the **DOS BUSY** flag. This is a flag set when the processor is executing DOS code, and translates to an absolute address as in the following illustration:

        0123:0321h

shift the segment value left:

```
  01230
 +0321
 -----
  01551
```

This same physical address could also be represented as **0155:0001h**, **0124:0011h**, and so on. Try the alternatives using **DEBUG**, or with your own debugging utility, and you'll see something like this:-

```
-d155:1
    0155:0000    07 0E 00 05 0D 01 00-00 00 00 00 00 00 00 0D    ...............
    0155:0010 BC 03 1C 01 01 00 00 00-00 00 00 00 00 01 00 00    ...............
    0155:0020 00 90 00 00 00 FF 02 15-2F 11 40 32 0D 02 07 00    ........./.@2....
    0155:0030 00 00 8A 00 29 00 00 00-20 00 C6 00 FF FF A7 05    ....).... .......
    0155:0040 80 00 00 00 10 00 CE 04-1E 00 00 00 01 00 00 00    ...............
    0155:0050 00 00 00 00 00 00 00 00-00 00 00 00 B8 19 06 BA    ...............
    0155:0060 CF 03 05 00 00 3B 06 02-00 72 1B B4 09 BA 18 01    .....;...r......
    0155:0070 CD 21 CD 20 4E 6F 74 20-65 6E 6F 75 67 68 20 6D    .!. Not enough m
-d123:321
    0123:0320    07 0E 00 05 0D 01 00-00 00 00 00 00 00 00 0D    ...............
    0123:0330 BC 03 1C 01 01 00 00 00-00 00 00 00 00 01 00 00    ...............
    0123:0340 00 90 00 00 00 FF 02 15-2F 11 51 3B 0D 02 07 00    ........./.Q;....
    0123:0350 00 00 8A 00 29 00 00 00-20 00 C6 00 FF FF A7 05    ....).... .......
    0123:0360 80 00 00 00 10 00 CE 04-1E 00 00 00 01 00 00 00    ...............
    0123:0370 00 00 00 00 00 00 00 00-00 00 00 00 B8 19 06 BA    ...............
    0123:0380 CF 03 05 00 00 3B 06 02-00 72 1B B4 09 BA 18 01    .....;...r......
    0123:0390 CD 21 CD 20 4E 6F 74 20-65 6E 6F 75 67 68 20 6D    .!. Not enough m
```

The above applies to 8086 processors through to i486 machines, running in real mode. In protected mode, 80286 machines operate somewhat differently. The 'segment' part of a segmented address is a 'selector' that represents an index into a segment descriptor table. Each descriptor in the table contains a 24-bit base address that indicates the actual start of the segment in memory. The resultant address is the sum of this 24-bit address plus the 16-bit offset. The 80386 and i486 support both 8086 and 80286 style addresses, but enhance this by being able to operate with 32-bit segment base addresses and 32-bit offsets.

In practice when you are programming at this level, it is best to keep segment addressing as constant, and conventional as possible, in particular if converting programs to run in 80286 protected mode where each different segment selector designates a different segment descriptor.

The Interrupt Vector Table

The interrupt vector table contains the addresses of up to 256 interrupts, or system functions, to provide communication with peripheral devices, like the keyboard, video display and disk drives. Most of the active vectors point to executable code, but others such as Interrupt 1Fh and Interrupt 43h point to data - in this case the bitmap patterns of video graphics characters. The code and data for these functions is loaded into memory at boot-up time, and the BIOS sets the interrupt vectors to point to the appropriate places in memory. Incidentally, in case you aren't already familiar with the term, the BIOS (Basic Input/Output Services) is the collective name for a set of instructions provided primarily by a Programmable Read-Only Memory (PROM) chip on your motherboard.

ROM BIOS Data Area

This area is reserved for use as a common data area which various system and interrupt routines access to communicate with each other. The idea is to provide a fixed space that all applications can rely on to access data which has a common value to all. One such fragment of data is the **master clock count** - 4 bytes stored as one 4-byte number, incremented once for each hardware timer tick - the result of a hardware interrupt occurring approximately 18 times a second.

You can access the ROM BIOS information either directly yourself, or in most cases, you can use the services of one of the interrupts referred to above.

Video RAM

It is important to understand the difference between the memory contained on your video adaptor card, and the memory in your computer. Your applications can't address memory on your video adaptor card directly, but instead share a common area of your PC's memory which both your CPU and the video BIOS address simultaneously.

The area at addresses A0000h-BFFFFh on your machine is reserved for this purpose. The area A0000h-AFFFFh is reserved for graphics modes, B0000h-B7FFFF for monochrome modes, and B8000h-BFFFFh for color text modes. This serves as a common memory area, which the video BIOS code and your program can share. At the same time, this memory area mirrors what you see on your screen. The easiest way to see this is in text mode. If you write instructions to move characters into the memory area reserved for your video in color text mode, you will see them appear immediately on your screen. Magic, when you see it happen for the first time! This is a very fast way to update your display, much faster than using the C functions `printf()` or `puts()`, but similar to using `poke()` (part of the Borland `DOS.H` header) the latter which writes one character-attribute pair at a time.

The difference is even more apparent in graphics mode. Video BIOS services are available which will write individual bits (pixels) on screen, but these are very slow compared with what can be achieved by writing directly to the screen. However, as you will learn in Chapter 3, this is not as straightforward as when you are dealing with text. For some graphics modes there simply isn't enough room in your computer's memory to hold the contents of a whole screenful of graphics data, so the necessary is achieved by what's known as **bank switching**. In one mode of operation, video memory, the memory on your video adaptor card, is configured to have four 64KB memory maps, spanning the same address in your computer's memory, and the color of each pixel on screen is composed of 1 bit from each map. The analogy is rather similar to the 'page frame' switching mentioned earlier, for swapping the contents of EMS into an area of 'real' memory to provide access within the existing 8086 address space.

At the other extreme, since many systems these days have a color monitor, the area reserved for the MDA (monochrome display adaptor) remains unused. Some memory managers may be able to make this area available as additional memory for applications, but be warned, this doesn't always work!

Using BIOS and Interrupts

Up to now, you may have got the impression that if you dabble with Assembly language, you have to do everything yourself. This is not so. Although you can, if you wish, take control of all system functions, including direct disk access, and hardware control, in some circumstances it is better to leave this to the BIOS. Your BIOS, augmented by code loaded at boot time, has dedicated code to access all the basic peripheral units attached to your PC, the Video, Keyboard, Disks, Printer and Serial Ports. This code is mapped to a reserved area in memory starting at address F0000h. In addition, your Video card has its own BIOS code, which is mapped to a reserved area in memory starting at address C0000h. Both of these memory areas are read only, so an application may not accidentally overwrite this code.

As you have already seen, during the boot up process, the BIOS sets the interrupt vectors to point to the interrupt handlers in memory (RAM or ROM). The interrupt vector table starts at address 0000:0000h. Each entry in the table is stored as a segment:offset pair, with the low order value placed first, as usual, or in other words, offset first and segment portion second. The values of the vectors can be changed to point to an additional or replacement interrupt handler, but when this occurs, it is usual to save the address to branch back to the original handler after the necessary additional work has been done.

Each peripheral unit has its own associated interrupt. Interrupts are generated by both hardware and software. For instance, typing a key at your keyboard generates a hardware interrupt which invokes code to direct the processor 'process this key now!'. Matching this, your program can invoke the companion software interrupt which directs the processor 'Give me the next key pressed, I want it now, and I will do nothing more until you give it to me!'

The hardware interrupt for the keyboard is 9 decimal, or 09h. The address of the routine to process keyboard input is at address 0000:0024 (9*4). The software interrupt for keyboard access is 22 decimal, or 16h.

There is no companion hardware interrupt for the video controller. The software interrupt for video control is 16 decimal, 10h.

One of the most important interrupts is Interrupt 21h, the DOS interrupt. The code in this handler performs a set of DOS specific instructions which augment the facilities available in the BIOS. It is beyond the scope of this chapter to provide a full list of all the functions that Interrupt 21h provides, but it is worth mentioning one of the more important ones, that of returning control to the system after your program is complete. Function 4Ch of Interrupt 21h not only ends a program and passes control back to the operating system, but also flushes file buffers, closes any open files, and frees all memory which was allocated.

The Assembly Language

The statements in an assembler source file may be classified into three general categories: Instruction Statements, Data Allocation Statements, and Assembler Directives.

Instruction Statement

The Instruction Statement uses an easily remembered name (called a **mnemonic**) to specify what machine instruction to generate.

The syntax of an instruction statement is as follows:

```
[label:] [mnemonic][operand] [;    comment]
```

where:

label   is the marker you choose to refer to that statement, so you can branch to it from elsewhere in your program, call it as a function, or define it as an external reference. A label is optional, but if used must be delimited by a colon (**:**).

Labels may consist of any alphanumeric characters, but must start with a letter (**A-Z**), **@** or underscore (**_**). Their maximum length will be dependent on the particular assembler you use, for example, Microsoft's MASM.

Note also that a label may not duplicate the name of a mnemonic operator or symbol otherwise reserved for use by the assembler.

mnemonic   is the name of the instruction you wish your machine to perform. There are some 100 unique instructions available on the 8086 family of processors, with additional ones special to the 80286 and 80386/i486 family.

In addition, there is a set of floating point instructions available for use if you have a maths co-processor, which is an additional 8087, 80287, 80387 chip, or inbuilt in i486 and DX processors.

operand is whatever item(s) of data or machine register(s) that you wish to operate on or with. Some instructions, such as **lodsb** don't need operands as the instruction itself defines the source and destination of the result, which in this case loads the contents of memory located at the address pointed to by the register pair DS:SI into register AL.

comment is simply a message to the programmer, and has no meaning to the Assembler, that is, it is simply useful to you, or to anyone who scrutinises your program, to explain what you are doing.

An instruction statement may consist of a lone label, a lone operator, a lone comment, or all of these, with an operand, as appropriate. All comments in your assembler source program should be preceded by a semi-colon (**;**).

Data Allocation Statement

A Data Allocation Statement has the following form:

```
[symbol] [type]      [value]
```

where:

symbol is the name you wish to use to refer to this piece of data.

type is the type of data. This roughly equates to the quantity of storage space or memory you wish to allocate rather than the contents. For instance, type **DB** (define byte) allocates storage in bytes, according to the *value* you specify. **DW** (define word) allocates storage in words (2 bytes). **DD** (define doubleword) allocates storage in doublewords (4 bytes), and **DQ** (define quadword) allocates storage in quadwords (8 bytes at a time).

value   is the initial value you wish to assign to your data. Character
data is defined by enclosing the characters you wish to assign in
single or double quotes (there is usually no distinction). Numeric
data may be assigned in different ways, as with any programming
language. In particular, hexadecimal values are defined by adding
the letter **h** to their hexadecimal representation. Several data items
may be assigned on the same line, with values separated by
commas.

Note that there is a special assembler directive for indicating a repeated initial
value - **dup**.

For instance the statement

```
FOO   DB    40 dup 0
```

generates 40 bytes of storage, filled with zero. You may also use a question
mark **(?)** to indicate that you want a certain amount of storage allocated,
but don't care what the contents are, as in:

```
FOO1   DB    99 dup (?)
```

Assembler Directive

An assembler directive is a statement which gives special instructions to your
assembler. For instance:

```
ITEM   equ   5
```

This is the equivalent of the C statement:

```
#define ITEM 5
```

However, assembler directives do much more than define values for symbols.
They can also define what memory model you want your program to be
assembled for, what processor type, or what address space to use for
individual parts of your program. In other words, they tell the assembler
how you want your program assembled.

For instance, in Chapter 14, you will find the following assembler directives:

```
.model large
.386      ; Pay attention to these lines.
.387      ; Only for 386+387 !!!
public _mult_matrix
```

The first statement tells the assembler to generate instructions appropriate to the large memory model. All programs in this book are written to be assembled using this option, so we will not discuss alternative memory models other than to explain that they exist; they also have relevance in Assembly language.

The second statement tells the assembler to accept instructions which may be performed on a 80386 compatible machine; the third statement says statements should be assembled taking into account there is a 80387 or equivalent co-processor available.

The fourth statement, **public**, allows you to specify explicitly that the symbol **_mult_matrix** may be used by other modules. In other words, you expect to have a program elsewhere which will refer to it as an external symbol.

The converse assembler directive is **extrn** (note, **not extern**). This indicates to the assembler that the variable you define is external to your current procedure, and that you expect the program to which it refers to be linked in from elsewhere prior to execution.

Note that unlike C, the case of symbols is, by default, not significant. If you do want the assembler to honor case, you can specify it as an option on the command line. For example, with MASM you would specify:

```
MASM /Mlxu ...
```

The /M indicates that you wish to preserve case of label, while the following letters specify further which labels: l All, x Globals, and u Uppercase Globals

You may use either upper or lower case for instructions and data statements - whichever you prefer.

Assembling your source program converts the assembler instructions into machine code instructions, based on any assembler directives you have given

it and then it performs the necessary calculations for program flow control, which may include branching to other places in your program or calling procedures, sometimes called subroutines. All assemblers will produce an **.OBJ** file as output, which can then be linked in with your existing high level language programs, or alternatively converted to a stand alone **.EXE** or **.COM** program.

Bits and Bytes

Before proceeding further with our discussion of Assembly language, we will pause briefly to consider how information is stored in a computer's memory. Indeed, it is essential to understand this, if you are to program in Assembly language effectively.

At the lowest level of storage, all values are represented by bit patterns formed of ones and zeros. A byte is 8 bits, 2 bytes make up what's known as a word (in C, a short integer), 4 bytes are a double word (in C, a long integer), and so on. 16 bytes are referred to a paragraph.

The printable part of the ASCII character set is represented by the values 32-127 (20h-7Fh hexadecimal). For instance, if when you see the character 'A' on your screen you were to locate the bit pattern for that character in the video RAM text buffer, you would find it's stored as the value 65, or 41h.

If you were able to look a little more closely at the individual bits, you would see the following pattern:

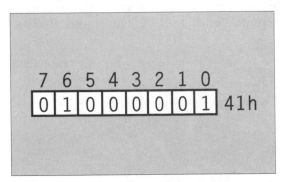

The convention used is to number the bits upwards from right to left. Therefore the high order bit is on the left, and the low order bit is on the right.

If instead of the letter A, we want to use this bit pattern to represent a signed arithmetic value, the leftmost bit, bit 7 is used to indicate the sign. If it's set to 1, the number is negative, if 0, the number is treated as positive. Negative values are stored in what's known as twos-complement notation. In practical terms, this means that if you want to know what the bit pattern of a negative number looks like, and you know what it looks like as a positive value, invert the bits and add 1.

To illustrate this, let's look at the integer value for 'A', 65.

First, invert the bits:

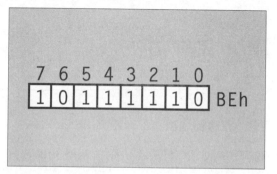

Now add a binary 1:

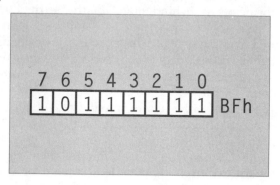

So, -65 has the same representation at machine level as the hex value BFh, which in unsigned decimal arithmetic would have the value +191. Notice also that if we add together BFh and 41h, we get zero with 1 bit to carry, that is, the result is 100h (256), as you might expect.

We will discuss the **carry bit** later, but firstly we will consider what happens when we move upwards from bytes to words. The 8086 processor has what at first appears to be a curious way of accessing values of more than one byte in length.

To illustrate this in action, suppose you assign the integer value 260 (104h) to a variable **ax**, using C as follows:

```
int ax;
ax = 260;      /* set ax to the value 260 (hex 104h) */
```

If you were able to look at the area where your computer has stored this value, you might get a surprise! The hexadecimal representation of **ax** stored in memory will look like this:

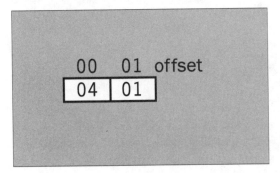

Notice the low order byte is on the left! The machine code instructions which store words into memory save the low order byte first, followed by the high byte. This is not true for all computers, but as we are talking about PC's... This fundamental principle is behind many of the arithmetic operations your computer performs, and if you are going to delve into your computer's memory, it is as well you understand it, as it is not immediately obvious or intuitive! The principal carries further for storing longer values; for instance the four bytes of the timer tick value (representing the number of seconds since midnight), stored at address 0040:006C, in the ROM BIOS data area, will be found with the low order word stored first, at location 0040:006C, and the high order word stored adjacent, at location 0040:006E.

The effect is simply that when you are examining memory, you will learn to read the values of numbers from right to left, instead of from left to right.

The Stack

The stack is a built-in feature of the PC architecture. It provides a convenient place both to store transient data, and to keep track of program execution. In C, as you may know, it is used when a function is invoked for storing local variables. However, it is also used implicitly every time a **call** or **int** instruction, two instructions that are used to pass control elsewhere, is executed in machine code. However, unlike the **jmp** instructions, which also pass control to other areas, invoking a **call** or **int** instruction means it's likely you'll want to return to the next instruction following the **call** or **int**. The **call** instruction implicitly 'pushes' the address of the next instruction, or **instruction pointer** onto the stack, and passes control to the required address. The **int** instruction also invokes other instructions, but has a special use: to call up one of the built in system functions, or interrupts. When the instruction **call** is completed, control is regained at the instruction following the **call** by executing the appropriate **ret** (return) instruction, which will 'pop' the return address off the stack.

For transient storage, there are two instructions, **push** and **pop**, to **push** (move) a value onto the stack, and **pop** (remove) it again. The stack increments downwards in memory, so '**pop**'ping restores the most recently '**push**'ed value, the Last-In, First-Out (LIFO) principle; the stack pointer decreases in value when a value is '**push**'ed, and increases when a value is '**pop**'ped. The place in memory which is used is determined by the value of the **stack pointer** register (**SP**), which usually points to the highest address in the **stack segment** (**SS**). It is also possible to increase or decrease the value of the stack pointer directly. In the former case, this results in losing one or more '**push**'ed values, as the contents of memory previously occupied by the value is destroyed.

Note that it is possible to **push** and **pop** both registers and memory contents.

Coding and Registers

The CPU uses a number of registers to perform its tasks, to pass values between memory and hardware, or to perform arithmetic and logical operations. There are 14 16-bit registers in all on an 8086 machine; on the 32-bit machines, 80386 and i486, 14 32-bit registers are available, with an additional segment register, **GS**.

We will describe just the 8086 16-bit registers; the 32-bit registers have the same names, prefixed by the letter '**E**', and are simply extended versions of the 8086 series, performing similar functions in 32-bit mode. The extra segment register, **GS**, for 32-bit mode operation, may be used in a similar way to the **DS** and **ES** registers we are about to describe.

Following on from the description of addressing, together with that on segment and offset registers, 4 (or 5 including **GS**) registers are designated specifically as segment registers, that is, used to contain the segment portion of addresses.

These segment registers are:

CS   Code Segment - this register holds the value of the segment where your program resides. This register may not be set explicitly but may be changed by a **far call** instruction, or system **interrupt**. **far** in this context means the procedure to be invoked is in a different segment, and so control needs to be passed to its address in memory using both segment and offset registers. The converse is **near** meaning that the procedure lies in the same segment.

DS   Data Segment - this register holds the value of the segment where your data lies.

> Note that data may be accessed using **far** or **near** pointers in the same way as instructions (code). In this case, the assembler directives **far ptr** and **near ptr** are provided when it's necessary to convey this fact explicitly to the assembler.

ES   Extra Segment - this register may be used for addressing data in other portions of memory.

SS   Stack Segment - this register defines the segment where your program stack is located.

Each of these registers has an offset register traditionally associated with it - although in some circumstances it is possible to override this with one of your own choice. These are:

IP   Instruction Pointer - the offset of the current instruction within your code segment. Like the **CS** register it is not possible to change the value of this register explicitly.

SI   Source Index - implicitly used in conjunction with the **DS** segment register in instructions for manipulating memory - **lods** (load data), **movs** (move string), **cmps** (compare string), **outs** (output string to port **DX**) but may also be used for general purpose addressing of data - for instance as an index into a data array.

DI   Destination Index - implicitly used in conjunction with the **ES** segment register in instructions for manipulating memory, **stos** (store data), **movs** (move string), **cmps** (compare string), **ins** (input string from port **DX**). Likewise it may be used for general purpose addressing, and note **DS:SI** and **ES:DI** form a complementary pair, used jointly in **cmps** and **movs** instructions.

SP   Stack Pointer - provides the offset into the stack segment. The value of **SP** gives the location of the top of the stack.

BP   Base Pointer - also provides the offset into the stack segment, but may also be used in conjunction with the **ES** register to address data.

In addition there are 4 'scratch pad' registers - used for arithmetic, comparisons, passing values between functions and procedures, etc. Although these registers are available for any kind of scratch-pad use, each has some special functions:-

AX   The Accumulator register - used implicitly for multiply and divide instructions, and in conjunction with **DS:SI** to load values from memory, and with **ES:DI** to store values in memory.

BX   The Base register - may be used as an index in addressing.

CX   Count register - used in **cmps**, **ins**, **movs** and **outs** instructions, coupled with the **rep** (repeat) prefix to indicate how many bytes to operate on, and in the **loop** instruction to perform sets of instructions repeatedly.

DX   General purpose Data register - also used in conjunction with the **AX** register for 32-bit multiply and divide.

The high and low byte of each of **AX**, **BX**, **CX** and **DX** can be accessed independently, using the notation **AH**(igh), **AL**(ow); **BH**, **BL**; etc.

Finally the 8086 processor maintains a series of control and status bits called **flags**. Flags indicate the result of operations. There are 9 in all: six status flags, and 3 control flags which are contained in a special register called the Flags Register. They can be saved and restored, '**push**'ed and '**pop**'ped from the stack as a set, and tested independently, but are of most use simply to control program flow - as a result of setting and clearing instructions, for instance after a comparison operation, when a branch (**jmp**) instruction may be executed on the basis of how the flags have been set.

These two sets of flags are:

Name	Description	Comment
SF	Sign Flag	Indicates result of signed result/ comparison
ZF	Zero Flag	Indicates zero result or equal comparison
AF	Auxiliary Carry Flag	Used in binary-coded decimal (BCD) or single byte arithmetic indicate adjustment needed
PF	Parity Flag	Indicates even parity - an even number of 1-bits
CF	Carry Flag	Indicates an arithmetic carry
OF	Overflow Flag	Indicates signed arithmetic overflow
DF	Direction Flag	Controls direction of string operations (**cmps**, *****ins**, **lods**, **movs**, *****outs**, **scas**, **stos**)
IF	Interrupt Flag	Controls whether interrupts are enabled
TF	Trap Flag	Controls single step operations (as used by debug) by generating an interrupt after every instruction

It is worth noting at this point that System Interrupts and DOS Function calls use, and expect values to be placed in some or all of these registers prior to invoking them. They also return results in both general registers and as flags to indicate the success or failure of an operation. It is beyond the scope of this chapter to give a full list of calling conventions, but in brief, **AH** (and sometimes **AL**) are used to specify what function you wish the service to perform, **BX** may be used as a general purpose register to pass status bits or values, **CX** is used for counting and **DX** is used to address data.

Here's an example of using the DOS Interrupt, 21h to request 20 bytes to be read from the standard input device:

```
mov   ah,3fh      ; DOS Interrupt 21h Function 3Fh, READ from file
mov   bx,0        ; File handle 0 - standard input (stdin)
mov   cx,20       ; number of bytes we are asking for
mov   dx,input    ; where we want DOS to put the data for us to use
int   21h         ; invoke DOS Interrupt
```

You will also meet other different kinds of registers in this book, such as color and palette registers used by your video processor, registers which perform a specific function for video control. However, they all have one thing in common - they form special channels for passing data around your machine's hardware.

Data And Its Structure

Data under the control of a program written in Assembly language has no inbuilt structure other than that which the programmer decides it should have. It is true that assemblers, like C Compilers, support data typing. By that we mean that the assembler expects a particular instruction to operate on a particular type of data defined at assembly time, and indeed may produce a syntax error if the data is not defined as such, but at run time, the contents of the same memory area may contain anything at all. Therefore the responsibility lies with the programmer to check the bounds of arrays, and to verify the contents and type of variables is as expected, especially whilst debugging. It is all too easy to crash your machine if you don't take these precautions. High level languages put in 'traps' for you, an example of which is if an instruction generates a Divide Exception caused by dividing by zero. When programming in Assembly language, you should expect to perform these checks for yourself.

For this reason, if you are going to program seriously in Assembly language, a debugger is a necessary tool. This is a utility which will allow you to single-step each instruction in your program, so you can verify it is doing what you want it to, and if not, stop it in time before your machine crashes. DOS itself has such a utility, called simply **DEBUG**, but you may well find a more 'user friendly' one bundled with your assembler.

Data Definitions

It is customary to place your data definitions at the start of your Assembly language source program, preceded by a **.data** directive. This tells the assembler to calculate the displacements of the variables you've defined relative to the value of **DS** register. Within the code segment, displacements are assumed to be relative to the **CS** register. If you are writing a stand-alone **.EXE** program, it will be necessary to load the address of the **DS** segment into **DS** as your first statement as follows:

```
.model   large
.data
store    dw   0
.stack
.code

testit   proc    far
    mov    ax,@data    ; '@data' is a special Assembler Directive
    mov    ds,ax       ; you may not move a constant value direct to ds
...
    mov    ax,4c00h
    int    21h
testit   endp
end
```

> Note that at the end of the procedure we use Interrupt 21h Function 4Ch to return to DOS. Alternatively, if you are coding a procedure to be invoked from a C language program, you would replace the INT 21h instruction with a **ret** - in this case, since you have defined your **proc**edure as **far**, the assembler will insert a **retf** instruction.

Also note that most assemblers support a **struc** directive to define structures similar to those in C, using the following notation:

```
viewporttype    struc
    left        dw 0
    top         dw 0
    right       dw 0
    bottom      dw 0
ends
```

Likewise you may access elements in your data area in a similar way to C, for example by the instruction **mov ax,viewport.left**.

Program Flow Control

When your program is loaded into memory, the **CS** or Code Segment register will contain the address of the segment your program occupies, and the **IP** or Instruction Pointer will contain the offset of the first instruction within this segment.

From this point, your assembler instructions will be executed in the order you have programmed them. As the CPU executes instructions, the **IP** register will increment according to the length of the instruction.

However, as you are now writing your first few lines of Assembly language program, you may begin to wonder where the excitement lies in simply executing instructions serially. You want to be able to do so much more, and indeed you can. The first feature of a high level language which you may find you need is an equivalent to the **for()** loop. Although you will have to manage the indexing yourself, help is at hand in terms of the **loop** instruction. This allows you to execute a portion of the program a specified number of times. You set the count in the **CX** register, and the **loop** instruction decrements this counter, and loops to the label you specify whilst the count is non zero.

For example, take this fragment of program:

```
    ...
    mov    cx,ffffh    ; load the maximum integer value, 65,335
repeat:
    loop   repeat      ; waste time
                       ; drop out here some time later
    ...
```

In fact this might seem a pointless piece of program at first glimpse, as it apparently does nothing useful, but in fact this method is used in some software to delay the CPU whilst something else is happening. This is why programs with sound effects produced by the PC's speaker sometimes sound differently on machines of different speeds, because the faster the machine, the slower the pauses between 'notes'.

> A more elegant method would be to examine the master clock count for a change of value, but in fact the graduation of it changing 'only' 18 times a second is too slow for some sound effects.

Also note the companion instructions, **loopz** (or **loope**) and **loopnz** (or **loopne**). These will branch as long as **CX** is non-zero and the results of a previous test return a result of equal, or not equal.

There is a special way of repeating the instructions which operate on strings, **cmps**, **movs** and **outs**. Again, place a count of the number of times you wish to execute the instruction in **CX**, and prefix the instruction with one of **rep**, **repz** (or **repe**), **repnz** (or **repne**), and your processor will execute the **cmps** or **movs CX** number of times, or in the case of **cmps** when the comparison of the strings produces a match (**repnz**), or mismatch (**repz**).

The Basic Instruction Set

Possibly the simplest, and perhaps the most often-used instruction is **mov**, which transfers an item of data from register to register, from register to memory, and from memory to register.

> Note that **mov** doesn't move data from memory to memory.

For instance, the following instruction:

```
mov    ax,store    ; equivalent to C language's ax = *store;
```

loads the word contained in the memory location labeled **store** into register **AX**.

If you want to load the address (offset relative to the current segment) of the variable **store** into **AX**, rather than the contents, you can use the instruction **lea** - Load Effective Address.

```
lea    ax,store    ; equivalent to C language's ax = &store;
```

The instruction

```
mov    ax,offset store
```

achieves the same effect.

For moving data between memory locations, use the instruction **movs** (**movsb**, **movsw, movsd**), when the register pairs **DS:SI** and **ES:DI** are used to contain the addresses of source and destination address respectively.

Further operations which the 8086 architecture can perform break down into just a few categories:

▲ Arithmetic (**add**, **sub**tract, **mul**tiply, **div**ide)

▲ Moving Data around (**lods**, **mov**, **movs**, **stos**)

▲ Logical operations on individual bits in memory (**and**, **or**, **xor** - eXclusive OR)

▲ Testing conditions on which branch (**jmp**) instructions can be executed

▲ Flow Control. The branching instructions themselves, such as **jmp** and **call**

▲ Stack operations (**push**, **pop**)

and last but not least, and probably most relevant to the topics discussed in this book:

▲ Operations to control hardware and circuitry within the PC - the **in**s and **out**s.

> Note that the following list gives each instruction in its most general form. The instructions with two operands will accept the forms [register, register], [register, memory]; [register, immediate]; or [memory, register] values, and [register] may be a 1- or 2 byte-type.

In the following lists, the instruction parameters are as follows:

First letter	Meaning	Second letter	Meaning
r	register	b	byte
e	effective	w	word
m	memory	d	double word
c	call (address)	m	memory
i	immediate		

Arithmetic

```
adc    rw,ew      ; add ew to rw then add the status of the Carry Flag;
                  ; and store result in rw

add    rw,ew      ; add ew to rw and store result in rw

sbb    rw,ew      ; subtract ew from rw then subtract the status of
                  ; the Carry Flag (Borrow) and store result in rw
sub    rw,ew      ; subtract ew from rw and store result in rw

cbw               ; Convert Byte to Word (AH = sign bit of AL)
cwd               ; Convert Word to Doubleword (DX = sign bit of AX)

dec    rw         ; decrement rw by 1. Note this instruction sets
                  ; the status of the Carry Flag but not the Sign Flag

div    ew         ; Unsigned divide DX AX by ew (AX=Quo DX=Rem)
idiv   ew         ; Signed (Integer) divide DX AX by ew (AX=Quo
                  ; DX=Rem)

inc    rw         ; increment rw by 1. Note this instruction sets
                  ; the status of the Carry Flag but not the Sign Flag

imul   ew         ; Signed (Integer) multiply (DX AX = AX * ew)
mul    ew         ; Unsigned multiply (DX AX = AX * ew)
```

Note the equivalent integer instructions **div**, **idiv**, **imul** and **mul** operate on the **AX** register only. For instance, **div eb** returns the Quotient in **AL** and the Remainder in **AH**.

```
neg    ew         ; Two's complement negate ew (word or byte)
                  ; (ew = -ew)
```

Moving Data

cld		; Clear direction flag - SI and DI will increment ; (bytes processed from left to right in memory)
lds	rw,ed	; Load ed (doubleword) into rw and DS register
lea	rw,em	; Load Effective Address (offset em), place in rw
les	rw,ed	; Load ed (doubleword) into rw and ES register
lgs	rw,ed	; Load ed (doubleword) into rw and GS register

> Note that there is no equivalent to store doubleword

lodsb		; Load word DS:[SI] into AX, advance SI by 1 byte
lodws		; Load word DS:[SI] into AX, advance SI by 2 bytes
mov	rw,ew	; Move a copy of ew into rw - ew is unchanged
movsb		; Move byte DS:[SI] to ES:[DI], advance SI and DI
movsw		; Move word DS:[SI] to ES:[DI], advance SI and DI
rep	(prefix)	; Repeat following string operation CX times
repe	(cmps, scas)	; Repeat following operation CX times or until ZF=0
repne	(cmps, scas)	; Repeat following operation CX times or until ZF=1
repnz	(cmps, scas)	; Repeat following operation CX times or until ZF=1
repz	(cmps, scas)	; Repeat following operation CX times or until ZF=0
std		; Set direction flag so SI and DI will decrement ; (cmps, lods, movs, scas operate right to left)
stosb		; Store AL to byte ES:[DI], advance DI by 1 byte
stosw		; Store AX to word ES:[DI], advance DI by 1 word
xchg	rw,ew	; Exchange contents of rw with ew (word or byte)
xlatb		; Set AL to memory byte DS:[BX + unsigned AL] ; (translate AL according to value in table[BX]

Logical Operations

and	*rw,ew*	; Logical-AND *ew* with *rw* - store result in *rw*
clc		; Clear carry flag
cmc		; Complement carry flag
not	*rw*	; Reverse each bit of *rw*
or	*rw,ew*	; Logical-OR *ew* with *rw* - store result in *rw*
xor	*rw,ew*	; Logical-exclusive OR *ew* with *rw* - store result in *rw*

Note in the following Shift instructions, the quantity to be shifted is either placed in the **CL** register, or assigned in the instruction. The standard 8086 instruction set only permits an immediate value of 1, but for 80286, 80386 and i486 processors, values other than 1 may be set.

---

rcl	*ew,x*	; Rotate register (**CF**, *ew*) Left *x* times

In the above instruction, the leftmost bit in the *ew* register replaces the Carry Flag; whilst the contents of the Carry Flag replace the rightmost bit in the register.

---

rcr	*ew,x*	; Rotate register (**CF**, *ew*) Right *x* times
rol	*ew,x*	; Rotate register *ew* left *x* times
ror	*ew,x*	; Rotate register *ew* Right *x* times
sal	*ew,x*	; Shift Arithmetic Left, *x* times
sar	*ew,x*	; Shift Arithmetic Right, *x* times

The above Shift Arithmetic Right instruction propagates the sign bit

---

shl	*ew,x*	; Shift Left logically, *x* times
shr	*ew,x*	; Shift *ew* Right logically, *x* times
stc		; Set carry flag

Testing Conditions

```
cmp     rw,ew        ; Subtract ew from rw - for flags only - rw remains
                     ; unchanged.

cmpsb                ; Compare byte(s) at ES:[DI] with DS:[SI], advance SI
                     ; and DI
cmpsw                ; Compare word(s) at ES:[DI] with DS:[SI], advance SI
                     ; and DI

lahf                 ; Load: AH = flags   SF ZF XX AF XX PF XX CF

sahf                 ; Store AH into flags   SF ZF XX AF XX PF XX CF

test    rw,ew        ; Logical AND rw with ew - for flags only
```

Flow Control

```
ja, jnbe             ; Jump short if above (CF=0 and ZF=0)
                     ; above=UNSIGNED
jae, jnb, jnc        ; Jump short if above or equal (CF=0)
jb, jc, jnae         ; Jump short if below (CF=1) below=UNSIGNED
jbe, jna             ; Jump short if below or equal (CF=1 or ZF=1)

jcxz                 ; Jump short if CX register is zero

je, jz               ; Jump short if equal (ZF=1)
jg, jnle             ; Jump short if greater (ZF=0 and SF=OF)
                     ; greater=SIGNED
jge, jnl             ; Jump short if greater or equal (SF=OF)
jl, jnge             ; Jump short if less (SF!=OF) less=SIGNED
jle, jng             ; Jump short if less or equal (ZF=1 or SF!=OF)

jmp                  ; Unconditional Jump

jne, jnz             ; Jump short if not equal (ZF=0)

jno                  ; Jump short if not overflow (OF=0)
jnp                  ; Jump short if not parity (PF=0)
jns                  ; Jump short if not sign (SF=0)
jo                   ; Jump short if overflow (OF=1)
```

```
jp            ; Jump short if parity (PF=1)
jpe           ; Jump short if parity even (PF=1)
jpo           ; Jump short if parity odd (PF=0)
js            ; Jump short if sign (SF=1)

call    cw    ; Call near segment, 2-byte address
call    cd    ; Call far segment, 4-byte address

cli           ; Clear interrupt enable flag; interrupts disabled

int     ib    ; Interrupt numbered by immediate byte
              ; (Call far segment with flags pushed first)

iret          ; Interrupt return (far return and pop flags)

loop    cb    ; Decrement CX; jump short if CX!=0
loope   cb    ; Decrement CX; jump short if CX!=0 and equal (ZF=1)
loopne  cb    ; Decrement CX; jump short if CX!=0 and not equal
loopnz  cb    ; Decrement CX; jump short if CX!=0 and ZF=0
loopz   cb    ; Decrement CX; jump short if CX!=0 and zero (ZF=1)

retf          ; Return from far call (pop offset, then segment)
ret           ; Return from near call (pop offset only)
retf    iw    ; Return (far), pop offset, segment, iw bytes
ret     iw    ; Return (near), pop offset, iw bytes pushed before
              ; Call

sti           ; Set interrupt enable flag, interrupts enabled
```

Stack Operations

```
  pop     rw    ; Load rw with value at top of stack, increment SP
                ; by 2
* popa          ; Pop All - DI,SI,BP,SP,BX,DX,CX,AX
                ; (SP value is ignored)
  popf          ; Load flags register with value at top of stack,
                ; increment SP by 2

  push    rw    ; Set [SP-2] to rw value, then decrement SP by 2
* pusha         ; Push All - AX,CX,DX,BX,original SP,BP,SI,DI

  pushf         ; Set [SP-2] to flags register, decrement SP by 2
```

Control of Hardware

The **in** and **out** instructions are used a lot in this book, so we will list the variants in full.

```
   in     AL,ib      ; Input byte from immediate port number ib into AL
   in     AL,DX      ; Input byte from port DX into AL

*  ins    eb,DX      ; Input byte from port DX into [DI]
*  ins    ew,DX      ; Input word from port DX into [DI]
*  insb              ; Input byte from port DX into ES:[DI]
*  insw              ; Input word from port DX into ES:[DI]

   out    ib,AL      ; Output byte AL to immediate port number ib
   out    ib,AX      ; Output word AX to immediate port number ib
   out    DX,AL      ; Output byte AL to port number DX
   out    DX,AX      ; Output word AX to port number DX

*  outs   DX,eb      ; Output byte [SI] to port number DX, advance SI
*  outs   DX,ew      ; Output word [SI] to port number DX, advance SI
*  outsb             ; Output byte DS:[SI] to port number DX, advance SI
*  outsw             ; Output word DS:[SI] to port number DX, advance SI
```

> Note: The instructions marked (*) aren't available on the 8086 processor.

Indexed Memory - Using the Index Registers

The 8086 processor supports an indexed addressing scheme, where a combination of base and index pointers may be used in instructions to calculate an effective address into memory. **BX** and **BP** are known as **base registers**, and **SI** and **DI** are known as **index registers**. An instruction may use one base register and one index register plus a constant run time displacement to calculate the address. For example:

```
    mov   ax,[bx]         ; transfer the contents of the location
                          ; at the offset in the data segment equal to
                          ; the value of register BX to AX.
```

```
        mov    [si+17],cx        ; transfer the contents of register CX to the
                                 ; location at the offset in the data segment
                                 ; calculated by adding 17 to the value of
                                 ; register SI.

        mov    ax,es:[bp+di+4]   ; transfer the contents of the location at the
                                 ; offset in the extra segment calculated by
                                 ; adding 4 to the sum of the values in
                                 ; registers BP and DI to register AX.
```

Note the latter example also illustrates the principle of using a **segment
override**. The default segment register for this instruction would be **DS**, but
we want to use **ES** instead. We can do this by adding the prefix **ES**: to our
base-displacement operand. From this point we shall assume the shortened
notation that a register, for example, **AX**, when used in an appropriate
operand position is interpreted as the contents of the register.

Macros

A macro in an Assembly language program is much like a macro in any
other language. If you are using the same fragments of code repeatedly in a
program, a macro gives you a shorthand way to tell the assembler 'do that
again'. Indeed, assemblers usually provide a full-featured macro language
which you can use to produce variations according to the conditions in use
at the time of assembly, not only in the same way as you would use #if..
#else... #endif in C, but by substituting values at assembly time for the
macro parameters you define.

Macros must always be defined before they are used. This may be either at
the beginning of your Assembly language source file, or in a library, which
you include in your program source.

An example of a macro definition follows. Note that any detailed syntax will
depend on the particular assembler you are using:

```
name  macro    parm1,  parm2...
      ...
endm
```

where:

name is the unique name you assign to the macro. Naturally this shouldn't be
the same as any existing label, or mnemonic, or reserved word.

parm1 the first symbolic parameter.
parm2 the second symbolic parameter.

and so on.

Here is an example (suitable for use with MASM):

```
swap    macro    x, y
   push   ax      ; preserve the contents of ax
   mov    ax,x    ; use ax as temporary storage for x
   mov    x,y     ; move the value of y to x
   mov    y,ax    ; move the value of x to y
   pop    ax      ; restore ax
endm
```

The above example may be used to swap the values of two registers, or a register with storage. For example,

```
swap bx,memory
```

generates the following instructions:

```
push   ax
mov    ax,memory
mov    memory,bx
mov    bx,ax
pop    ax
```

Note this is included simply as an example, and in fact the same effect can be achieved in one instruction:

```
xchg bx,memory
```

See Chapter 3 for a further example; the macro **PixelAddress**. Note that this macro has symbolic parameters **Y** and **X**, which will be replaced by specific numeric values at assembly time each time the macro is invoked.

Also note that invoking a macro differs from calling a function because the assembler substitutes the macro instructions you have defined each time the macro appears in the source program. Invoking a function means the function's instructions appear only once in the program, and program flow branches to it at execution time, and returns on completion.

Floating Point

If you have a maths co-processor, which is an extra chip on 8086, 80286 and 80386 machines, but is included as standard in i486/DX processors, you will be able to take advantage of floating point arithmetic; let's refer to this as the Floating Point Unit (FPU). The FPU has its own register set, containing 8 floating point numbers occupying 10 bytes each, plus 14 bytes of status and control information. Many of the FPU instructions cause the numbers to act like a stack. The standard name for the top of the stack is **ST** or **ST(0)**; the others are named **ST(1)** through **ST(7)**.

You can use the FPU by loading numbers from memory to the FPU by using **fld** instructions, perform the necessary calculations and store the results back in memory using **fst** and **fstp**.

Note that **ftsp** pops the value off the 'stack'. The instruction set also supports some mathematical functions, such as **sqrt**, while on 387 and i486/DX machines the FPUs also supports **sin**, **cos**, **tan** and **arctan**, as well as various logarithmic operations.

The easiest way to learn about floating point is to jump right in and try it. See Chapter 14 for instructions about using floating point arithmetic.

A Word Of Warning

If you are using an 8086 CPU with a 8087 FPU you should be aware that once control is passed to the FPU, the 8086 processor can carry on quite happily with the next instruction - indeed, that is why it is called a co-processor! This is fine, provided the next instruction isn't another floating point operation which depends on the result of the previous! To overcome this problem, some assemblers may insert an **fwait** (wait for FPU ready) instruction prior to each floating point instruction, so you don't need to worry about such a problem and in any case, it has been overcome on later FPUs.

Emulating Floating Point By Software

If you don't have an FPU, there is a software package provided with many compilers, for example, Borland's Turbo C, and most Microsoft compilers, which will emulate the FPU's instruction set. The emulator is implemented so that you need not know whether you are using a FPU or not. This is achieved by your link utility which replaces all floating point instructions with a call to a special interrupt handler which processes the instructions in software.

Floating Point Instructions

Below is a list of some of the Floating Point instructions available on 8087 processors, including the instructions used in this book. This is by no means a comprehensive list, but is intended to give you an idea of the scope of instructions available. Please consult your assembler manual if you are interested in pursuing floating point arithmetic further.

```
fadd                ; st(1) = st(1) + st(0), pop
fadd    st(i)       ; st(0) = st(i) + st(0)
fadd    st(i),st    ; st(i) = st(i) + st(0)
fadd    mem         ; st(0) = st(0) + mem
faddp   st(i),st    ; st(i) = st(i) + st(0), pop

fcom                ; compare st(0) - st(1)
fcom    st(i)       ; compare st(0) - st(i)
fcom    mem         ; compare st(0) - mem
fcomp               ; compare st(0) - st(1), pop
fcomp   st(i)       ; compare st(0) - st(i), pop
fcomp   mem         ; compare st(0) - mem, pop
fcompp              ; compare st(0) - st(1), pop both

fdiv                ; st(0) = st(1) / st(0), pop
fdiv    st(i)       ; st(0) = st(0) / st(i)
fdiv    mem         ; st(0) = st(0) / mem
fdivp   st(i),st    ; st(i) = st(i) / st(0), pop

fdivr               ; st(1) = st(0) / st(1), pop
fdivr   st(i)       ; st(0) = st(i) / st(0)
fdivr   mem         ; st(0) = mem / st(0)
fdivrp  i,0         ; st(i) = st(0) / st(i), pop

fld     st(i)       ; push, st(0) = old st(i)
fld     mem         ; push, st(0) = mem
fld1                ; push, st(0) = st(1).st(0)
fldz                ; push, st(0) = +0.0
```

```
fmul                   ; st(1)  =  st(1)  *  st(0), pop
fmul    st(i)          ; st(0)  =  st(0)  *  st(i)
fmul    mem            ; st(0)  =  st(0)  *    mem
fmulp   st(i),st       ; st(i)  =  st(i)  *  st(0), pop

fsqrt                  ; st(st(0))  =    square root of  st(0)

fst     st(i)          ; st(i)  =  st(0)
fst     mem            ; mem  =  st(0)
fstp    st(i)          ; st(i)  =  st(0), pop
fstp    mem            ; mem  =  st(0), pop
fstsw   AX             ; AX  =    status word

fsub                   ; st(1)  =  st(1)  -  st(0), pop
fsub    st(i)          ; st(0)  =  st(0)  -  st(i)
fsub    mem            ; st(0)  =  st(0)  -    mem
fsubp   st(i),st       ; st(i)  =  st(i)  -  st(0), pop

fwait                  ; wait for 87 ready
```

Interfacing with C

By now, you may be asking yourself 'but how does my C language program communicate with the assembler instructions which I'd like to write?' The easiest way is to include the assembler instructions within your C program source file. Note that most C compilers have the option to assemble inline assembler language instructions. This is a quick and convenient way if, for example, you wanted the Video BIOS to provide a service which isn't available directly from a standard C language library, such as scrolling the contents of the screen up or down (Interrupt 10h, Functions 06h and 07h), or, as in Chapter 6, to access the BIOS screen font, the address of which is contained in interrupt vector 43h.

The alternative is to write your Assembly language program to act as a function invoked directly from a C program, in the same way you would call any function. However to do this, you need to know the calling conventions which C compilers adopt.

The requirements are different according to the memory model you are using. The basic models, small, compact, medium and large result in the following use of memory:

Memory model	Code segment	Data segment
small	single code segment	single data segment
compact	single code segment	multiple data segments
medium	multiple code segments	single data segment
large	multiple code segments	multiple data segments

If your function has no parameters it's relatively straightforward. Simply write your assembler program, and at the end, include a **ret**, or **retf** (return far) instruction, which will return control to your C language program. Whether you choose a **ret**, or **retf** instruction depends on the memory model you are using, but in fact your assembler will usually generate the appropriate **ret** instruction according to the **proc** definition you gave it.

> **retf** is necessary for memory models medium and large, which both use multiple code segments and for which your C compiler will have generated a far **call**.

If your function has parameters, the C compiler will generate instructions to push the values onto the stack prior to executing a **call** instruction to your Assembly language program. If using multiple data segments, parameters are passed as segment:offset pairs. If using multiple code segments, calling the assembler program generates a far **call**, resulting in both the segment (**CS**) and offset (**IP**) of the return address being pushed onto the stack after the calling parameters. The first parameter address is therefore offset 4 from this position on entry to the program.

Conventions are often boring, but they are also the easiest to follow in the first instance. In our case, it is customary to use the register pair **SS:BP** within the Assembly language program to access parameters pushed onto the stack. The initial assembler instructions should first save the existing value of **BP**, then load the stack pointer (**SP**) register to **BP**, in order to load the values of parameters which may be accessed relative to **BP** at a later date.

So the typical fragment of Assembly language program might be:

```
        .model   large
        .code
        testit   proc   far
            push bp              ; save existing contents of the bp register
            mov  bp,sp           ; now use bp as base pointer to access the stack
```

```
    lds    si,[bp+6]   ; load the segment:offset address of first
                       ; parameter into the register pair ds:si.
    ...
    ret                ; the assembler generates a RETF instruction
testit   endp
end
```

> Note that since the value of **BP** has been pushed onto the stack, the first parameter is now offset 6 from the parameter list.

In the large memory model, and for a function which expects two parameters, the sequence of values on the stack is as follows:

Address	High Memory
BP+12	Value of parameter 2 (segment)
BP+10	Value of parameter 2 (offset)
BP+8	Value of parameter 1 (segment)
BP+6	Value of parameter 1 (offset)
BP+4	CS Return Address
BP+2	IP Return Address
BP+0	Previous BP

Low Memory

How Parameters are Passed by C Language to an Assembler Program

It is the programmer's responsibility to ensure parameter types and values are consistent between the C language program and the Assembly language program.

Pascal uses the same calling convention as C. FORTRAN and BASIC follow the opposite convention of pushing parameters onto the stack in reverse order, and it is the responsibility of the called Assembly language program to clear the stack before returning. This is achieved by executing a **ret** *n*2* (or **retf** *n*4*) instruction, where *n* is equal to the number of parameters pushed onto the stack.

Microsoft's MASM version 6 and Borland's Turbo Assembler (TASM) version 3.0 provide macros which will generate the necessary Assembly language instructions for you. For the large memory model, define your procedure as **far**, and the parameters as far pointers, as follows:

```
myproc    proc   C far uses ax,bx,cx,dx,
                 parml: far ptr word, parm2: far ptr word
```

Summary

Hopefully by now you will have learnt enough about your computer's memory requirements, how data is stored and addressed and about the Assembly language itself to enable you to understand the fragments of Assembly language programs within this book, and to make small modifications to meet your own requirements.

However, if you now want to learn more about Assembly language you would be advised to consult one of the many excellent specialist Assembly language books such as 'The Revolutionary Guide To Assembly Language'.

PC Video Architecture

In this chapter, we are going to cover the most fundamental part of all bitmapped graphics systems - the video display hardware. Unfortunately, there is a huge range of display electronics in the marketplace. Each type of computer has its own way of driving the display-some use off-the-shelf chips, while other companies design custom chips to do the job. We are going to cover the VESA standard for AT compatible computers, as we believe that with this knowledge, you will be able to explore the rest of the video hardware market with confidence and authority.

Chapter Contents

In this chapter, we will cover:

- An Overview of Video Hardware Types

- An Outline of PC Video Architecture

- BIOS Programming

- Memory Structure

- Advanced Programming of the VGA

- Direct Memory Techniques

- SVGAs without VESA Support

The Mysterious World of PC Video Hardware

We will provide you with a short and concise introduction to the dark and mysterious world of PC video hardware as well as device level programming. Our aim is not to demystify video hardware programming, nor do we want to cover the subject inside out; it would be impossible to do so in so few pages anyway. Instead, we will try to do the following:

 Give a full, but compact, description of the different methods of hardware-level programming from 16-color up to TrueColor video modes. We will base our descriptions on memory model classification rather than on device details.

Provide tested and optimized examples of the basic techniques, which will lay the foundations for subsequent chapters. We hope that you will be able to put these examples, together with the examples from other chapters, to good use, maybe as a prototype of your own graphics library.

Give our point of view on video hardware programming and its future.

Overview of Video Hardware Types

We'll start with a quick overview of the types of video cards available. As it happens, it's also a history lesson, as the details appear in chronological order. Every graphics-related book looks at this sort of thing, so we'll try to add something different.

The IBM Enhanced Graphics Adapter (EGA)

The IBM Enhanced Graphics Adapter was released in early 1985. It's called 'enhanced' because, unlike its predecessors, it can display 16 color text and graphics images with a resolution of up to 640×350. Although the resolution and color capabilities of the EGA are no longer anything to write home about, they were considered to be a break-through at the time. However, IBM failed to improve on the lack of colors, making available only 16 from a possible 64. Programmers were also left with unreadable registers and non-square pixels.

Nevertheless, the availability of inexpensive EGAs and color software based on the adapter's capabilities rapidly made the EGA the de facto standard, at least for a few years.

The Multi Color Graphics Array (MCGA)

The Multi-Color Graphics Array, introduced in 1987 is the video subsystem used in the junior models (25 and 30) of the PS/2 series. A key difference between the MCGA and EGA is that the MCGA generates analog RGB video signals, so with its 6-bit Digital to Analog Converter (DAC), the MCGA can display as many as 256 different colors at once from a palette of 262,144 (2^{3*6}) colors.

The Video Graphics Array (VGA)

The Video Graphics Array which was also introduced in 1987 was, strictly speaking, a chip in the video subsystem of the PS/2 Models 50, 60, and 80. Nevertheless, the abbreviation VGA is now used to refer to the video display which has become standard in graphics programming circles. The VGA interface is almost identical to that of the EGA, but the VGA supports a higher display resolution, 640×480 in 16-color mode.

Like the MCGA, the VGA uses a video DAC to generate up to 256 colors at a time from a possible 262,144. It includes readable registers, hardware detection using BIOS (VGA BIOS Extension), and has more space for fonts. This last point means that different fonts can be displayed at the same time. But as you know, standards come and go, yet VGA is still here. This is because it has a good balance of features, and 16 colors is usually enough for most business applications.

> Note that you can always increase the number of colors by dithering. We will look at this in Chapter 4.

The following table goes some of the way to explaining why VGA is still an acceptable video display:

Mode#	VESA#	Number of Colors	Resolution	Display Mode
0/1	-	16/256K	320×200	Text
2/3	-	16/256K	640×200	Text
4/5	-	4/256K	320×200	Text
6	-	2/256K	640×200	Text
7	-	mono	720×350	Text
0D	-	16/256K	320×200	Graphics
0E	-	16/256K	640×200	Graphics
0F	-	mono	640×350	Graphics
10	-	16/256K	640×350	Graphics
11	-	2/256K	640×480	Graphics
12	-	16/256K	640×480	Graphics
13	-	256/256K	320×200	Graphics
-	10A	16/256K	1056×350	Text
-	109	16/256K	1056×350	Text
-	100	256/256K	640×400	Graphics
-	101	256/256K	640×480	Graphics
-	102(6A)	16/256K	800×600	Graphics
-	103	256/256K	800×600	Graphics
-	104	16/256K	1024×768	Graphics
-	105	256/256K	1024×768	Graphics
-	106	16/256K	1280×1024	Graphics
-	107	256/256K	1280×1024	Graphics

Continued

Mode#	VESA#	Number of Colors	Resolution	Display Mode
-	111	64K/64K	640×480	Graphics
-	114	64K/64K	800×600	Graphics
-	110	32K/32K	640×480	Graphics
-	113	32K/32K	800×600	Graphics
-	10D	32K/32K	320×200	Graphics
-	10E	64K/64K	320×200	Graphics
-	10F	16M/16M	320×200	Graphics
-	112	16M/16M	640×480	Graphics
-	117	64K/64K	1024×768	Graphics
-	170	32K/32K	512×480	Graphics
-	171	64K/64K	512×480	Graphics

VGA and VESA Video Modes

> In the Number of Colors column, the first number indicates the number of colors which can be displayed at any time, while the second number indicates the total number of colors to chose from.

The 'Super' VGA

The 'Super' VGA appeared around the end of 1987. You could say that NEC Home Electronics created the first SVGA, with an adapter supporting a 800×600 resolution with 256 colors. IBM replied with the 8514/A which offered an even higher, though interlaced, resolution of up to 1024×768, with an onboard graphics co-processor.

Interlacing is a method of increasing the output resolution of a graphics card. It works by using two frames to display a single computer frame: the first frame displays all the even lines, the second frame all the odd lines. This leads to a noticeable flicker of the monitor's screen. Modern, and therefore expensive, video cards have the hardware capabilities to display the highest resolutions without resorting to interlacing the display.

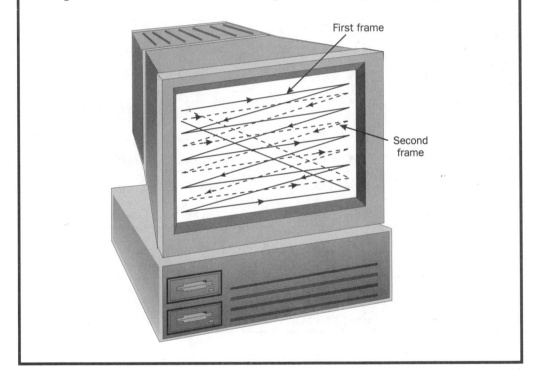

First frame

Second frame

Unfortunately, IBM didn't publish the hardware specification for the 8514/A, but instead offered programmers a set of software hooks called the Application Interface. Could this have been one of the reasons why the 8514/A failed as an industry standard? Whatever the reason, it failed and other manufacturers were ready with their SVGA cards. We started our experiments with the Prisma VGA ART 800.

There was a complete lack of order in the jungle of SVGAs which caused a great many problems for those who worked in the industry. The following table illustrates exactly what we mean.

Firm	Video mode #
ATI Technologies, Inc.	65h
Chips & Technologies	72h
Oak Technology	56h
Realtek Semiconductors Co. Ltd.	27h
Trident Microsystems	5Fh
Western Digital	5Dh

1024×768 16 Color Video Mode Numbers for Different SVGAs

Everyone was waiting for IBM to put an end to this chaos with its XGA standard, but this failed to be a success.

The Video Electronics Standards Association (VESA)

The Video Electronics Standards Association was given the task of setting the SVGA standard. The VESA standard versions 1.0, 1.1 and 1.2 (1989 -1991) defined 8 calls for interrupt INT 10h, function 4Fh which are now referred to as the VESA BIOS Extension. The main advantages of the VESA BIOS Extension are as follows:

▲   Its information service cuts out the problem of hardware detection almost completely.

▲   You can obtain and set all accessible video modes including vendor specific ones and also get all the information you need for programming.

▲   And last but not least, you can use bank switching either with a special call or by getting the address of a vendor specific function and doing it yourself (probably the faster method).

> Bank switching is important because the PC architecture only works in pages of 64Kb, and a screen mode like 1024 x 768 in 256 colors needs 768Kb (to access it all, the hardware must switch in 12 banks of memory, one at a time).

We'll give a detailed description of the VESA BIOS Extension in Appendix A. Since almost all modern SVGAs now support the VESA standard (version 1.2) it is worth devoting a few pages to this subject.

> Older non-VESA cards will also support VESA with a suitable TSR program. These TSR programs are available 'at no extra charge' in the public domain.

Accelerators

Today, only lazy software publishers fail to give their products an array of buttons, icons and windows. Whether you like it or not (and personally we're not that keen), the great commercial success of MS Windows has made this style a kind of de facto standard. The Graphic User Interface (GUI) is not only a fashionable accessory for users, it's a new whole way of doing things. However, because of its flexibility, the GDI (Graphic Driver Interface, the 'video heart' of MS Widows) is rather slow. Therefore it can, and does, benefit from the special clone of video systems, Windows accelerators.

Sophisticated graphics co-processors have a long history but they were always deemed to be a special class of video device reserved solely for image processing, animation, and so on. Almost all of them supported a built-in system of basic graphics primitives, such as line and circle drawing, polygon filling, zooming and so on. IBM's 8514/A, mentioned earlier, was one of the first intended for common use. Texas Instruments TMS34010 and TMS34020 chip, and Hitachi's HD 63484 were also popular on the graphics co-processor market.

Since the arrival of MS Windows, the number of video adapters of this kind has doubled each year. The most popular chips are S3 86C928 and CL-GD5426, while the most powerful systems, both supporting TrueColor mode, are probably Diamond Stealth Pro and Genoa Windows VGA24, although by the time you read this, they will probably have been superseded as the technology is moving at break-neck speed.

An Outline of PC Video Architecture

The following figure shows the anatomy of a modern video system. All PC systems have a monitor, as this is how the computer communicates information to the user. The monitor is connected to a video card.

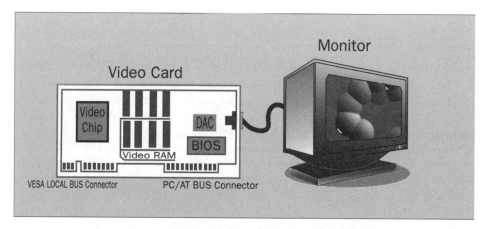

The Structure of a Modern PC Video System

The Monitor

This chapter describes video hardware from a programmer's point of view. You don't need a detailed understanding of the monitor to create good graphics. What you do need to know is where and how your program can exploit the hardware to produce video output in the most efficient way.

To really appreciate this chapter you should have a video display in front of you, preferably something like a SVGA analog multisync monitor. As it differs a little from a TV screen, it's worth saying a few words about it.

Most SVGA monitors are analog because this allows you to produce an almost unlimited number of colors, and you only need one wire for each RGB component. We assume that you are familiar with the red, green and blue components of a video signal. Most SVGA monitors are also multisync which means they can support resolutions up to 1280×1024.

There are many types of display available for all of the various graphics systems on the market. The picture quality of a display depends on many factors which we won't worry about here. We're sure your local dealer will be more than willing to give you all the details you need. We will only discuss the technical details of electron beam driving, timing and so on where absolutely necessary.

The Video Card

The card contains several components such as a video chip, some memory and BIOS. The video chip contains all the hardware to convert the image stored in the memory into signals that the monitor can then decode. It also contains all the control systems required to keep the card running smoothly. As we have mentioned, some video chips include support for primitives. Although most video chips contain a DAC, some do support external DACs. The DAC is better and faster at doing the conversion than the video chip. This means that the board, providing it has the memory, can have high resolutions and more color. The RAM normally comes in one of three configurations; 512KByte, 1MByte or 2MByte. Some of the really expensive cards support 4MByte. The amount of RAM is usually the deciding factor on the video modes available to the user. The BIOS chip handles all the communications between the CPU and the video chip and memory. Communications is through the Bus connector. These days, video cards have an additional connector, either VESA Local Bus or PCI (Peripheral Components Interconnect) Bus. This allows a faster transfer of information between the CPU and the video card.

BIOS Programming

It is hard to believe that there was once a time when programmers relied on video BIOS to perform most graphics hardware programming. Today, BIOS is mostly used for information purposes, say to detect hardware, and for controlling adapters, when setting video modes, but not really for drawing. Unfortunately, you can't even rely on BIOS to set a single pixel in HighColor or TrueColor modes. However, it's not much fun to have to control all the registers when setting new video modes yourself, which is where BIOS (or its VESA extension) comes into play.

The VGA BIOS provides 23 basic functions that work with the display. Twenty are inherited from EGA (0-13h), and VGA added 1Ah-1Ch. However, only a few of them are for the graphics mode. You can use **PutPixel** (function Ch) or

GetPixel (function Dh), but you should check to make sure that they are supported by the modes you wish to use. We doubt that any of these BIOS functions except **SetVideoMode** (function 0h) and maybe **SetPalette** (10h) have ever been used in 'serious' programming.

> The BIOS is written to work with a variety of different modes, and so the code contained on the chip is big and therefore slow. If you are working with a DOS screen, then the tendency is to choose and from then on remain loyal to one video mode. This means that you can write code to directly access the video memory which is optimized for that mode, making it a lot faster. Doom would never have been written if it had to use the video BIOS to update the display.

There is also a VESA BIOS extension for SVGA adapters, including 8 calls for function 4Fh, which we describe in detail in Appendix A.

The actual call to the video BIOS is simple. First, the desired function number is placed into the Ah register, and other registers are set if necessary. Then the ROM BIOS function is called by executing interrupt 10h.

```
mov    ax,0013h    ; Setting video mode 13h
int    10h         ; 320x200 , 256 colors
```

You'll find some examples of BIOS calls that work with color registers, and therefore function 10h, later on in this chapter.

Compatibility Between Hardware

Obviously, if you are designing complicated applications to sell, you would have to consider compatibility with different hardware configurations, future upgrades and so on. From the very beginning, IBM suggested BIOS style programming as the easiest solution to these problems. However, this idea has become less useful with the introduction of a new generation of hardware and software.

With the prevalence of MS Windows, there is now a better way. Windows give the programmer the GDI (Graphical Driver Interface). This uses a virtual device context or DC for short, which is an area of memory which you use as the video memory. You, as a programmer, do all the drawing to this DC, and then the GDI handles the conversion between the DC and the actual video

card. The GDI takes into account the fact that the DC can be bigger than the window it represents and that there is one DC for every window. The GDI builds up the display, and passes the information to the video card through the device driver written for that video card by the manufacturer. As you may guess, this makes the GDI rather slow, and you no longer have direct access to the video hardware. The benefit of this is that you are using a part of MS Windows which will be uniform on all machines rather than the video card which could be one of hundreds.

However, if you are using DOS, then you don't have this luxury, and you must write software to detect the available modes of the graphics cards, and then write code which is specific to the mode that you use.

At least, this is what we thought until we tested the performance of some SVGA adapters. The results differed drastically between MS Windows and when we used direct memory writing. Moreover, we couldn't find any correlation between them. There were 'gaps' for almost every card on the 'mode scale' or 'operation scale' (polygons, text scrolling, patterns, and so on) in which operation speed vanishes. Yes, Windows accelerators are definitely optimized, but for the needs of Windows, not for ours. Where do they hide this artificial intelligence? Your guess is as good as ours!

Memory Structure

The video RAM, or VRAM, is a part of the video subsystem where the data to be displayed is stored. The video memory of modern adapters can be as much as 2Mb or more. A quick calculation will tell you why it needs to be so big. Suppose you want TrueColor at a resolution of 1024×768 then it would need 1024 * 768 * 3, which works out to be about 2.3 Mb.

There is a special window in the address space of the CPU which is used to access the video memory. The segment address of the window starts at A000h and the size of the window is 64K. Once upon a time IBM considered 128K enough and reserved the addresses A000h:BFFFh for video; 64K for each adapter of a possible two-monitor system. So if you want to read from or write to a video memory 2MB in size, you have to use a sophisticated addressing method, such as bank switching.

Bank Switching

This is a term we'll use dozens of times throughout the book, so for those of you who may be unfamiliar with it, a quick explanation. The general idea is that you have an address space that is less than the accessible memory. Thus you need to shift the beginning of the window to access certain parts of the memory. For **PutPixel**, it means that all you need is the bank number and the offset within the bank.

The logical structure of the video memory (by which we mean the way in which a VRAM's bytes construct pixels of a raster) varies for different video modes. If you want to use the direct memory technique, it's crucial that you have a really good understanding of how the video memory is organized. It is a bit like using the hard disk - to work with files in DOS you don't need to know the details of the FAT, ROOT and so on. However, as soon as you need to write special bytes directly to special sectors, for example, for copy protection, you have to master DOS's innards.

The next four figures show several methods in which memory may be organized in the different memory models.

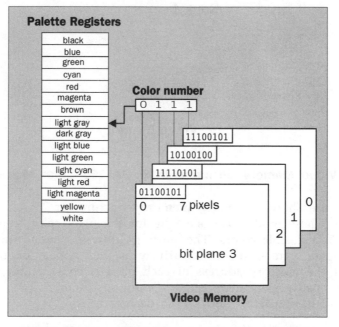

Video Memory Structure in 16 Color Modes

The figure on the previous page illustrates the structure of the video memory in the 16-color modes. In these modes the video memory is arranged as four bit planes. Each plane contains one bit of the pixel color 'code', and therefore you have 2^4 = 16 colors. Adapters 'decode' a particular color by referring to a special table called the palette. All four planes have the *same* address space, starting at A000h:0. It's a rather cruel way to cripple a programmer's mind, so we'll delay the details for a while.

For 16 color SVGA modes exceeding 800×600, say 1024×768 or 1280×1024, you have to deal with bank switching as well. Real programmers will enjoy creative programming in these modes.

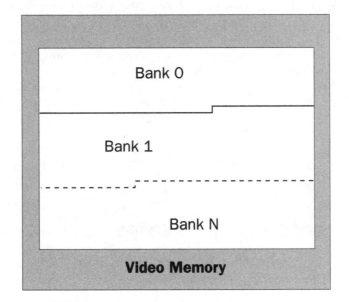

Video Memory Structure in SVGA 256 Color Modes

The above figure shows the video memory structure for 256-color VGA and SVGA modes. These modes use one byte for the pixel color 'code', so you have 2^8 = 256 accessible colors. The starting address remains the same, A000h:0. All pixels are stored consecutively as they appear on the screen. The calculation of the memory address of each pixel is considerably simplified by one byte per pixel organization and a continuous memory map. These are the easiest and most useful modes ever designed.

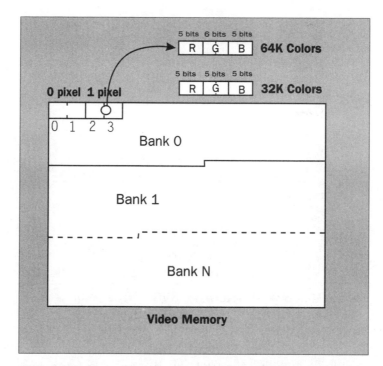

Video Memory Structure in SVGA HighColor Modes

Here is the illustrative figure for the VRAM structure for SVGA HighColor video modes. This system has a new level of mysterious coding, with a word (2 bytes, 16 bits) for each pixel. There is no palette; the two byte pixel 'code' simply contains different intensities of the red, green and blue components of the color. However, it is not quite so simple; for 32K color modes, it's 5 bits per RGB component and the sixteenth bit isn't used; for 64K color modes, the green component occupies 6 bits with red and blue at 5 bits each. It seems the world is greener than we thought!

The reason for this is actually based on human physiology. The eye is more sensitive to the green region of the spectrum, so it makes sense to have a greater range for the green component.

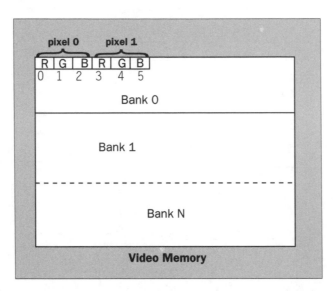

Video Memory Structure in SVGA TrueColor Modes

The final figure is for SVGA TrueColor modes. Again it's fairly simple; 3 bytes for each pixel, 8 bits per RGB component. If you have 24 bits per pixel this is called twenty four bit graphics and you can use 2^{24} = 16,777,216 colors simultaneously, or at least you could do, if you had that many pixels on the screen.

Advanced Programming of the VGA

Introduction to the VGA Register Set and Register Programming

Each graphics adapter has several registers which organize its internal functions. The registers which are common to all VGAs fall into six major groups:

 Sequencer registers which control memory access, timing, and data flow among the other registers

 CRTC (Cathode Ray Tube Controller) registers which deal with the timing related to the monitor

 External registers which provide miscellaneous functions

▲ Graphics Controller registers which support graphics mode functions

▲ Attribute Controller registers which handle the color palette selections

▲ DAC (Digital to Analog Converter) registers which convert the color 'code' to a voltage for your analog monitor

The external registers and the Color Select Registers block in the Attribute Controller are accessed directly, as each of them has a unique host port. All the others are accessed indirectly.

There is a special address register for each group which is used to select the register to be modified. Each of the indirectly addressed registers has a unique index within the group. This index is written to the address register of the corresponding group, and then the desired register is addressed, as shown in the following table:

Register Group		Direct I/O port	Address port	Data port
Sequencer		------	3C4h	3C5h
CRTC	Mono	------	3B4h	3B5h
	Color	------	3D4h	3D5h
External	Mono	3BAh,3CAh	-----	3C2h,3CCh
	Color	3DAh,3CAh	-----	3C2h,3CCh
Graphics Controller		------	3CEh	3CFh
Attribute Controller		------	3C0h	3C1h
DAC		3C6h,3C7h	-----	3C8h,3C9h

Addresses of Register Groups

Have a look at the following simple example of addressing the Graphics Controller:

```
mov    dx,3CEh      ;Graphics Controller addressing register
mov    al,8         ;Index of bit mask register
out    dx,al        ;select this register
inc    dx           ;Graphics Controller data register
mov    al,0EFh      ;AL = data (the mask)
out    dx,al        ;set bit mask
```

The following does the same but is a little bit shorter and therefore faster:

```
mov    dx,3CEh      ;Graphics Controller Addressing register
mov    ax,0EF08h    ;AL = index, AH = value
out    dx,ax        ;set bit mask
```

Before we dive into more detail there are some important points to note:

- ▲ You can read and write to all VGA registers except for the Attribute address register and input status registers. This is one advantage that VGA has over the EGA.

- ▲ Some VGA registers must be read and written at different port addresses, an example of which is the external register 3C2h that reads from 3CCh.

There is a simple, but very useful rule to remember when changing a register's state (essential for tricky programming); the port should be read, only the desired bits modified, and the result written back to the port.

Also note that once the index of the Address Register has been set, it will remain in effect until it is changed, the only exception being the Attribute Register. Therefore, if you are changing the same registers repeatedly, you can set the index outside the loop, something like this:

```
       mov    dx,3CEh      ;Graphics Controller Addressing register
       mov    al,8         ;Index of bit mask register
       out    dx,al        ;select this register
       inc    dx           ;Graphics Controller data register
       mov    cx,100h      ;CX = counter
next:
       ...
       mov    al,[di]      ;AL = mask
       out    dx,al        ;set bit mask
       ...
       inc    di
       loop   next         ;load next mask
```

Most programmers think that register programming is the basis for each and every sophisticated or tricky technique in graphics. And they aren't wrong; however, there are registers and Registers.

Attractive Graphics

You can make your programs really attractive by juggling colors. If you really know how to work with your DAC and Attribute Controller, fading, glimmering, translucency and a whole host of other effects are there for the taking. If you use direct memory techniques, it usually means you'll be working with the Graphics Controller and possibly the Sequencer's Map Mask Register, both of which we'll discuss in a moment.

There are several entries in the Sequencer Registers group and in the CRTC that would be worth looking at, but it would be beyond this book to go into great detail. Instead we'll just introduce the helpful features of the Sequencer and CRTC and you'll find some examples of splitting and panning in Chapter 5. After that we'll forget about them.

The CRTC is used for low-level control of the CRT. It can be used for a lot of things, but most people only really work with the Start Address (index 0Ch for low bytes and 0Dh for high), Offset (index 13h) and Line Compare (index 18h) to produce effects like smooth scrolling and screen splitting.

The Sequencer's primary task is to control the data flow. Timing, memory models and the like are really only for experienced programmers. However, you can switch your screen on and off if you have a reason to.

Anyway, it's best not to touch these registers, unless you like creating video modes of your own, such as a 543×210, 256 color, chain 4 memory mode!

Palette and Colors

A color palette is a special table used to translate a pixel color 'code' into the color of a pixel on the CRT. You'll need a palette table if your hardware can display more colors than your pixel encoding technique permits. For instance, VGA can display 256K different colors (6-bit DAC registers, 2^{3*6} = 256K). However, in 16-color modes (4 bits per pixel) a pixel can be any of 16 different colors. Therefore, you need a palette to define which 16 of the 256K possible colors will be used. This explains why no palette exists for the TrueColor mode; you use straightforward pixel encoding (24 bits per pixel) and your hardware can display as many colors as you need at the same time. In theory, you could have a palette for HighColor mode that would choose 64K from a possible 16M, but it would have to be a rather large table.

There are some pretty tricks you can do thanks to this palette. The key idea is that you can affect lots of pixels at once by changing 256, 16, or even 1 register. We'll show you some techniques in the examples later, but first back to business.

There are two groups of registers which are responsible for colors in VGA. We've mentioned both briefly in the previous section. Now let's have a look in more detail.

DAC Registers

The Digital to Analog Converter (DAC) registers are used to convert the color code information of the pixels into analog signals for the CRT. The DAC contains 256 Color Registers, each defining one color. Each Color Register consists of 3 parts which correspond to the red, green and blue components. Each part is 6 bits wide making it possible for any of the components to have a maximum of 64 levels of brightness. Thus you can get any of the 262,144 (2^{3*6}) available colors by mixing the RGB components.

For Color register management the DAC has four registers as shown below:

Address	Read/Write	Function
3C8h	Read/Write	PEL Address Register when write
3C7h	Write	PEL Address Register when read
3C7h	Read	DAC State Register
3C9h	Read/Write	PEL Data Register
3C6h	Read/Write	PEL Mask Register

DAC Registers

The PEL Address Register is used to select a particular Color Register with which to work, as well as to choose the operation (read or write) to perform. A funny technique is used to select the operation. It depends on what you are going to do, read or write. You either send the Color Register's address to port 3C7h or 3C8h, and reading or writing is done through the PEL Data Register. Further, any reading or writing consists of three sequential operations, one for each of the RGB components. After each 'full' operation, by which we mean one that contains three sequential operations for each of the RGB components, the PEL Address Register automatically increments itself to address the next PEL Data Register.

It was thought that a delay of about 240 nanoseconds was needed between successive read or write operations. However, our own experience shows that this delay may be omitted, depending on the video hardware. If you get funny color effects, you will need to put in a delay using one or several **nop**s. When the Color Registers are modified, 'snow' may appear on the screen. To avoid this complication, you should change the Color Registers only when the display is in the retrace period, or in other words for a 4 millisecond period when the electron beam is moving back to the top of the screen.

Examples of Color Register Setting

An example of Color Register setting with a delay of about 240ms:

```
        mov     cx,Count        ;CX = amount of Color Registers to be set
        mov     dx,3dah         ;DX = Input Status Register #1
                                ;3bah-for monochrome displays,3dah-for color one
@ActWait:                       ;wait for vertical retrace
    in      al,dx               ;AL = status
    test    al,8                ;test bit 3
    jz      @ActWait            ;loop while not in vertical retrace

        mov     dl,0c8h         ;PEL Address register
        mov     al,First        ;AL = first Color Register to be set
        out     dx,al
        inc     dx              ;PEL Data Register
        lds     si,Palette      ;ES:[DI] points to array of R,G,B value
        cld                     ;clear direction flag
        cli                     ;disable interrupts

next_col_reg:
        outsb                   ;set Red component
        jmp     $+2
        jmp     $+2             ;short delay
        outsb                   ;set Green component
        jmp     $+2
        jmp     $+2             ;short delay
        outsb                   ;set Blue component
        loop    next_col_reg    ;set next Color Register
        sti                     ;enable interrupts
```

and without delay:

```
        mov     cx,Count        ;CX = amount of Color Registers to be set
        shl     cx,1            ;CX = CX * 2
        add     cx,Count        ;CX = CX * 3
        mov     dx,3dah         ;DX = Input Status Register #1
```

```
@ActWait:               ;wait for vertical retrace
    in    al,dx         ;AL = status
    test  al,8          ;test bit 3
    jz    @ActWait      ;loop while not in vertical retrace

    mov   dl,0c8h       ;PEL Address register
    mov   al,First      ;AL = First Color Register
    out   dx,al
    inc   dx            ;PEL Data Register
    lds   si,Palette    ;ES:[DI] point to array of R,G,B value
    cld                 ;clear direction flag
    cli                 ;disable interrupts
    rep   outsb         ;to make it shorter
    sti                 ;enable interrupts
```

DAC State Register

The DAC State Register is used to determine whether the DAC is in read or write mode. If the first two bits (0,1) of the DAC State Register are both set to 1, then the DAC is in read mode. If both are set to 0, then the DAC is in write mode.

The PEL Mask Register is set to FFh by BIOS and its better not to touch it. It's a rather mysterious piece of silicon, we've never heard of anybody using it.

The Attribute Controller includes the second group of registers that deal with colors in 16 color mode. There are 16 Palette Registers (index 0 - 0Fh), the Color Select Register (index 14h) and the seventh bit of the Mode Control Register (index 10h). The last determines which method of 'color decoding' will occur, and so two of them exist:

- ▲ The first method of color decoding is where the seventh bit of the Mode Control register is set to 0. The pixel's 4-bit color 'code' points to one of 16 Palette Registers, which, in turn, contains the 6 lower bits of the Color Register's address. The 2 upper bits of this address are taken from the Color Select Register (bits 2 and 3).

- ▲ The second method differs a little. Only the 4 lower bits of the Color Register's address are taken from the Palette Register, while 4 upper bits of this address are taken from the Color Select Register (bits 0-3).

> The only use we can imagine that justifies such 'creative design' is the ability to perform a very quick change of all the colors displayed on the screen.

The access to the Attribute Controller Registers is a bit like a Chinese puzzle. The following example of setting the Attribute Controller register:

```
    mov   dx,3dah          ;DX = Input Status Register #1
    in    al,dx            ;IN from Input Status Register #1
                           ;will always set the port 3c0h to the Address mode
    mov   al,RegNumber     ;AL = register index
    mov   dx,3c0h          ;DX = Attribute Address Register
    out   dx,al            ;set register index and
                           ;now port 3c0h set to the Data mode
    mov   al,Value         ;AL = new value of register
    out   dx,al            ;set register

    mov   al,20h           ;set bit 5
    out   dx,al            ;enable display
```

Modifying the Color Registers using BIOS calls

Additionally, the Color Registers can be written to or read from by using some BIOS calls. Programmers may set or read a single Color Register or a group of Color Registers, or they may select or read the color subset. For a list of the BIOS calls related to the Color Register, see the following table:

Subfunction	Description
10h	Set individual Color Register
12h	Set block of Color Registers
13h	Set color subset
15h	Get individual Color Register
17h	Get block of Color Registers
1Ah	Read color subset
1Bh	Sum DAC registers to gray shades

BIOS Calls that Deal with Color Registers, Function 10h

There is a 'disadvantage' in using the BIOS functions to change color registers. The BIOS functions are written so that the change to the register is held until the retrace period. This means that some of the more fancy color changes can't be done with the BIOS and you have to resort to modifying the registers directly.

Note that function 12h (BL=31h) is used to set the default palette.

An example of Color register setting by means of the BIOS:

```
    mov    ax,1012h      ;AH = Function 10h
                         ;AL = Subfunction 12h (Set block of Color registers)
    mov    bx,First      ;BX = start Color Register
    mov    cx,Count      ;CX = number of Color Register
    les    di,Palette    ;ES:[DI] point to Palette table (R,G,B value)
    int    10h           ;do it
```

Direct Memory Techniques

This section is one of the most important in the whole chapter. Why? We will only be showing how to Put and Get pixels to video memory, although we will be using various graphics modes up to TrueColor. BIOS can do this too but not up so far as HighColor and TrueColor modes. However, this technique, although useful in itself as you very often only need to put a pixel or two, is the foundation for understanding the 'kernel' of graphics programming.

The section is arranged according to the video modes and memory models rather than the types of adapters. This is because we are studying direct memory techniques, and the memory addressing that is different between the video modes.

Pixel Addressing

In any mode, before setting a pixel, you must calculate the address in video memory to write to. Usually the pixel on the screen is addressed by means of X, Y coordinates. Y is the number of the row and X is the pixel's position in this row. Both X and Y are counted from 0 and the pixel with coordinates (0,0) lives in the upper left corner of the screen.

In all modes, and for all adapters described here, the pixels are stored in video memory consecutively, as they appear on the screen, from left to right within the row, from the top to bottom, row after row. So, to determine the 'address' of the pixel you should simply add the row offset in video memory (calculated using Y) and the offset of the pixel from the beginning of the row (calculated using X).

The crucial thing when calculating the pixel address is how many bytes of video memory is required for each row of screen. Let's call it **BytesPerLine** and we will use this acronym in all the examples below. For instance:

▲ in 640×480, 16-color mode
BytesPerLine = 640/8 = 80 bytes

▲ in 320×200, 256-color mode
BytesPerLine = 320 bytes

You should multiply **BytesPerLine** by the Y coordinate to get the offset of the beginning of the row. The offset along the row depends on the video mode.

16 Color Modes

As was mentioned before, in 16 color mode, video memory is constructed as four bit planes which are addressed in parallel. Each plane contains one bit of the pixel color 'code'. You may think that you need four read/write operations to get/put a pixel. However, as we'll show below, it can be done more briefly.

For the video modes considered, each byte of the video memory corresponds to 8 pixels. The more to the left a pixel lies on the screen, the higher the bit of the byte used. **BytesPerLine** is 8 times less than the number of pixels in line, for example:

▲ in 800×600 mode
BytesPerLine = 800/8 = 100 bytes

The quotient of the integer division X by 8 gives the offset of the byte from the beginning of the row, or in other words, how many bytes along the row, while the remainder gives the number of the bit in the byte, or in other words, its significance. So the expression for the pixel's 'address' calculation is as follows:

```
addr = Y*BytesPerLine + X / 8
```

To address a particular pixel from this byte, you'll need to use a special mask in which the corresponding bit is set to 1 and the others to 0.

Here is an example of the pixel's address calculation:

```
PixelAddress    macro    Y,X
    mov    ax,Y          ;AX = Y Coordinate
    mov    bx,X          ;BX = X Coordinate
    mov    cl,bl         ;Save in CL low byte of BX
    mul    BytesPerLine  ;AX = row offset in video memory (Y * BytesPerLine)
    shr    bx,3          ;BX = byte offset in row X / 8
    add    bx,ax         ;BX = byte offset in video memory
    and    cl,7          ;CL = CL & 7
    xor    cl,7          ;CL = number of bits to shift left
    mov    ax,0a000h
    mov    es,ax         ;ES = video memory segment
    mov    al,1          ;AL = unshifted bit mask
    shl    al,cl         ;AL = bit mask
                         ;ES:[BX] pointer to byte in video memory
    endm
```

This macro will come in useful later.

It is the Graphics Controller (GC) that manages all the data transfer operations in 16-color modes. We've met it briefly before, but now let's get to know it a bit better. It has always been difficult for us to understand why they designed it in the way they have. In fact, in this mode, you don't use direct memory techniques. We are going to clarify the mystical way to get around this problem, but you'll have to touch on something more complicated than memory mapping, namely the internals of the VGA. So fasten your seat belts and be patient.

The Internals of VGA

The Graphics Controller has 9 registers, which are addressed through port 3CEh, while the port for data is 3CFh, as shown below:

Index	Function
0	Set/Reset
1	Enable Set/Reset
2	Color Compare
3	Data Rotate/Function Select
4	Read Map Select

Continued

Index	Function
5	Mode
6	Miscellaneous
7	Color Don't Care
8	Bit Mask

VGA Graphics Controller Registers

All of them, except the 6th, are designed to be used just in 16-color modes.

There are some specific **read** and **write** modes which control the way the data is transformed in your adapter and these will restrict your possible actions. The VGA has four **write** modes and two **read** modes.

Write Mode 0

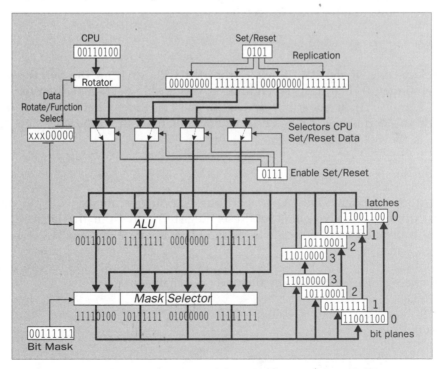

Scheme to Illustrate the VGA's Work in Write Mode 0

This write mode is the most difficult to understand as you can see from the previous figure. Firstly, we will describe what's what in the figure. We don't know for sure whether the elements within the figure have silicon analogs in a real chip, but we'd just like to help your understanding.

Latches

The latches are four 8-bit registers, one for each of the bit planes. When executing a CPU read operation, the four bytes from the bit planes are transferred to the corresponding latches. The data stays in the latches, and so it may be used for something else during further write operations, as you will see in the next few pages. To provide this every time you are writing data to an address in video memory, you must first read the contents of the memory. It isn't necessary to use the data read, it's only a way to update the latches.

Rotator

This shifts the CPU byte clockwise by the number of bits set in the Data Rotate / Function Select Register (index 3 bits 0..2). It's hardly ever used, (or we don't know how) so let's forget it.

Selector - CPU or Set/Reset

This selects one of the data flows - from the CPU or from the Set/Reset Register (index 0, bits 0..3) depending on the Enable Set/Reset Register setting (index 1, bits 0..3). If some bits in the Enable Set/Reset Register are 0, then data for the corresponding plane is taken from the CPU, otherwise the data source is the Set/Reset Register.

ALU

The Arithmetic Logic Unit (ALU) performs logical operations with the data coming from the CPU (or the Set/Reset Register) and from the latches. The ALU is controlled by bits 3 and 4 of the Data Rotate/Function Select Register. In particular:

00 - Replace, CPU or Set/Reset data pass unchanged
01 - AND
02 - OR
03 - XOR

Mask Selector

The Mask Selector doesn't allow data bits forbidden by the Bit Mask Register (index 8) to be placed into video memory. More precisely, if some bits of the register are 1, corresponding bits for each bit plane are taken from the ALU, and if they are 0 then they are taken from the latches. Thus, as the latches normally contain the same data as in the video memory, the Mask Selector only lets you modify the desirable pixels of the 8 pixels addressed.

There are two approaches to working in the Write Mode 0: color-oriented and byte-oriented. The first one may be used, for example, to place a pixel or fill an area with a certain color. To implement it, you should set all bits of the Enable Set/Reset Register to 1. In this case, the color 'code' from the Set/Reset Register is considered as the source of data. Each bit of this register expands into 8 bits: 0 into 00h and 1 into FFh. As a result, you have 32 bits which then come into the ALU. The desired logical operation under 32 bits from the latches is executed in the ALU as well. Those bits of the result which pass through the mask are placed in the video memory.

Example: Write Pixel in write mode 0, color logic - XOR

```
    PixelAddress 100,200        ;calculating pixel address with coordinates
                                ;X=100, Y=200
                                ;ES:BX points to byte in video memory
                                ;AL = bit mask
    mov    dx,3ceh              ;Graphics Controller addressing register
    mov    ah,al                ;AH = bit mask
    mov    al,8                 ;AL = Bit Mask register index
    out    dx,ax                ;set bit mask

    mov    ah,PixelColor        ;AH = pixel color (0 - 15)
    mov    al,0                 ;AL = Set/Register register index
    out    dx,ax                ;set draw color

    mov    ax,0f01h             ;AL = Enable Set/Reset register index
    out    dx,ax                ;AH = 0fh bit mask for Set/Reset register
    mov    ax,1803h             ;AL = Data Rotate/Function Select register index
                                ;AH = 18h (bits 3,4 function select)
    out    dx,ax                ;set XOR operation
    xchg   es:[bx],al           ;use advantages of xchg instruction to
                                ;update bit planes (one instruction performs
                                ;both read & write of data)
```

To follow the byte oriented approach, you should set all bits of the Enable Set/Reset Register to 0. In this case a byte from the CPU first passes through the Rotator and then goes to the ALU, where the desired logical operation is performed; the result is then masked and written to the bit planes. It may be used to send an image previously saved in conventional memory to the screen.

You may put something more sophisticated than just 0000 or 1111 into the Enable Set/Reset Register. It won't scare the Graphics Controller and it will send data from the CPU to certain bit planes and data from the Set/Reset Register to others. But to be frank, we don't know whether anybody would find it of any use.

It should be mentioned that refreshing the latches before a write operation isn't the Eleventh Commandment, it's only a common technique. If you'd like to update all 8 pixels corresponding to some byte, and you don't need any of the logical combinations that are usually on offer, then you needn't spend time making the CPU read. But if you'd like some of the bits (pixels) masked or are going to use any type of color logic, you have to execute a read first.

Write Mode 2

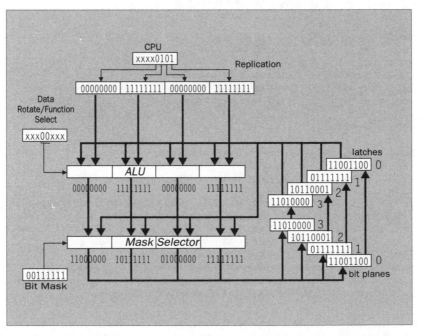

Scheme to Illustrate the VGA's Work in Write Mode 2

The way this mode is normally used is very much like the color-oriented approach in the write mode 0. The only difference is that instead of using the

Set/Reset Register you use the 4 low bits of the CPU byte. The ALU and the Bit Mask Register perform the same actions as in the write mode 0.

Example of writing a pixel in write mode 2, color logic - AND:

```
        PixelAddress 100,200        ;calculating pixel address with coordinates
                                    ;X = 100, Y = 200
                                    ;ES:BX point to byte in video memory
                                    ;AL = bit mask

        mov     dx,3ceh             ;Graphics Controller  addressing register
        mov     ah,al               ;AH = bit mask
        mov     al,8                ;AL = Bit Mask register index
        out     dx,ax               ;set bit mask

        mov     ax,0205h            ;AL = Mode register index
                                    ;AH = 2(write mode 2)
        out     dx,ax               ;set write mode 2
        mov     ax,0803h            ;AL = Data Rotate/Function Select register index
                                    ;AH = 08h (bits 3,4 function select)
        out     dx,ax               ;set AND operation

        mov     al,PixelColor       ;AL = pixel color
        xchg    es:[bx],al          ;update bit planes
```

Write Mode 3

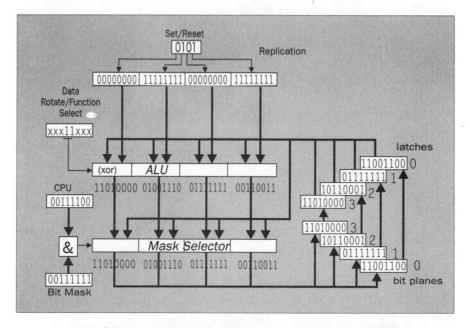

Scheme to Illustrate the VGA's Work in Write Mode 3

This mode is accessible only for VGA cards. The 'code' of the color is taken from the Set/Reset Register. The settings of the Enable Set/Reset Register don't have any effect. The ALU still works like it did in the mode 0. The CPU byte passes through the Rotator and bit by bit is ANDed with the value of the Bit Mask Register. The result works just as the mask does in write mode 0. So it's possible to save one **out** instruction, as you needn't update the Bit Mask Register, but don't forget to preset the Bit Mask Register to 0FFh.

Example of writing a pixel in write mode 3

```
    PixelAddress 100,200        ;calculating pixel address with coordinates
                                ;X = 100, Y = 200
                                ;ES:BX point to byte in video memory
                                ;AL = bit mask
    mov    cl,al                ;CL = bit mask
    mov    dx,3ceh              ;Graphics Controller addressing register
    mov    ax,0305h             ;AL = Mode register index
                                ;AH = 3 (write mode 3)
    out    dx,ax                ;set write mode 3

    mov    ah,PixelColor        ;AH = pixel color
    mov    al,0                 ;AL = Set/Reset register index
    out    dx,ax                ;set draw color

    mov    ax,0ff08h            ;AL = Bit Mask register index
                                ;AH = 0ffh (the real mask in CL)
    out    dx,ax                ;set bit mask
    xchg   es:[bx],cl           ;update bit planes
```

Write Mode 1

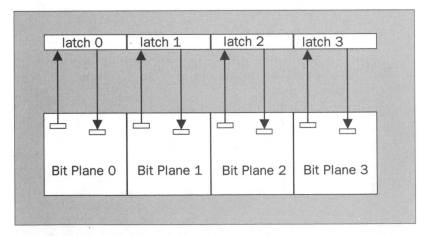

Scheme to Illustrate the VGA's Work in Write Mode 1

This mode is extremely useful for fast copying within the video memory. When the CPU reads, information is moved to the latches, and when it writes, data is transferred from the latches into video memory. The settings of the Set/Reset Register, Bit Mask Register and the value of the CPU data, don't have any influence in this mode.

Example of coping contents of the 1st row to the 9th row:

```
        mov     dx,3ceh       ;Graphics Controller addressing register
        mov     ax,0105h      ;AL = Mode register index
                              ;AH = 1 (write mode 1)
        out     dx,ax         ;set write mode 1

        mov     ax,0a000h
        mov     es,ax
        mov     ds,ax         ;ES = DS = video memory segment

        xor     si,si         ;sourse offset (0 row)
        mov     di,800        ;target offset (9 row)
        mov     cx,80         ;counter moved bytes

        rep     movsb         ;move data from DS:[SI] to ES:[DI]
```

The Sequence Map Mask Register

There is one other register, the Sequencer Map Mask Register (Sequencer Register 02h, bits 0..3) which may be used to enable/disable data writes to the bit planes. A 1 in any of its bits enables writing to the corresponding bit plane and a 0 disables bit plane updating. It should be noted that this register is active in ALL write modes so don't forget about it, especially when using the write mode 1.

Example of writing a pixel in write mode 0 using the Sequencer Map Mask Register:

```
    PixelAddress 100,200      ;calculating pixel address with coordinates
                              ;X = 100, Y = 200
                              ;ES:BX point to byte in video memory
                              ;AL = bit mask
        mov     dx,3ceh       ;Graphics Controller  addressing register
        mov     ah,al         ;AH = bit mask
        mov     al,8          ;AL = Bit Mask register index
        out     dx,ax         ;set bit mask

        xchg    es:[di],ah    ;zero masked bits in all planes
```

```
        mov     dl,0c4h          ;Sequencer addressing register
        mov     ah,PixelColor    ;AH = pixel color
        mov     al,2             ;AL = Map Mask register index
        out     dx,ax            ;set map mask

        mov     es:[bx],0ffh     ;update bit planes
```

Now we will look at the two read modes, before finally saying 'farewell' to 16-color modes.

Read Mode 0

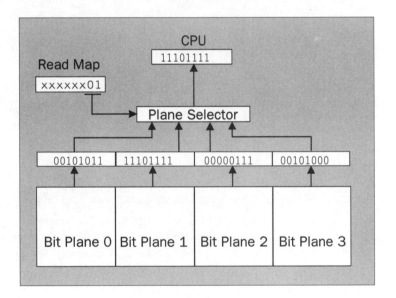

Scheme to Illustrate the VGA's Work in Read Mode 0

In this mode the CPU reads the contents of one of the 4 latches. The number of the latch read is taken from bits 0 and 1 of the Read Map Select Register (index 4). Thus to obtain the color of a pixel you have to execute four CPU read operations.

Example of how to read in Read Mode 0.

```
                         ;ES:[DI] points to byte for read in video memory
                         ;DS:[SI] points to bytes array
        mov     dx,3ceh  ;Graphics Controller  addressing register
        mov     al,4     ;AL = Read Map Select register index
```

```
        out    dx,al
        inc    dx              ;Graphics Controller data register
        mov    cx,4            ;bit plane counter
        mov    al,0            ;first read from 0 bit plane

next_bit_plane:

        out    dx,al           ;select bit plane for read
        mov    al,es:[di]      ;read byte from bit plane
        mov    [si],al         ;save byte somewhere
        inc    si
        inc    al              ;read next bit plane
        loop   next_bit_plane
```

Read Mode 1

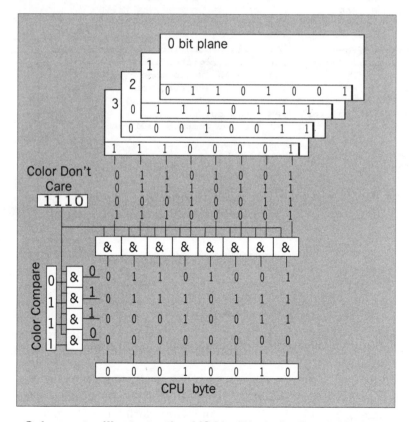

Scheme to Illustrate the VGA's Work in Read Mode 1

In this mode the CPU gets the result of comparing the color held in the Color Compare Register (index 2, bits 0..3) and the latches. If the colors are the same, the corresponding bit of the CPU byte is set to 1, otherwise to 0. The Color Don't Care Register excludes some bits of the color code (some bit planes) from the comparison. If any bit of the Color Don't Care is 0, then the corresponding bit of the pixel's color is ignored. Thus if the Color Don't Care Register is 0000, then the CPU always gets 0FFh and the colors are considered the same, just like gray cats in the dark.

It's not so easy to find an example of Read Mode 1 usage. You may find it useful to change one color to another.

```
        mov     ax,0a000h
        mov     es,ax           ;ES = video memory segment
        mov     di,800
        mov     si,di           ;SI = DI = offset 9 row

        mov     dx,3ceh         ;Graphics Controller  addressing register
        mov     ax,0b05h        ;AL = Mode register index
                                ;AH = 1011h (write mode 3, read mode 1)
        out     dx,ax           ; set write and read mode 1

        mov     ah,OldColor     ;AH = old color
        mov     al,2            ;AL = Color Compare Register
        out     dx,ax

        mov     al,0            ;AL = Set/Reset register index
        mov     ah,NewColor     ;AH = new color
        out     dx,ax

        mov     ax,0ff08h       ;AH = 0ffh (bit mask)
                                ;AL = Bit Mask register index
        out     dx,ax
        mov     cx,80           ;bytes per one row
        rep     movsb           ;fire !
```

SVGA - Modes Above 800×600

When using SVGA with modes above 800×600, the programming techniques remain the same, although pixel addressing is more complicated because of the need for bank switching.

An example of the pixel's address calculation for SVGA 16-color modes above 800×600, where the bank size is 64K, and Granularity is 64K follows:

```
PixelAddress    macro   Y,X
    mov     ax,Y            ;AX = Y coordinate
    mov     bx,X            ;BX = X coordinate
```

```
    mov   cl,bl           ;Save in CL low byte of BX
    mul   BytesPerLine    ;AX = row offset in video memory from the
                          ;beginning of the bank Lo(Y * BytesPerLine)
                          ;DX = bank number Hi(Y * BytesPerLine)
    shr   bx,3            ;BX = byte offset in row X / 8
    add   bx,ax           ;BX = byte offset in video memory from the
                          ;beginning of the bank
    adc   dx,0            ;catching bank-split-row occasion
    and   cl,7            ;CL = CL & 7
    xor   cl,7            ;CL = number of bits to shift left
    mov   ax,0a000h
    mov   es,ax           ;ES = video memory segment
    mov   al,1            ;AL = unshifted bit mask
    shl   al,cl           ;AL = bit mask
                          ;ES:[BX] pointer to byte in video memory from the
                          ;beginning of the bank
                          ;DX = bank number
endm
```

256-Color Modes

In comparison with 16-color modes, the programming techniques for 256-color modes is a piece of cake for a programmer. Pixel addressing is the simplest method to use when considering all the video modes, as there is one byte per pixel. The only problem is the palette.

First, let's have a look at the VGA standard video mode 13h (320×200). Video memory may be thought of as an array of bytes with the dimension [320][200], while the pixel addressing is thought of as being equivalent to the process of accessing an element of such an array. Therefore, calculating the pixel address is done like this:

addr = Y * BytesPerLine + X

where **BytesPerLine** = 320

> For any 256-color mode **BytesPerLine** is equal to the X resolution (one byte per pixel).

Example of writing a pixel in 320x200 256 color mode:

```
    mov   ax,Y           ;AX = Y coordinate
    mov   bx,X           ;BX = X coordinate
    xchg  al,ah          ;AX = Y * 256
    add   bx,ax          ;BX = X + Y * 256
    shr   ax,2           ;AX = Y * 64
    add   bx,ax          ;BX = byte offset in video memory
                         ;(Y * 256 + Y * 64 + X) = (Y * 320 + X)
```

```
        mov    ax,0a000h
        mov    es,ax         ;ES = video memory segment
        mov    al,Color      ;AL = pixel color
        mov    es:[bx],al    ;set pixel
```

You may be upset, but no color logic is supported by hardware in this mode. So the mov instruction should be changed with xor, or or and to provide it.

For SVGA, the programming technique is still the same, and bank switching is still required.

Example to write a pixel in 256-color SVGA modes:

```
        mov    ax,Y          ;AX = Y coordinate
        mov    bx,X          ;BX = X coordinate
        mul    BytesPerLine  ;AX = row offset in video memory from the
                             ;beginning of the bank Lo(Y * BytesPerLine)
                             ;DX = bank number Hi(Y * BytesPerLine)
        add    bx,ax         ;BX = byte offset in video memory from the
                             ;beginning of the bank
        adc    dx,0          ;bank-split-row catching
        mov    ax,0a000h
        mov    es,ax         ;ES = video memory segment
        call   SwitchBank    ;look at Note below

        mov    al,Color      ;AL = pixel color
        mov    es:[bx],al    ;set pixel
```

Note that this procedure implements bank switching. For an explanation of the code see Appendix A, VESA BIOS Extension (function 5h).

HighColor & TrueColor Modes

You do remember video memory structure in HighColor and TrueColor modes, don't you? Video memory may be considered as an array of words (2 bytes) for HighColor modes and of 3 bytes (24 bits) RGB structures for TrueColor.

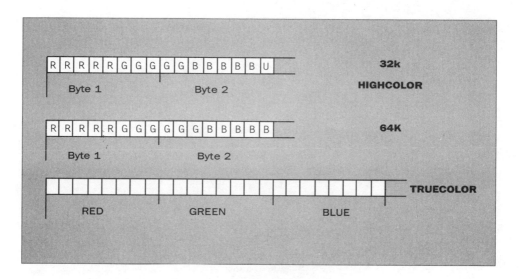

The formulas for pixel addressing look like this:

```
HighColor_addr  =  Y  *  BytesPerLine  +  X*2.
BytesPerLine  =  X_Resolution  *  2.
TrueColor_addr  =  Y  *  BytesPerLine  +  X*3.
```

BytesPerLine should be taken from the VESA SVGA information service (See Appendix A for details).

> Tip: The TrueColor modes we've explored have **BytesPerLine** equal to a multiple of 1024 bytes as it's convenient. For most video modes, this means that the number of bytes per line is in fact less than **BytesPerLine**. For example, 640 x 480 uses 640*3 bytes, or 1920 bytes, so **BytesPerLine** is set to 2048, and the last 128 bytes are forgotten. This method prevents the beginning of a bank from splitting a row.

Example of writing a pixel in HighColor modes:

```
mov    ax,Y        ;AX = Y coordinate
mov    bx,X        ;BX = X coordinate
mul    BytesPerLine ;AX = row offset in video memory from the
                    ;beginning of the bank Lo(Y * BytesPerLine)
                    ;DX = bank number Hi(Y * BytesPerLine)
```

```
        shl    bx,1              ;BX = X * 2 (word per pixel)
        add    bx,ax             ;BX = word offset in video memory from the
                                 ;beginning of the bank
        adc    dx,0              ;bank-split-row catching
        mov    ax,0a000h
        mov    es,ax             ;ES = video memory segment
        call   SwitchBank
        mov    al,Blue           ;AL = blue component of pixel color
        mov    ah,Red            ;AH = red component of pixel color
        shl    ah,3              ;shift by 2 if 32K colors, by 3 if 64K
        movzx  bx,Green          ;BX = green component of pixel color
        shl    bx,5
        or     ax,bx
        mov    es:[bx],ax        ;do it
```

Example of writing a pixel in TrueColor modes:

```
        mov    ax,Y              ;AX = Y coordinate
        mov    bx,X              ;BX = X coordinate
        mul    BytesPerLine      ;AX = row offset in video memory from the
                                 ;beginning of the bank Lo(Y * BytesPerLine)
                                 ;DX = bank number Hi(Y * BytesPerLine)
        shl    bx,1              ;BX = X * 2
        add    bx,X              ;BX = X * 3 (tree bytes per pixel)
        add    bx,ax             ;BX = word offset in video memory from the
                                 ;beginning of the bank
        adc    dx,0              ;bank-split-row catching
        mov    ax,0a000h
        mov    es,ax             ;ES = video memory segment
        call   SwitchBank
        mov    ah,Green          ;AH = green component of pixel color
        mov    al,Blue           ;AL = blue component of pixel color
        mov    es:[bx],ax        ;putting red and green bytes
        mov    al,Red            ;AL = red component of pixel color
        mov    es:[bx],al        ;now blue byte personally
```

SVGAs without VESA Support

We still have a little gap on the 'adapters' side of this chapter because there are some old SVGA adapters which don't have either VESA extensions in the BIOS or a VESA driver. Is there any way to make these boards show more colors in higher resolutions? Certainly. Will it be easy? Certainly, not, but you could try.

The key issue is still how to master the vendor specific function for bank switching and to gather knowledge of the video mode numbers. There are three possible scenarios:

1   You have such a card of your own and have decided to tame its SVGA modes for your own purposes. In this case you'd should look through your SVGA card manual, or any given example code that uses the appropriate modes, to find the key information. As soon as you get it, try and you'll succeed. It's reasonably simple, because there should be plenty of drivers available.

2   You are writing a commercial application and you would like it to support such SVGAs. This case is much harder to solve, but even in this case there is a recipe for success. You need to gather the necessary information about such SVGAs and implement it in your application code, driver, or whatever else. Next, don't bore the user with questions like 'Pick your SVGA from the list below..', especially as you can 'easily' perform this yourself. There is usually a unique system for recognizing each card. As soon as you find out which SVGA you face, tune the application for it and let it fly.

3   Find a TSR which gives your old non-VESA card full VESA capability and use that. To help you do this, we've included a selection of them on the CD-ROM.

Summary

A few words before we depart from low-level video hardware programming. It would seem some kind of apology is required.

When we planned the contents of this book, it was absolutely clear that some kind of hardware dictionary was necessary for the completeness of the book. But how to make it SI_LI_CON? To cover PC video hardware in detail would require a book by itself, as the topic is really huge. However, we've made an attempt, and to be frank, we are satisfied with the result, or at least we believe that the explanation of the 16-color modes is the most honest ever written and the tips on TrueColor should also be quite useful to you.

In the next chapter, armed with the knowledge garnered from this together with the last chapter, we will give a detailed look at the subject of color, paying particular attention to the theories of color and the use of palettes. After all, without color the world would be a dull place to be!

CHAPTER

4

Colors and Palettes

In this chapter, we'll cover the basics of color theory, and then move back into the realms of computing to show you how to work with the palette registers. We will also show how, with a limited palette, you can obtain more 'colors' using a technique called dithering.

Chapter Contents

In this chapter, we will cover:

 What is Color?

 Color Models

 Getting More Colors - Dithering

 Getting Less Colors - Palette Transformation

 A Color Manipulation Example

What is Color?

Most people feel that they understand what color is. This understanding is based on perceptual experience, and does not involve any formal definition of the term 'color'. So how could we define color? Maybe it is:

▲ a specific distribution of wavelengths

▲ or the hue, brightness, and saturation of light

▲ or the hue, lightness and saturation of objects.

In fact it is all of these. The first definition is the most precise from a scientific point of view, the others come from art or everyday life. Nevertheless, all three are correct to some extent; color can be described and discussed from a number of perspectives. In fact, each of the descriptions emphasizes different aspects of a complicated phenomenon. Because of this, we need to consider a number of theories, each covering one or more aspects of this thing called color. We hope it will be useful, at least for those who want to know the answers to the following questions:

▲ What is so unique about red, green and blue?

▲ Why do we need **three** base colors?

▲ What do the magic spells CMYK, YIQ, HSV mean?

If you already know the answers, or don't need them, you may skip the next few pages.

Color Models

We'll start with the first definition. The figure on the next page shows three different colors, purple, green and red.

> Note that the figures on the CD-ROM are in glorious technicolor!

These colors are made up from different wavelengths of light, and it is a certain mixture of these that creates a particular color. This is known as the spectral distribution, otherwise called the spectrum, and can be looked at using a spectrometer. You can imagine an almost infinite number of such graphs and that's why there is an ocean of color.

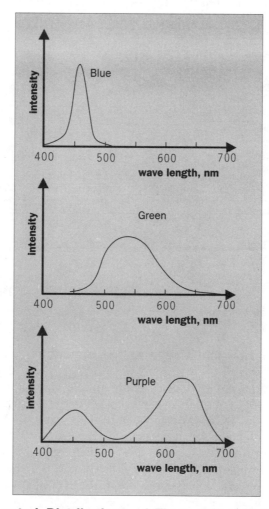

Spectral Distributions of Three Different Colors

Another way of describing color is with hue, luminosity and saturation (HLS). The hue is an indication of the wavelength, though only an indication because, strictly speaking, most colors are made up from a mixture of different wavelengths. Saturation is an indication of the purity of the hue,

moving from gray to the pure color and luminosity is the brightness of the color, in the range from black to white. This system is based on how the brain perceives color. For a color based on a 'single' wavelength, the following figure shows the relationship between HLS and the spectrum:

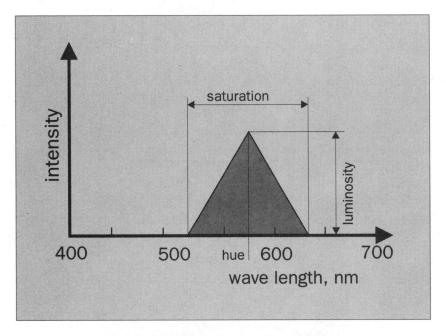

HLS in Relation to the Spectrum

The HLS system is fine, but it doesn't relate to the way a monitor works, or for that matter, the way a human eye works. A better system is for representing color is the RGB system, as it has it's basis in the eye. There are three different types of color-sensitive cells in the eye's retina: blue, green and red, which are optimally stimulated at wavelengths of approximately 440, 545 and 580 nanometers respectively. Each color is perceived *separately*. The following figure shows the average color sensitivity of a human eye to blue, green and red light.

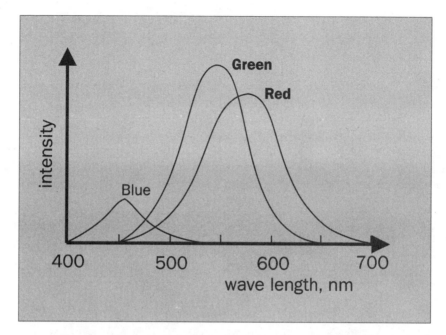

Average Sensitivity of a Human Eye to Blue, Green and Red Light

This theory is the foundation of **additive color models**, in which a color is represented as the sum of its components, for instance red green and blue (RGB). You should note that at the moment we are talking about emission spectra, or in other words, created light. Your monitor emits light, and it is the sum of the light emitted from the dots of red, green and blue phosphor on the screen that generates the color. Most of the colors that you see in the world are actually the result of absorption. The ink that makes up these letters are not black - they don't emit black - but rather, they absorb all the visible light that falls on them. This text is blue because the ink absorbs every wavelength except for that which corresponds to blue. The remaining light is then reflected into the eye, thus causing the text to appear blue.

Therefore, any color that can be perceived by the human eye can be made up from different intensities of blue, green and red with wavelengths of around 440, 545 and 580 respectively.

Nevertheless, the idea of a uniform representation of color was too attractive to be forgotten. In 1931, the Comission Internationale de I'Eclairage, or CIE, established a color standard which has almost cleared away the problems of representing, measuring and mixing colors.

The CIE standard uses three basic pseudo-colors which are more convenient to operate. These colors are usually referred to as XYZ. They are added together to give a particular color, in a similar way to the RGB system.

However, CIE is usually used in the form of a special graph or nomogram. How do you get this graph? We'll imagine a pile of color triangles in XYZ 3D color space. Each of the triangles contains every possible combination of hue and saturation for a given brightness. When projected on to some plane (for instance XY) each of the triangles (for instance the one formed by the points (1,0,0), (0,1,0), (0,0,1)) may be used to interpret colors. Then you only need some way to represent brightness, as shown in the figure below:

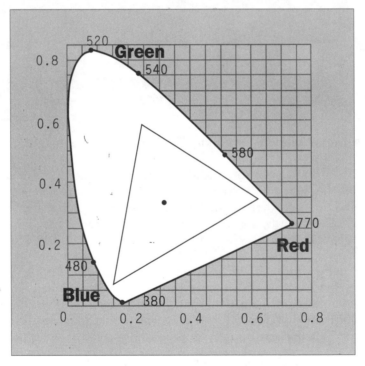

CIE Color Graph (Nomogram)

Coordinates x and y of the CIE color graph are defined using the following formulas:

x=X/(X+Y+Z)
y=Y/(X+Y+Z)
z=Z/(X+Y+Z)

where x + y + z = 1

The center of the CIE color graph is the standard white.

> It should be understood that there are, in fact, quite a few different 'whites'.

Values on the border of color triangles are the wavelengths that correspond to the various indicated colors.

The CIE color 'triangle' has numerous valuable uses. We've decided to illustrate only two of its magnificent features: color mixing and color inclusion. Mixing colors of the same brightness is simple - just add appropriate proportions of each. If the brightness differs, or you'd like to mix different 'weights', you'd should use the routine **mixcolors** provided below. Color interpolation will be referred to throughout the book, especially in the second part, no matter what you're doing. From image processing to morphing, it's one of the basic tools.

```
void mixcolors(float x1,float y1,float z1,
               float x2,float y2,float z2,
               float &x12,float &y12,float &z12)
{
   float t1,t2;
   t1 = z1/y1; t2 = z2/y2;
   x12 = (x1*t1 + x2*t2)/(t1 + t2);
   y12 = (y1*t1 + y2*t2)/(t1 + t2);
   z12 = z1 + z2;
}
```

Color Inclusion

Color inclusion is closely connected to color mixing. Using weighted mixing, you can pick up all colors which 'lie' on the line connecting two distinct points within a CIE color triangle. If you choose three different points, you can obtain all the colors which 'lie' within the triangle defined by these three points. You simply mix two of them, and then add the third to the 'mixture'. If you place three points corresponding to RGB into the CIE triangle, you'll see which colors can and which can't be represented in the RGB model. The triangle in the figure above roughly shows RGB color within the CIE color graph. You can see that there are a lot of colors beyond the RGB triangle.

You may want to move between the two systems of color representation and so, to make your job a little easier, we have provided two conversion routines, one for CIE to RGB, and one for RGB to CIE:

```
void CIE2RGB(float x,float y,float z,float &R,float &G,float &B)
{
    float x1,z1;
    x1 = x*z/y;
    z1 = (1 - x - y)*z/y;
    R = 2.739*x1 - 1.145*z - 0.424*z1;
    G = - 1.119*x1 + 2.029*z +0.033*z1;
    B = 0.138*x1 - 0.333*z + 1.105*z1;
}
```

```
void RGB2CIE(float R,float G,float B,float &x,float &y,float &z)
{
    float x1,z1,sum;
    x1 = 0.478*R + 0.299*G + 0.175*B;
    z = 0.263*R + 0.655*G + 0.081*B;
    z1 = 0.020*R + 0.160*G + 0.908*B;
    sum = x1 + z + z1;
    x = x1/sum;
    y = z/sum;
}
```

There are other color models, each with their own advantages and disadvantages. For completeness, we'll describe the following color models:

- additive - RGB and YIQ;

- subtractive - CMY and CMYK;

- 'human adapted' HSV and HLS;

We'll also provide a small, but thoroughly tested 'library' of procedures to convert colors between RGB and each of the other representations. This is a simple idea, but we've never seen one without errors!

RGB

Imagine a three-dimensional color cube (or better still, look at the figure opposite), with red along the x-axis, green along the y-axis, and blue along the z-axis. Any color possible in RGB can be defined within this cube by its red, green, and blue 'coordinates'. The origin at (0,0,0) is black. The opposite vertex, (1,1,1), is white. The brightest red is (1,0,0) and the axis (x,0,0) contains different shades of pure red. The same is true for blue (0,0,1) and green (0,1,0). The brightest magenta (purple), which is red plus blue, is

(1,0,1) and the line (x,0,x) contains different shades of this color. And so on, and so forth.

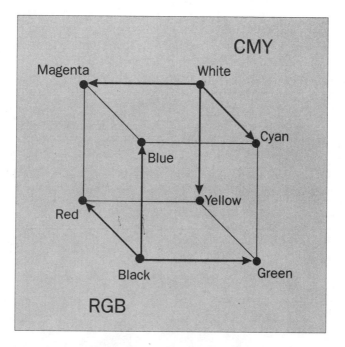

RGB and CMY Color Cube

The most important feature of RGB is that it's an additive color model. So red and blue are added together, in some proportion, to produce magenta. Red, green, and blue added together in equal quantities produce white. Not every color can be reproduced within the RGB color model, but it suffices. In fact the RGB model is widely used. Your color monitor and TV set exploit RGB, so does anybody need any more evidence?

RGB is simple - that's its advantage. However, the model's underlying assumption, that everything about color is linear, is too simple to be completely true. In practice, problems arise. It's difficult enough to make the phosphors of RGB triads really shine linearly so that (0,0,255) produces a blue that is 255 times as bright as that produced by (0,0,1). And it's twice as difficult to make the human eye believe this. Human perception of light is really more logarithmic than linear.

CMY and CMYK

Computer monitors are additive, but colors on a sheet of paper are generally subtractive. Instead of combining red, green and blue spots of phosphors, the artist coats his paper with paint (colored pigment) which absorbs some part (color) of the light. Therefore, the paint subtracts some colors from the white (which is the sum of all colors) and the remaining colors are visible. Adding another paint subtracts more colors from the white. This is how artists mix colors.

Cyan, magenta, and yellow (CMY) are the complements of red, green and blue. For example, magenta is white without green. So if white light is reflected off a magenta-painted wall, the green is absorbed (subtracted), and the wall looks magenta. To get the color red, you have to deposit magenta (which absorbs green) and yellow (which absorbs blue).

The CMY cube is the opposite of the RGB cube (see the figure above). White is (0,0,0) and black is (1,1,1) Cyan is (1,0,0), magenta is (0,1,0), green is (1,0,1),and so on. Converting from RGB to CMY is easy:

```
void RGB2CMY(float R,float G,float B,float &C,float &M,float &Y)
{
    C = 1 - R;
    M = 1 - G;
    Y = 1 - B;
}
```

Many printers use a four-color process by adding black ink. This is because combining all three CMY pigments in real life usually looks more like gray than black.

The CMYK color model, for cyan-magenta-yellow-black ('K' is used instead of 'B' to avoid confusion with blue) is defined as follows:

K=minimum (C,M,Y)
C=C-K
M=M-K
Y=Y-K

Here is the conversion routine:

```
void RGB2CMYK(float R,float G,float B,float &C,float &M,float &Y,float &K)
{
    RGB2CMY(R,G,B,C,M,Y);
    K = min3(C,M,Y);
```

```
      C = C - K;
      M = M - K;
      Y = Y - K;
   }
```

Adding Vs Subtracting, or Colors in Light and Colors on Paper

The combination of RGB lights of phosphors on a screen or CMYK inks on a paper are usually referred to as colors in Computer Graphics. However they are two quite different things. What do we actually mean when we talk about color as 'the combination of lights on a computer monitor or inks on paper?' How does color work in light as opposed to paint?

RGB is the model for your computer's screen. It refers to the way these three colors of light are combined to produce the rainbow myriad of different colors on a color monitor (which will be in TrueColor mode). Each pixel on the screen is made up of phosphor triads (four or forty of them depending on the current resolution). Each phosphor emits the light of a single color. The intensity of the light emitted can be varied for each type of phosphor in every individual pixel.

RGB color is an additive process, emitting and combining different intensities of red, green, and blue light to produce the appearance of various colors.

> CRT screens emit X-rays too, not to mention that annoying blinking of interlaced modes. Remember that looking into the Dragon eye of a CRT screen is a task for a Real Warrior!

The color illustration on the cover of this book is printed using the CMYK color model. CMYK is the abbreviation for cyan, yellow, magenta, and black. It refers to the way these ink colors are combined to produce different colors on paper, and is the reason why it is known as the four color separation process.

By varying the amount of each ink applied to the page, the printer can produce almost any color desired. CYMK color is a subtractive process, absorbing (or subtracting) some of the light and reflecting the remaining colors to produce an assortment of colors on the page.

*The subtractive process for producing color is certainly more powerful than the additive. There are color pigments (paints or inks) that reflect very narrow bands of wavelength. By mixing them together one can obtain almost any imaginable color. To achieve this in an additive process you would have to use **laser beams** for mixing.*

HSV

Red, green and blue light may be perceived by the retina of your eye, but it is not the image you get in your mind. Instead, we think of color as a hue, which is the mean (average) wavelength of the light. We see the luminance, or brightness, which is a measure of the intensity of the light. The higher the intensity , the brighter it appears. We also see the saturation, or purity, of the color.

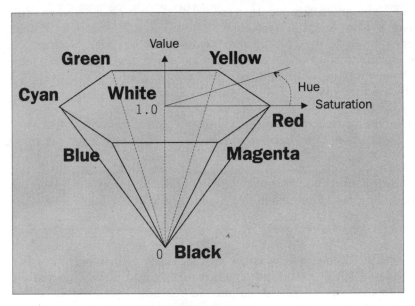

HSV Color Hexcone

The figure above shows a hexcone, a graphical representation of the **Hue**, **Saturation**, and **Value** color model. H is represented as an angle about the vertical axis between 0 to 360 degrees. S and V vary between 0 and 1. Pure red, which is 1,0,0 in the RGB model, is (0 degrees,1,1) in HSV. Pure blue is (240 degrees,1,1) in HSV.

The HSV color model makes color selection more intuitive. Starting with a pure hue, you can add white and black by changing the S and V parameters, until the color is perfect.

The following C++ routines convert from RGB to HSV and then back again:

```
// values: H within 0..360 or UNDEFINED if S = 0
// L,S, R,G,B within 0..1

#define UNDEFINED -400
#include <math.h>

void RGB2HSV(float R,float G,float B,float &H,float &S,float &V)
{
   float Cr,Cg,Cb,min,d;

   V = max3(R,G,B);    // max3, min3 return maximum or
   min = min3(R,G,B);    // minimum value among 3 arguments

   if (V != 0) S = (V - min) / V;
   else S = 0;          // saturation calculation

   if (S == 0) H = UNDEFINED;
   else          // hue calculation
   {
      d = V - min;
      Cr = (V - R)/d;
      Cg = (V - G)/d;
      Cb = (V - B)/d;

// hue lies between yellow and magenta
      if (R == V) H = Cb - Cg;
      else
// hue lies between blue and yellow
         if (G == V) H = 2 + Cr - Cb;
         else
// hue lies between magenta and blue
            if (B == V) H = 4 + Cg - Cr;

      H *= 60;                  // convert hue to angular degrees
      if (H < 0) H = H + 360;// make the result positive
   }
}

void HSV2RGB(float H,float S,float V,float &R,float &G,float &B)
{
   float f,j,k,l;
   long i;

   if (S == 0)
```

```
    {
        if (H == UNDEFINED) //achromatic case
        {
           R = G = B = V;
           return;
        }
        else return;              // OOPS - you can't have a hue in B&W
    }

//chromatic case
    if (H < 0) H += 360;         //if hue < 0 we still work
    if (H == 360) H = 0; else H = H/60;

    i = floor(H);              //largest integer < H
    f = H - i;
    j = V * (1 - S);
    k = V * (1 - S * f);
    l = V * (1 - S * (1 - f));

    switch (i)
    {
        case 0 : R = V; G = l; B = j; break;
        case 1 : R = k; G = V; B = j; break;
        case 2 : R = j; G = V; B = l; break;
        case 3 : R = j; G = k; B = V; break;
        case 4 : R = l; G = j; B = V; break;
        case 5 : R = V; G = j; B = k; break;
    }
}
```

HLS

The hue, luminosity, and saturation (HLS) color model is quite similar to the HSV. Neither of them has any significant advantage over the other. H is still the hue. Luminosity ranges between 0 (black) and 1 (white). Saturation still specifies the relative purity of the color, but the meaning is a little bit different in this case. Pure red is (0 degrees, 0.5,1) and pure green is (120 degrees,0.5,1). Here are the conversion routines:

```
// values: H within 0..360 or UNDEFINED if S = 0
// L,S, R,G,B within 0..1

#define UNDEFINED -400
#include <math.h>

void RGB2HLS(float R,float G,float B,float &H,float &L,float &S)
{
    float min,max,D;
```

```
    max = max3(R,G,B);        // max3, min3 return maximum or
    min = min3(R,G,B);        // minimum value among 3 arguments
    L = (max + min) / 2;      // lightness calculation
    if (max == min)
    {
        S = 0;
        H = UNDEFINED;
    }    // achromatic case (R=G=B)
    else              // chromatic case
    {
        D = max - min;

// saturation calculation
        if (L <= 0.5) S = D / (max + min);
        else S = D / (2 - max - min);

// hue calculation
// hue lies between yellow and magenta
        if (R == max) H = (G - B) / D;
        else
//hue lies between blue and yellow
            if (G == max) H = 2 + (B - R) / D;
            else
//hue lies between magenta and blue
                if (B == max) H = 4 + (R - G) / D;

        H *= 60;            // convert hue to angular degrees
        if (H < 0)  H += 360;        // make the result positive
    }
}

void HLS2RGB(float H,float L,float S,float &R,float &G,float &B)
{
    float m,n;

    if (L <= 0.5) n = L * (1 + S);
    else n = L + S - L * S;

    m = 2 * L - n;

    if ((S == 0) && (H == UNDEFINED)) // achromatic case, Hue undefined
        R = G = B = L;
    else              // chromatic case
    {
        R = value(m,n,H+120);
        G = value(m,n,H);
        B = value(m,n,H-120);
    }
}

float value (float a,float b,float hue)
{
```

```
        if (hue > 360) hue = hue - 360;
        else if (hue < 0) hue = hue + 360;

        if (hue < 60) return(a + (b - a) * hue/60);
        else if (hue < 180) return(b);
        else if (hue < 240) return(a + (b - a) * (240 - hue)/60);
        else return(a);
}
```

HSV and HLS may be considered more 'humanistic' in contrast to the 'technological' RGB and CMYK. The first pair also provides the basis for the Color Wheel - a mystic amulet that helps you to select a suitable color. But for anything beyond selecting, that is for real color tricks like fading and transparency, it's better to use RGB, CMYK and the most technological model of all - YIQ.

YIQ

YIQ is the color model used in US television. It was designed to be backwards-compatible with black-and-white TV sets. Y stands for luminance, or brightness, just like CIE's Y. Note that this Y is greenish gray, so it's slightly different from the V in HSV and the L in HLS. I and Q contain color information, and are called the 'chromaticity'. You can convert from RGB to YIQ using the following routines:

```
void YIQ2RGB(float Y,float I,float Q,float &R,float &G,float &B)
{
    R = Y + 0.956*I + 0.623*Q;
    G = Y - 0.272*I - 0.648*Q;
    B = Y - 1.105*I + 1.705*Q;
}

void RGB2YIQ(float R,float G,float B,float &Y,float &I,float &Q)
{
    Y = 0.299*R + 0.587*G + 0.114*B;
    I = 0.596*R - 0.274*G - 0.322*B;
    Q = 0.211*R - 0.522*G + 0.311*B;
}
```

The constants used assume the standard RGB NTSC phosphor, but we've tested them for our SVGA monitors and it works fine. Of course, the third decimal place is mostly decorative.

YIQ is also important because it forms the basis of the JPEG graphic compression technique. You will find details of this in Chapter 7, but the main idea is simple - it deals primarily with Y because it contains most of the video information. You can distinguish almost 255 'shades' of Y, and barely 25 'shades' of Q.

And one more interesting tip. As you may have noticed (routine `RGB2YIQ`), green is much more important in determining luminosity than blue. You remember HighColor mode memory mapping (from the previous chapter); it usually reserved 6 bits for green and 5 for red and blue. In fact, the human eye is far less sensitive to blue light than it is to red or green light.

Getting More Colors - Dithering

Business applications look fine in only four colors, and 16 will take care of your day to day needs most of the time. However, you can be sure that within a year or two most PC screens will be windowing into the High or even TrueColor realms.

In High/TrueColor modes, the graphic system has to work four to six times harder and so you'll need it to be much faster. Superficially, it will be of little benefit, because you'll have far more colors than can be seen at once. But it will remove the problems of color conversion, common palette construction and so on. However, until then, the more colors you can achieve, the better your graphics will look.

A common technique to increase the number of colors is called **dithering**. What does this mean? You simply apply spatial resolution to colors in just the same way that your color display works (in a grid fashion). So dithering is a method of systematically or randomly combining pixels of the basic colors to produce more shades of color or gray.

In order to clarify this idea, let's look at the simplest method, which is pattern dithering. You probably know, that a pixel in most of your CRT color modes isn't the same as one RGB triad - in 320×200 mode, for example, there are many triads in one pixel. So when using pattern dithering, you can think of the **dither cell**, usually with 4×4 or 8×8 hardware pixels in it, as your 'pixel'. The mixed color of such a 'pixel' is generated just as the RGB triad mosaic generates the colors of hardware pixels.

This simple technique is in fashion at the moment mainly because of MS Windows. However it was invented and perfected long ago as a method of halftoning for black and white or color printing. When printing, this technique is essential because it's so difficult to provide many shades of color or gray for printers. Dithering must be used, and the fewer shades available on the printer, the more sophisticated the algorithms that are applied. You'll meet them and become familiar with them in Chapter 9.

Below we'll describe the details of pattern dithering for implementation in 16-color modes. We will also touch slightly on 256-color modes. In both modes the technique of pattern dithering may provide almost as many colors as HighColor. But first we'll hear from the Graphics Guru.

Dithering is a powerful technique. However, it isn't a magic wand, particularly in its simplest form, pattern dithering. You must be clear about what you gain and what you lose. Which mode is better, 640×480 256-color by 8×8 dither cell or 320×240 of 256 real colors? When used in games or image processing the first usually appears worst. There are plenty of ways of getting a magnificent visual effect with a small number of colors. Pattern dithering is the simplest in implementation and the fastest in operation.

Pattern dithering is a kind of compromise between resolution and colors. So the best application for it is in GDI-like systems, where it helps **hardware-independent color processing**. In reality, an 8×8 dither cell in 16-color modes and a 4×4 one in 256 give you at least HighColor.

16 Colors, 8×8 dither cell

By combining 8×8=64 color dots in 16-color modes you can, in theory, provide a huge number of colors. In practice, a kind of creative combination is needed, even to map 256K colors. There are many possible approaches to dither programming. However, our experience shows, that on the whole, the best palette map of an 8×8 dither cell is the one exploited by MS Windows.

There are two stages in the implementation of dithering:

▲ 'geometrical' - this means inventing the cell patterns

▲ the color mixing method

The first just requires you to spend time in the creative, but boring pursuit of pattern creation (as in the REVERSI game). So the GG proposes that you use a ready-made set of cell patterns. However, we shall outline the key ideas.

What do we mean by a dither cell pattern? Imagine a chessboard (it's 8×8 too!) on which the white squares are made up of bright color dots and the black ones are made up of dark color dots. You can use a set of 'chessboards' with a smoothly increasing '**density**' of white dots (or decreasing 'density' of black) as cell patterns for dithering. The original chessboard is the famous pattern usually referred to as 50% Gray, so it is the 'middle of the road' from dark to light.

The patterns must have a smoothly increasing density of white dots. But they also should have this 'density' uniformly distributed, and in such a way that allows systematic combination of dither cells. This means that when two cells are placed next to each other, there shouldn't be any dark or light line on the border.

Dither cells in our implementation are 8×8, but this is mostly in order to make dithering faster. You may remember the amazing write modes of 16-color modes from the previous chapter. But adding one light or one dark dot in an 8×8 matrix does not have a noticeable effect on the dithering. Therefore, we've made the 'density' increase by two dots each time. So there is a sequence of 32 patterns. The figure below presents the first four and last four patterns. Don't you think that they are a little symmetrical?

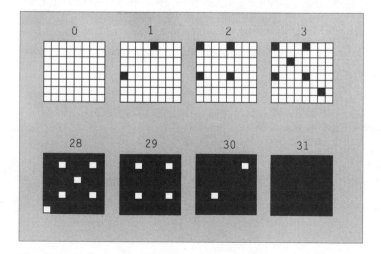

The First Four and Last Four Patterns for an 8×8 Dither Cell

Now that we have prepared the patterns, what about the colors? You can use numerous models for color mixing within a dither cell. We'll describe the most artless, but nevertheless (or perhaps consequently) the most popular one.

In 16-color mode, we have two pairs of intensities for each color of the RGB model, for instance, dark blue and bright blue. Each of the pairs, when used as the base for dithering, can produce 32 shades of the corresponding color. Altogether, we obtain 64 shades for each of RGB. Then we simply mix them in the same way that RGB are usually mixed. For each color dot of the dithering pattern, the RGB mixture is calculated and shown.

There are some shortcomings. It's assumed that Blue + Bright Red or Bright Blue + Red when mixed in the same color dot, generate Bright Magenta as well as Bright Red + Bright Blue. We would encourage you to choose the one you prefer.

How many colors have we gained? We have 32*2 shades for each of RGB, 6 bits per component, so theoretically we should have $2^{6*3} = 256K$ colors. However some of them are identical, so about 160K distinct colors are actually available. It's not TrueColor yet, but it still seems enough.

A similar technique may be applied to 256-color mode. In this case the dither cell should be 4×4, so that a row of the cell would fit into a double word! Four pairs of intensity provide 4*8 = 32 shades, presuming that the pattern's 'density' is increased by two for each pure color, resulting in 128K colors. Just like the 16-color mode, though much more colorful.

We'll now look at 16-color dithering implementation in more detail. The following listing contains the Assembly code of the routine **_setrgbcol** which generates a tiny bitmap, one dither cell 8×8, according to the RGB representation of a particular color.

```
; base colors - number of "pure" colors in system palette
; (numbers of palette registers)
Red          EQU     4
LightRed     EQU     12
Green        EQU     2
LightGreen   EQU     10
Blue         EQU     1
LightBlue    EQU     9
```

```
    RGBcolor struc                    ; 8x8 bitmap structure
       Plan0 db 8 dup (?)             ; 8 bytes per each bit plane
       Plan1 db 8 dup (?)
       Plan2 db 8 dup (?)
       Plan3 db 8 dup (?)
    RGBcolor ends

    .data
    fillRGBcol     RGBcolor <0>      ; allocate memory for bitmap in data segment

    .code

    ; R,G,B components [0..63]
    B        EQU byte ptr [bp+10]
    G        EQU byte ptr [bp+8]
    R        EQU byte ptr [bp+6]

    _setrgbcol     proc far
       push  bp
       mov   bp,sp
       push  di                       ; preserve caller registers

       mov   ax,@data
       mov   es,ax
       lea   di,fillRGBcol.RGBcolor.Plan0 ; ES:DI point to bitmap

       cld                            ; clear direction flag
       mov   cx,16                    ; CX = word in bitmap
       xor   ax,ax                    ; AX = 0
       rep   stosw                    ; zero bitmap

       lea   di,fillRGBcol.RGBcolor.Plan0
       add   al,R                     ; AL = Red component
       jz    no_red                   ; jump if R = 0
       mov   cl,0                     ; CL = 0 (Black)
       mov   ch,Red                   ; CH = number of "Red" register
       cmp   al,32                    ; if R < 32 then will be mixed
                                      ; Black and Red colors
       jb    BlackRed
                                      ; mixed Red and LightRed colors
       mov   cl,ch                    ; CL = number of "Red" register
       mov   ch,LightRed              ; CH = number of "LightRed" register
       sub   al,32                    ; AL = 0..31
    BlackRed:
       call  CalcMaskColor            ; create mask for the first four
                                      ; rows of bitmap
       call  CreatBitMap              ; create the first four rows
                                      ; of bitmap
    no_red:
       mov   al,G                     ; AL = Green component
       or    al,al
```

```
    jz     no_green              ; jump if R = 0
    lea    di,fillRGBcol.RGBcolor.Plan0
    mov    cl,0                  ; CL = 0 (Black)
    mov    ch,Green              ; CH = number of "Green" register
    cmp    al,32                 ; if G < 32 then will be mixed
                                 ; Black and Green colors
    jb     BlackGreen
                                 ; mixed Green and LightGreen colors
    mov    cl,ch                 ; CL = number of "Green" register
    mov    ch,LightGreen         ; CH = number of "LightGreen" register
    sub    al,32                 ; AL = 0..31
BlackGreen:
    call   CalcMaskColor         ; create mask for the first four
                                 ; rows of bitmap
    call   CreatBitMap           ; create the first four rows
                                 ; of bitmap
no_green:
    mov    al,B                  ; AL = Blue component
    or     al,al
    jz     no_blue               ; jump if B = 0
    lea    di,fillRGBcol.RGBcolor.Plan0
    mov    cl,0                  ; CL = 0 (Black)
    mov    ch,Blue               ; CH = number of "Blue" register
    cmp    al,32                 ; if B < 32 then will be mixed
                                 ; Black and Blue colors
    jb     BlackBlue
                                 ; mixed Blue and LightBlue colors
    mov    cl,ch                 ; CL = number of "Blue" register
    mov    ch,LightBlue          ; CH = number of "LightBlue" register
    sub    al,32                 ; AL = 0..31
BlackBlue:
    call   CalcMaskColor         ; create mask for the first four
                                 ; rows of bitmap
    call   CreatBitMap           ; create the first four rows
                                 ; of bitmap
no_blue:

; make last four rows of bitmap

    lea    di,fillRGBcol.RGBcolor.Plan0
    mov    dl,4                  ; plan counter
    mov    cl,4                  ; shift counter
shift_next_plan:
    mov    ch,4                  ; row counter
shift_row:
    mov    al,es:[di]            ; AL = row from first half of bitmap
    rol    al,cl                 ; shift AL at 4
    mov    es:[di+4],al          ; create row the second half of bitmap
    inc    di                    ; DI point to next row
    dec    ch
```

```
      jnz   shift_row              ; shift next row

      add   di,4                   ; DI point to next bit plane of bitmap
      dec   dl
      jnz   shift_next_plan        ; next bit plane
debug_exit:
      pop   di
      pop   bp                     ; restore registers
      ret                          ; and return
_setrgbcol    endp


; subroutine for creating the first four rows of bitmap
; input: DL,DH,BL,BH - masks for corresponding rows
CreatBitMap    proc near
      call  CalcBitMap             ;first row
      mov   bl,bh
      inc   di
      call  CalcBitMap             ;second row
      mov   bl,dl
      inc   di
      call  CalcBitMap             ;third row
      mov   bl,dh
      inc   di
      call  CalcBitMap             ;fourth row
      ret
CreatBitMap    endp

; subroutine for creating one row of bitmap
; input: BL - mask for that row
;     CL,CH - base colors
CalcBitMap     proc near
      push  dx
      mov   dl,8                   ; bit counter
      mov   ah,1                   ; unshifted bit mask
next_bit_mask:
      push  di
      mov   al,cl                  ; AL = base color 1
      shr   bl,1                   ; by shifting BL we can
      jnc   color1                 ; monitor the CF flag to see which
                                   ; color to use
      mov   al,ch                  ; AL = base color 2
color1:
      mov   dh,4                   ; plane counter
next_bit_plane:
      shr   al,1                   ; load AH to bit planes in
      jnc   no_or                  ; accordance with four lower
      or    es:[di],ah             ; bits AL (base color)
no_or:
      add   di,8                   ; DI = points to next bit plane
      dec   dh
```

131

```
        jnz     next_bit_plane

        pop     di
        shl     ah,1                    ; next bit
        dec     dl
        jnz     next_bit_mask
        pop     dx
        ret
CalcBitMap      endp

; masks table (32 items)
DitherTable:    db 08,0,0,0
                db 88h,0,0,0
                db 88h,0,20h,0
                db 88h,0,22h,0
                db 0a8h,0,22h,0
                db 0aah,0,22h,0
                db 0aah,0,0a2h,0
                db 0aah,0,0aah,0
                db 0aah,0,0aah,40h
                db 0aah,0,0aah,44h
                db 0aah,1,0aah,44h
                db 0aah,11h,0aah,44h
                db 0aah,11h,0aah,54h
                db 0aah,11h,0aah,55h
                db 0aah,51h,0aah,55h
                db 0aah,55h,0aah,55h
                db 0bah,55h,0aah,55h
                db 0bbh,55h,0aah,55h
                db 0bbh,55h,0eah,55h
                db 0bbh,55h,0eeh,55h
                db 0fbh,55h,0eeh,55h
                db 0ffh,55h,0eeh,55h
                db 0ffh,55h,0feh,55h
                db 0ffh,55h,0ffh,55h
                db 0ffh,55h,0ffh,75h
                db 0ffh,55h,0ffh,77h
                db 0ffh,0d5h,0ffh,77h
                db 0ffh,0ddh,0ffh,77h
                db 0ffh,0ddh,0ffh,0f7h
                db 0ffh,0ddh,0ffh,0ffh
                db 0ffh,0fdh,0ffh,0ffh
                db 0ffh,0ffh,0ffh,0ffh

; load to DX and BX masks for the first four rows of bitmap
; input: AL - mask number
CalcMaskColor   proc near
        cbw                             ; AX = mask number
        mov     bx,Offset DitherTable   ; CS:BX - point to masks table
        shl     ax,2                    ; AX = AX*4
```

```
        add     bx,ax                   ; BX = points to mask ???
        mov     dx,cs:[bx+2]            ; DX = masks for first and second rows
        mov     bx,cs:[bx]              ; DX = masks for 3rd and 4th rows
        ret
    CalcMaskColor    endp
    end;
```

We've omitted the implementation of dithering in 256-color mode just to avoid boring repetition. In addition, you may think it too ambitious. Do the authors really not consider 256 colors from 256K palette to be enough? Frankly, they do, but let's ask GG's advice.

*The dithering technique implemented above for both 16- and 256-color modes makes **uniform color processing** possible. This means wherever you work with colors, you can represent them as if you are using HighColor, whether this mode is supported by particular hardware or not. Surely HighColor is enough.*

Getting Less Colors - Palette Transformation

The title of this section may cause surprise, especially after those creative efforts of dithering implementation. Nevertheless this problem really exists, and is quite a complicated one. So what do we mean?

Suppose you have a TrueColor image, and you want to process it in 256-color mode. Most TrueColor pictures still look fine in 256 colors, but only if the palette (256 of 256K) is properly chosen. But how can you select these 256 colors from the possible 16.7 million in TrueColor? This is quite a task. Try your favorite image processor, say Corel PhotoPaint, displayed at TrueColor and try a 256-color mode conversion. Do you think it will succeed?

The problem could be even trickier. Imagine you have two images, both in 256 colors but using different palettes. How do you combine or mix them (you may already have had this problem)? Surely you can convert them both into TrueColor, combine them and then bring them back. Isn't that the straightforward solution?

We've decided not to bother you with this puzzle right here and now. Chapter 7 is the place to look for the answers.

Color Manipulation: Some Examples

Fading

You have no doubt seen a color picture smoothly vanishing, a technique usually seen in games. This is called fading, and is a simple but pretty trick. In this area, our comprehensive knowledge of color models will be tested.

Fading usually means a smooth reduction in lightness, so the first model coming to our aid is HLS. We'll show that YIQ plays this game with greater honesty. We'll also broaden the field of application for fading. You'll be able to speed the onset of twilight or indeed induce the effects of sun rise by fading certain components of colors.

The method is actually quite simple. We'll take the palette, which is stored as RGB values, convert these into either HLS or YIQ values, then reduce the L or Y value smoothly to zero. At each decrease, we'll convert back to RGB and change the palette accordingly.

Here are the details:

```
typedef struct { unsigned char R,G,B;} paltype;
typedef struct { float Y,I,Q;} YIQtype;
typedef struct { float H,L,S;} HLStype;

// the following routine provides smooth palette
// transformation using YIQ color model
// you should input the palette range to be transform
// and the number of conversion steps

void fadeyiq(unsigned char first,unsigned char last,
            unsigned char step,paltype *pal,paltype *pal1)
{
   float D,R_,G_,B_,Y,I,Q;
   int j,i;

   YIQtype YIQ[256];
   YIQtype DYIQ[256];

   for (j=first;j<=last;j++) // calculate array of increments
   {
// for call RGB2YIQ normalize R,G,B values
      RGB2YIQ((float)pal[j].R/63,(float)pal[j].G/63,
             (float)pal[j].B/63,YIQ[j].Y,YIQ[j].I,YIQ[j].Q);
```

```
        RGB2YIQ((float)pal1[j].R/63,(float)pal1[j].G/63,
              (float)pal1[j].B/63,Y,I,Q);

      DYIQ[j].Y = (YIQ[j].Y - Y)/step;
      DYIQ[j].Q = (YIQ[j].Q - Q)/step;
      DYIQ[j].I = (YIQ[j].I - I)/step;
   }

   for (i=1;i<step;i++)        // do the fade (step - 1) times
   {
      for (j=first;j<=last;j++) // calculate intermediate palette
      {
         YIQ[j].I = YIQ[j].I-DYIQ[j].I;
         YIQ[j].Y = YIQ[j].Y-DYIQ[j].Y;
         YIQ[j].Q = YIQ[j].Q-DYIQ[j].Q;

         YIQ2RGB(YIQ[j].Y,YIQ[j].I,YIQ[j].Q,R_,G_,B_);

         pal[j].R = R_*63;
         pal[j].G = G_*63;
         pal[j].B = B_*63;
      }

      setDACblock(first,(last-first)+1,pal);// set VGA palette
   }
// set VGA palette with last palette
   setDACblock(first,(last-first)+1,pal1);
}

// the following routine provides smooth palette
// transformation using HLS color model

void fadehls(unsigned char first,unsigned char last,
            unsigned char step,paltype *pal,paltype *pal1)
{
   float D,R_,G_,B_,H,L,S;
   int j,i;

   HLStype HLS[256];
   HLStype DHLS[256];

   for (j=first;j<=last;j++)      // calculate array of increments
   {
      RGB2HLS((float)pal[j].R/63,(float)pal[j].G/63,
            (float)pal[j].B/63,HLS[j].H,HLS[j].L,HLS[j].S);
      RGB2HLS((float)pal1[j].R/63,(float)pal1[j].G/63,
            (float)pal1[j].B/63,H,L,S);

// being aware of critical situation with Hue (negative or
// UNDEFINED)
      if ((HLS[j].H != UNDEFINED) && (H != UNDEFINED))
```

```
        {
           D = HLS[j].H - H;
           if (D > 0)
              if (D > 180) DHLS[j].H = -(360 - D)/step;
              else DHLS[j].H = D/step;
           else if (abs(D) > 180) DHLS[j].H = (360 + D)/step;
           else DHLS[j].H = D/step;
        }
        else
        {
           DHLS[j].H = 0;
           if (HLS[j].H == UNDEFINED) HLS[j].H = H;
        }
        DHLS[j].L = (HLS[j].L - L)/step;
        DHLS[j].S = (HLS[j].S - S)/step;
     }

     for (i=1;i<step;i++)        // do fade (step - 1) times
     {
        for (j=first;j<=last;j++)    // calculate intermediate palette
        {
           HLS[j].H = HLS[j].H-DHLS[j].H;
           HLS[j].L = HLS[j].L-DHLS[j].L;
           HLS[j].S = HLS[j].S-DHLS[j].S;

           HLS2RGB(HLS[j].H,HLS[j].L,HLS[j].S,R_,G_,B_);

           pal[j].R = R_*63;
           pal[j].G = G_*63;
           pal[j].B = B_*63;
        }
        setDACblock(first,(last-first)+1,pal);    // set VGA palette
     }
// set VGA palette with last palette
     setDACblock(first,(last-first)+1,pal1);
}
```

And here is an example of when you could use such routines:

```
   paltype palette[256];
   paltype palette1[256];

   unsigned int i,j;

   void main(void)
   {
// You may use any picture you like. We simply fill the screen
// with horizontal lines of different colors in
// 320x200 256-colors mode
     asm
```

```
    {
      push  di
      mov   ax,0x13
      int   0x10
      mov   dx,200
      mov   ax,0xa000
      mov   es,ax
      xor   ax,ax
      xor   di,di
    }
nr:
  asm
    {
      mov   cx,320
      rep   stosb
      inc   al
      dec   dx
      jnz   nr
      pop   di
    }

// create source palette - reddish
  for(i=0;i<256;i++)
    {
      palette[i].R = 63-i/4;
      palette[i].G = 0;
      palette[i].B = 0;
    }
// create destination palette - greenish
  for(i=0;i<256;i++)
    {
      palette1[i].R = 0;
      palette1[i].G = i/4;
      palette1[i].B = 0;
    }
// choose the method you prefer by uncommenting

  fadeyiq(0,255,60,palette,palette1);
// fadehls(0,255,60,palette,palette1);

  getch(); // wait for key pressed
}
```

 The authors have taken a risk by showing you such an odd example involving floating point arithmetic leaving you to convert to integers yourself. The results won't disappoint you. By the way, you do see the difference between color wheel rolling and YIQ's straight way through the color space don't you?

Summary

So what have you gained from reading this chapter?

The combination of color phosphors on the screen, or inks on paper is what we perceive as 'color'. The most important thing to be remembered about colors is that we all perceive and respond to them in different ways. Therefore, all theories about colors are of relative value. However, you need some framework upon which to build.

To deal with colors, computer systems use three elements:

   input devices such as a scanner

   output devices such as a monitor and printer

▲   software in between.

Each of these three elements can increase or restrict the ability of your computer to produce and process color.

Just as humans do, every computer system has its own way of producing and describing color. The electronics of the system determine which actual color is associated with each RGB or CMYK combination. This means that colors of one system are not identical to the 'same' color of another system. For example, the colors your color printer outputs most probably will not match the colors on the screen, and the same RGB value will probably produce different colors on different computer systems.

Just as the hardware does, the software you use also affects your ability to produce and process colors. Software can enhance, but usually it limits access to color. Chapters 3 and 4 were intended to help enhance your software rather than limit it. We've shown hardware level access to High (True)Color modes as well as a SI_LI_CON software trick that allows you to do the same. By means of simple pattern dithering with different combinations of the seven colors, you can produce about 160K shades of colors. This should be plenty from which to choose.

With most personal computers, people now play with images of 256 colors. But we are ready to bet that, in a year or two, HighColor will become the standard. This will encourage further competition between hardware manufacturers and remove the headaches from software engineers.

And nobody will talk about the number of colors that a particular computer can display. There will be more of them than anyone can take in at the same time.

Chapter 4

CHAPTER 5

Fast Algorithms for Basic Constructs and Techniques

This chapter is the heart of the book, as everything hangs on graphics appearing quickly when the Go button is pressed. As you may have guessed the 'Tools..' part of the book was intended to be a bedrock for your shining progress in fractals, image processing, 3D, and so on. The tools, although scattered across eight chapters, make up the whole complex world of practical graphics programming. We call it the **Graphics System** and it's designed to cover almost every routine job in graphics. But in this chapter, we cover the system's internal structure and talk about the basic set of drawing primitives that we will use in the rest of the book.

Chapter Contents

In this chapter, we will cover:

- Making a Comprehensive Graphics System
- Bresenham Line-Drawing Algorithm
- Clipping
- Anti-Aliasing
- Filling Polygons
- Circle, Ellipse, Curve
- System Settings

Fast Algorithms and a Little History

An interesting point to note is that most of the primitives and routines mentioned here are classical, they've been implemented for about 25 years and have been described over and over again. We're under no illusions that what we will say will be something new or better, but we can't miss it out completely. We can only try to make our discussion as short and consistent as possible.

Making a Comprehensive Graphics System

Once upon a time, when the term 'dialog' was associated with text screens rather than a resource workshop, and before the mouse pointer acquired the habit of hiding under the cover of the hourglass every minute, a graphics system, by which we mean a library, a unit and so on, was an essential, albeit auxiliary, part of each and every compiler package on the market. No matter what your favourite compiler was, be it Turbo Prolog or Quick Pascal, it had to provide you with access to graphics, and it did just that. It let you draw graphs, bar charts and pie-charts in 16-color mode, but hardly ever anything beyond that.

Each graphics system attempts to be complete and universal, or in other words, its components are chosen and designed to match every user demand. That's why the list of primitives (routines) which every graphics system supported, as well as the logical structure of the system, had become a kind of established tradition, a tradition shown in the table below. Each system is usually constructed as follows:

 A low level driver, hardware and/or video mode dependent, including fundamental primitives, such as Pixel, Rectangle and Line

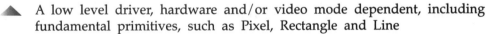 An almost independent graphics kernel, carrying the rest of the primitives as well as data structures and **Set**/**Get** procedures.

Primitive/routine	Description
InitGraph	Switches the video system to a specified graphics mode
Get/**Put** Pixel, Image	Raster primitives
Draw/**Fill** Line, Bar, Polygon, Ellipse.	Vector primitives
OutText	Raster and vector fonts (see Chapter 6)
Set/**Get** Palette, ViewPort, FillStyle.	System settings

The Summary of a Typical Graphics System

We should stress that this structure is logically consistent and fairly applicable, therefore we'll only touch on some technical topics, such as:

 The possible ways to organize a system to work in a wide range of video modes, from 16-color up to TrueColor and HighColor

 A few minor changes in the primitives, that we found reasonable

 How to make it faster

However, we'll describe it as though we are creating a real comprehensive graphics system. After all, MS Windows, although a graphical operation environment itself, still allows you to have and use your own graphics routines.

Whole System Structure

It was not so long ago when graphical applications were a kind of specialized software (image processing, CAD systems, specially featured databases). These days, the simplest note pad program may look and act more graphically than 3D-Studio and still the typical internal structure of a

graphical application remains the same. The only difference is that most driver functions may now be performed by the graphical operational environment itself, at the kernel level, especially if we are talking about MS Windows.

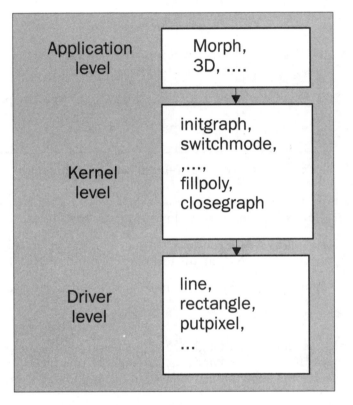

The Structure of a Typical Graphical Application

The application level contains routines and primitives specific to the particular field, such as fractal pattern generation, morphing or ray tracing. We'll discuss some of these techniques later on, but in this chapter, we'll focus our attention at the levels of graphics driver and graphics kernel, what we call our **graphics system**. The following figure shows the internal structure of the graphics system.

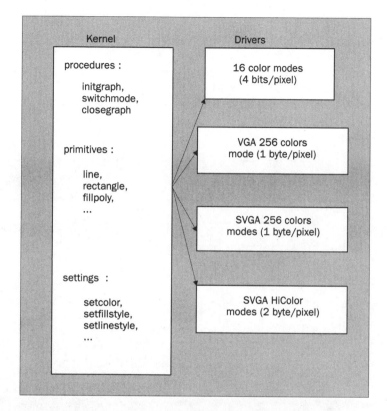

Internal Organization of the Graphics System

This system supports a wide range of video modes including those usually referred to as SVGA. However, the system only provides access to SVGA modes if it finds a VESA compatible adapter installed, or a VESA driver loaded. If your particular video adapter is incompatible with VESA, you should be able to find a suitable VESA driver on the accompanying CD-ROM. We've also added shareware drivers for some of the popular video cards.

The Driver Level

Historically, the low-level, hardware dependent graphics drivers were named according to, and designed for, a specific video standard, such as **HERC.BGI**. But it was the organization of the video memory that made the generic, hyperthetical driver, **SVGA.WRX** into an unobtainable dream. We believe that the acronym SVGA unites too many video modes and memory mapping

models (Chapter 3). It would be a mistake to combine, 16 and 256 color modes in the same driver, for instance. The actual implementation of low-level primitives for these modes varies drastically, which makes even more detailed grading a definite requirement. It appears that video modes that work without bank switching should be separated from the high resolution modes, in order that you don't have to waste time checking for the bank border crossing. The following table shows you our classification of drivers by video modes:

Name	Description	Bank switching
VGA16	All 16-color modes up to 800×600	No
VGA256	VGA 256-color mode 320×200	No
SVGA256	8-bits-per-pixel modes except 320×200	Yes
HighColor	All 16-bits-per-pixel modes	Yes
TrueColor	All 24-bits-per-pixel modes	Yes

VGA & SVGA Drivers, Possible Classification

As you can see, we've left out 16-color SVGA modes exceeding 800×600, as bit planes + bank switching = too much headache, too little speed. If you need a resolution beyond 800×600, you'll have to put up with 256 colors.

One thing we should make clear is our use of the term 'driver', which we are using here to mean the low-level part of the system. This does not presume a particular method of implementation, and as a matter of fact, we rather prefer to link 'drivers' into the application body. This practice helps reduce the number of files and also makes the hacker's life a little harder.

Primitives

Now we are going to go into more detail about which particular primitives should be included in the driver. Speed and mode dependence are the key issues here.

There is no doubt that the right place for Pixel is in the driver. But what about Line or Polygon? We could just draw them both via the Pixel primitive, a much slower, but more generalized approach. And so, here as everywhere, we have the choice between speed and universal appeal. We found it reasonable to include the following primitives in the driver:

 Pixel

 Put Row (of pixels)

 Get/Put Image (rectangular area on the screen)

▲ Bar

▲ Line (with all special cases monitored)

▲ Fill Polygon (without a border)

When we say 'include', we mean that only the hardware dependent part of each primitive's code is implanted in the driver. We're not talking about including clipping, rasterizing or the like in the driver - these routines are general and should reside in the kernel.

 Among the listed primitives the first three are pure 'raster' and the last three are more or less 'vectorian'. When drawing straight lines or curves by pixels of a rectangular grid, the best you can do is achieve a close visual approximation. Raster conversion or rasterizing is the most complicated problem when showing vector primitives on the raster.

The Kernel Level

In the kernel of the system, we can distinguish:

▲ General procedures such as `graphinit`

▲ The high-level parts of all primitives

▲ The block system settings

We'll consider a routine to be a general procedure only if it affects the whole system. And so, we can say that the general procedures are engaged to operate with specific video modes.

As we've said above, the code associated with some primitives is split between the driver and the kernel. Usually rasterizing and clipping belong to the kernel level while all incarnations of pixel updating routines belong to the driver level.

Every graphics system contains a list of simple routines that let the programmer **set** and **get** the system settings. Color, line_style, view_port, and palette are all examples of system settings. We should separate these routines into a special part of the kernel.

So now, let's start building our system, from procedures through primitives, and ending with a little section on the system settings.

Procedures

There are only a few procedures in our graphics system - three to be exact, **graphinit**, **switchmode** and **closegraph**. The system was designed to support a wide range of video modes from EGA 640×350 16-color up to TrueColor modes in high resolution. The following code is the **graphinit** routine, which we think is worth including here in the text:

```
int graphinit(void)
{
   WORD device;

   asm    mov ah,0xf         // preserve the current video mode
   asm    int 0x10
   asm    mov oldmode,al

   device = testadapter();   // check for EGA or VGA

   switch (device >> 8)
   {
      case -1 : return(-1);
      case 2  : mono = TRUE;
   }

   switch (device & 0x00ff)
   {
      case -1 : return(-1);
      case 3  :
// graphinit() fills the table of supported video modes
// just for you to choose from
```

```
// VGA:
// standard VGA modes : (640x350x16) 640x480x16 or 320x200x256
          activemode = arraymodeset[VGA16];
          modelist.modes[0].mode = EGA16;
          memcpy(modelist.modes[0].name,
                  arraymodenames[EGA16],sizeof(arraymodenames[0]));
          modelist.modes[1].mode = VGA16;
          memcpy(modelist.modes[1].name,
                  arraymodenames[VGA16],sizeof(arraymodenames[0]));
          modelist.modes[2].mode = VGA256;
          memcpy(modelist.modes[2].name,
                  arraymodenames[VGA256],sizeof(arraymodenames[0]));
          modelist.numberofmodes += 3;

// Check for VESA compatibility and go on with mode table
          SVGAsearch();
          break;

// EGA:
      case 2 :
          activemode = arraymodeset[EGA16];
          modelist.modes[0].mode = EGA16;
          memcpy(modelist.modes[0].name,
                  arraymodenames[EGA16],sizeof(arraymodenames[0]));
    }

// Set default video mode to EGA 640x350, VGA 640x480 via INT 10
   _AH = 0;
   _AL = activemode.BIOSmode;
   asm int 0x10;

// default system settings
   setviewport(0,0,activemode.width-1,activemode.height-1);
   line = normalline;
   drawcolor = 15;
   fillcolor = 15;
   backcolor = 0;
   bytesperline = activemode.bytesperline;
   linepattern = 0xffff;

// now we allocate the scan line buffer (for polygon)
   if ((ArrayScanLinesPtr = (int *)
        malloc(activemode.height*sizeonerow)) == NULL)
   {
     printf("Not enough memory to allocate buffer\n");
     return(-1);
// terminate if out of memory
   }
   return(0);
}
```

This routine tests the hardware and prepares all the system settings. It also fills the supported video modes table, ready for the **switchmode** routine. The table contains mode names and some useful information about colors and resolution.

The **switchmode** routine does just that, switches the video mode to one which is supported by the video card. If there is an error, then the function returns **-1**, otherwise a zero.

The **closegraph** routine simply tidies up when you have finished, returning the computer to the original state.

Primitives

If you have a look at the **GRAPH.C** program on the CD-ROM, you'll notice that there are quite a lot of routines there. We won't go into detail, or print here each and every one of them, as most of them are quite simple. However, where applicable, we will discuss the technique behind the routines.

putpixel and getpixel

The Pixel is the basic primitive of bitmap graphics and its implementation is really video mode dependent, and this is why the driver level is the proper place for pixel manipulation. Putting a pixel in various video modes is not as simple as it may seem. However, we've already described this in enough detail in Chapter 3 to illustrate how various hardware works, so we won't repeat it here. The driver source code obviously contains the **PutPixel** routines for all supported modes. A sample call looks like this:

```
void putpixel(int x, int y, BYTE color);
BYTE getpixel(int x, int y);
```

where **x** and **y** are the screen co-ordinates.

 I strongly recommend you to avoid using putpixel.

putrow

putrow is a kind of intermediate between a single pixel and a rectangular pixel block. We invented them just to make the raster subset of the primitives list logically complete. All you can expect to get is a single row of pixels, generated from one function call, but we find this technique useful for various purposes. When you work with an image which is organized, obtained or treated row by row, you'll appreciate that using **putrow** provides fast output. The following is an example of using putrow:

```
void putrow(rowptr row, int x, int y, int xcount);
```

where:

rowptr is the pointer to the row of pixels;

x and **y** are the screen co-ordinates of the row's leftmost pixel;

xcount is the number of pixels in the row.

putimage and getimage

The **getimage** and **putimage** routines operate with rectangular blocks of pixels. You can read, preserve or write with them. But what tasks can you put them to? Well, anything really. You may need to work with part of an image, save it to disk or, at least, manage the undo list. However, this technique is most frequently used for preserving a part of the background image covered by a moving object (see Chapter 8) or a pop-up menu. In this case, you definitely need fast-working **getimage** and **putimage** routines.

There is a simple trick that can drastically improve the performance of these routines in 16-color modes, especially when saving and restoring the background. It is so pretty and illustrative that we can't help describing it in detail.

The usual practice presumes that when you get an image from the screen you convert it to byte-aligned. That is, you shift all the pixels of the image so that the image starts at the start of a byte, as shown below. That's why when you put it back, you have no choice other than to shift every row, or usually every byte, of the bitmap an appropriate number of bits - and this takes time. There are certainly enough reasons for doing it this way, it can make the routines more logical, or more generalized, presuming that you usually put the image to some other place, it makes almost no difference. Nevertheless, in that special case when your only purpose is to restore a background, it is pointless.

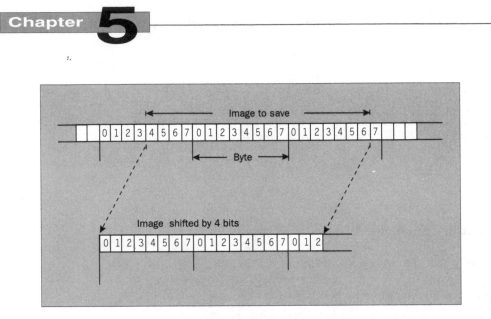

The Usual Practice of Byte-Aligning the Image

In our implementation, we get the image as it is, without any shift. In the header, along with the image size, we store the actual start position of the image within the leftmost byte. Therefore, when putting the image back, we only have to mask the leftmost byte column and not shift at all. If we move the image to another location, we still have to perform the necessary shift just like any ordinary implementation. But even then we don't waste time pre-converting the image.

This simple trick can make your procedures, when dealing with 16-color modes restore the background twice as fast as before. The calls look like this:

```
getimage(int x1, int y1, int x2, int y2, void* buffer);
```

and

```
putimage(int x0, int y0, void* buffer);
```

where:

buffer is the pointer to the image

x1, **y1**, **x2**, **y2** are the screen co-ordinates of the upper-left and lower-right corners of the image

x0 and **y0** are the screen co-ordinates of the upper-left corner of the image

bar

bar is a term for the graphical primitive usually meaning a rectangular area on the screen filled with a color or pattern. **Bar** is the simplest primitive which is, to some extent, transitional between raster and vector types. You will not find anything new and exciting in the implementation of **bar**. You should just create one scan line and then repeat it for every pixel of your bar's height. The declaration is as follows:

```
bar(int x1, int y1, int x2, int y2);
```

where:

x1, **y1**, **x2**, **y2** are the screen co-ordinates of the upper-left and lower-right corners of the bar.

What you end up with also depends on the fillstyle setting.

line

This section is the first in which we must recollect vector graphics (see Chapter 1) and we do so with little bitterness. **line** is the basic vector primitive, and maybe that's why in raster representation it causes so many complications. Of course, the line can be drawn, pixel by pixel, on a solid mathematical basis from line equation:

$$y = ax + b$$

For each x you can calculate the corresponding y-coordinate which will give you everything you need for pixel addressing. This way is too accurate to be fast, as you'd have to perform floating point multiplications, but it is easy to implement. You can be sure that for arbitrary curves, we'd apply exactly this technique.

You should be careful if you want to use this technique. If you consider the case where a equals 2, it is obvious that for an increase in x of 1, y increases by 2. In other words in the y direction there is a gap between each pixel. The way to avoid this is to check the value of a, if it is greater than 1, then use the equation:

$$x = (1/a)y - b$$

and calculate x for each value of y.

However, for straight lines, you'd really appreciate something faster and more creative. 'Would I?', you may well ask. The answer must be 'yes' since **line** is the most frequently used graphical primitive and it must be fast enough to keep all the routines that rely on it operating quickly. We'll leave the rest of the primitives for now, at least until we have discussed some other important techniques.

Bresenham Line-Drawing Algorithm

Surely repeatedly calculating the y co-ordinate of each pixel in the line from scratch looks a bit odd. However, with a straight line, there is a kind of order that lets you formulate an iterative rule to calculate the y co-ordinates of pixels. Such a method promises to be more efficient. There are several approaches to doing this but we'll just describe the Bresenham algorithm used in our system.

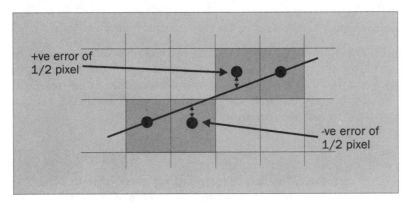

Bresenham Line-Drawing Algorithm

This algorithm was introduced by J.E. Bresenham in 1965. The important and key idea is simple but very clever. As our respectable GG has said, all we need when drawing vectors using rasters is a fast and precise method of approximation, and approximation always produces error, but it's actually the error estimation that provides the basis for the Bresenham algorithm.

To visualize the way it works, take a close-up look at a portion of a line. After placing the ith pixel, the algorithm determines whether the next pixel should be put into the same vertical scan line or the next. The decision is made on the basis of the continuously corrected error. The error is usually initialized by 1/2 in order to compare the sign of the error rather than the number.

We'll illustrate this algorithm using a tiny code fragment, which draws the set of pixels that lies on the closest line between two given pixels, (**X1,Y1**) and (**X2,Y2**), assuming that **X1** is less than **X2** and that the slope of the line is between 0 and 1.

```
int X,Y,Er,DX,DY;

Y = Y1; DX = X2 - X1; DY = Y2 - Y1;

Er = 2 * DY - DX;

for(X = X1; X <= X2; X++)
{
   PutPixel(X,Y);
   if (Er >= 0)
   {
      Y = Y + 1;
      Er = Er - 2 * DX; // Er = Er - 1.0 in the floating point version
   }
   X = X + 1;
   Er = Er + 2 * DY;    // Er = Er + DY/DX in the floating point version
}
```

Note that you should try to avoid floating point arithmetic as we have done here. This makes the routine as fast as possible. Doing this also facilitates the conversion of your routines into Assembly language.

For other octants and $|DY/DX| > 1$ you should change **x** for **y** (or increment for decrement). Look through the code on the CD for more details.

The resulting algorithm is efficient, because it doesn't need complicated floating-point calculations. However, there is still room for improvement.

Optimization

After implementing such a clever algorithm for line approximation, it would be absurd to lose efficiency in tedious pixel address calculations. So, the first step of optimization should be more efficient pixel addressing.

The pixel address calculation should itself be iterative. After calculating the address of the first pixel in the line, you can easily find its neighbors in the video buffer. Calculating pixel addresses incrementally is very much faster than

calculating each (X,Y) pair in the line from scratch. Actual implementation depends on video memory organization, therefore you'll have to look through the supplied code to find out the details.

Special Cases

For further improvement, you should consider special line drawing cases. A special purpose routine can draw horizontal lines 10 times faster than a general purpose procedure for arbitrary lines. As you probably remember, a horizontal line is stored in the video memory as a contiguous series of bytes. You can fill them with a single **rep stosb** instruction, which runs much faster than the iterative loop of a general line-drawing routine.

For vertical lines, a special purpose routine is about 25% faster. No logic is required to determine the pixel locations when drawing vertical lines; you simply increment the pixel address. Again, the resulting code is simpler and faster.

And yet another trick: for lines with a slope of less than 1, the algorithm usually produces a sequence of horizontal lines. Note that if the slope is small these lines can be quite long. In 16-color modes it's worth making the algorithm a bit more complicated to draw these horizontal lines without solving the line equation.

The situations where the special line routine is used aren't unique. Remember the procedure **putimage**? *You could create an excellent universal algorithm which may turn out to be useless because, in fact, you only needed one or two simple and fast special routines. So the time spent on accurate analysis of special cases almost always works. In many applications, these special cases account for a surprisingly high percentage of the total calls to the primitives.*

And now some more line-related topics.

Clipping

Clipping is the process of truncating a primitive because it does not fit onto the screen. Clipping is not always done if you are using a GDI, as you tend to draw everything and not worry whether it can be displayed or not. The reason for this is that the display system will automatically clip the image for you. In the case of MS Windows, not applying the clipping process means that the window can be scrolled around the image, and you don't have to re-draw the part just uncovered. However, drawing the whole image, including those areas that can't be seen is slow, and if you are doing animation, then it can be unacceptably so.

Clipping by Pixel

The simplest and the most general way to clip your diagram is to include a clipping test in each pixel update routine of the graphics system, so that before putting any pixel, your routine compares the current pixel address with the system viewport limits. Of course, such an approach may seem tedious, but for arbitrary clipping limits it may be the only available choice. However, there are much more efficient algorithms for clipping a line in a rectangular window.

As a rule, you should avoid including condition checking in low-level routines, regardless of how efficiently it's written. Only include it if you are absolutely sure that a particular routine will never limit overall performance, or that you'll never need the routine to work without the checking.

A More Line-Specific Approach

Another way to clip a line is to use its equation to calculate where, if anywhere, the line intersects the boundaries of the clipping region. If the clipping window is rectangular this calculation shouldn't be too complicated.

To calculate the co-ordinates of the intersections, you should put the co-ordinates of the window's boundaries (X for vertical and Y for horizontal ones) one by one into the line equation, solve the equation and see if the intersection point lies within the line segment to be drawn, as well as within the rectangle.

Although the actual calculation of intersection points is relatively simple, this approach takes more time, primarily because the whole calculation cycle is performed four times for every line segment you draw. Furthermore, you have to handle the special cases of horizontal and vertical lines.

A More Case-Sensitive Algorithm

We can make the previous algorithm more efficient by first sorting out the lines we want to clip. By comparing the co-ordinates of the line endpoints with the boundaries of the rectangular region you can skip the lines that don't need clipping. The Sutherland-Cohen algorithm uses this method and is well known for its simplicity and efficiency.

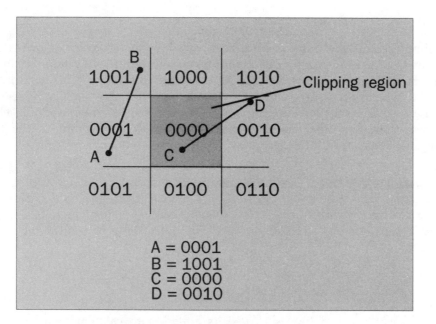

Sutherland-Cohen Coding

First, you code the endpoints of the line depending on its position in the clipping window. Each endpoint of the line segment to be clipped falls into one of nine possible subregions, as shown above. The algorithm uses a computational shortcut to mark the relative location of the line segment. Each endpoint is coded with a 4-bit code representing the subregion to which it belongs. Every line segment is identified by the codes of its endpoints. The location of a line segment relative to the rectangular clipping window can then be quickly estimated by simple logical operations on the codes, allowing you to quickly identify the lines that need to be clipped.

Endpoint codes		OR	AND	Meaning
0000	0000	0000	0000	No clipping
0001	0001	0001	0001	No clipping
1001	0001	1001	0001	No clipping
1001	0100	1101	0000	Partly visible (clipping required)

Examples of the Endpoint Codes

So, if the logical OR of two codes is 0, as shown in the first row of the table, both endpoints are within the window, and no clipping is needed. If the logical AND of the codes is non-zero, both endpoints fall outside the window, and again no clipping is required. These checks can be performed quickly, by the **or** and **and** instructions.

If it happens that a line segment is partly visible, and therefore needs clipping, then the values of the endpoint codes determine which edge of the window is crossed by the line. The resulting intersection point becomes a new endpoint of the line segment. The following is a sample code fragment to illustrate this method:

```
x1      EQU word ptr [bp+6]
y1      EQU word ptr [bp+8]
x2      EQU word ptr [bp+10]
y2      EQU word ptr [bp+12]
flag    EQU byte ptr [bp-2]


_normalline    proc far
   push   bp
   mov    bp,sp
   sub    sp,2
   push   ds
   push   si
   push   di

   mov    ax,SEG graphdata
   mov    ds,ax

   mov    flag,1              ; flag = 1 (slanted line)

   mov    ax,word ptr viewport.left
   add    x1,ax               ; x1 += viewport.left
   add    x2,ax               ; x2 += viewport.left
```

```
    mov    ax,word ptr viewport.top
    add    y1,ax              ; y1 += viewport.top
    add    y2,ax              ; y2 += viewport.top

    mov    si,x2
    sub    si,x1              ; SI = dx
    jnz    no_flag
    mov    flag,-1            ; flag = -1 if x2 = x1 (vert line)
no_flag:
    mov    di,y2
    sub    di,y1              ; DI = dy
    jnz    no_flag1
    mov    flag,0             ; flag = 0 if y2 = y1 (horiz line)
no_flag1:
    mov    ch,0               ; ch - edge counter
next_edge:
                             ; calculate endpoints codes
    xor    bx,bx              ; BL = code for point x1,y1
                             ; BH = code for point x2,y2
    mov    dx,32768
    mov    ax,x1
    add    ax,dx
    cmp    ax,word ptr viewport32767.left
    rcl    bl,1
    cmp    word ptr viewport32767.right,ax
    rcl    bl,1
    mov    ax,y1
    add    ax,dx
    cmp    word ptr viewport32767.bottom,ax
    rcl    bl,1
    cmp    ax,word ptr viewport32767.top
    rcl    bl,1

    mov    ax,x2
    add    ax,dx
    cmp    ax,word ptr viewport32767.left
    rcl    bh,1
    cmp    word ptr viewport32767.right,ax
    rcl    bh,1
    mov    ax,y2
    add    ax,dx
    cmp    word ptr viewport32767.bottom,ax
    rcl    bh,1
    cmp    ax,word ptr viewport32767.top
    rcl    bh,1

    or     bx,bx              ; completely visible check
    jnz    prob_part_vis      ; jump if line is not completely visible
                             ; draw line
    mov    ax,SEG proctable
```

```
        mov    ds,ax
        lea    si,proctable
        les    si,[si]
        push   y2
        push   x2
        push   y1
        push   x1
        call   dword ptr es:[si+1*4]
        add    sp,8
        jmp    exitpr
prob_part_vis:
        mov    ax,bx
        and    ah,al              ; check for partly visible
        jz     part_vis

        jmp    exitpr             ; exit if line is invisible
part_vis:
        mov    dx,0101h
        mov    cl,3
        sub    cl,ch
        shl    dx,cl
        mov    ax,bx
        and    ax,dx
        jnz    no_loop            ; jump if line is partly visible

        inc    ch
        cmp    ch,4
        jne    part_vis

        jmp    exitpr             ; exit if line is invisible
no_loop:
        test   bl,dh
        jnz    no_swap
                                  ; swap x1 y1 and x2 y2
        mov    ax,x2
        xchg   ax,x1
        mov    x2,ax
        mov    ax,y2
        xchg   ax,y1
        mov    y2,ax
no_swap:
        mov    ax,word ptr viewport.left
        cmp    flag,-1
        je     go
        cmp    ch,1
        ja     go
        jne    no_1
        mov    ax,word ptr viewport.right
no_1:
        mov    dx,ax
```

```
    sub    ax,x1
    mov    x1,dx
    xor    dx,dx
    imul   di
    idiv   si
    add    y1,ax
    jmp    end_loop
go:
    mov    ax,word ptr viewport.bottom
    cmp    ch,2
    je     go_ok
    mov    ax,word ptr viewport.top
go_ok:
    cmp    flag,0
    jz     end_loop
    mov    dx,y1
    mov    y1,ax
    js     end_loop
    sub    ax,dx
    xor    dx,dx
    imul   si
    idiv   di
    add    x1,ax
end_loop:
    inc    ch
    cmp    ch,4
    je     all_edge
    jmp    next_edge
all_edge:
                          ; draw the visible part of
                          ; the line
    mov    ax,SEG proctable
    mov    ds,ax
    lea    si,proctable
    les    si,[si]
    push   y2
    push   x2
    push   y1
    push   x1
    call   dword ptr es:[si+1*4]
    add    sp,8
exitpr:
    pop    di
    pop    si
    pop    ds
    mov    sp,bp
    pop    bp
    ret
_normalline    endp
```

Line Attributes

The line as a graphic primitive can have the following attributes:

- Color
- Pattern
- Width

The color attribute is the simplest of the three; you simply transfer the desired color to the pixel-putting part of your routine. This part of the routine will arrange everything itself, even if you want a 'dithered' color.

In some applications, you may wish to draw dashed lines or multicolored lines that incorporate a pattern of pixel values. To do this, modify the inner loop of your line-drawing routine to select pixel values from a circular list of possible values. Rotate the list each time you set a pixel to get a different color.

And lastly consider width. Sloped lines that are one pixel wide appear less bright than horizontal or vertical ones. You can fatten diagonal lines by modifying the inner pixel-putting loop of a Bresenham line-drawing routine so that it always puts 2 pixels if the error is about 0. The resulting lines looks fatter, but this routine is slower.

To draw lines 2 or 3 pixels wide, you can simply draw neighboring parallel lines. You can also take a wide line to be a polygon and use the `fillpoly` routine to draw it.

Anti-Aliasing

As we have already mentioned, the rasterizing of a vector primitive always causes errors. With lines and smooth curves, these errors make the image on the screen appear jagged, and no matter how precise your approximation is, this effect remains. In the figure on the next page, you can see the classical illustration of this phenomenon, a nearly horizontal line, as denoted by the black squares. The only way to display such a line on a rectangular grid is as a series of connected horizontal line segments, which makes it looks rough.

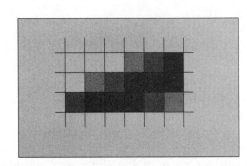

Anti-Aliasing Applied to an Almost Horizontal Line

The most reasonable solution must be to use a video mode (adapter, monitor) with a higher resolution. However, you may often appreciate something more creative, especially if you have to work in a low resolution video mode like 320×200. And fortunately, such a technique exists. It makes the line look smoother by adding *lighter* pixels to the corners of the ragged lines, as you can see. You can modify Bresenham's algorithm slightly to make it do this. Of course, it will still run slower, but the speed is still acceptable.

However, there still remains the problem of color for those lighter pixels. The way to do this is to use the fading technique from chapter 4 to get a couple of colors between the line color and the background color. You can then place a couple of extra pixels at the end of each segment. The only problem with this is deciding whether to apply this technique vertically and/or horizontally.

Due to the fact that this slows the line algorithm, we have decided to exclude it from the implementation.

Oh sorry, nearly forgot! You can get your line as follows:

```
line(int x1, int y1, int x2, int y2);
```

where **x1**, **y1**, **x2**, and **y2** are the screen co-ordinates of the beginning and end of the line.

You should remember that what you'll see on the screen also depends on the line style setting.

Filling Polygons

The most sophisticated primitive that we cover is derived from a technique based on filled polygons. The pressures of space mean that we'll just give you a 'conveyor belt' of the procedures performed, and leave out the details of the actual implementation. Remember that you can easily find them in the code on the CD-ROM.

The system has a pre-allocated data buffer (created during **graphinit**) which can be addressed via the pointer **ArrayScanLinePtr**. This buffer is used to scan convert a polygon (or any other primitive). The structure of the scan line buffer is shown below.

first scan row	**Num_of_points**	**Xin, Xout**	...	**Xin, Xout**
second scan row	**Num_of_points**	**Xin, Xout**	...	**Xin, Xout**
...				
...				
Ymax-th scan row	**Num_of_points**	**Xin, Xout**	...	**Xin, Xout**

Num_of_points is the number of intersections of each scan line with the polygon, and **Xin** and **Xout** are the X co-ordinates of both the entry and exit points. The figure below provides you with more detail:

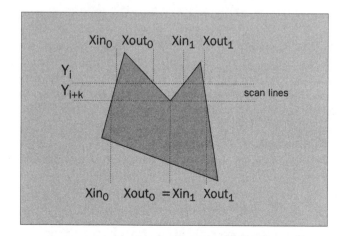

The Scan Conversion of a Polygonal Region

The buffer can initially store **Ymax** scan rows and up to 8 intersection pairs for every row, but the size of the buffer is increased by the system when necessary.

Each time you need a filled polygon, the system rasterizes it by performing a scan conversion. It starts from the first vertex you specify and moves to the next one, filling the scan line buffer.

It moves round the polygon from vertex to vertex, writing the X co-ordinate into the corresponding Y row of the scan line buffer for each point of the polygon's border. It also determines the maximum and minimum Y co-ordinates of the polygon, as we need the Y range of the polygon to set the limits for the filling cycle. Scanning is also the right time to clip Y co-ordinates, as you can just stop writing to the scan line buffer when the current Y goes beyond the clipping window boundaries. When scanning is complete, each row must contain an even number of intersection co-ordinates, which should then be sorted into ascending order.

> Note that there are some special cases to be checked for when scanning polygon boundaries. A vertex which is a local minimum, which means that it has smaller Y co-ordinates than its neighbors, or a local maximum, it has greater Y co-ordinates than its neighbor, must be written into the scan line buffer twice.

Now all we have to do is clip each row. This is easy because the X co-ordinates are sorted. The algorithm checks each scan line interval from the beginning and changes the X co-ordinates of the intervals that clip off to -1. If it finds an interval that is only partly visible it updates **Xin** or **Xout** with the left or right X co-ordinate of the clipping window.

So, we've prepared the scan line buffer, by rasterizing the polygon and there's nothing else left but to transfer it to the low-level routine which will show all the scan lines.

You can get a polygon by calling the following:

```
fillpoly(WORD numpoints, void* polypoints);
```

where:

numpoints is the number of points in the polygon
polypoints is the pointer to the points array

There's also a routine for drawing the outline of a polygon:

```
drawpoly(WORD numpoints, void* polypoints);
```

with the same interface.

 In computer graphics, filling is a much wider subject area than just polygon filling. There are, for instance, algorithms that fill an arbitrary shape, starting from a single point inside the shape, which is known as flood filling. However, the technique of rasterizing that we've described seems to be one of the most common and it'll be referred to many times in this book. TrueType fonts, sprite animation, and many other techniques are based on some kind of rasterizing method. The differences lie in the condition to be checked when the rows are scanned and how the scanning is organized.

Circle, Ellipse, Curve

We are used to thinking that circles and ellipses are exotic graphics elements, only needed for special software, like image editors and CAD systems, and never for GUI purposes. However, it has become an established tradition to include these primitives into each and every graphics system, especially as you need them to draw the ever-popular pie-chart.

This section describes traditional techniques for circles, ellipses, and curves. These techniques are very much like the algorithms for straight lines. However, to draw a smooth curve around an arbitrarily complex set of points, we have to solve the equation for every given point.

In this section, we won't distinguish the circle as a specific case. In raster depiction, you encounter the problem of pixel scaling to get something that appears as a circle on the screen. This is because in some graphics modes the horizontal scale in which pixels are displayed differs from the vertical scale, or in other words, the pixels aren't exact squares. If you display a 'speculative circle' whose pixels are calculated with no regard to the actual scaling in the particular video mode, what you get is an ellipse. That's why we'll start with the ellipse-drawing secrets and then to draw a circle that really looks round we draw an ellipse with major and minor axes at the same ratio as the pixel co-ordinate scaling factor.

The Ellipse Drawing Algorithm

Again you can use the algebraic formula derived from the ellipse equation to compute the X and Y co-ordinates of the pixels. If we were producing our system from scratch, this is the way we'd probably choose to do it, ignoring the computational overhead, and to be perfectly honest, two multiplications, one division, and a square root for each pixel is too much.

However, there are many widely available ellipse-drawing algorithms, so we'll use one of them and make a few minor changes. The one we'll use here takes its origin from one of GG's books: 'Fundamental Algorithms for Computer Graphics', Springer-Verlag 1985.

Midpoint Algorithm

It is quite easy to imagine a kind of incremental algorithm for drawing ellipses similar to the Bresenham line algorithm. In fact, there does exist a Bresenham version of the circle-drawing algorithm. However, we've chosen a slightly different version.

The midpoint algorithm is incremental, so it works in the same old way. After drawing the ith pixel, the algorithm selects the next pixel by calculating whether the midpoint between the current pixel's two neighbors lies inside or outside the ellipse. So it needs something analogous to the 'error' in the Bresenham line-drawing algorithm, and again it's better to compare the sign rather than the value.

And here comes the beauty of the midpoint algorithm, which was the main reason for us choosing it. We'll find the mid point between the two adjoining pixels and then calculate whether or not it lies within our ellipse. To do this we just have to put the co-ordinates of the mid point into the ellipse equation and do the necessary calculations. The difference that we obtain will give us the decision value. There is a mathematical trick that allows you to simplify the calculations and make them work faster, especially as we can do without equation solving. The actual implementation of this is included on the accompanying CD-ROM.

If the value is negative, then the midpoint is inside the ellipse; if the value is positive, the midpoint is outside the ellipse. So, the algorithm can choose which of the two pixels lies closer to the ellipse by examining the sign.

Now we are only one step from success. We just have to determine which pair of neighboring pixels the algorithm will analyze at each step of the iteration. Take a look at the following figure, as its worth a thousand words:

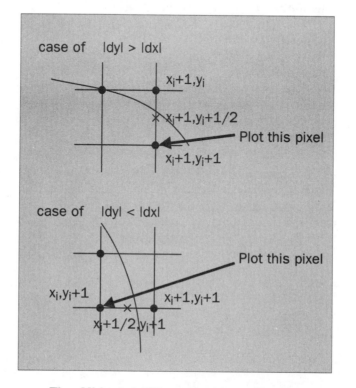

The Midpoint Ellipse-Drawing Algorithm

Note that the algorithm only needs to work in the first quadrant; the other three parts of the ellipse can be drawn by symmetry.

Clipping

The only place to perform clipping when drawing an ellipse is in the put pixel routine. You simply clip each pixel's co-ordinates before putting it. This may seem artless but it works, and anyway we don't really think that an ellipse-drawing algorithm is a good place for complicated clipping.

Optimization

For many applications, a high-level language implementation of ellipse-drawing routines is fast enough. However, you can make it at least twice as fast by writing the routine in Assembly language.

We considered this possibility but decided to leave it as it was. Even now, we don't know what is so great about ellipses. Maybe people are simply tired of straight lines or the edges of polygons, perhaps they just want something a little rounded. If so, you may appreciate the following primitive that we've added to our system.

Curves

Smooth curves form a large topic stuffed full of simple, but tiring mathematics. Therefore, we'll have a superficial look at just a single representative of the smooth curves family, **B-splines**. We'll do this mainly because they're the smoothest and we'll use them again in other chapters.

We'll presume that we have our curve parametrically determined:

$$X(t) = A_3 {}^*t^3 + A_2 {}^*t^2 + A_1 {}^*t + A_0$$

$$Y(t) = B_3 {}^*t^3 + B_2 {}^*t^2 + B_1 {}^*t + B_0$$

or better still:

$$X(t) = ((A_3 {}^*t + A_2) {}^*t + A_1) {}^*t + A_0$$

$$Y(t) = ((B_3 {}^*t + B_2) {}^*t + B_1) {}^*t + B_0$$

and we want to obtain $A_3..A_0$ and $B_3..B_0$ co-efficients to approximate our curve between two points $X_n Y_n$ and $X_{n+1} Y_{n+1}$. We therefore need an equation. We'll use an old mathematical trick: at the point where two segments join, the curve must have equal values up to the second power derivative. This will guarantee the smoothness of the curve and give us enough conditions to construct equations.

We'd like to skip the details of actual mathematical cerebration. However, we should mention that we need **four** controlling points to obtain B-spline parameters between two central ones. Here we'll just give you the code fragment to illustrate the idea:

```
void B_spline(WORD numpoints,WORD step,pointtype* polyp)
{
    float x,y,t,xa,xb,xc,xd,ya,yb,yc,yd;
    float a0,a1,a2,a3,b0,b1,b2,b3;
    int i,j,first=1,N;

    if (step != 0)
    {
        for(i=1;i<numpoints-1;i++)
        {
            xa=polyp[i-1].x;xb=polyp[i].x;
            xc=polyp[i+1].x;xd=polyp[i+2].x;
            ya=polyp[i-1].y;yb=polyp[i].y;
            yc=polyp[i+1].y;yd=polyp[i+2].y;

            a3=(-xa+3*(xb-xc)+xd)/6;      // Here are the formulas
            b3=(-ya+3*(yb-yc)+yd)/6;      // for the coefficients,
            a2=(xa-2*xb+xc)/2;            // skipped in the text
            b2=(ya-2*yb+yc)/2;            // as they are readible
            a1=(xc-xa)/2;                 // enough.
            b1=(yc-ya)/2;
            a0=(xa+4*xb+xc)/6;
            b0=(ya+4*yb+yc)/6;

            N = floor((abs(xc-xb)+abs(yc-yb))/step);
// N is the number of curve points to be inserted (interpolated)
// between each pair of controlling points.
// The more is N the smoother curve you'll get.
// We decided to control this by the step parameter that
// has the meaning of "step" between neighboring curve points.

            if (N == 0) N = 1;

            j=0;
            t=(float)j/(float)N;
            x=((a3*t+a2)*t+a1)*t+a0;
            y=((b3*t+b2)*t+b1)*t+b0;
            moveto(x,y);

            for(j=1;j<=N;j++)
            {
                t=(float)j/(float)N;
                x=((a3*t+a2)*t+a1)*t+a0;
                y=((b3*t+b2)*t+b1)*t+b0;
                lineto(x,y);    // Now we connect the points with a line
            }
        }
    }
}
```

171

And now just to tidy up a few loose ends, let's turn to the Graphics Guru for the answers to some questions that you may have

Question: Why do you use the cubic polynomial? Why not something simpler, the square one, for instance?

To make the curve really smooth, there are a lot of conditions that need to be satisfied. The cubic polynomial is the simplest one which provides enough suitable parameters to do this.

Question: Will the curve contain all of the points specified in the function call?

It may contain some but usually none of them. They are the controlling points, just like the focuses of the ellipse. If you want the spline to pass through the points you'll have to do it yourself.

Question: Once again, why is the term 'step' parameter used?

Assume that the distances between your controlling points are not equal. In this case, if you put the same (N) number of intermediate points, the curve will appear rougher between distant controlling points. Parameter **step** *allows you to make it more uniformly smooth.*

One more thing - it may happen that you'd like your B-spline routine to make a continuous, closed curve. If so, you should specify the first three and last three controlling points as the same.

The following is a tiny example of using the B-spline routine:

```
    ...

    pointtype manyangle[10] = {{0,0},{120,120},{300,30},{300,300},
                               {20,310},{0,0},{120,120},{300,30}};
    void main(void)
    {
        int i;

        graphinit();
        drawpoly(5,manyangle);
```

```
    for(i=100;i>=20;i-=10) B_spline(7,i,manyangle);
    getch();
    closegraph();
}
```

System Settings

This section is merely a vocabulary of the system settings. There's sometimes one or two creative ideas about how they influence the system, but there's really nothing interesting in how they are set or retrieved. So here they are:

```
setviewport(int x1, int y1, int x2, int y2);    //Set the clipping window.
        //x1, y1, x2, and y2 are the coordinates of the
        //upper-left and down-right corners of the window.

setcolor(BYTE color);              //Set the drawing color.
setbkcolor(BYTE Color);            //Set the background color.

setlinestyle(WORD linestyle,       //Set the line style,
        WORD pattern,              //the line pattern (user defined),
        BYTE wline);               //and the line width.

setfillstyle(BYTE pattern, BYTE color);   // pattern type
                                           // preset or user defined

setfillpattern(BYTE* pattern);  // Set user defined pattern (8x8).

setwritemode(BYTE wrmode);       // Set write mode logic (XOR, OR, etc.)
setglassflag(BYTE glflag);       // Set the background glass flag.
```

Most of the procedures have equivalent **Get...** counterparts.

Summary

So, there you have it, a fast and flexible graphics system. And yet we're far from regarding it as the ultimate word in computer graphics programming. Feel free to enhance it, or expand it. Over the page are just a few figures to show you the kind of things that could be enhanced. The table presents the results of simple performance tests: the BGI graphics system versus ours. We tested the two systems on a 486DX, 33MHz, with a VESA Local Bus. The results are given in seconds.

Primitive	Test details		BGI in 16 colors	This system in 16 colors	256 colors
Bar	1000 bars 200×200	Solid	3	1.3	4
		Pattern	7	6	23
Polygon	1000 polygons	Solid	21	10	16
		Pattern	27	17	50
Line	5000×Hi slope, Low slope, hori,vert total = 20000		5	3.5	2.5
GetImage	1000		22	13	13
PutImage	same posit.& 500 different		51	43	5

The Results of the Performance Tests

Of course, an applicable graphics system must have routines to display text, manipulate colors and palettes, and support various printers. It's also true that no one would object to it providing support for different formats, such as GIF, TIFF, PIF, PAFF and so on, as well as covering animation and image processing. So we encourage you to pick out these techniques from other chapters of this book and assemble your own graphics library to suit your own tastes. Learn by doing, and vice versa.

Now that we have covered the topic of various graphics primitives, it is to time to move onto the subject of fonts and displaying text, as covered in the next chapter.

Raster and TrueType Fonts

In this chapter we'll discuss various types of fonts used on the PC, and give you optimized routines that you can incorporate into your programs. These routines range from simple and fast bitmap fonts to complex and flexible vector ones. We'll also discuss the specifics of using all types of Windows fonts (including TrueType).

Chapter Contents

In this chapter, we will cover:

▲ Fonts On The PC Display

▲ Fonts In Your Programs

▲ Getting More Out Of Bitmap Fonts

Fonts on the PC Display

Whatever graphics software you write, you inevitably have to deal with the problems of displaying text. Even with the modern icon-button GUI style, and other means of expression such as sound cards, most dialog with the user is still carried out via screen text. Some applications just need any old 'text' to communicate with the user, while others, such as publishing systems, for example, require multiple typesets and font sizes.

Fonts, What Are They?

A font is a complete set of characters that have a common style. The design of a font includes its weight (light, normal, or bold), shape (round, oval, or straight), posture (oblique or italic), and the presence or absence of serifs, which are the short crosslines at the end of the main strokes. Fonts are grouped in families. An example of such a grouping is Times, a font family that consists of face names such as Times Bold, Times Italic, and so on. Face names generally denote weight and posture but not size.

Fonts have been designed and used for centuries, right back from when books were printed on parchment and had wooden covers. Guttenberg certainly had no computer to help him! But with changing times and improving technology, fonts began to appear in the world of computers. Now that the PC is equipped with a graphics display, it can work with many fonts at the same time. Nowadays desktop publishing produces most printed materials, from books (like the one you're reading now) to newspapers.

Every day, millions of people switch on their PCs to work on their texts, spreadsheets, databases, as well as other types of programs, and sit looking at just one typeface on the screen all day long, as if it was as unchangeable as a typewriter's font. Strange, but true. A very simple raster font is built into the video adapter BIOS, and we can't, for instance, make it look bolder or change its size.

On the other hand, in Windows documents we can see many type styles and letter sizes, and in the **WINDOWS\SYSTEM** directory, there are megabytes of font files. We look at them every time we clean out our winchester and... let them live. Although we don't use them all ourselves (preferring an old-fashioned DOS mode text processor), it's nice to read someone's letter with the full WYSIWYG.

WYSIWYG stands for What You See Is What ~~~~~~~~~~~~ ample, it more like WTMIWIS - What they meant ~~~~~~~~~~~~~~~~~~~

There are three kinds of fonts used i~~~~~~~~~~~~~stry:

▲ Raster (sometimes referre~~~~~

▲ Vector

▲ TrueType

The following subsections explain the di~~~ence between these categories.

Raster Fonts

Historically, these are the first breed of fonts that appeared on computer displays. Even now such fonts are widely used. Simple and compact, they are built into devices like video adapters or printers to provide the fastest text output possible.

As you may have guessed by the name, the raster font maps the pixel layout of each character exactly as it should appear on the display. Every pixel that will be put on the screen is represented by one bit in the bitmap. The table below illustrates an example of how this technique works, using the capital letter 'I'. We've assumed that the font letters are 8 pixels square

Offset	Hex value	Binary value
0	00h	00000000
1	3Ch	00111100
2	18h	00011000
3	18h	00011000
4	18h	00011000
5	18h	00011000
6	3Ch	00111100
7	00h	00000000

An Example of a Raster Font Bitmap

Characters in raster fonts are of fixed width and height. Bitmaps of each separate letter are stored in a font one by one, so the offset of the first byte of a character can be calculated as follows:

Offset = (ASCII code) * (Bytes per character)

Therefore, the letter 'A' in an 8×8 font starts from the offset 520 (65×8)

Raster fonts have the following advantages:

- They are efficient in terms of the memory that they use.

- Speed. They can be created very quickly.

- It's very easy to create and modify them.

To illustrate the last point, we remember how some 4 years ago, one of the authors wrote a Binary Editor, a utility that displays and edits files in binary format. Browsing through .**EXE** files and drivers, he could easily recognize and freely modify raster fonts. This was quite a problem for us Russians, because back then popular western software didn't support the Cyrillic alphabet.

However, not all is joy and happiness when it comes to raster fonts. As they are mosaically composed of individual pixels, you can't scale a character to an arbitrary ratio, since it will probably turn out very distorted. Of course, it's possible to enlarge a character several times by substituting each pixel with two or three, but again it will look untidy and blocky. To solve this problem, vector fonts were invented.

Vector Fonts

Vector fonts make much more use of a computer's processing power than raster fonts. They don't simply code shapes of letters, but rather describe them in terms of a sort of language. This language consists of commands like 'Line', 'Curve', and 'Polygon' to draw symbols. These primitives naturally have co-ordinates relative to a rectangular area occupied by the symbols. The routine that displays text translates primitives, and physically draws the characters on the screen.

As the vector font only knows relative co-ordinates and not pixels, letters can easily be scaled and still retain their original proportions, and their shapes will still be as smooth as the screen resolution allows. You just have to recalculate the relative position of each primitive component. You can also create some special effects like bending, curving, rotating, perspective, and so on.

You may ask, 'If we gain more flexibility and smoothness, do we lose speed?' Let's see what the Graphics Guru has to say about it:

Yes, generally some loss is inevitable. If you need to show a letter of normal size, e.g. 8x16, it's faster to use a bitmap rather than fiddle around drawing lines and curves on one spot. But as size increases, the vector technique rapidly overhauls raster.

Is it possible to combine high speed and flexibility, the advantageous features of the two sytems? Some systems can do this by rasterizing vector font outlines.

A rasterizer is a program module that creates a bitmap image of a vector font, scaled as necessary. The prepared bitmap is then shown on the screen like a raster font.

So, it looks like vectors are really good, but...

Using vector fonts can result in serious typeface distortion when scaling down to relatively small sizes.

The problem is that while they have enough space, lines and curves can run freely. If crowded on one spot, they get mixed up and even drop out of the pixel grid.

> Imagine if the recalculated size of the dot of an 'i' becomes smaller than a pixel - it will, in effect, disappear completely, the poor little thing! But don't panic, all is not lost.

True Type Fonts

The TrueType font (TTF) is a logical derivation from the vector concept. Letter outlines are made up of lines and quadratic spline curves and, in addition to these vector based advantages, TTFs are smart enough to give instructions to a graphics system to compensate for the low screen resolution. It's this unique hinting mechanism that provides the convincing WYSIWYG font in Windows 3.1.

Each TrueType font remembers ideal outlines of perfectly shaped glyphs. It's as if it dreams of some time in the future when an output device with a resolution of thousands of dpi will be able to reproduce this artwork. Until this day, it patiently uses hints to adapt the fine typeface for our poor SVGAs.

So what's inside this treasure box?

A glyph outline consists of a series of connected contours and lines, which are defined by a series of points interpolated by quadratic B-splines. There are two types of point, those that are ON the curve and those that are OFF. These two types may be freely combined to make the desired curve shape. Straight lines are defined merely by their endpoints.

Positions of points are coded in font units, or FUnits. A FUnit is the smallest measurable unit in the em square, which is an imaginary Cartesian co-ordinate square in some abstract high resolution space that is used to store, resize and align glyphs.

> Why 'em'? This was historically inherited from the real world typography, where it meant the space occupied by the capital 'M'.

The greater the dimension of this M-space, the more precise the point addressing and outline scaling must be. You should note that outline scaling will be faster if the units per em chosen is a power of 2 (usually 2048).

Up to now we've just discussed how TrueTypes are organized. Now we'll see how Windows brings them before our eyes:

1 It loads the font

2 It transfers it to the rasterizer

3 The outline is scaled to the actual point size for the given resolution of the output device

4 Hints are applied to the outline, transforming the contours to build what is known as a gridfitted (or hinted) outline

5 A gridfitted outline is filled with pixels, creating solid letter bitmaps

6 A scan for dropouts is performed, if required by the nature of the font

7 The raster bitmap is cached.

8 And finally, the raster bitmap is transferred to the display.

Why are hints necessary if scaling can be done with much better precision than the display allows? The question in a way contains the answer.

Consider the following figure. The scaled letter 'M' is laid over the pixel grid. The GDI's rasterizer uses a simple rule to determine which pixels to turn on or off. If the center of the pixel falls inside the outline, it's turned on, otherwise it's turned off. You will notice that the left vertical stem of the 'M' encompasses the centers of two pixel columns, so it'll be two pixels wide. However, the right vertical stem only covers one pixel column, and so will be half the thickness of the left stem, even though both stems are exactly the same width in the original outline.

Outline to Pixels: Possible Distortion

As a result, we would see a rather clumsy font on the screen, which changes its style at its own will as we try different sizes. But this is where hints come into play.

They instruct the GDI how to modify an outline in a systematic way to produce agreeable-looking letters. In our case, if we move the right stem slightly further to the right, it will fall on two pixel columns, just like the left one, as shown below:

The Hinted Outline

Naturally, hints become less important at higher resolutions and greater font sizes, as one pixel error produces less relative asymmetry. However, they are still used even at 300 dpi.

As you can see, outline adaptation takes a lot of intelligence, especially from such a non-intuitive thing as a PC. That's why hints are described in great detail using a special language, very similar to Assembly language. These instructions are stored in each particular TrueType font program. Moreover, each glyph has its own program portion. The rasterizer interprets hint instruction codes like the CPU interprets machine code.

Each time you change the size of a character, the resolution of the device, or rotate the outline, you have to re-hint that specific raster bitmap, which means that you have to execute the hint program once more.

Rasterising a vector outline can produce an even more unpleasant effect than asymmetry, known as dropout. Some parts of a glyph, or even whole glyphs like hyphens or apostrophes can literally drop out of sight. To see this in action, look at the following figure that shows how a Latin capital "F" can appear like a Greek capital gamma:

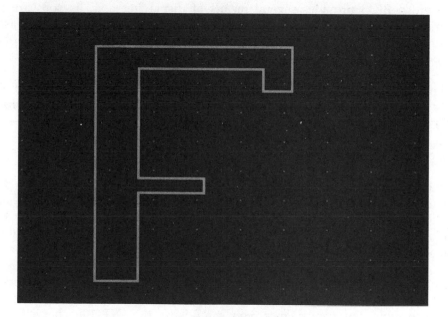

A Dropout

As you can see, the small horizontal stem of the 'F' happens to fall in between two rows of pixel centers, and so no pixels are turned on for it. Although in this particular case the letter can be recovered by hints, it's not so easy with thin curves passing between pixels in a diagonal direction.

But the GDI's rasterizer helps to solve the problem. It is equipped with algorithms which scan hinted, filled bitmaps, looking for dropouts to cure. Only the font itself can hold the information on whether it requires scanning or not. Some simple fonts like sets of block characters are safe from dropouts. Finer typefaces almost always need this additional correction.

All this should enable you to understand the importance of font caching used in Windows. As so much work is carried out to rasterize a font properly, it would be too time-consuming to repeat this from scratch every time a font is used. Consequently, all TrueType fonts are kept in the memory, by which we mean virtual memory, including the swap file on disk, and only discarded when the memory becomes full.

BIOS Support

The video BIOS provides several means of displaying text. Its software character generator allows you to set up a dynamic raster font which is used whenever INT 10h functions 09h, 0Ah, 0Eh, and 13h are called in graphics modes.

Originally in IBM PC and AT models, the software character generator used only the 8×8 characters defined in the ROM at F000:FA6E (ASCII 0 through 127) and at the address pointed to by interrupt vector 1Fh (ASCII 128 through 255). When DOS was started, the upper half of the character set was undefined, and had to be installed by the DOS **GRAFTABL** utility.

BIOS versions in EGA, VGA and PS/2 use a font table for the entire character set to which interrupt vector 43h points, while the character height is stored in BIOS variable POINTS (WORD) at 0040:0085. When you boot up your PC and initialize the graphics mode, these BIOSs set vector 43h to point at a font in the video ROM.

You can use the BIOS software character generator to display characters from any raster font table by modifying the appropriate interrupt vectors to point to the new table. For convenience, you should use the INT 10h character generator function 11h to do this.

Then, when you've installed your custom font, you simply use BIOS interrupt 10h functions to display text. In the days of our apprenticeship, the Graphics Guru advised using function 13h (available on EGA and VGA):

```
Interrupt 10h (Video Service)
Function 13h (Display string)

On entry:
        AH = 13h
        ES:BP = address of string to display
```

```
CX = character count
DH, DL = row, column to start the string
BH = video page number
BL = color attributes
AL = 0
```

It should be said that I didn't recommend the BIOS text output functions very often!

Indeed, though it's very convenient and saves endless amounts of coding, the BIOS mechanism has a few disadvantages. It supports only fonts 8 bits wide and displays characters byte aligned, or in other words, the possible X co-ordinates are 0, 8, 16, 24, and so on. It's also not the fastest way to do the job. And don't expect BIOS to support text output in HighColor or TrueColor video modes.

So, if you're writing a small utility program in graphics mode, which does not have a great deal of dialog, you can survive using BIOS. In a complex environment with a control panel metaphor, graphs, text editing and a modern user interface all at the same time, you'll most probably need a slightly more sophisticated technique.

Now we'll see what can be done without BIOS. In the following section we've included a more flexible routine, optimized for speed, to display custom fonts in graphics mode, which is worth keeping hold of.

Fonts in Your Programs

Storage: Linking or Loading?

Although we quickly got used to having a choice of fonts in most Windows applications, there is still a place under the sun for SI_LI_CON programs that don't open a screen-long list from which you have to select a typeface.

Sometimes you can make do with three or four raster fonts. Link them up and forget about it! It will slightly increase the data segment of your program, but it will make managing them simpler. You should always sacrifice 4-8 Kb to make life a little easier.

And what if you have to provide access to lots of fonts? Obviously, they should be loaded from disk, but to load an outline and scale and rasterize it every time you select a particular font in your program would not be a particularly good solution. Window's policy of keeping rasterized images of fonts in the memory works well, with virtual memory extended onto the hard disk.

In addition you may implement bitmap compression in your font system, so that output routines decompress bitmaps on the fly. That would slow down the output slightly, but may save some extra memory for other program blocks and data.

The Code Behind The Font

Now it's time to write something. Displaying raster fonts is no harder than displaying a bitmap picture, and in fact, it may even be easier. You simply replace the appropriate pixels in the video buffer according to the bit patterns in a character table. Then sending one byte from a character bitmap you update eight pixels at once, after selecting a corresponding mask.

Since graphics modes allow the arbitrary positioning of text on the screen, your routines have to check whether a character falls into the video buffer within the boundary of a single byte or crosses it. If one part of a character falls in one byte and the rest in another, you should transfer these two parts separately, shifting and masking the bit patterns properly.

You should also check the output for clipping. Practically all the output must be clipped if not to some square (or more complex) window, then at least to the entire screen area, for example, if you write an 8-bit wide letter at the position (636,200) near the right edge of display in 640×480 mode, then only 4 bits of the pattern can fit on the screen. Therefore, you must output exactly 4 bits, or else the remaining 4 will wrap to the left edge, which is not particularly useful. To clip characters horizontally, you should mask the part of the bit pattern which doesn't fit, so that it doesn't update the video buffer.

Vertical clipping is easier. Just don't transfer those bytes which would end up beyond the screen limits.

The program code shown below is not just any old sample code. It's what we at Control-Zed actually use, and naturally, we've optimized the routine to make it as fast as possible. We hope you'll find it useful, and if you improve it even further, we'll be even happier.

```
; This program defines procedure OverlapString, that displays
; a text string on EGA/VGA in 16 colors graphics mode using specified
; raster font.

.model large

.data
   BytesPerLine dw 80
   FontColor    db 15

; Output is clipped to the view port defined below
   ViewPortleft    dw 0
   ViewPorttop     dw 0
   ViewPortright   dw 639
   ViewPortbottom dw 479

public _OverlapString
.code

; Call: OverlapString(int X, int Y, void* StrVar,void* CurrentFontPtr,
;                     int CharHeight, int CharWidth);

X               EQU word  ptr [bp+6]
Y               EQU word  ptr [bp+8]
StrVar          EQU dword ptr [bp+10]
StrVarAOffs     EQU word  ptr [bp+10]
CurrentFontPtr  EQU dword ptr [bp+14]
CharHeight      EQU byte  ptr [bp+18]
CharWidth       EQU byte  ptr [bp+20]

; Local variables:

OurCharHeight     EQU byte ptr [bp-1]
OurCharWidth      EQU byte ptr [bp-2]
VBOffs            EQU word ptr [bp-4]
Bchar             EQU byte ptr [bp-5]
OurStrLength      EQU byte ptr [bp-6]
BCMask            EQU byte ptr [bp-7]
ECMask            EQU byte ptr [bp-8]
DecBytesPerLine   EQU word ptr [bp-10]
SolidFColor       EQU byte ptr [bp-11]
AbsCharHeight     EQU byte ptr [bp-12]
VideoSelector     EQU word ptr [bp-14]

_OverlapString    proc far
   push  bp
   mov   bp,sp
   sub   sp,14
   push  ds
   push  di
   push  si
```

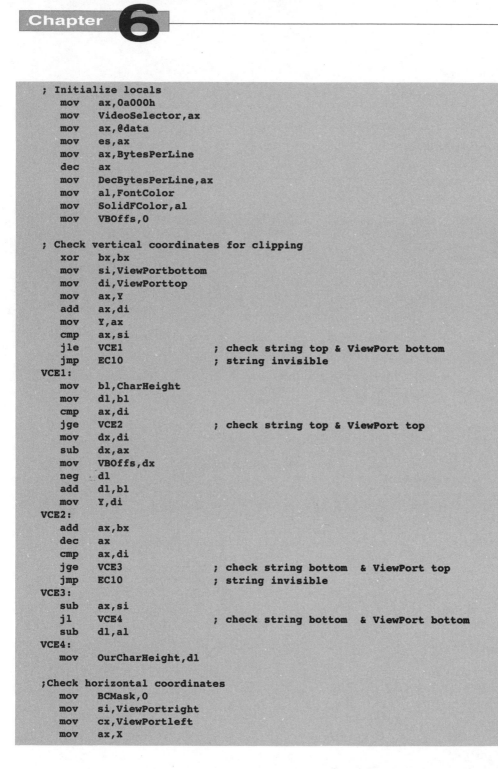

```
    ; Initialize locals
        mov     ax,0a000h
        mov     VideoSelector,ax
        mov     ax,@data
        mov     es,ax
        mov     ax,BytesPerLine
        dec     ax
        mov     DecBytesPerLine,ax
        mov     al,FontColor
        mov     SolidFColor,al
        mov     VBOffs,0

    ; Check vertical coordinates for clipping
        xor     bx,bx
        mov     si,ViewPortbottom
        mov     di,ViewPorttop
        mov     ax,Y
        add     ax,di
        mov     Y,ax
        cmp     ax,si
        jle     VCE1              ; check string top & ViewPort bottom
        jmp     EC10              ; string invisible
    VCE1:
        mov     bl,CharHeight
        mov     dl,bl
        cmp     ax,di
        jge     VCE2              ; check string top & ViewPort top
        mov     dx,di
        sub     dx,ax
        mov     VBOffs,dx
        neg     dl
        add     dl,bl
        mov     Y,di
    VCE2:
        add     ax,bx
        dec     ax
        cmp     ax,di
        jge     VCE3              ; check string bottom  & ViewPort top
        jmp     EC10              ; string invisible
    VCE3:
        sub     ax,si
        jl      VCE4              ; check string bottom  & ViewPort bottom
        sub     dl,al
    VCE4:
        mov     OurCharHeight,dl

    ;Check horizontal coordinates
        mov     BCMask,0
        mov     si,ViewPortright
        mov     cx,ViewPortleft
        mov     ax,X
```

```
        add    ax,cx
        mov    X,ax
        cmp    ax,si
        jle    HCE1                   ;check string left & ViewPort right
        jmp    EC10                   ;string invisible
HCE1:
        mov    BChar,bl               ;store AbsCharHeight
        les    bx,StrVar              ;ES:BX -> String
        push   bx
        mov    dl,0

; Find terminating zero and initialize char counter
find_0:
        mov    dh,es:[bx]
        or     dh,dh
        jz     end_line
        inc    dl
        inc    bx
        jmp    short find_0
end_line:
        pop    bx
        mov    dh,dl
        mov    OurStrLength,dh        ;char counter
        mov    dl,CharWidth
        mov    OurCharWidth,dl
        mov    ECMask,dl
        mov    di,ax
        cmp    ax,cx
        jge    HCE2                   ;check string left & ViewPort left
        neg    ax
        add    ax,cx
        div    dl
WCut:
        cmp    al,dh
        jl     HCPE
        jmp    EC10                   ;string invisible
HCPE:
        mov    di,cx
        and    ah,ah
        je     BMzero
        mov    BCMask,ah
        inc    al
BMzero:
        xor    ah,ah
        mov    cl,dh
        sub    cl,al
        mov    OurStrLength,cl
        add    bx,ax
HCE2:
        mov    cl,OurStrLength
        mov    al,dh
```

```
        mul    dl
        add    ax,X
        dec    ax
        sub    ax,si
        jle    AllChEnd
        div    dl
        cmp    ah,0
        je     WCut2
        inc    al
        sub    ECMask,ah
WCut2:
        sub    cl,al
        mov    OurStrLength,cl
AllChEnd:
        push   ds
        mov    StrVarAOffs,bx
        mov    dx,3ceh
        mov    ax,0805h
        out    dx,ax              ;Set write mode 0 (normal)
        mov    ax,010ffh
        out    dx,ax              ;Enable Set/Reset
        dec    al
        mov    ah,SolidFColor
        out    dx,ax              ;Set color
        mov    al,8
        out    dx,al              ;Set register index to Mask Register

;Calulate start offset in video buffer
        mov    bl,cl
        mov    ax,Y
        mul    BytesPerLine       ; YCoord * BytesPerLine
        mov    dx,di
        mov    di,ax
        mov    ax,dx
        mov    cl,3
        shr    ax,cl
        mov    cx,dx
        and    cx,7
        add    di,ax

        lds    si,CurrentFontPtr
        add    si,VBOffs
        mov    al,BChar
        mov    AbsCharHeight,al

        mov    al,ECMask
        sub    al,OurCharWidth
        or     al,BCMask
        jnz    CharCuting         ;Clip to view port
HSpeedDC:
        mov    dx,3cfh
```

```
        mov     ax,StrVarAOffs
        xor     bh,bh
        add     bx,ax
        xchg    bx,ax
        mov     VBOffs,ax

;Main loop (string output)
PutEGALoop:
        push    si
        push    es
        push    di
        call    PutEGAChar          ;char by char
        pop     di
        pop     es
        pop     si

        add     cl,OurCharWidth
        cmp     cl,08
        jl      OldVByte
        inc     di
        and     cl,07
OldVByte:
        inc     bx
        cmp     bx,VBOffs
        jl      PutEGALoop          ;Next char
By_By:
;Restore default ports values
        mov     dx,3ceh
        mov     ax,0001h
        out     dx,ax
        mov     ax,0FF08h
        out     dx,ax
        mov     ax,0005
        out     dx,ax
        pop     ds
EC10:
        pop     si
        pop     di
        pop     ds
        mov     sp,bp
        pop     bp
        ret                         ;Return from OverlapString

;Character fragment output (clipped)
CharCuting:
        or      bl,bl
        jl      EandBcon

        mov     BChar,cl
        mov     X,di
```

```
        mov    dh,BCMask
        or     dh,dh
        jz     EMaskDrwng
        mov    dl,OurCharWidth
        mov    bx,StrVarAOffs
        dec    bx
        push   es
        push   si
        call   SpecPutEGAChar
        pop    si
        pop    es

        mov    di,X
        add    cl,OurCharWidth
        sub    cl,BCMask
        cmp    cl,08
        jl     EMDg
        inc    di
        and    cl,07
        mov    X,di
EMDg:
        mov    BChar,cl
EMaskDrwng:
        mov    dl,ECMask
        mov    al,OurCharWidth
        cmp    dl,al
        je     RestorePars
        mov    dh,OurStrLength
        mul    dh
        mov    dh,al
        mov    ch,cl
        mov    cl,03
        shr    ax,cl
        add    di,ax
        and    dh,07
        add    dh,ch
        mov    al,dh
        cbw
        shr    ax,cl
        add    di,ax
        mov    cl,dh
        and    cl,07
        xor    dh,dh
        mov    bx,StrVarAOffs
        add    bl,OurStrLength
        adc    bh,00
        push   es
        push   si
        call   SpecPutEGAChar
        pop    si
        pop    es
```

```
       mov    di,X
       mov    cl,BChar
RestorePars:
       mov    bl,OurStrLength
       or     bl,bl
       jz     ABy_By
NIncDI:
       jmp    HSpeedDC
EandBcon:
       mov    dh,BCMask
       mov    dl,ECMask
       mov    bx,StrVarAOffs
       dec    bx
       push   es
       call   SpecPutEGAChar
       pop    es
ABy_By:
       jmp    By_By
_OverlapString    endp


;----------        PutEGAChar

PutEGAChar    proc near
       xor    ax,ax
       mov    al,es:[bx]
       mul    AbsCharHeight
       mov    ch,OurCharHeight
       add    si,ax
       mov    es,VideoSelector

       or     cl,cl
       jnz    NonByteAlign
ByteAlignLoop:
       mov    al,[si]
       out    dx,al
       xchg   es:[di],al
       inc    si
       add    di,BytesPerLine
       dec    ch
       jnz    ByteAlignLoop
       jmp    Happy
NonByteAlign:
       xor    al,al
       mov    ah,[si]
       shr    ax,cl
       xchg   al,ah

       out    dx,al
       xchg   es:[di],al
       inc    di
       mov    al,ah
```

```
    out    dx,al
    xchg   es:[di],al
    inc    si
    add    di,DecBytesPerLine
    dec    ch
    jnz    NonByteAlign
Happy:
    ret
PutEGAChar    endp

;--------------- SpecPutEGAChar

SpecPutEGAChar    proc near
    xor    ax,ax
    mov    al,es:[bx]
    mul    AbsCharHeight
    mov    ch,OurCharHeight
    add    si,ax
    mov    es,VideoSelector

    mov    ax,0FF00H
    xchg   cl,dl
    shr    ah,cl
    not    ah
    mov    bl,ah               ;Zero-shr mask
    mov    bh,dh

    mov    cl,dl
    mov    dx,3cfh
    or     cl,cl
    jnz    SNonByteAlign
SByteAlignLoop:
    mov    al,[si]
    and    al,bl
    xchg   bh,cl
    shl    al,cl
    xchg   bh,cl
    shr    al,cl
    out    dx,al
    xchg   es:[di],al
    inc    si
    add    di,BytesPerLine
    dec    ch
    jnz    SByteAlignLoop
    ret
SNonByteAlign:
    xor    al,al
    mov    ah,[si]
    and    ah,bl
    xchg   bh,cl
    shl    ax,cl
```

```
     xchg  bh,cl
     shr   ax,cl
     xchg  al,ah
     out   dx,al
     xchg  es:[di],al         ; first half of char
     inc   di
     mov   al,ah
     out   dx,al
     xchg  es:[di],al         ; last half of char
     inc   si
     add   di,DecBytesPerLine
     dec   ch
     jnz   SNonByteAlign
     ret
SpecPutEGAChar    endp
end
```

The next program listing demonstrates using this routine. The font is taken
from the BIOS variable vector 43h, and the character height from the BIOS
variable known as POINTS (word at address 0040:0085):

```c
/* This sample program demonstrates use of OverlapString,    */
/* an external procedure from putstr.ASM.            */

#include <dos.h>
#include <conio.h>
#include <stdlib.h>
#include <graph.h>

extern "C" void OverlapString(int,int,void*,void*,int,int);
char str[] = "Hi, folks, I am a raster font!";

/* Pointer to character table */
void *fontptr;
int char_height;

void main(void)
{
   if (graphinit() < 0)
      exit(0);
   asm
   {
      push si
      mov ax,0
      mov es,ax
      mov si,0x43*4   // Vector 43h - pointer to the current BIOS font
      mov ax,es:[si]
      mov word ptr fontptr[0],ax
      mov ax,es:[si+2]
```

...

...

```
        mov word ptr fontptr[2],ax
        mov ax,0x40
        mov es,ax
        mov ax,es:[0x85]   // 0040:0085 - character height
        mov char_height,ax
        pop si
    }
    OverlapString(100,100,str,fontptr,char_height,8);
    getch();
    closegraph();
}
```

Getting More Out of Bitmap Fonts

Bolder! Bolder!

You can employ a simple trick to embolden a raster font - display a line of text once, increase its horizontal position by 1 and then display it again. You'll see that the vertical stems of the letters swell, while the horizontal ones look nearly the same. At Control-Zed, we happily use this naïve method, and it looks quite consistent with all fonts. Of course, it takes twice as long, but output is still fast enough.

```
    DisplayString( 100, 200, 'Get bolder!', black);
    DisplayString( 101, 200, 'Get bolder!', black);
```

If you're hot after all the speed you can get then modifing the bitmap itself is no problem. Every byte in the font's bitmap should be ORed with its shifted right copy. The essential Assembly code for the emboldening routine looks as folllows:

```
    mov    cx,FontSize      ; initialize the counter
    xor    di,di            ; start from offset 0
NextByte:
    mov    al,[Font+di]     ; get a byte
    shr    al,1             ; shift it right one bit (one pixel)
    or     [Font+di],al     ; store back to the font
    inc    di               ; next byte
    loop   NextByte
```

As often happens, faster performance means a larger amount of data. The choice is yours.

...

The Shadow Effect

Objects can cast shadows in many ways, depending on the position and structure of the light source, and surface qualities. Most image processing programs have a number of text shadowing options, but in the case of relatively small raster fonts you shouldn't expect a successful 'midday', 'sunset', or any other complex shadow.

There is, however, a simple simulation that works fairly well. You display dark text and then the same text in a bright color one pixel higher and to the left. The result makes it look as if the letters are raised above the background, as seen on embossed coins, for instance:

```
DisplayString( 100, 200, 'Just me and my shadow...', black);
DisplayString( 99, 199, 'Just me and my shadow...', yellow);
```

Alternatively, if you make the underlaid text brighter and the covering text darker, and display the latter one pixel lower and to the right, the letters appear engraved on the surface:

```
DisplayString( 100, 200, 'Sir Crouchback, Esq', light_red);
DisplayString( 101, 201, 'Sir Crouchback, Esq', black);
```

Summary

So now your graphics programs can be equipped with that highly useful module, the character generator. Writing titles on icons and buttons, subscribing axes, or browsing through pages of text in a window should no longer be a problem. Using BIOS variables, you have access to ready-made character sets, so if you are short of memory or data space, you can use them without problems. The code itself is fast and compact.

If your software needs a multifont environment, then frankly we would recommend writing a Windows-based application. Windows is often criticized for faults and flaws in its internal organization, but with TrueType they've really done well. The rasterizer tries its hardest to be even cuter than the fonts themselves.

Take it all and may your programs read better both from the inside and outside!

Graphics File Formats

Up until now, we have concentrated on the techniques and processes for creating an image on the monitor. Some of these processes can take quite a long time, and therein lies the problem. What happens at the end of the day when you want to go home? Without some means of saving the image to a file, all the work will be lost. Therefore, in this chapter we are going to rectify this omission, and give you the tools to both save and load images from a file.

Chapter Contents

In this chapter, we will cover:

- A Plethora of Formats
- Common Encoding and Compression Techniques
- Paletted Images - Quantization
- How To Choose An Image Format
- The Image Formats - Examined Are BMP/DIB, PCX, TARGA, GIF and JPEG
- Reading and Writing Graphics Files

A Plethora of Formats

It has become a kind of established tradition, to recollect the legend of the Tower of Babel each time someone writes about graphic file formats. Are there any reasons for this? Unfortunately, there are...

The modern version of the ancient myth might sound something like this. In the days of GG's youth, everyone in computer graphics understood everyone else and everybody spoke the same language (**.PCX**, **.PIC**, or the like), and the Graphics Tower nearly reached Heaven. To avoid complications the Sovereign of all mysteries tempted the graphics community with the idea of a universal image file format. And so there came **GIF**, **TIFF**... and **JPEG**. Isn't progress fun?

In this chapter, we want to show you the common techniques of handling generic image formats. Obviously, we can't even dream of covering the whole topic; for instance, the most advanced software package for image format conversion (Image Alchemy by Handmade Software) at present reads and writes about 30-40 different dialects. We had quite enough to choose from and our choice was mostly determined by our own experience and the mid-range PC platform upon which we work, and to make matters worse, we also want to illustrate some data compression techniques.

The PC Explosion

In recent years, the field of computer graphics has exploded, or rather, has been affected by the explosion in the personal computer market. Every PC user now has his SVGA plugged in and ready to go, and wishes it to display what only **SIGGRAPH** could do not so long ago. Today, more graphical applications are being created every week than during the whole of 1989. These applications need some means of saving and exchanging pictures for manipulation and display.

With so many widely-accepted standards, it's so hard to resist the temptation to invent one of your own, just to support your own applications. These innovated or slightly modified formats vary only a little bit. However, this difference is quite enough to cause overheating if you want to read all the dialects of **PCX**, for instance.

More than that, almost every one of the graphic formats use this or that data compression technique, and some of them are really complex. So, let's go and find out if there's actually that much need for creative programming.

Common Encoding and Compression Techniques

Hopefully you should now understand how to store a color bitmap image. For each pixel you should save a set of three values, corresponding to the intensities of the primary colors (RGB, YCbCr, HSV) of the color representation.

> YCbCr is similar to YIQ, the coefficients of the conversion equations differing slightly.

This set can be organized in two different ways. The difference is pretty simple:

- ▲ The first way is by pixels; for TrueColor it gives ((R1,G1,B1)...(Ri,Gi,Bi)..).

- ▲ The second way is by color planes; the TrueColor version looks like this: ((R1..Ri),(G1..Gi), (B1..Bi)).

No matter how you write your RGBs, a 640×480, 24-bit bitmap uses up about 1 MByte when uncompressed, which pushes us towards starting with a short overview of compression techniques. You see, bitmap files are unnecessarily large. There are only a few common data compression techniques used for bitmaps, but nevertheless, there are quite a lot of slightly different ways that the graphics data is encoded.

Theoretically, the compression algorithm must be accurately described in a file format specification. However, there's always a lot of subtle details and enough room for different interpretations. Before we look at some examples though, let's give an overview of the common coding/compression techniques.

Compression Techniques

There is a kind of solid mathematical bedrock for each and every compression method. In general, the compression of a bitmap means that for each small fragment of the image, which is usually one pixel, you write a binary code smaller in length than the initial bitmap representation. The coding algorithm you choose must allow you to decode, or restore the original bitmap. The decoding process for most traditional techniques works without any loss of information, or in other words, it restores exactly what was coded. However, with pictures, you can afford to lose some information without serious distortion, and so **lossy** image compression methods, such as JPEG, (the file format from the Joint Photographic Experts Group) are thought to be very promising.

Almost every compression algorithm is complicated; the fact is it has to be, just to be able to work fast and efficiently. Anyway, the basic idea they are based upon is usually pretty simple.

Huffman's Coding (Code Length Optimization)

It was discovered long ago that some characters of the alphabet are used more often than others, so if those more frequently met had shorter codes, it would result in a significant compression.

Two quite different questions arise each time Huffman's method is implemented:

- ▲ How to create the optimal code table for the given data flow.

- ▲ How to implement coding/decoding routines if the code length isn't fixed.

Strictly speaking, the first one is optional, as you can use predefined code tables. It has one more advantage, in that it allows single-pass operations. However, for small files as well as for certain kinds of text, such as Assembly source code or a bitmap, an adaptive code table may provide a significantly better compression ratio.

We decided to omit the details of Huffman's coding as it's rarely used in graphic formats. As far as we know the only occurrence is JPEG where it's applied to the sequence of Fourier co-efficients. However, one thing that should be mentioned is that Huffman's coding has a theoretical upper compression ratio limit. Since you can only code a symbol with an integer number of bits, a text with 8 bits per symbol, which equates to a 256 letter alphabet, can't be compressed any more than 8:1.

Run-Length Encoding (RLE)

RLE is the simplest and the most child-like of data compression techniques, however it handles the situation it was designed for excellently. What do we mean? I'm sure that sometimes you've noticed fragments in your data that look like **aaaaaaaaabbbbbbb**. You intuitively feel that these fragments can be written a bit shorter - **9a7b** maybe or perhaps just one symbol and the repeater (the number of recurrences of this symbol).

By the way, both Huffman's and LZW compression techniques don't find this sort of data chain particularly easy to compress. Moreover, if you think the RLE technique is inefficient, you are quite mistaken. It actually works pretty well, especially in graphics. The fact is, most graphic file formats use RLE coding.

We're sure you could easily implement this outstanding method by yourself. Of course, you have to define some kind of specific attribute for the repeater. Let's suppose that it has the following format:

The two high-order bits in the repeater byte are set to 1, leaving 6 free bits to specify the number of recurrences. This means we can represent up to 63 repeating symbols. The byte following the repeater is the value that needs to be repeated.

> Therefore, in binary notation, the repeater byte is 11000000 plus the number of symbols that are repeated. This equates to C0h plus the number of symbols to be repeated in hexadecimal.

For example, if the initial data is 3Eh, 3Eh, 3Eh, then the compressed result would be:

    C3h, 3Eh

and if the initial data is 3Ah, 3Ah, ... repeated 18 times, then the compressed result will be:

D2h, 3Ah

> Here D2h is the repeater. Written in binary, 11010010, we can see how it is constructed. The first two bits specify that it is a repeater and the remaining 6 specify the number of recurrences.

The **.PCX** graphic format works in this way, but there are variations such as the TARGA graphic format, which use one major bit marker and so can code up to 127 recurrences.

There is, however, the problem of what to do with those bytes which initially have their two high-order bits set to 1. The easiest way is to add a repeater with the number of recurrences equal to 1 before each of these bytes. This method was chosen for PCX implementation.

Unfortunately, with some data sets, this method will actually produce a compressed file bigger than the uncompressed one! If the initial data looks like:

FFh, 00h, FFh, 00h

compression will result in:

C1h, FFh, 00h, C1h, FFh, 00h

A percentage compression of -50%!

> The C1h is inserted before each FFh, otherwise the FFh (or 11111111 in binary) could be mistaken for a repeater.

To get around this problem of data explosion, with the aid of our 'compression' algorithm, we must include the following rule. For any series of identical bytes that are shorter than two items long, do not use the compression algorithm. The implementation of this algorithm is illustrated on the next page.

Input data:

08h, 08h, 3Ah, 3Ah, 3Ah, 3Ah, D4h, D4h, D4h, ...

Compressed data:

08h, 08h, C4h, 3Ah, C3h, D4h, ...

The first two bytes, both 08h, could have been compressed to C2h, 08h, but this is pointless from a space saving point of view and would actually slow the algorithm runtime right down as the repeater has to be decoded.

However, you can't mix two systems when you are talking about a computer that can only follow a simple set of commands. And so, because of this, we're going to have to use two sorts of repeater:

1??????? for compressed (repeated) bytes,

0??????? for the following bytes to be output as they are.

This allows you to code up to 127 recurrences and also makes it possible to detect the presence of repeaters in the code, or perhaps more importantly, the lack of them. Using this improvement on the previous two examples we get:

FFh, 00h, FFh, 00h

04h, FFh, 00h, FFh, 00h

The initial 04h means that the next 4 bytes are output as they are. The amount of data has still increased, but not by such a drastic amount as before.

08h, 08h, 3Ah, 3Ah, 3Ah, 3Ah, D4h, D4h, D4h, ...

82h, 08h, 84h, 3Ah, 83h, D4h, ...

This time we have had to use a repeater for the first two bytes, otherwise the first 08h would have been mistaken to mean that the following 8 bytes should be output as they are.

One word of warning: beware of using such a technique for your own 'new PCX incarnation'. Bear in mind those who will have to decode it. By the way, such a technique has already been implemented in the RLE version of the TARGA graphic format.

Lempel-Ziv-Welch (LZW) Algorithm

LZW is a compression technique based on the coding of repeated data chains or patterns in graphics.

Consider the following situation. Suppose you are packing only text files and you have a vocabulary of the 65536 most frequently used words. In this case, you can code each word in the text with two bytes - its index in the vocabulary. This method would compress your text by at least a factor of two. Unfortunately, the vocabulary file turns out to be too large, but the idea is too good to be forgotten.

The **LZ77** and **LZSS** versions of the Lempel-Ziv algorithm work in a very similar manner to our vocabulary example. The difference is in the vocabulary, they simply use a block of initial text without any reordering for this purpose.

LZW avoids the problem of a huge predefined vocabulary in a more sophisticated way. Usually LZW implementations build their own adaptive code tables, that contain the data chains (or successions of pixels. The compressor takes data from the incoming data flow and constructs the table of chains.

The algorithm starts with the **minimum code length** and uses it while there's still enough room in the table, then the code length is increased by one bit, and again and again until the maximum length, which is usually 12 bits, is reached. None of the 'code length overflow' markers are used. The decompressor itself finds out when the limit of the code length has been reached. As a matter of fact, during decompression the same table of chains is accurately restored from the coded data flow. That's why if the minimum code length is defined, the LZW algorithm doesn't need a predefined code table at all!

> Note that in graphics, the minimum code length is usually the number of bits per pixel +1.

There is, however, an important thing to watch out for: code table overflow. The usual solution to this problem is simple; you must watch the current code length and the number of free entries in the table of chains. Remember that the table size is determined by the maximum code length of 12 bits, or in other words, 4096 entries. Once you've used the last free entry, you have to finish coding and output the specially reserved **Clear Code** (an analog of EOF) to inform the decompressor that it has to interrupt the decoding process here and reinitialize all the tables and variables. You can find details of LZW on the accompanying CD (**.GIF** format reader/saver).

Arithmetic Coding

Huffman's coding technique, although logically grounded, suffers from one small shortcoming. You can only code a symbol with an integer number of bits. Suppose that in a paragraph of text, you wanted to count the number of times that each individual character occurred, and you were going to count the occurrences in full groups of five in order to save space in memory. In general, there would be no problem, but in certain cases, for example in the case of the letter 'z', the number of occurrences would not reach the required level to form one bit, and a dilemma would have to be faced. There's no way you could accurately code the letter with less than one bit, and you would have to decide which side of the fence to fall, no occurrences or one group of five counted.

Arithmetic coding manages this situation, and therefore in general, is much better. This method is based on the idea of transforming the incoming data flow into one rational number or, to be more precise, into a rational interval. The longer the incoming data, the more precisely boundaries of the interval are defined. Like Huffman's coding, it could be used as the last step of the JPEG coding chain to compress Fourier coefficients. However, it does seem that this really nice idea vanished due to patent limitations.

Paletted Images - Quantization

We don't know who was the first to apply the color palette representation in bitmap graphics, but whoever he was, it was a great idea. Unfortunately, the problems match the deed. Palette color representation doesn't simply mean that your image has a limited number of colors. As you will remember, in a paletted image, a pixel value isn't the actual color, it's a reference to the palette table. The data file must, therefore, include not only the pixel data, but also the table of palette data, and you must be sure that this palette is unique.

No matter what the actual reason for it is, there's a problem in representing an existing TrueColor image with a smaller number of colors, and the problem sometimes occurs when using a limited color space, for example when converting a TrueColor, 16Megacolor image into 256 colors of 256Kilocolor space. Generally speaking the problem falls into two parts:

▲ Selecting the appropriate palette.

▲ The actual transforming of the initial image according to the palette selected at the first stage.

We can eliminate both problems at once if we are prepared to tolerate acceptable, and not excellent, image representation. This sort of poor man's solution is called the **uniform palette**. First we'll construct it by simply taking, for instance, 8 levels for green, 8 for red and 4 for blue (8*8*4 = 256) and dividing the whole color space into 256 boxes. And so this construction of the palette solves the first problem. So far, so good.

The second problem is greatly simplified, too, as we can treat every RGB separately. Moreover, we can use the dithering technique (see Chapter 4 for details). By the way, a specially constructed predefined palette provides the best way to use pattern dithering. The results you get are almost always acceptable, and you can make them even better by applying an **error transferring** algorithm, such as Floyd-Steinberg (see Chapter 9 for FSA implementation).

If the 'poor man's' solution doesn't suit you, then you have to undertake the whole quantization routine. The following description is based on Heckbert's two-pass quantizer implementation belonging to the JPEG group; an excellent piece of software, by the way. We have made some minor changes and (we think) corrections. Most of the ideas used here though can be traced back to the following paper: Heckbert, Paul. "Color Image Quantization for Frame Buffer Display", Proc. SIGGRAPH '82, Computer Graphics v.16 #3 (July 1982), pp 297-304.

Therefore, color reduction is performed by a two-pass algorithm.

Palette Construction

During the first pass over the image, we accumulate a histogram showing the usage of each possible color. To keep the histogram to a reasonable size, we reduce the precision of the input; typical practice is to retain 5 or 6 bits per color, so that 8 or 4 different input values are counted in the same histogram cell. Generally speaking, the quantizer can work in any kind of color space, but RGB is one of the most inconvenient. The YCbCr color scheme is much better as it's closer to perceptual practice. Unfortunately RGB-to-YCbCr transformation is too expensive for everyday use, except in the case of JPEG decompression. Certainly, the color space you work in should be properly scaled. We use a factor of 1.5 for R and 2 for G.

Next, the color-selection step begins with a box representing the whole color space, and repeatedly splits the 'largest' remaining box until we have as many boxes as desired colors.

Heckbert-style quantizers vary a good deal in the way they choose the 'largest' box and how they decide where to split it. The 'largest box' can be selected according to either its volume or 'weight'. What is meant by volume is clear. To calculate the 'weight' of a box you can count either the number of colors, or in other words, non-zero histogram cells within the box, or the number of pixels. Our forerunners from the JPEG group decided that counting colors was best. We, however, stand by pixels. Nevertheless, their heuristic decision to use weight as the box selection criterion on the first half of the palette and volume on the second half is fine, and we are quite happy to go along with this.

Well, we've chosen the box to be cut out, but how should we split it? The simplest, and most natural way is to take the longest side and split it in two, or you may decide to split the box into two subboxes with equal weights, but we hope you don't. Each time we split the box we should 'press out the air', or in other words, make the box as small as we can, without losing any of non-zero cells.

Now we have to choose the **mean color** for each remaining box, by which we mean one of the possible output colors. The mean color is calculated as the mass center of the box. So, at last, the palette is complete.

Color Mapping

The second problem is to map each pixel of the initial image to the closest output color (palette entry). Logically, this mapping seems quite trivial. However, it's the most time consuming part of the routine, so we really need a piece of algorithmic art to make it fast enough.

Three basic ideas are used.

1. The Reverse Color Map

We should use a **reverse color map**, as a cache for the results of nearest-color searches. This means that each time we map a pixel color to a palette entry we retain the result in a special table, so the calculations are only performed once. The most natural way to arrange the table is to use a 3D array similar to our histogram. You can even utilize this particular data structure.

> Why do we call it reverse? A palette itself is a color map, which sets the relationship between a color and an entry index; the table we use sets the relationship between the entry index and the pixel color.

2. A Locally Sorted Search

The second idea is a **locally sorted search** as described by Heckbert. It's a kind of simple mini-max criterion, but it's efficient enough for our algorithm. Again, we split the initial color space into subboxes, but this time we make them equal. The optimum size of a sub-box is a matter of empirical judgment, it could be, for instance, 1/512th of the color space, 1/8th in each direction.

Now, for any sub-box we can easily eliminate the entries which are too far away and won't be used to map the colors of the sub-box. For each of the color entries we should calculate the minimum and maximum distance between it and the sub-box, calculations being performed based on the vertices of the sub-box. Then we find the minimum among the maximums. Now, every color entry which has a minimum distance bigger than mini-max will be thrown away. Typically, 3/4 of the entries don't fit this criterion. Obviously a sub-box should only be processed if there are cells in it, so you never need to bother with empty color space regions.

3. Incremental Distance

The last trick is the **incremental distance** calculation described by Spencer W. Thomas in Chapter III.1 of Graphics Gems II (James Arvo, ed. Academic Press, 1991). Actually, the distances between a given color map entry and each cell of the color space can be computed incrementally; the differences between distances to adjacent cells differ by a constant. It's more convenient to apply this incremental rule as the last step of color mapping within each subbox.

That's all then. We hope you've managed to grasp at least a general understanding of how it works. One more thing - you may never work with TrueColor images and still find the quantization technique useful. "Useful for what?", you may ask. Imagine you have a set of paletted images and you wish to show them simultaneously or in fast succession. If the palettes of the images are different, as they normally are, you may get a very impressive picture if you display them together. In fact, it will be a pretty weird one. To avoid this problem you must remap the palettes of all your images into one. Only the quantizer can help you do this.

How To Choose An Image Format

Choosing a particular format, or formats, for your application isn't as easy as it may seem. Certainly your boss (who knows best anyway!) will say, ".**PCX** and .**DIB**" or, "we must support JPEG because everyone does". But if you have to make the decisions yourself, you'll probably find the following set of comparative criteria useful.

Throughout this chapter, we evaluate different formats according to their:

▲ Flexibility

▲ Efficiency (compression and calculations)

▲ Support

Flexibility

By flexibility, we generally mean the video range covered by a particular graphic. We also take into account, to some extent, the facilities provided to specify aspect ratio, alpha channel information, and so on.

Efficiency

In our estimation, the efficiency criterion relates to both the media space and computing resources required to process a single image. You should remember, the more powerful the image compression technique you use, the greater computing time you need for encoding and decoding. Moreover, each image compression algorithm suits a particular class of images. The highest prize for efficiency we award to JPEG, and it's clear why we were quite impressed by its results. The JPEG compression ratio can exceed 100:1, but don't expect to squeeze your 256 color image of 100Kb down to 1k.

Generally speaking, there are three major kinds of bitmap image and three common compression techniques, and this is how they relate;

▲ 16 colors, 4 planes   - RLE, working on separate planes

▲ 256 colors paletted   - LZW

▲ True (actual) color   - JPEG compression chain

and we have tried to take this into account when classifying the formats.

Support

For most project managers and programmers, the key issue is, 'Which applications support this format?', and 'How widely is it used?'. The answers to these questions are of extreme importance when a particular format is being considered.

However, you should note that there's another question connected with this, namely, 'Will it take much to support this format?'. There are supports and SUPPORTs. Some programs can only read a given format, some can only write it. Certain features of some formats can, and should be, skipped. Moreover, graphics formats are a matter of continuous improvement. Almost every one of them has two or more versions and you can't be sure that the user will always utilize the latest one.

That's why, when we classify the formats by 'support', we not only consider how widely a particular format is used but also how much it would cost to provide real support for it. This is only one of the reasons why we evaluated support for PCX to be less than that for GIF.

So, for each of the following descriptions, we'll start with a format 'identification card' containing:

▲ The format's full title.

▲ The owner's (creator's) name

▲ The compression technique used

▲ The range of video modes covered

▲ Its usual 'occupation', or in other words, where it is usually employed

This is followed by a table containing our star rating for flexibility, efficiency and support, as well as a description of the file format, and any notes we think you should be aware of.

BMP/DIB

Name:	Microsoft Windows Device Independent Bitmap. (`.BMP`, `.DIB`)
Owner/Creator:	Microsoft.
Compression:	RLE or none.
Video Range:	Whole, from 1 to 24 bits per pixel.
Occupation:	Image display and interchange under MS Windows.

Flexibility	* * * *
Packing Efficiency	* *
Support	* * *

DIB File Header

Offset bytes	Size (bytes)	Description
FILE HEADER		
0	2	ASCII string "BM"
2	4	Size of the file in bytes
6	2	Reserved - 0
8	2	Reserved - 0
10	4	Image offset, counting in from the beginning of the file
IMAGE HEADER		
14	4	Size of the image header (always 40 bytes)
18	4	Image width in pixels
22	4	Image height in pixels
26	2	Number of planes, always 1
28	2	Bits per pixel (1,4,8,24 possible)
30	4	Compression type (0 = uncompressed, other = RLE)
34	4	Compressed image size, in bytes
38	4	Horizontal resolution, in pixels per meter
42	4	Vertical resolution, in pixels per meter
46	4	Number of colors (palette entries) used
50	4	Number of the most important colors (first in the palette)
54	4*N	Color map (palette)

Normally N may be 2, 16 or 256 for 1, 4 or 8 bits per pixel (24 bits per pixel stands for the direct colors). The palette entry is 4 bytes long and contains RGB components, but in reverse order, i.e. B,G,R. The fourth byte is reserved, perhaps for the alpha channel.

Format Details

DIB is an excellent format across the Windows world, sometimes even supported abroad, for example, 3D Studio 3.0. You'll certainly find it convenient, except for its compression algorithm. You just need to remember that, in order to be able to display it properly, an image is written from the bottom to the top.

Format Traps

There is a strange trap with the image row length in DIB. The size is accurately specified in the header - OK, no problem. However, each line is padded to a 4 byte boundary. Some applications pad by adding bytes while others prefer to truncate lines. If you rely on just adding, you risk getting your image 'sheared'. The only reliable approach we know works in this way:

```
Line length(in bytes) = (File size(in bytes)-Image offset) / Image height.
```

Compression Details

The MS Windows DIB format is meant to support four and 8-bit RLE compression. However, we find this version of RLE decompression too sophisticated to implement. Most MS Windows applications have their own, usually unique, interpretation of DIB's RLE. Some of them don't even read the compressed DIBs that they themselves write.

PCX

Name:	PCX (.PCX)
Owner/Creator:	ZSoft.
Compression:	RLE or none.
Video Range:	Whole, from 1 to 24 bits per pixel (except for 15 and 16 bits/per pixel HighColor).
Occupation:	Image display and interchange across the PC world.

Flexibility	* * *
Packing Efficiency	* * *
Support	* * * *

PCX is one of the oldest formats still extensively in use on the PC. Originally created by ZSoft for their paint software, the PCX format can at present be read and written by almost any PC graphics software. A new version of the PCX format even supports 24 bits per pixel. A PCX file starts with a header of 128 bytes.

PCX File Header

Offset bytes (bytes)	Size	Description
0	1	Zsoft Flag (0Ah)
1	1	Version (always 5 so far)
2	1	Always 1 (means RLE encoded)
3	1	Number of bits per pixel for each plane
4	2	X Left
6	2	Y Upper
8	2	X Right
10	2	Y Lower
12	2	Horizontal resolution (dots per inch)
14	2	Vertical resolution (dots per inch)
16	48	Palette (see below)
64	1	Reserved, always 0
65	1	Number of planes
66	2	Bytes per each plane line

Continued

Offset bytes	Size (bytes)	Description
68	2	Header palette interpretation, rarely used 1
70	2	Screen size X (seems used only by PaintBrush 4)
72	2	Screen size Y
74	54	Zeros down to the end of the header.

Palette and Image Practice

The PCX format covers the widest range of video modes amongst the formats we are reviewing in this chapter, which is surely an advantage. However, the PCX file format provides next to nothing when you are considering the image type. To help you out, first find out which particular image type you are going to operate upon, and then look at the table given below:

Bits/pixel /plane	Number of planes	Description
1	1	Monochrome
1	2	4 colors (is it still used?)
2	1	4 colors
1	4	16 colors 4 planes, standard mode,
4	1	16 colors 2 pixels in each byte,
8	1	256 colors, palette in the end of file
8	3	16.7M-colors no palette, TrueColor

PCX Image Type Interpretation

We've marked the most popular image types saved by the PCX format.

> Note that the 4 plane, 1 bit per plane, 16-color mode is the best for PCX.
> It's main advantage is that separate planes are more easily compressed by
> the RLE algorithm. That's why we consider choosing 1 plane, 4 bits per
> pixel (two pixels in each byte), 16-color images type a mistake. In our
> opinion, it's the worst way to store a 16-color image. However, there are
> painting programs that prefer this way of storing images.

The PCX format provides two ways of storing the image palette. The first is
the EGA/VGA standard palette which resides in the header - 48 bytes starting
from 16 and going up to 63. It's arranged in triads, 1 byte per RGB
component. For VGA modes you have to divide the value of components by 4,
and by 64 for EGA, if you want to obtain the levels of intensity.

For 256-color images, the whole palette must have 256 3-byte entries. There
isn't enough space in the header, and therefore the palette lies at the end of
file. It starts 768 bytes before the end of the file with the marker 0Ch. Again,
the value of each byte should be divided by 4.

Format Traps

Some applications pad each line of each plane to a word (two-byte) boundary.
Again, the only reliable way involves some simple calculations:

```
Line length (in bytes) = ((XRight-XLeft+1) * Bits per pixel+ 7) / 8
```

Then you can compare the obtained value with the bytes-per-line field. If they
are the same then OK, but if not, then during the decompression, you should
skip the last byte of each plane line.

> Never believe anyone who says that the image scan lines, or plane scan
> lines, in PCX are always separated. Sometimes they are, but be prepared to
> face a PCX dialect which separates only image scan lines or even writes
> the continuous byte stream.

In general, the PCX format suffers from its great age. Since it was first introduced in the early 80s, too many graphics standards have been established and too many versions of the format implemented. So the plain and short decompressing code introduced by ZSoft at present looks like a Chinese puzzle. (See the PCX reader on the accompanying CD-ROM.) We can't be sure that it covers all dialects, but at least it shows any PCX file we've ever seen. By the way, the compression ratio (if any) is poor for 8- and 24-bit images.

TARGA

Name: TARGA (.**TGA**)
Owner/Creator: Truevision, Inc.
Compression: RLE or none.
Video Range: Highend, 8, 15, 16, 24, and 32 (Alpha channel) bits per pixel.
Occupation: Image storage and interchange, used by highend graphics software and some scanners.

Flexibility	* * *
Packing Efficiency	* *
Support	* * *

TARGA files may contain:

 A fixed size (18 bytes long) header

 An optional ID string of variable size up to 255 bytes

 An optional color map

 An image section

 An optional footer

TARGA File Header

Offset bytes	Size in bytes	Description
0	1	ID filed length
1	1	Color map flag (1 = paletted image, 0 = TrueColor)
2	1	Image type (see table overleaf)
COLOR MAP SECTION		
3	2	First color map entry
5	2	Color map size
7	1	Color map entry size
IMAGE DATA SECTION		
8	2	X Left
10	2	Y Upper
12	2	Image width in pixels
14	2	Image height in pixels
16	1	Number of bits per pixel
17	1	Image descriptor byte. (See below)

The image type field specifies the type of image and the compression method employed, which is always RLE but maybe... one day... See the following table for details:

Code	Description
0	No image
1	Color mapped (palette), uncompressed
2	TrueColor (no palette), uncompressed
3	Black and white, uncompressed
9	Color mapped (palette), RLE coded
10	TrueColor (no palette), RLE coded
11	Black and white, RLE coded

Codes Used In The Image Type Field

The Bit Codes Of The Image Descriptor Byte

Bits	Meaning	Values
0-3	Number of attributes bits per pixel (Alpha chan.)	
4-5	The order in which the pixels are stored	00 - left to right, bottom to top
		01 - right to left, bottom to top
		10 - left to right, top to bottom
		11 - right to left, top to bottom
6-7	Scan line interleave	00 - no interleave
		01 - two way interleave
		10 - four way interleave

Palette and Image Practice

If the color map flag is set to 1, the image has the color map, if it's set to 0, there is no palette and the image contains actual color, and if so, all bytes of the color map section must be zeros. At present TARGA files are hardly ever paletted. If, however, you face a TARGA file with the color map flag set, then:

- ▲ First color map entry   - the smallest pixel value in the file
- ▲ Color map size   - specifies the range of pixel values
- ▲ Color map entry size   - may be 15, 16, 24 or 32 (bits)

For 15- and 16-bit color map entry sizes, the two byte entry looks like this: **ARRRRRGG   GGGBBBBB** - 5 bits per RGB component. The **A** attribute is optional and may be set to 0 (as you can guess **A** is for Alpha). A 24-bit entry contains 3 bytes: **B**, **G**, **R** in this order. A 32-bit entry is similar to 24-bit plus one byte for the alpha channel: **B**, **G**, **R**, **A**.

The Image Itself

Color mapped images are usually a byte per pixel. You have to read the corresponding palette entry to get the actual color.

Pixels of TrueColor images contain from 15(16) to 32 bits each and have a structure similar to a palette entry:

Bit (Byte) to color map	Image type
ARRRRRGG GGGBBBBB	for 15, 16 bits per pixel
B, G, R	for 24 bits
B, G, R, A	for 32 bits per pixel

Some applications, and therefore manufacturers, prefer the reverse order of **R**, **G**, **B**, **A** or **A**, **R**, **G**, **B**, just to make things confusing. We don't know any reliable method of detecting the RGB component order.

Format Details

TARGA files of the version 2.0 format allow a footer containing additional data, such as aspect ratio, gamma and color correction information, and even a 'postage stamp' version of the image, which is not larger than 64×64 pixels. However, only a few programs at present can read, write and use the footer information correctly.

Compression Details

TARGA format provides probably the best implementation of RLE compression. It is so good, we used it to illustrate RLE in the 'Common Encoding and Compression Techniques' section earlier. This is quite ironic because the TrueColor images TARGA usually deals with are almost incompressible by RLE.

Format Traps

However, even TARGA is not blemish-free and the trap is typical of RLE implementations. Yes, you've guessed it, line termination. Never believe that each row is compressed separately.

GIF

Name:	Graphic Interchange Format, (.**GIF**)
Owner/Creator:	CompuServe
Compression:	LZW
Video Range:	Low end, from 1 to 8 bits per pixel.
Occupation:	Image display and interchange under MS Windows.

Flexibility	* * *
Packing Efficiency	* * * *
Support	* * * * *

GIF files were originally developed by CompuServe as a machine independent image file format. GIF files are the most popular way of storing 8-bit, scanned or digitized images. Moreover, the compression ratio provided by GIF's LZW algorithm is usually better than any other for 8-bit formats.

We can't, shouldn't, and won't provide the full GIF specification, including plain text, graphics control and application extensions. Anyone who really feels they are deprived without this information can contact CompuServe for details. Unfortunately, we have never met any `.GIF` file with these parts included. In this section, we'll just give you the information necessary to show images.

GIF appears to be a more sophisticated format than the previous ones. Its organization is strictly sequential; understandable, as it was designed for transmitting rather than for storage. GIF has five sections, all of which are usually present:

▲ The header

▲ The logical screen descriptor ›

▲ The global color table (optional)

▲ The data section (image descriptor, local palette, image data)

▲ The trailer (terminating code)

Each section consists of one or more blocks.

GIF File Header

The 6-byte-long header identifies the Data Stream as GIF, the first 3 bytes always contain the ASCII string 'GIF'. The last 3 are used to specify the format version, which is ASCII '87a' or ASCII '89a' for the latest version.

The Logical Screen Descriptor

This section, and only this section must be in the file. It contains the parameters for the image display. The details are in the following table:

Offset bytes	Size in bytes	Description
0	2	Logical screen width (in pixels)
2	2	Logical screen height (in pixels)
4	1	Packed fields byte (see below)

Continued

224

Offset bytes	Size in bytes	Description
5	1	Background color index
6	1	Pixel aspect ratio. Actual aspect ratio is calculated as: (Pixel Aspect Ratio +15)/64, (if the field isn't zero, of course)

GIF, The Structure Of The Logical Screen Descriptor

The Bit Codes Of The Packed Fields Byte

Bits	Meaning	Values
0-2	size of global palette, $3*2^{(\text{field value} + 1)}$ bytes	
3	sort flag	0 = not sorted
		1 = sorted palette
4-6	bits per primary color -1	
7	global palette flag	0 = not present
		1 = global palette present

Global Color Table (Palette)

If the global palette flag is set, then the global palette is present and it immediately follows the logical screen descriptor. It's arranged in exactly the same way as all palettes are, one byte for each primary (RGB) color. The number of global palette entries (for instance RGB triads) is defined by the size of global palette field as shown in the table below, and so GIF files can only store palette size as the nearest power of 2.

Data Section

Image Descriptor

The image descriptor contains the set of parameters necessary to handle the image. There must be exactly one descriptor per image in a **.GIF** file. The details are included in the table below.

Offset bytes	Size in bytes	Description
0	1	Image separator (always 2Ch)
1	2	Image left position (in pixels)
3	2	Image top position (in pixels)
5	2	Image width (in pixels)
7	2	Image height (in pixels)
8	1	Packed fields byte (see below)

The Structure of The Image Descriptor

The Bit Codes Of The Image Descriptor Packed Fields Byte

Bits	Meaning	Values
0-2	size of local palette, $3*2^{(\text{field value} + 1)}$ bytes	
3-4	reserved	
5	sorted flag	0 = not sorted
		1 = sorted palette
6	interlaced flag	0 = not interlaced
		1 = the image is interlaced
7	local palette flag	0 = not present
		1 = global palette present

Local Color Table (Palette)

If the local palette flag is set, then the local palette is present and it immediately follows the image descriptor. It's organized in exactly the same way as the global palette, and affects only the image that follows it.

Image Data

The image data section begins with a 1-byte field which holds the LZW Minimum Code Size, the details of which we have already covered. Then comes the data sub-blocks, each starting with a 1-byte field which specifies the size of the sub-block, which must not be larger than 256 bytes. The data blocks contain LZW encoded pixel values with indices in the global or the local palette. The pixels are organized from left to right, top to bottom. There is a problem in the way GIF packs LZW variable length codes into bytes. The codes within each byte are packed from right to left. Look at the following example, where 5-bit code is assumed:

11111 is the first code, 22222 is the second...

```
Byte 1          Byte2    ...
22211111        43333322 ...
```

The Trailer

This single-byte block merely terminates GIF Data Stream. It always has the value 3Bh.

Format Details

The GIF format has two versions, referred to in the header as 87a and 89a. The newer, 89a version provides a set of additional facilities, unfortunately, they are almost unused. Although the syntax of the header, logical screen descriptor, and image descriptor remains the same, there are many programs that fail to read GIFed images of the 89a version. So, maybe, you'd better use the older one.

Compression Details

The LZW algorithm, used by GIF, appears to provide the best way of compressing a byte per pixel image. It competently handles the patterns which stall the RLE compression algorithm.

JPEG

Name: JPEG (`.JPG`)
Owner/Creator: Joint Photographic Experts Group (JPEG).
Compression: Sophisticated, four-step coding routine.
Video Range: Highend, usually 24 bits per pixel or gray scale.
Occupation: Storage and interchange of the photorealistic images.

Flexibility	* *
Packing Efficiency	* * * * *
Support	* * *

JPEG is a new type of image file format that uses a lossy compression technique to achieve high compression ratios. It's used mostly for photographic images.

In this section we will venture to give an overview of the JPEG compression method, the representation being mostly based on the JPEG group shareware source code and it's description.

The JPEG compression method is a kind of multi-pass routine including a series of reasonably complex mathematical transformations of the initial image:

 Color space conversion

 Discrete cosine transforms

▲ Quantization

▲ Entropy (usually Huffman) coding

Color Space Conversion

The image is converted to a YCbCr color space with separate luminance (Y) and chrominance (CbCr) components. The YCbCr color system differs from the YIQ system that we discussed in Chapter 4. The formulas for RGB to YCbCr transformation look like this:

```
Y  = 0.299 * R + 0.587 * G + 0.114 * B;
Cb = 0.169 * R - 0.331 * G + 0.5 * B;
Cr = 0.5 * R - 0.419 * G - 0.081 * B;
```

The third digit is surely for decorative purposes only, and sometimes they even give four.

Generally speaking, this transformation isn't lossy yet, since you still have all the information in the YCbCr triads that you had in RGB. However, in the RGB color system, the components, or primary colors, are almost all of the same importance, while in YCbCr one Y 'color' holds the main part of the video information. This is based on the idea that the human eye is more sensitive to variations of brightness than variations of color. Therefore, we can use significantly less Cb and Cr samples, scarcely affecting the resulting image.

The reduction of the number of samples for a color component is called **downsampling**. It's the first real lossy step of the JPEG compression. It's usually performed in the following way. For each 2×1 (2×2, or even 4×4) rectangular block of pixels, only one Cb and one Cr sample are used. This step gives the compression ratio 2/3, 1/2 for 2×2 downsampling.

Discrete Cosine Transforms

This step usually looks like the most complicated in the JPEG algorithm, but the key idea is pretty simple. Photorealistic images consist mostly of areas with smooth variations of brightness and/or color, and it is this structure that JPEG takes advantage of. The luminance and chrominance information is separately transformed to the **frequency domain** using two dimensional discrete cosine transformation (DCT) operating on 8×8 pixel blocks. After DCT, we get a 8×8 matrix of 'intensities' of different spatial frequencies. Because of the smoothness of realistic images, in most transformed blocks only the upper-left corner significantly differs from zero. The upper-left corner of the transformed block indicates the lower spatial frequencies. The following figure shows two sample pixel blocks and their frequency representation.

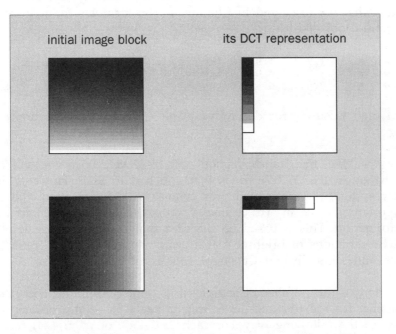

initial image block   its DCT representation

Pixel Blocks and their Representation after DCT

Quantization

The transformed data is then quantized, so adding one more lossy step. The 'higher frequencies' are quantized using fewer levels than lower frequencies, and it is here that you can control the quality and compression ratio by scaling a set of quantization levels. JPEG uses the linear quantization which means that each DCT co-efficient is divided by the value of the quantization level and rounded to an integer. JPEG operates using an 8×8 table of quantization levels, one number for each spatial frequency. As a matter of fact, there are usually two tables, one for Y and another one for Cb and Cr. The tables are stored in the JPEG file to be used during decompression.

And because of this, the 'higher frequencies', which are normally weak, are cut down even more by quantization.

Entropy (Usually Huffman) Coding

Next the quantized data is compressed using an entropy coder. Normally Huffman coding is used, even though arithmetic coding would be significantly better. But before coding, the DCT co-efficients are reordered to the specific 'zigzag' order.

Unfortunately, arithmetic coding can't be used because of patent limitations.

Typical block representation
in frequency domain.

The darker the color,
the greater the amplitude

Reordering DCT Co-efficients before Entropy Coding

The reason for such a mysterious operation becomes obvious if you look at the two figures given above. The 'tail end' of the reordered table usually contains only zeros.

Huffman coding of the reordered co-efficients can be performed using either a predefined coding table or an image-specific one. A custom table produces a slightly better compression, but it does require a two-pass operation.

Some Format Tips

Since JPEG compression was designed for continuous tone photographic images, don't be surprised by poor results when compressing line drawings or the like.

Due to JPEG compression working on 8×8 pixel blocks it may produce a parquetry effect, especially for higher compression ratios. The boundaries of the blocks are visible, but smoothing can attempt to reduce this phenomenon.

When you decompress a JPEG image, you get an image that is not quite the same as the original which is why JPEG compression is lossy. However, the loss is generally very small and, as a matter of fact, almost every image conversion operation is lossy to some degree.

JPEG is designed to work mostly on TrueColor images, or at least it hasn't been adapted to operate on paletted ones. If you engage the usual JPEG compressor to work on a 256-color paletted image, it first converts it to actual colors, making it 3 times larger, and then tries to compress it. This doesn't seem to be the best way to use such a great technique.

Reading and Writing Graphics Files

At first we decided not to provide any code fragments in this chapter. There are many problems surrounding image file formats, and none of them are worth separate consideration except, maybe, for the compression techniques and the quantizer. On the other hand, the niceties of implementing these helpful routines are beyond this book. After all, the source code is on the CD-ROM, and is well-commented.

But in this section, we've changed our minds and have decided to give you code fragments. They are simply three headers of objects which we use for graphics formats reading/writing/converting. However, these tiny pieces of code illustrate the whole process, or at least we hope they do:

```
#define BUFF_SIZE 30000 // size of object's input buffer

enum image_type {MONOIMG, COLOR16IMG, GRAY256IMG, COLOR256IMG,
                 TRUECOLORIMG};

enum image_extention_type {NO_EXTENTION, MONOGIF, COLOR16_2PIXEL,
                           COLOR16_1PIXEL, COLOR16_PLANE,
                           RGB15,RGB16,BGR24,RGB24,BGRA32,RGBPLANE24};

int get_bitsperpixel(image_type it,image_extention_type iet);

//this object is just the abstract father of the clone of some
//graphic file format readers and savers
class graph_file_abstract
{
protected:
   FILE *the_file;
   BYTE *buffer;
   WORD buff_offset;
   BOOL usebuffer;
public:
   BOOL file_ok;
   BOOL top_to_bottom,left_to_right; // pixels order
   int width,height;
   int bytesperline;
   int line_n;         //current line number
   long colors;

   graph_file_abstract();
// closes file and disposes buffer
   virtual ~graph_file_abstract();
   long image_size();
// procedure for constructors, call with file opened!
// if (usebuffer_) allocates buffer
// otherwise - buffered file
   void init_buffer(BOOL usebuffer_);

// WARNING:
// in the last case procedure calls fseek(0,SEEK_SET);
// for savers call only after file has been opened!
};

class graph_file_reader: public graph_file_abstract
{
protected:
   long data_begin;    // don't forget to set it, descendants!!!
public:
   BGRpalette palette;
   image_type source_type;
   image_extention_type source_ext_type;
```

```
    BYTE *source_line;
    graph_file_reader() {}; // formal
    graph_file_reader(char *fname);      // opens the file

// seek image start
// normally constructors calls seek_start()
    virtual void seek_start();

// if buffer is almost cleared
// reads new block of data
    virtual void fresh_buffer();
// returns -1 if file is finished
    virtual int get_next_line();
};

// some graphics format file saver
class graph_file_saver: public graph_file_abstract
{
protected:
    BGRpalette *palette;
public:
    image_type dest_type;
    image_extention_type dest_ext_type;

    graph_file_saver() {}; //formal
    graph_file_saver(char *fname, BOOL usebuffer_, image_type dest_type_,
                     image_extention_type dest_ext_type_, int width_,
                     int height_, void* pal);
//returns -1 if  some error occurs
    virtual int put_next_line(BYTE *line);
// writes acumulated buffer in file
    virtual void flush_buffer();
};
```

Summary

It seems to us that, although relevant, this chapter has turned out to be too dry. It's our fault, but we've failed to find anything funny or amusing about graphics formats. Unfortunately, it's a complex, although routine, thing which is needed every day.

We have also acutely felt the lack of GG's assistance - he refused any participation in this chapter. At first we didn't understand why, but now we do. The motive was his own experience with graphics formats, which is usually a royal pain. Our experience isn't much fun, either. Working with the standard version of any graphics format is simple until you decide to support all the 'dialects'. Still, the clone of format 'readers' and 'writers' included on the CD-ROM has been tried and tested on every format dialect we could get hold of.

We have a bit of advice before we part with this topic. You should always try to select the proper format for your particular work:

- ▲ PCX is the best for 16-color, 4-plane images, its RLE implementation treats each plane separately and therefore it usually compresses 16 colors well.

- ▲ GIF is certainly the best for 256-color paletted images, its LZW technique manages them really well.

- ▲ JPEG is for photos - no doubt about that.

- ▲ DIB is for MS Windows (but beware of its compressed version; even now some Windows applications fail to read the compressed DIB files they have written themselves).

- ▲ Lastly, what about the TARGA format? We like it simply for convenience. But it's a personal opinion with which you may or may not agree.

CHAPTER

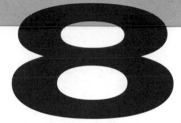

Animation

In this chapter, we'll try and tempt you into the world of computer animation. We are not going to go into too much detail, and this chapter is definitely not about writing games! It is more to give you a signpost in the direction that you may wish to travel. Most of the techniques we have covered already apply to animation, as the main consideration is speed, but we'll cover some new ones here.

Chapter Contents

In this chapter, we will cover:

- ▲ PC Animation - What is it?
- ▲ Windowing
- ▲ Modeling
- ▲ Some Animation Techniques
- ▲ Slide Show Effects
- ▲ Sprite Techniques

PC Animation - What is it?

Almost everyone comes across animation on the PC screen at some point. As we've already mentioned, computer animation is one of the most tempting areas in bitmap graphics, and can be found in any place you care to look: science, education, adventure and role-play games, company presentations - the list is endless. Animation is everywhere, or at least it tries to be.

What does animation mean? It's maybe something that's living, moving and impressive, but what exactly is it, particularly on the PC? Perhaps it's:

 Drawing smoothly moving figures on a background picture (an image or frame), from the simplest Captain Cosmic, to the handsome and skillful Prince of Persia.

Filmed or computer generated video, running in a small window on the screen.

Virtual Reality with all its miraculous inhabitants, as typified by the Star Trek - Next Generation Holodeck.

No doubt, each of these definitions could apply, and many others would do as well. Nevertheless, even though we specified three quite different things, all the definitions are correct. Computer animation (and even its smallest part, animation on the PC) is a field vast enough to be lost in definitions. However, we'll try to make some sense of it.

Different Approaches

Formally speaking, animation is based on a peculiarity of human vision. If you view a series of specially created images in fast enough succession, your brain perceives them as smooth continuous motion. This is just how your monitor works; the frames are shown fast enough so that you don't see any flicker.

But what is meant by fast enough? The number of pictures, or frames, that needs to be shown per second varies from one person to another, but it's usually about 12. The greater the number of frames per second, the more perfect the illusion of motion. However, increasing the frame rate beyond 30 frames per second (NTSC standard) is usually considered useless.

So, what's so great about these 'motion' pictures? Aren't there any problems at all? Of course, there are. In fact, there are quite a lot of them at every stage of the animation life cycle, especially if you choose the PC to do it with.

The table below lists the stages of a computer animation cycle from cre
displaying, just to give you a feel for the problems associated with eac

Animation stage	Key Problem	Solution	
Creation	Too many frames	Key framing, modeling	
Storage	Huge media space	Compression (FLC, M	
Display	Fast transmission	New generation of I	

The Key Problems of Computer Animation and Possible Solutions

Imagine you decide to animate something. The first difficulty you face is the huge number of frames you have to create. Each minute of animation would require from 720 (60*12 frames per second) to 1800 frames (60*30), depending on the smoothness of motion you want to achieve. Drawing this number of pictures by hand is a pretty big task, and is a rather boring form of entertainment, as most of the frames are nearly identical.

Suppose you've created the number of frames required for one minute of animation (by employing artists or purchasing Autodesk Animator, for instance), in 640×480, 256-color graphics mode. If you estimate the amount of storage space you need for this one minute, you'll get:

640 * 480 * 1800 = 550 Megabytes.

Just right for one CD-ROM. So you decide to moderate your appetite and make it a more 'reasonable' 320×200, still using 256 colors but only 20 frames per second. Now you have 77M of animated bytes to be stored somewhere, just for one minute of your cartoon. From these figures, you can really see the need for a huge amount of media space when working in animation.

Finally imagine your animation is ready, stored and you are about to show it to the world. You need a high enough transfer rate to move the successive frames to the video system of your computer. It's fairly difficult to estimate the exact figures as, to some extent, they depend on bus, processor and video adapter type. So we decided to run a simple test.

We used the simplest and fastest assembly routine we could write that just moves data blocks 64K in size from conventional memory to the video buffer.

The overall time for 1000 transfers was measured. Why 64K? This is the whole screen, or in other words, a single frame in 320×200 256-color video mode, which means we could measure the transfer rate directly in frames per second. We created two versions of the test routine, one for word and another for double word transfer. We tested various computers, the results of which you can see below.

CPU type	Freq	Cache size	Bus type	Video adapter	Frames per second 640×480, HighColor	
					Word	DWord
386/SX	33	0	ISA	VGAArt 800	3.05	3.11
386/DX	20	0	ISA	WD90C3X	5.00	6.02
386/DX	40	128K	ISA	Realtec	1.04	1.12
486/DX	33	128K	VLB	TGUI 9400	10.38	**18.94**
486/DX	33	128K	VLB	CVGA- 26VL	**15.5**	15.5

Transfer Rate from Elsewhere to Video Memory

Well, what can we glean from this? The figures show the upper limit of the PC's performance applied to animation. Sad, but true, that only 486 machines with VLB (VESA Local Bus) provide an adequate transfer rate. However, if the HDD is used as a data source (which is most natural) the results are much worse.

What was the point of this test? We simply wanted to show that even if Real Time Video is somehow created and stored, it can't be shown on a modern PC without special equipment. If it could, this whole chapter would comprise of just program code a couple of pages long.

From the animation artist's point of view the main problem in animation is the number of frames to be drawn (media space and transfer rate shouldn't bother him). There are two completely different ways to get round this problem.

The first 'simply' increases artist productivity by the computer aided generation of [be]**tweens**. This is called **keyframing**. What is meant by keyframing? Most of the frames in cartoons can be routine, incremental changes of figures on the picture (like a bullet flying across the screen or an arm stretching out), or background scrolling (like moving trees behind a car).

You can get software that can 'interpolate' handmade keyframes to produce all the needed tweens. Of course, the artist has to write the local scenario in order to specify each character's motion, transformation and maybe action. The language of these descriptions is rapidly developing as new 'words' and 'expressions' are added, such as precise perspective projection, stretch morphing, biomechanically realistic motion and so on. You never know, maybe sooner or later the artist will only have to type one word 'Aladdin' to get a complete 'ready to go' cartoon.

The second way is a kind of modeling. The artist defines 'nature', creates the rules, invents the characters and lets them get on with their own lives. For us mortal beings, creation is no easy job. However, for interactive animations such as games, tutorials and simulators, modeling is the only way.

From a programmer's point of view the three main problems of computer animation can be solved in two different ways:

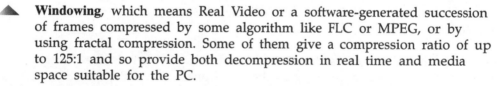

- ▲ **Windowing**, which means Real Video or a software-generated succession of frames compressed by some algorithm like FLC or MPEG, or by using fractal compression. Some of them give a compression ratio of up to 125:1 and so provide both decompression in real time and media space suitable for the PC.

- ▲ **Modeling**, which needs a kind of sophisticated Virtual Reality engine that calculates graphics fast enough to look like video.

Both approaches are described below, but first a few words from the Graphics Guru:

Computer animation has two strata. The first is governed by the logic of means (possibilities), the second by the logic of ideas (wishes). The PC platform lies on the first. Once upon a time it was difficult to create any working animation at all, but things are changing rapidly and in the not-so-distant future, Real Time Video will be a kind of routine feature of every PC. And it is because of this that my advice is you'd be better off concentrating your attention on modeling.

Windowing

It seems the first windowing technique that became a de facto standard was **flic**, designed by Jim Kent for Autodesk Animator. A flic file is a sequence of images or frames which can be shown rapidly enough to achieve the illusion of movement - a purely software equivalent of the video. Although flics are limited to 256 colors and don't contain sound, the speed and simplicity of preparation and playback has made them the format of choice for multimedia and game developers.

Flic files use **delta compression** in order to get the required hardware through-put. This is a pretty simple trick, which means that you only store the image areas that are changed from one frame to the next. Since only the parts of the screen that have changed need to be updated, delta compression allows animations to be displayed on even the slowest hardware.

Overview of File Structure

There are two types of flic files; **.FLI** and **.FLC**. The **.FLI** files are older and are limited to 320x200 resolution. The newer **.FLC** format uses a faster compression method, has a slightly different header, and can have any resolution.

A flic file is built of hierarchically nested chunks. The whole file is a chunk itself, every frame is a chunk, and there are types of chunks that don't contain any data, such as WIPE, the chunk then clears the screen. The file structure looks like this:

```
Flic chunk (the whole file with the header)
    prefix chunk (.FLC only)
        settings chunk (reserved for Animator Pro)
            position chunk (Offset of the window on screen)
    First frame chunk
            postage stamp (icon-sized first frame, .FLC only)
            palette (256 colors)
            image data
  . . .
    Intermediate frame chunks
            palette (only colors that change)
            image data (delta encoded)
```

```
   . . .
ring frame chunk (difference between the first and the last)
       palette (only colors that change)
       image data (delta encoded)
```

The ring frame is intended for smoothly looped playback. When it loops to the beginning of the animation, the first frame is skipped, but recreated by updating the last frame with the ring frame. This works much faster than unpacking the whole, possibly large, first frame.

Each chunk contains the size of itself, the type, and the appropriate data.

How to Show a Flic

To show a flic, you have to read all the chunks one by one, in the following order:

1   Read the 128-byte file header, and check the type field (see the table below). If the type is **.FLI** file, convert the speed field from 1/70th to 1/1000th of a second. If it's an **.FLC** file, you have to skip the prefix chunk to move to the first frame position as defined by the oframe1 field of the header.

2   Read a 16-byte frame chunk header. You can check if this is a valid frame, by which we mean the type must be 0F11Ah.

3   Allocate buffer according to the frame size field in the header minus 16 (the size of the header itself), and read the rest of the frame chunk into the buffer.

4   Go through each subchunk in the buffer: read a 6-byte subchunk header (DWORD size and WORD type), and pass the subchunk to the processing routine specific for this type. Then go to the next subchunk, etc.

5   Go to the next frame.

6   When you have shown the ring frame, return to the second frame, and repeat the process.

Now for the tables of flic header, prefix header, and frame header:

Offset	Size	Name	Description
0	4	size	Size of entire file
4	2	type	File-format identifier (0AF12h for **.FLC**, 0AF11h for **.FLI**)
6	2	frames	Number of frames
8	2	width	Window width in pixels
10	2	height	Window height in pixels
12	2	depth	8 (bits per pixel)
14	2	flags	3
16	4	speed	Time delay between frames. For **.FLI** files, in units of 1/70 second; for **.FLC**, in milliseconds.
20	2	reserved	0
22	4	created	MS-DOS-formatted date and time of file's creation for **.FLC**, 0 for **.FLI**
26	4	creator	used by Animator Pro. Set to 0 and ignore
30	4	updated	MS-DOS-formatted date and time of file's last update for **.FLC**, 0 for **.FLI**
34	4	updater	used by Animator Pro. Set to 0 and ignore
38	2	aspectx	X-aspect ratio of display where the file was created for **.FLC**, 0 for **.FLI**
40	2	aspecty	Y-aspect ratio for **.FLC**, 0 for **.FLI**
42	38	reserved	0
80	4	oframe1	Offset of the first frame in the file for **.FLC**, 0 for **.FLI**

Continued

Offset	Size	Name	Description
84	4	oframe2	Offset of the second frame in the file for `.FLC`, 0 for `.FLI`
88	40	reserved	0

Total Size =	128 bytes (80h)		

Flic Header Structure

Offset	Size	Name	Description
0	4	size	Size of prefix chunk, including subchunks
4	2	type	0F100h (Prefix chunk identifier)
6	2	chunks	Number of subchunks
8	8	reserved	0

Total Size =	16 bytes (10h)		

Prefix Header Structure

Offset	Size	Name	Description
0	4	size	Size of frame chunk, including subchunks and this header
4	2	type	0F1FAh (Frame chunk identifier)
6	2	chunks	Number of subchunks

Continued

245

Offset	Size	Name	Description
8	8	reserved	0

Total Size =	16 bytes (10h)		

Frame Header Structure

Processing Chunks

The following table lists the variety of subchunk types that can be in flics:

ID	Type	Description
4	COLOR_256	256-level palette (.FLC only)
7	DELTA_FLC	Delta compression (.FLC only).
11	COLOR_64	64-level palette (.FLI only)
12	DELTA_FLI	Delta compression (.FLI only)
13	WIPE	Clear screen
15	BYTE_RUN	Byte run-length compression (first frame)
16	LITERAL	Uncompressed image
18	PSTAMP	Icon-size image of flic. Ignore it.

Frame Subchunk Types

Now we have a comprehensive list of all the data types, let's look at them in more detail.

Chunk Type 4 (COLOR_256)

This is a 256-level map of the colors that are to be modified in this chunk. The data is organized in packets. The first word after the chunk header is the number of packets in the chunk. Each packet consists of a 1-byte color-index skip count, a 1-byte color count, and three bytes of RGB components for each color. Each component can range from 0 to 255.

When you begin processing the chunk, the color index is assumed to be 0. Then you skip some colors, by increasing the index, while others are modified. The following sample chunk illustrates this point, by updating colors 3, 4, and 120:

```
2                          ; number of packets
3, 2, (r3,g3,b3), (r4,g4,b4) ; skip 3, change 2 (3 and 4)
115, 1, (r120, g120, b120)  ; skip 115, change 1 (120)
```

Chunk Type 7 (DELTA_FLC)

This covers word-oriented delta compression. This format contains the difference between the previous frame and the current one. The data is organized into lines, and each line is organized into packets.

The first word in the data contains the number of lines in the chunk. Each line can begin with some optional words that are used to skip lines or set the last byte in the line. These optional words can be distinguished by two highest bits, as shown in the table below, and are followed by a count of the packets in the line. The line count includes only the lines that are actually updated.

Bit 15	Bit 14	Meaning
0	0	Packet count. Can be 0 (when only last pixel on a line is updated). Packets, if any, follow this word.
1	0	Low-order byte of this word is to be the last byte of the current line. Packet count must always follow this word.
1	1	Line skip count. Number of lines to skip is the absolute value in this word (so -5 means skip 5 lines). Can be followed by any control word.

Control Words in a Word Compressed Chunk

Now for the structure of a packet; the first byte is a column-skip count, while the second byte holds the type. If the type byte is positive, the packet type is a count of words to be copied directly from the packet to the image (uncompressed). If the type byte is negative, the packet contains one word which is to be replicated, and the absolute value of the type byte is the number of replications.

Chunk Type 11 (COLOR_64)

This contains a 64-level color map. The same as FLI_COLOR256 with a minor difference: the values for the RGB components are in the range of 0 to 63.

Chunk Type 12 (DELTA_FLI)

This deals with byte-oriented delta compression. This chunk contains the difference between the previous frame and the current one.

After the chunk header, the first word contains the offset of the first updated image line, or more precisely, the number of lines to skip from the top of the window. The second word is the number of lines in the chunk. These two words are followed by the lines' data. Each line begins with two bytes, the first byte is the number of packets for the line, the second is apparently unused.

Next go the packets. The first byte in each packet is column skip, the second is the packet type/size byte. If the type is positive, it is a count of pixels to be copied directly from the packet to the image. If the type is negative, the packet contains a single pixel which is to be replicated; the absolute value of the type byte gives the number of replications.

Chunk Type 13 (WIPE)

This chunk fills the screen with pixels of color code 0 (which is normally black).

Chunk Type 15 (BYTE_RUN)

This chunk contains information about byte run-length compression. This chunk contains the whole image in a compressed form. This type of chunk is usually used for the first frame.

As in other compressed chunks, the data is organized into lines, and subsequently each line into packets. Lines go from the top of the image to the bottom. The vertical size of the image is determined by the height of the flic. The first byte of each line historically contains a count of packets in the line, but you should ignore it, because there can be more than 255 packets in a line. You have to use the width of the flic window as the criterion for the decompressing routine; just keep reading and unpacking packets until you reach the right edge of the window, then proceed to the next line.

Each packet consist of a type/size byte, followed by one or more pixels. If the type/size byte is positive, it's a count of pixels to be copied directly from the packet to the image. If the type/size is negative, it contains a single pixel that is to be replicated, and the absolute value of the type/size is the number of replications to be made.

Chunk Type 16 (FLI_COPY)

This final chunk gives information about the raw image, before it was compressed. You have to fill the flic window with the pixel values that follow the header, left to right, from the top to the bottom. So the count of pixels to be read is width*height.

General Notes about Flics

In the worst case, where no delta compression is possible, a flic will require a bit more media space for a frame than the frame image itself. This situation will happen when you digitize real video or use scanned photos as frames. But luckily, when you draw frames in a graphical editor or generate them by software means, your images usually compress O.K.

Anyway, flic is one of the most traditional formats of digital animation on the PC. After all, a number of modern multimedia applications, including Microsoft's Video for Windows, support flics, or at least on the import/export level.

Video for Windows

Video for Windows is just another attempt to make digital video possible. It's based on the multimedia features of Windows 3.1. Microsoft have 'simply' defined a new RIFF (resource interchange file format) file for video information called AVI (audio-video interleaved). An AVI file interleaves waveform audio in the standard form supported by Windows 3.1 together with video data.

The most pretty feature of the Video for Windows architecture is its scalability. Digital video files can be played back under any Windows 3.1-equipped multimedia PC without **any** additional hardware. Moreover, the video sequences can be enlarged and accelerated, based on the particular characteristics of the playback machine. This standard is also intended to work with a wide variety of video capture boards.

Digital Video Capturing

Getting video on a PC requires that it's captured by some means and digitized. Here we omit the possibility to compute the whole image sequence, although, this was particularly how we prepared our sample videos.

The basic concepts of digital video are fairly simple. You run analog video and audio signals, such as those from a VCR or a camcorder, into some PC hardware that converts the video signal to a series of bitmaps and the audio signal into digitized waveform samples. What you get is stored in a file. To play back the file, you display the successive bitmaps on the PC screen simultaneously playing the waveform samples through a sound card.

That's why, capturing your own .AVI files requires a video capture board, which is sometimes also called a 'frame grabber'. A video capture board uses a composite video signal as input. It converts the analog video signal into a bitmap image, usually up to 640x480 for compatibility with VGA displays, and usually with a color encoding called **YUV**, which is conceptually similar to **YIQ** (see chapter 3 for details).

By the way, some video boards, like the Video Blaster, also support video-in-a-window capability. That means, they can merge a VGA signal with the undigitized analog video signal, providing a full-motion, full-color, full-resolution video image on your VGA display.

Digital Video Playback

Real-time digital video playback is mostly limited by CD drives transfer rate, because by now, CD is the only reasonable media that provides enough space for digital video. Let's once again calculate what can be shown through this 300KB per second (double-speed) bottle-neck. Well, instead of demanding a 640x480 window, we have to have 1/16 of this, which brings it down to 160x120. And instead of 30 (or 25) frames per second, we have to put up with 15 (or even 12). True color also seems too generous, so we can store the color in 8 bits using an optimized palette.

And so, what do we get?

160 * 120 * 1 * 15(fps) = 288 Kb/sec.

That's 288,000 bytes per second. We have 12 Kb/sec left for sound at 11000 samples per second with 1 byte per sample (a telephone-like sound, but still audible).

This is the standard for software-only **uncompressed** digital video in QuickTime for the Macintosh, and Video for Windows; 160x120 resolution with 15 frames per second and 8-bit palettized color. Audio plays at an 11 KHz sampling rate with 8 bits per sample, mono. Until your video hardware becomes faster, most .AVIs you can watch will be in this format.

Of course, one way out of this problem is to use compression, but the more sophisticated the compression, the longer it takes to compress and decompress the data.

Compression Methods

Video sequences are compressed and decompressed by routines called **codecs** (short for compressor/decompressor). Video for Windows provides special hooks for third party codecs, which can be software only, hardware assisted, or hardware only. A codec is responsible for compressing raw video data into a format suitable for distribution. When the user plays back the compressed video, the codec performs a reverse function, converting the compressed data into images.

Video for Windows includes several codecs, each with its advantages and disadvantages. When choosing a codec, you should consider the following factors:

▲   **Quality**: how well the codec reproduces the original colors, motion, and image details.

▲   **Media space required**: how much storage space is saved as a result of compression.

▲   **Data transfer rate** (DTR): does the codec reduce the required DTR to an acceptable level? (usually, it's DTR which is the bottle-neck for digital video on the PC).

The following compression methods are available now with Video for Windows:

▲ **Microsoft RLE** - A fast compression method useful for computer-generated animation, screen capturers, and other sequences with areas of uniform color. Quality and size reduction drop rapidly if there are many changes from frame to frame (for example, as would be the case in a sequence captured from videotape). The RLE method is limited to 8-bit video sequences.

▲ **Microsoft Video 1** - This method combines good playback quality with relatively quick compression times. The video sequence is stored in either 8-bit or 16-bit format. Using the 8-bit format, you can specify which palettes to use in the video sequence, so if your sequence is playing strictly on 256-color video cards, Video 1 provides better control over the palette colors than compression methods that use an automatic dithering technique.

▲ **Intel Indeo Video R3.1** - This method provides high-quality video (320x240 frame size and 15 frames per second), using an asymmetric compression technique. Indeo 3.1 uses a 24-bit color format. When played on 256-color video cards, Indeo dithers 24-bit colors to 8-bit format.

▲ **Intel Indeo Video Raw** - This method covers the uncompressed YUV format produced by the Intel Smart Video Recorder capture board. Capture in this format if you want to use another compressor other than Indeo 3.1.

You can experiment with several compression methods to see which works best with your video. Don't forget, most methods result in some loss of quality. So save the original uncompressed version of your video before experimenting with different compression settings.

On the accompanying CD you can find 3 differently compressed **.AVI** files, presenting the same video sequence. Consider the difference:

▲ **DRAGON1.AVI** was created using Microsoft Video 1 with default settings;

▲ **DRAGON2.AVI** is compressed using Intel Indeo(TM) Video R3.1 technique;

▲ **DRAGON3.AVI** is produced using Microsoft Video1 with the highest compression possible.

We understood that zooming a fractal image would be rather a difficult test for video compression techniques, but what we saw was hardly any video at all.

Even with all Microsoft's magic, Video for Windows still doesn't manage full-screen broadcast-quality digital video on your SVGA monitor, unless you have additional hardware (say, a MPEG board) installed. But for incorporating short and small video clips in your multimedia Windows-based application, Video for Windows is quite acceptable. By the way, media Player 2.0 is also an OLE server, so you can incorporate windowed video sequences, match box in size, and other multimedia data into your other documents.

Modeling

Modeling is the oldest but still the freshest idea in computer animation. Why? Because it's primarily a paradigm and only secondarily a method.

You need a lot of creative programming and expert knowledge of PC video subsystems to create any working animation. But you need twice as much to create a worthy animation program based on modeling; you need time to model your pictures and time to show them. Therefore, most of our discussion of the subject will be based on theory, and so you will find some practical recipes in the section 'Sprite Techniques'.

Maybe you've played, or seen someone playing, the game 'Alone in the Dark'. If so, you may remember that it features 'polygonal' robot-like characters. Everyone we asked easily, and correctly, distinguished them as models. But here's another question: what about those uninhabitable vaults in which the 'polygonal warriors' combat evil, aren't they a kind of model too? Indeed they are, and in fact, even if you animate the 'Enterprise' flying in a completely empty space, you still need a background model. The qualitative difference lies in whether you use the 'superlight override' formulas for a particular model or something simpler.

Polygonal constructions came before all other models (certainly from CAD systems), and they brought with them the polygonal shadowing technique that is still very popular in games, just because of its simplicity and speed. Polygonal landscapes and other objects are more or less detailed **meshes**, that is, systems of connected polygons that define modeled surfaces, which are relatively easy to project and shadow. However, it's rather difficult to make a polygonal model of a human being look natural, no matter how smoothly it moves.

You need something more creative to generate surface texture. For this you could choose to use B-splines, which is a computer generated method for drawing curved lines through several given points, applied to a polygonal framework, like skin pulled over a mannequin. Splines themselves are rather complicated, and would require even more artful projecting and shadowing (like Guru and Phong techniques). So they aren't really applicable to real time animation, even on present day high-end graphics workstations and, on top of everything else, you need some inventive methods to manage object structure and features. This is actually starting to happen in games these days on some of the new 3D simulators.

When the knights of computer animation have perfected the reality of their models, it'll be possible to master any kind of imaginary reality. Certainly they work towards this goal. Here is a quotation we like, by Alvy Ray Smith (we found it in 'Omni' December, 1989):

"Once you can do a silk scarf falling on a wood table, you can do a wood scarf falling on a silk table. That's when it gets interesting. These worlds will not be precisely realistic, but they will be realistically consistent and therefore as authentic on their own terms as our own world is on its."

Some Tips to Remember

We decided to finish this section with some heuristic recipes taken mostly from the notes of the Graphics Guru:

Computer animation is 'just a trick of the mind'. It is based on a trick and thus can be assisted by means of art rather than technology. Here are some simple rules which you are encouraged to remember and use when creating 'real' animation.

Space and Motion

A moving object usually attracts our attention so we keep our eye on it. Sometimes, however, motion may be so fast that you can't follow it. There are 'normal', fast and extra fast types of motion and specific effects to express each of them.

Normal Motion

There's a lot of Disney-like tricks to make 'normal' motion appear more natural. Unfortunately, most keyframing software usually leaves this work to you. The brave who venture to build a 'hand-made' cartoon by computer, will, of course, look through the special publications available. We wish to mention just one thing: the motion of a living being should never be as mathematically precise as the bounce of a rubber ball, and so, 'humanize' in computer-generated motion should actually be translated as randomize.

This is also true for view point movement. It has become an established tradition in computer animation to destroy the illusion of reality by this fluid, slow, dream-like flight (surely manifesting human aspirations to fly). Make it slightly random and you'll see a real difference.

Rapid (Stroboscopic) Motion

Some motions are so fast that you have no time to follow them. What you can see are separate phases of motion. A pretty trick of this stroboscopic motion is widely used in cartoons to express 'being in a hurry'. But be careful! This trick can easily wreck the impression of reality in your animation. And anyway, your animating software usually provides you with enough stroboscopic motion, even if you don't want any.

Fleet (Blur) Motion

Slurred, 'ghostly' motion is a solid and impressive trick, and we wholeheartedly encourage you to use it. Superlight flight of the Enterprise, Formula I racing... it's a pity, but there are too few examples.

 Just one last piece of advice. Be very careful when selecting or recording a soundtrack for your animation because nothing ruins the reality of animation so much as weird synthesized humming or screeching that bears no relation to the show.

Some Animation Techniques

We'll now go into some details on techniques that you can employ to obtain a complete animation. The first of these techniques makes use of the palette.

Palette Trick

In Chapter 4, we introduced you to picture fading, simple magic which is usually used to smoothly hide something. As you may remember, we supplied you with a flexible tool for handling the palette in 256-color modes; a routine called **SetDACBlock**. In this section we'll show you how this, as well as a new 'magic spell' **ColorWheel**, can be used in 'animation'. It's a trick technique that only works in 256-color modes, but it's simple and inspiring. You might find it useful for something, maybe a screen saver or the like.

The key idea is very simple. By changing a single DAC register you can affect many pixels almost immediately; by changing the palette continuously you can create a good illusion of motion. In fact, nothing really moves in this case. As you play with the palette you continuously show and hide 'frozen' frames. All you need is a picture prepared in a special way. The figure below shows how to prepare the screen for palette-changing animation. The video buffer is filled with either rectangular or striped areas.

Preparing for Palette Animation

After you have prepared your screen, you just let the **ColorWheel** spin, by which we mean run cyclical, smooth modifications of the palette colors and we promise that you'll see something moving.

The following is the **ColorWheel** routine, the basis for most palette tricks. It simply cyclically shifts the palette table values to the right, from **first** to **first + count**.

```
void ColorWheel(int first,int count,void *Pal)
{
   asm
   {
        cld                    // clear decrement flag
        push   ds              // preserve registers
        push   di
        push   si
        les    di,Pal          // ES:DI -> palette
        mov    ax,es
        mov    ds,ax
        mov    ax,first
        add    ax,ax
        add    ax,first
        add    di,ax           // ES:DI -> Pal[first]
        mov    si,di
        add    si,3            // DS:SI -> Pal[first+1]
        mov    bx,[di]
        mov    dl,[di+2]       // save Pal[first] in BX & DL
        mov    cx,count
        add    cx,cx
        add    cx,count        // CX = byte counter
        rep    movsb           // shift palette
        mov    [di],bx
        mov    [di+2],dl       // load Pal[first+count] from BX & DL
        pop    si              // restore registers
        pop    di
        pop    ds
   }
}
```

The figure shows two possible methods of preparing the screen for palette-changing animation. We encourage you to experiment and to have fun inventing your own pictures. They will depend, of course, on the way you modify the palette. You could increase or decrease the color number by some multiple, maybe adding a slight randomization. Look through the following code examples which contain various routines for screen filling and palette animation.

```
typedef unsigned char MixRow[320];
typedef MixRow *MixBuffer;

typedef struct
{
   unsigned char r,g,b;
} colortype;

colortype Pal[256];

int _r, _g, _b, r0, g0, b0;
const Cyclelen = 20;
const PaletteLen = 201;
const MaxDer = 25;

// prepare color increments
void calccolorinc(void)
{
   _g = random(MaxDer*2) - MaxDer;
   _b = random(MaxDer*2) - MaxDer;
   _r = random(MaxDer*2) - MaxDer;
}

// calculate new value for a color
void increment(void)
{
   r0 += _r;
   if (r0 > 255) r0 = 255;
   else if (r0 < 0) r0 = 0;

   g0 += _g;
   if (g0 > 255) g0 = 255;
   else if (g0 < 0) g0 = 0;

   b0 += _b;
   if (b0 > 255) b0 = 255;
   else if (b0 < 0) b0 = 0;
}

void PaletteDemo(void)
{
   int i, j, index;
   index = 0;
   r0 = g0 = b0 = 128;

   for(i = 0; i <= 20; i++)    // initialize the palette
   {
      calccolorinc();
      for(j = 0;j <= 10; j++)
      {
```

```
            Pal[index].r = r0/4;
            Pal[index].g = g0/4;
            Pal[index].b = b0/4;
            index++;
            increment();
      }
   }
   setDACblock(10, 220, Pal);   // set VGA palette

// screen filling (four rectangles), corresponding to figure
   for(i = 0; i <= 50; i++)
   {
      if (i > 47) setcolor(211);
      else setcolor(i+10);
      rectangle(i, i, 159-i, 99-i);
   }
   for(i = 0; i <= 50; i++)
   {
      if (i > 47) setcolor(211);
      else setcolor(110 - i);
      rectangle(160+i, i, 319-i, 99-i);
   }
   for(i = 0; i <= 50; i++)
   {
      if (i > 47) setcolor(211);
      else setcolor(i+110);
      rectangle(160+i, 100+i, 319-i, 199-i);
   }
   for(i = 0; i <= 50; i++)
   {
      if (i > 47) setcolor(211);
      else setcolor(210-i);
      rectangle(i, 100+i, 159-i, 199-i);
   }

   index = 0;
   do        // the main cycle
   {
      index++;
      if (index == Cyclelen)
      {
         calccolorinc();
         index = 0;
      }
      increment();
      Pal[PaletteLen].r = r0/4;
      Pal[PaletteLen].g = g0/4;
      Pal[PaletteLen].b = b0/4;
      memcpy(&Pal[0], &Pal[1], PaletteLen*3);// shift colors
      setDACblock(10, PaletteLen, Pal);    // set new palette
      delay(3);                  // short delay
```

```
   } while (!kbhit());
}

// Actually chaotic screen filling. Nevertheless, it
// makes an illusion of motion

void colwheeldemo1(void* v)
{
   int i,j;
   memset(Pal, 768, 0);
   for(i = 127; i <= 191; i++)    // initialize the palette
   {
      Pal[i].r = 60;
      Pal[i].b = 0;
      Pal[i].g = i - 127;
   }

// fill the screen with random color values
   for(i = 0; i <= 199; i++)
      for(j = 0; j <= 319; j++)
         *&MixBuffer(v)[i][j] = random(64) + 127;
   do
   {
      setDACblock(0, 191, Pal);    // Set VGA palette
      colorwheel(127, 64, Pal);    // rotate palette
   } while (!kbhit());
}

// striped screen filling, corresponding to figure
void colwheeldemo2(void* v)
{
   int i,j,k,l;
   memset(Pal, 768, 0);

// initialize palette
  for(i = 127; i <= 191; i++)
   {
      Pal[i].r = 60;
      Pal[i].b = 0;
      Pal[i].g = i-127;
   }
   for(i = 192; i <= 252; i++)
   {
      Pal[i].r = 60;
      Pal[i].b = 0;
      Pal[i].g = i-192;
   }

// striped screen filling
   for(l = 0; l <= 19; l++)
      for(i = 0; i <= 19; i++)
```

```
        for(j = 1*10; j <= 1*10+9; j++)
            for(k = i*16; k <= i*16+15; k++)
                if ((1 % 2) == 0) *&MixBuffer(v)[j][k] = random(63)+i*10;
                else *&MixBuffer(v)[j][k] = 252-(random(63)+i*10);

    do
    {
        setDACblock(0, 246, Pal);    // set VGA palette
        colorwheel(10, 246, Pal);    // rotate palette
        delay(10);            // soft dealy
    } while (!kbhit());
}
```

The same technique can be applied to a real picture. The result is unpredictable but usually very exciting. We recommend that you run the demo.

You can use this technique for any cyclic type of animation. For instance, a bouncing ball can be done by drawing a picture containing all the balls, each with a different color, as shown in the figure below. Then by setting all the colors you have used to the background color, apart from one, and then cycling through them, you get animation!

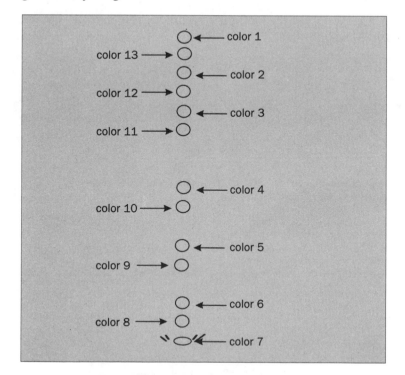

Graphic Required for Bouncing Ball

Slide Show Effects

We hope that the previous section has proved that animation can be produced very simply; no moving parts! In practice, you may find another kind of animation trick useful. One picture changes into another with a sort of 'animation-like' effect. All you need is a set of pictures and a kind of scenario specifying the order and method of how one picture changes into another.

So, we are now ready to present you with the most comprehensive collection of slide show effects from the simplest, such as **Slide**, to quite complicated ones, such as **Jalousie**, **RandomFillArea** and **Gone_with_the_wind**.

Here, we'll only show one representative of each class according to a simple classification. The rest of them, as well as a demo example, are included on the accompanying CD-ROM. All routines are designed to work not only on the full screen but also in an arbitrary chosen window. This enables you to make them work in any video mode you need (here they are written for 320×200, 256-color mode, VGA standard). So here we go!

All effects are based on the buffering technique, so first, a simple help routine and some declarations:

```
typedef unsigned char MixRow[320];
typedef MixRow *MixBuffer;

typedef struct
{
  int  x ;
  int  y ;
} pointtype;

pointtype arrp[32*20*7]; // 10x10 cell  320x200 mode}
unsigned char arrhits[32*20*7];

void ShowBuffer(int x1,int y1,int x2,int y2,void *p1,void *v)
{
   int i;
   for(i = y1; i <= y2; i++)
     memcpy(&MixBuffer(v)[i][x1], &MixBuffer(p1)[i][x1], x2-x1+1);
}
```

Simple Sliding Effects

In the figure below you can see a diagram of some simple sliding effects: **Slide**, **Explode**, **show_from_center**, and **show_to_center**.

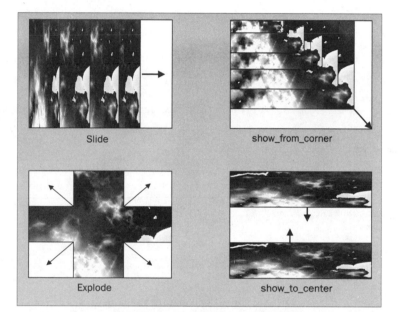

Slide

show_from_corner

Explode

show_to_center

Diagram of Sliding Effects

Here is just the simplest one - **Slide**:

```
// x1,y1,x2,y2, screen relative coordinates of a rectangular
// area "effected"
// step - affects the motion speed,
// U(p)L(eft)R(ight)D(own) defines the direction of movement
// p1 - pointer to source image buffer (usually in RAM)
// v - pointer to target image buffer (usually in video memory)

void Slide(int x1,int y1,int x2,int y2,
           int step,int ulrd,void *p1,void *v)
{
   int dx,i,j;
   dx = x2 - x1 + 1;
   switch (ulrd)
   {
      case 0 : //from up to down
         for(i = 0; i <= (y2-y1+1)/step-1; i++)
```

```
               for(j = 0; j <= i*step; j++)
                  memcpy(&MixBuffer(v)[j+y1][x1],
                         &MixBuffer(p1)[y2-i*step+j][x1], dx);
            for(j = y1; j <= y2; j++)
               memcpy(&MixBuffer(v)[j][x1], &MixBuffer(p1)[j][x1], dx);
            break;

         case 1 : //from down to up
            for(i= y1; i <= y2/step; i++)
               for(j = y1; j <= i*step + y1; j++)
                  memcpy(&MixBuffer(v)[y2-i*step+j][x1],
                         &MixBuffer(p1)[j][x1], x2-x1+1);
            for(j = y2; j >= y1; j--)
               memcpy(&MixBuffer(v)[j][x1], &MixBuffer(p1)[j][x1], x2-x1+1);
            break;

         case 2 :  //from right to left
            for(i = 1; i <= dx/step; i++)
               for(j = y1; j <= y2; j++)
                  memcpy(&MixBuffer(v)[j][x1+dx-i*step],
                         &MixBuffer(p1)[j][x1], i*step);
            showbuffer(x1, y1, x2, y2, p1, v);
            break;

         case 3 : //from left to right
            for(i = 1; i <= dx/step; i++)
               for(j = y1; j <= y2; j++)
                  memcpy(&MixBuffer(v)[j][x1],
                         &MixBuffer(p1)[j][x1+dx-i*step], i*step);
            showbuffer(x1, y1, x2, y2, p1, v);
   }
}
```

Jalousie is a more complicated class of effects:

```
// x1,y1,x2,y2, screen relative coordinates of a rectangular
// area "effected"
// step - stripes counter
// direct -
// p1 - pointer to source image buffer (usually in RAM)
// v - pointer to target image buffer (usually in video memory)

void Jalousie(int x1,int y1,int x2,int y2,int step,
              int direct,void *p1,void *v)
{
   int dx,dy2,dy,i,j;

   dx = (x2 - x1 + 1);
   dy = (y2 - y1 + 1);
   dy2 = dy/step;
```

```
   if (direct == 0)
   {
      for(i = y1; i <= step - 1 + y1; i++)
      {
         for(j = 0; j <= dy2 - 1; j++)
            memcpy(&MixBuffer(v)[i+j*step][x1],
                   &MixBuffer(p1)[i+j*step][x1], dx);
         if (dy % step != 0 && i+j*step <=  y2)
            memcpy(&MixBuffer(v)[i+j*step][x1],
                   &MixBuffer(p1)[i+j*step][x1], dx);
         delay(10);
      }
   }
   else
   {
      for(i = step-1+y1; i >= y1; i--)
      {
         for(j = dy2-1; j >= 0; j--)
            memcpy(&MixBuffer(v)[i+j*step][x1],
                   &MixBuffer(p1)[i+j*step][x1], dx);
         if (dy % step != 0 && i+(j+1)*step <= y2)
            memcpy(&MixBuffer(v)[i+(j+1)*step][x1],
                   &MixBuffer(p1)[i+(j+1)*step][x1], dx);
         delay(10);
      }
   }
}
```

RandomFillArea effects:.

```
// x1,y1,x2,y2, screen relative coordinates of a rectangular
// area "effected"
// dx,dy - size of the fill cell
// p1 - pointer to source image buffer (usually in RAM)
// v - pointer to target image buffer (usually in video memory)

void RandomFillArea(int x1,int y1,int x2,int y2,
                    int dx,int dy,void *p1,void *v)
{
   int counter,i,j,sx,sy;

   counter = 0;
   sx = (x2-x1)/dx + 1;
   sy = (y2-y1)/dy + 1;
   for(j = 1; j <= sy*sx; j++) arrhits[j] = 0;
   for(i = 0; i <= sy-1; i++)
      for(j = 1; j <= sx; j++)
      {
         arrp[i*sx+j].x = x1+j*dx-dx;
         arrp[i*sx+j].y = y1+(i+1)*dy-dy;
      }
```

```
            do
            {
               do
               {
                  j = random(sy*sx);
                  if (j == 0) continue;

                  if (arrhits[j] == 0)
                  {
                     arrhits[j] = 1;
                     break;
                  }
                  else
                     continue;
               } while (1);
               counter++;

               if (x2 - arrp[j].x < dx && y2 - arrp[j].y < dy)
                  for(i=0;i<=y2 - arrp[j].y;i++)
                     memcpy(&MixBuffer(v)[arrp[j].y+i][arrp[j].x],
                            &MixBuffer(p1)[arrp[j].y+i][arrp[j].x],
                            x2 - arrp[j].x+1);
               else if (x2 - arrp[j].x < dx)
                  for(i = 0; i <= dy-1; i++)
                     memcpy(&MixBuffer(v)[arrp[j].y+i][arrp[j].x],
                            &MixBuffer(p1)[arrp[j].y+i][arrp[j].x],
                            x2 - arrp[j].x+1);
               else if (y2 - arrp[j].y < dy)
                   for(i = 0; i <= y2 - arrp[j].y; i++)
                      memcpy(&MixBuffer(v)[arrp[j].y+i][arrp[j].x],
                      &MixBuffer(p1)[arrp[j].y+i][arrp[j].x], dx);
               else
                  for(i = 0; i <= dy-1; i++)
                     memcpy(&MixBuffer(v)[arrp[j].y+i][arrp[j].x],
                            &MixBuffer(p1)[arrp[j].y+i][arrp[j].x], dx);
               if (counter > sx*sy-5)
               {
                  for(j = 1; j <= sy*sx; j++)
                     if (arrhits[j] == 0)
                        if (x2 - arrp[j].x < dx && y2 - arrp[j].y < dy)
                           for(i = 0; i <= y2 - arrp[j].y; i++)
                              memcpy(&MixBuffer(v)[arrp[j].y+i][arrp[j].x],
                                     &MixBuffer(p1)[arrp[j].y+i][arrp[j].x],
                                     x2 - arrp[j].x+1);
                        else if (x2 - arrp[j].x < dx)
                           for(i = 0; i <=dy-1; i++)
                              memcpy(&MixBuffer(v)[arrp[j].y+i][arrp[j].x],
                                     &MixBuffer(p1)[arrp[j].y+i][arrp[j].x],
                                     x2 - arrp[j].x+1);
                        else if (y2 - arrp[j].y < dy)
                           for(i=0;i<=y2 - arrp[j].y;i++)
```

266

```
                    memcpy(&MixBuffer(v)[arrp[j].y+i][arrp[j].x],
                           &MixBuffer(p1)[arrp[j].y+i][arrp[j].x], dx);
               else
                   for(i = 0; i <= dy-1; i++)
                       memcpy(&MixBuffer(v)[arrp[j].y+i][arrp[j].x],
                              &MixBuffer(p1)[arrp[j].y+i][arrp[j].x], dx);
           break;
           }
      delay(1);
      } while (1);
}
```

The next example is pretty simple as it's based on the idea of simple numbers:

```
// x1,y1,x2,y2, screen relative coordinates of a rectangular
// area "effected"
// divisor - control number
// p1 - pointer to source image buffer (usually in RAM)
// v - pointer to target image buffer (usually in video memory)

void Develope(int x1,int y1,int x2,int y2,
              int divisor,void *p1,void *v)

// divisor should be a simple number else the window may be
// filled partly
{
   long l,dx,dy,i,j;

   dx = x2 - x1 + 1;
   dy = y2 - y1 + 1;
   l = 0;

   do
   {
      i = ((l/dx) % dy) + y1;
      j = (l % dx) + x1;

      *&MixBuffer(v)[i][j] = *&MixBuffer(p1)[i][j];

      l += divisor;
   } while (!(l/divisor > dx*dy));
}
```

And lastly the **Gone_with_the_wind** effect:

```
// x1,y1,x2,y2, screen relative coordinates of a rectangular
// area "effected"
// p1 - pointer to first source image buffer (usually in RAM)
// p2 - pointer to second source image buffer (usually in RAM),
```

```
//      which will be shown the first
// v -  pointer to target image buffer (usually in video memory)

void Gone_with_the_wind(int x1,int y1,int x2,int y2,
                        void *p1,void *p2,void *v)
{
   int count,l,k,i,j;
   int arrx[200];
   arrx[y1] = random(20);

   for(i = y1+1; i <= y2; i++)
   {
      arrx[i] = arrx[i-1] + random(4)-2;
      if (arrx[i] < 0) arrx[i] = 0;
   }

   for(i=y1;i<=y2;i++)
   {
      memcpy(&MixBuffer(v)[i][x1+arrx[i]],
             &MixBuffer(p1)[i][x1], (x2-x1+1)-arrx[i]);
      memcpy(&MixBuffer(v)[i][x1],
             &MixBuffer(p2)[i][x1], arrx[i]);
   }

   do
   {
      k = 0;
      for(i = y1; i <= y2; i++)
      {
         l = (int(random(32001)) - int(16000))/8000;
         k += l;
         arrx[i] += k+5;
         if (arrx[i] < 0) arrx[i] = 0;
      }
      for(i = y1+1; i <= y2-1; i++)
      {
         arrx[i] = (arrx[i-1] +2*arrx[i]+ arrx[i+1])/4;
         if (arrx[i] < 0) arrx[i] = 0;
      }
      count = 0;
      for(i = y1; i <= y2; i++)
      {
         k = (x2-x1+1) - arrx[i];
         if (k < 0) k = 0;
         l = arrx[i];
         if (l > (x2-x1))
         {
            l = (x2-x1);
            count++;
         }
         memcpy(&MixBuffer(v)[i][x1+l],
```

```
                          &MixBuffer(p1)[i][x1], k);
              memcpy(&MixBuffer(v)[i][x1],
                          &MixBuffer(p2)[i][x1], l+1);
          }
      } while (!(count >= y2-y1-1));
  }
```

Slide show effects can be applied cyclically to successive areas of the screen which lets you apply effects upon effects. The following is the code of the examples which are used in the demo program for this chapter. Again we encourage you to invent something fresh of your own.

```
  for(i = 0;i <= 7; i++)
      RandomFillArea(i*40, 0, i*40+39, 199, 2, 40, p2, v);
```

```
  for(i = 0; i <= 9; i++)
      Slide(50, i*20, 300, i*20+19, 1, 2, p2, v);
```

```
  for(i = 0; i <= 19; i++)
      if (i%2 == 0)
          Slide(i*16, 0, i*16+15, 199, 2, 0, p1, v);
      else
          Slide(i*16, 0, i*16+15, 199, 2, 1, p1, v);
```

Sprite Techniques

A commonly used technique for simple animation is the **sprite technique**. For the PC, we guess it was introduced by IBM's StoryBoard sometime around 1984. But if you think that sprites are only for the history books, you're wrong. Thoroughly OOPed (Object-Orientedly Programmed) and enhanced by ideas of modeling, the sprite technique can be perfectly practical now and well into the future.

What is a sprite? I checked in my on-line thesaurus: "Sprite - a benevolent mystical being". OK. Quite a fitting term for computer animation. But what does our Graphics Guru have to say about it?

A sprite is an animation object, able to show a certain phase of its motion or projection in a certain place on the screen. Sprites (or more frequently, sprites and masks) is also the group name for animation techniques usually applied to situations where the object is to be moved across a complex background.

Right, this sounds more to the point, but are there any particular ways to implement them? Sure there are, but first, let's get some answers to questions you might have, from our Graphics Guru:

Question: What is the key problem of sprite implementation?

 The key thing is to preserve the background overlapped by the picture and to restore it after the picture is moved.

Question: Can you give some practical examples of where this technique is used?

 A mouse cursor, any other Drag & Drop, characters in most games, moving decorative elements in some presentations.

Question: How can it be done?

 There are quite a few possible techniques, including XOR animation, 'Get-Put' animation and Sprite animation.

XOR Animation

The first uses the advantages of the **XOR animation** method (showing the picture twice with XOR restores the background (see Chapters 4 and 5)). This technique is excellent for cursors and things like that, but it's restricted by the rather 'ghostly' way that XOR makes things look and the absence of XOR hardware support for video modes above 16 colors.

'Get-Put' Animation

The **second** technique doesn't really have a name, but we'll call it **Get-Put** animation. Usually a procedure looks like this:

 Copy the target rectangular area of the background to a memory buffer (Get)

 Show the image (Put) and pause for a short time

 Copy the background back to the video buffer (Put)

To achieve a respectable result, you simply have to do it fast enough. The only restriction stems from the fact that the moving picture has to be rectangular, or more precisely, this technique doesn't allow the background to be seen through the sprite. The Get-Put method works well with moving icons (Drag&Drop) or cards in Solitaire, where the moving object itself is rectangular.

However, it may happen that the image to be moved is too large or the speed required is too high (if it's controlled by the user, he'll more than likely try to push your routine to its limit), but there are some solutions if this is the case. You can make the motion step depend on the speed (the higher the speed, the larger the step). You can also show only a certain part of the image in the tween phase of the motion.

Sprite Animation

The third technique is the **sprite animation**. It lets the background be visible through a moving figure, so the animation looks much more real. To do this, you must control the output of the rectangular sprite picture in some way, so that some background pixels are replaced by sprite pixels and others remain unchanged.

There are two possible ways of doing this:

- Prepare a **mask** for the sprite.

- Use **interval coding** to specify which pixels are to be changed.

Masks

A mask is a bit array of exactly the same size as the sprite, where value 1 means 'output the corresponding pixel of the sprite' and value 0 means 'leave the pixel as background'. It's like a silhouette of the sprite, an idea illustrated below.

In 16-color video mode, you can use hardware (mask register) to mask the background. Before writing every 8 pixels of the sprite to the video buffer, you send a corresponding byte from the mask array to the mask register.

There is a trick that makes transfer faster when using EGA and VGA modes, where there are normally unused parts of the video memory which you can use for buffers. The image is built up in this unused video RAM, then copied

rapidly to the displayed video RAM using write mode 1. Write mode 1 allows the processor to transfer 32 bits of data, or in other words, one byte from each of the four planes, in one instruction between locations that are both in the video RAM area. This is four times faster than copying it byte by byte.

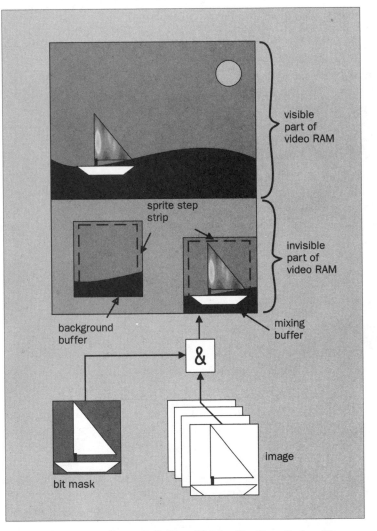

Using Masks for 16-Color Mode Sprite Animation

Interval Coding

This technique works better in modes above 16-color where there's no hardware support for masking. The sprite area is divided into rows of pixels, and in every row we find continuous intervals of pixels that should replace the background.

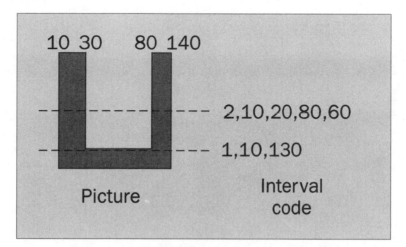

Interval Coding

Interval coding is a general idea that can be used in areas other than animation (see Chapter 5).

To create a sprite image, we assume that one color is 'transparent', by which we mean that the background will be seen through it. Then we scan the 256-color bitmap and code every interval of the transparent color. The following code fragment illustrates the actual technique (the encoding part).

```
// format of row coding looks like :
// N,(offset1, repeat count1,..., offsetN,repeat countN),
// where
// N - number of the intervals in row,
// offset - offset from the beginning of a row
// repeat count - bytes to be copied

// tmpp - pointer to the intervals array
void Createofmask(void *tmpp)
{
    void *maskp;
```

```
   unsigned char repcount,offset,counter,j,i,flag;
   unsigned int k,commonk;

   commonk = 0;
   maskp = malloc(65000);

   for(i = 0;i <= SizeY-1; i++)
   {
      offset = counter = flag = 0;
      k = commonk+1;
      for(j = 0; j <= SizeX-1; j++)
      {
         if(*&bytesptr(DataPtr)[i*SizeX+j] != _BackColor && flag = 0)
         {
            repcount = 0;
            counter++;
            *&bytesptr(maskp)[k] = offset;
            flag = 1;
            k++;
         }
         if(*&bytesptr(DataPtr)[i*SizeX+j] = _BackColor) && flag != 0)
         {
            flag = 0;
            *&bytesptr(maskp)[k] = repcount;
            k++;
         }
         repcount++;
         offset++;
      }
      if(flag == 1)
      {
         *&bytesptr(maskp)[k] = repcount;
         k++;
      }
      *&bytesptr(maskp)[commonk] = counter;
      commonk = k;
   }
   tmpp = malloc(commonk);
   memcpy(maskp,tmpp,commonk);
   free(maskp);
}
```

And so, on to the last question:

Question: Suppose we have two or three moving figures one closer to the observer and the others further away. How do they manage this?

It's easy. You should use a special 'Z'-organized mixing buffer to assemble the scene in advance. All the figures, sprites, models or whatever else, first show themselves on this 'dark' screen in 'Z' order of more distant first, less distant last, then this buffer is copied to the screen.

Sprites and Modeling

It may seem that sprites and modeling are opposing techniques, but they can, in fact, be combined. This is because modeling is mostly an idea, so it can involve different methods of practical implementation, for instance, sprites as animated objects of the modeled reality. And if the sprites are considered as objects, they can naturally be expressed by object-oriented programs.

Possible OOPed Realization of Sprites

One possible way to organize sprites using objects is to use the ability of a class to contain, not just the data for the sprite, but also the model of it's movement, the routine to display itself, and so on. A valuable feature would be if you had an animated sprite. The class could contain a cyclically linked list of frames, and the draw method would simply use the next frame from the list.

Also, if you are using multiple sprites, then you could produce a linked list of sprites that are ordered in the Z plane. This would be part of a controlling class, which maintained the ordering of the list, as well as telling the sprites to display themselves.

The following code fragments are the declarations of such classes, although obviously, it is up to you, the programmer, how you would implement such classes:

```
struct frame {
    void **mask;    // mask data for the frame
    void **bitmap;    // bitmap of the frame
};

class animation;
class animation {
private:
    animation *nextframe;    // pointer to the next animation frame
    frame *thisframe;    // pointer to the data for this frame
public:
// method that displays the frame at the passed x, y position and
// returns the pointer to the next frame
    frame * displayframe(int, int);
    void killframe(int, int);    // removes frame from display

    animation();
    ~animation();
};
```

```
class sprite {
private:
   int x, y, z;    // sprites position on the screen
// pointer to the animation sequence for this sprite
   animation *currentframe;
public:
// calles the displayframe method of sequence and
// updates currentframe with the returned value
   void displaysprite();
// changes the x, y and z values by the passed values,
// then calls displaysprite (or displayframe)
   void movesprite(int, int, int);
// moves the sprite one step along a pre-determined path
   void step_path();
// sets the initial position of the sprite
   void setposition(int, int, int);

   sprite();
   ~sprite();
};
```

The controlling class would look something like:

```
class spritelist {
private:
   int no_sprites;
   sprite * list;
public:
   void maintainlist();    // keeps list in Z order
   void update_sprites(); // calls each sprite's step_path method
}
```

The **main** function of a program that uses these declarations could simply call the **update_sprites** method on a regular basis to produce quite complex animation sequences.

Summary

When we planned this book, the Animation Chapter was considered to be an easy one. We were encouraged by our own experience in sprite animation, and we'd also discussed the subject lots of times within our circle (and outside it, too). But as soon as we faced a blank sheet of paper, we also faced a problem.

It seemed that we didn't know any firm classifications for the world of computer animation. Do you really see anything that is still on your PC screen? So many different things can be associated with animation that we couldn't squeeze them all into the structure of this short chapter. Maybe some other time we'll try it again and write a whole book about it. For now, we've just provided you with a bunch of techniques that work; after all, you need someplace to start.

Using simple palette-changing and slide show effects you'll be able to make your company presentation, or whatever else, animated enough. Sprites upon a fractal landscape (see Chapters 11 and 14) will let you make something like a 'Commanche' of your own, although the combat might be too much! It may not be as fast but it will work.

As is too often the case, your hardware may limit your capabilities for producing animation. The PC platform is still a little bit weak on handling digital video. This is the way it is at present. In a year or two, the problem of Real Time Digital Video on the PC (no matter whether Pentium, Alpha or PowerPC based) will be solved by some hardware manufacturers. So don't waste your time trying to increase the speed of your favorite triple-buffer technique... Next year you'll buy some Graphics Processor 2000 Pro Plus and it will have half this chapter inside it. You'd be better off concentrating on modeling which will always be at the forefront of interactive animation. After all, this will allow you to add combat to your hypothetical 'Commanche'.

In the next chapter we'll move away from the video hardware, and cover the difficult subject of printing out of your graphics.

Printing Bitmapped Images

So, you tried your hardest to produce something worth looking at and hopefully you did it! The picture looks pretty good but it seems there's nothing else you can do with it. But suddenly a thought springs to mind (if it hadn't already). You wonder if it's possible to transform the magic dance of electronic beams into something more solid. It's not a bad idea to get some kind of hard copy of any soft image you already have (though the glass of your screen is certainly hard enough). We hope that your modest intentions will become bolder as you read through this chapter. Yes, we are going to talk about printing and printers.

Chapter Contents

In this chapter, we will cover:

- ▲ Hardware Overview: How Printers Work
- ▲ How We Interpret the Image
- ▲ Processing an Image for Printing
- ▲ Dithering
- ▲ Halftoning
- ▲ Shade Conversion
- ▲ The Optimal Choice
- ▲ Hints and Tricks for Writing Drivers

Printing Pictures

If you feel up to printing, you should be aware that getting pictures (or any other graphics) printed isn't that straight-forward. You may well get depressed by the mountain that you must climb, a climb which is rather unknown to many PC 'artists'. This area often means a lot of boring and tiresome work, but you only win the race by running it. All we want to do is arm you with everything you need, and the rest is up to you. The main principle of any job remains the same; it's practice which makes perfect, not books or advice.

First, we'll brief you on the various types of printers most frequently used nowadays. Then, we're afraid, we'll have to give you some theory (just a little bit) about how, and by what means, graphical images can be converted into clear pictures on paper. We'll finish with a description of the basic printing techniques for each type of printer mentioned.

We presume we don't have to remind you which cables and connectors are used to connect your printer to your PC, and so...

Hardware Overview - How Printers Work

Before we talk about the specifics of printing an image, it is necessary to gain an understanding of the hardware involved. Nearly all printers work on the same principle, they place dots on a piece of paper. The only exceptions we can think of are plotters and those which use either a golf-ball or daisywheel, but we aren't going to worry about them. The difference between printers is then how they put the dot onto the paper, and related to this how many they can put in an inch.

Dot Matrix Printers

Dot matrix printers are known by this term because they form images by printing series of dot columns. The term dot matrix can be accurately applied to all the printers we describe here, but we'll use it to mean the impact type. The print head comprises either 9 or 24 separate pins arranged in a vertical line, as shown opposite.

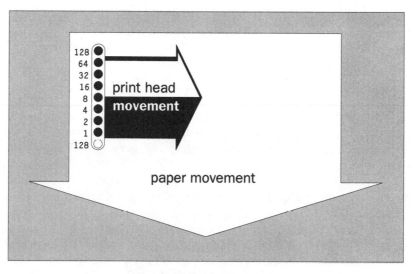

Matrix Printer Head

The best horizontal resolution achieved on 9-pin printers is 240 dpi (dots per inch). 24-pin printers can achieve up to 360 dpi. Vertical resolution depends on the space between dots in the printer head and the best numbers here are 72 and 180, for 9- and 24-pin printers respectively. Some printers can feed paper in tiny steps which are two or three times smaller than the distance between the dots, which means that the vertical resolution can be increased up to 200-360 dpi (see the section Hints and Tricks for Writing Drivers for details). But beware, our own experience tells us that even if some printers promise such high resolution, they may not support it.

For many years, dot matrix printers were happily used by the great majority of PC owners. Printer manufacturers have done much to improve these devices and their printing techniques. But no matter how great the technology is, dot matrix printers are still just a means of printing out text data line-by-line. Yes, sure, they can print graphics, but much slower and, together with the piercing noise, this makes the process torturous, and not only for people with a good ear for music. Also think about what kind of patience you'd need if you were to print pictures on a color dot matrix printer, which passes over the line an extra time for each color. Especially when new technology has made hard copying easy, very productive and far more fascinating.

Although this chapter will show you how to achieve newspaper quality on a 9-pin matrix printer, if your work involves some serious printing, you'd better persuade your boss to put an extra two hundred dollars on the right horse.

Inkjet Printers

Inkjet printers actually squirt tiny drops of ink (black or color) on the paper through a set of jets. The print head itself doesn't touch the paper (hence the name non-impact printing), so these printers are very useful for printing on transparent films.

Jet printers are more picky than their dot matrix forebears. The jets can be easily obstructed and the ink has a habit of spreading and absorbing into the paper, which may cause the image to appear fuzzy. But if your printer is handled with courtesy and tenderness and fed with special paper and ink, it will let you print nifty black and white, as well as color pictures with an agreeable resolution. For example, the Hewlett-Packard DeskJet-550 C model, gives you 300×300 dpi. A bit later we'll return to the 550 C to illustrate the capabilities of inkjet printing.

Laser Printers

The fact that dust and similar garbage always stick to statically charged things has being known for time immemorial. You also might have noticed just this phenomenon if you forget to wipe your video monitor. That's probably why nobody paid the slightest attention to the invention of a Bulgarian engineer who, at the beginning of the century, proposed a device which worked on a principle similar to that of the well-known Xerox. The invention was only appreciated fifty years later, and based upon similar technology, laser printers soon followed.

The way that laser printers work is very simple, like all great things in this world! To keep it simple, a light beam (normally a laser beam) scans the cylindrical surface of an elongated drum and charges it with static electricity. Then the drum goes through toner powder which sticks to the charged areas of its surface. Then the drum is rolled over a sheet of paper. The toner passes to the paper and, after heat treatment, gets fused onto it:

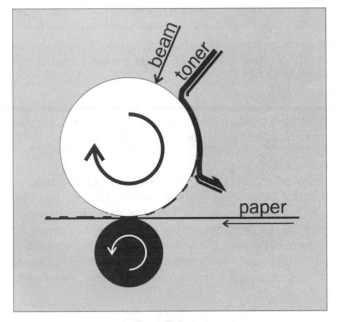

Laser Printer

The laser beam scans along the drum axis and forms an image with separate dots. Therefore, horizontal resolution is determined by how frequently the beam blinks, or makes a dot on its way across the drum. The cheapest laser printers make 300 dpi and the more expensive models 600 dpi. Each time the beam has passed over the drum, it turns by 1/300 inch. This minimal drum shift determines vertical resolution which is usually 300 dpi. A doubled resolution of 600 dpi can be obtained by using special tricks.

A laser printer prints out page-by-page. This means that it won't begin printing before it gets all the data for the whole page. This is possible thanks to its large memory, of at least 512K. But even these 512K aren't enough if you want to print a picture with a resolution of 300×300 dpi. Normally you will need about 1Mb for full page graphics at a resolution of 300 dpi, on a page format of A4 (you can easily calculate the precise figures yourself, one bit per dot).

To discuss the special techniques of laser printing, we'll take a HP LaserJet 4L as an example, because other manufacturers' laser printers emulate Hewlett-Packard models and understand their control language (PCL-5 in our example).

This doesn't apply to Canon printers because according to their joint agreement, Canon doesn't have the right to build HP emulators into its laser printers. (What is more interesting though, Canon supplies many world-wide manufacturers with driving engines for their printing and copying machines, including Hewlett-Packard.)

> Talking of printing control, we won't discuss other printer languages because the control possibilities they give are similar to those of PCL.

We can't help mentioning here one piece of printing technology which has become very popular since 1990 with the instruction of the HP LaserJet III series printers. It is called Resolution Enhancement Technology (RET) and is used in laser printers to print vector-based images as opposed to raster, or bitmap-based images. This involves changing the dot sizes on the picture without changing the actual resolution and makes it possible, for example, to sharpen letter edges or avoid toner amassing where lines cross, as shown below:

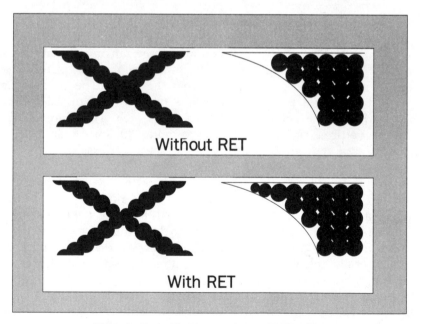

Resolution Enhancement Technology

Thermal Printers

We'll end our overview of printing devices with heat treatment technology printers, of which there are two types.

Printers of the first type, known as thermal-wax transfer printers, produce images on the paper by means of wax ink transfer. A large number of heating elements in the printer head affect a ribbon with thermal-wax ink, as opposed to heat-sensitive paper in fax machines. When heated, the ink is transferred from the ribbon to the paper. Now there are even printers whose head (and ribbon) are the same size as the paper used by the printer.

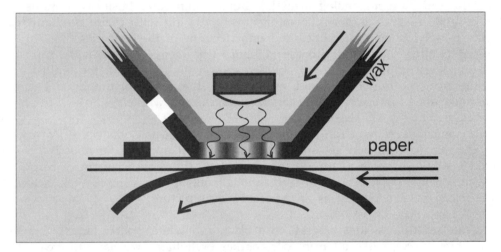

Thermal-Wax Printer

Printers of the second type known as dye sublimation printers, use dyes instead of wax on the ribbon. The heating elements vaporize the dyes onto the paper and then the paper is chemically treated to accept the dyes. Dyes of the three primary colors are mixed together in the required proportion which makes it possible to produce color pictures of exceptional quality.

The resolution in both cases depends on the density of the heating elements and is usually up to 300 dpi. It is obvious that, because of their special features, these printers are seldom used in usual everyday printing. But if you can afford to buy one, you'll get the best color print quality you can expect from a desktop printer.

How We Interpret the Image

When man interacts with a computer, the major problem, which spawns endless minor ones, is the contradiction between the discrete nature of the machine and human's analog mentality. But the computer business continues to thrive, and, as often happens, manufacturers carry on with their less-than-ideal products, relying on the abilities and imperfections of the human senses. In the case of printing (not only with the PC, but in newspapers, and in the case of TV, too) these imperfections and abilities are, on the one hand, the limited resolution of the human eye and, on the other, the ability of human sight and consciousness to integrate and recognize images as a whole.

On the micro level, you can see minute details, like color dots on a TV screen. On the macro level, you get an idea of reality as it appears. So nobody actually tends to see a picture in the New York Times as a swarm of black, gray, and white dots. And similarly, although only printing black dots, a matrix printer can print a bitmap as an agreeably clear picture.

To create multiple shades of gray on a black and white printer (strictly black and white, because it can't print dots darker or lighter), we have to create zones with different concentrations of dots on the paper. For darker areas in the picture we print dots more often, for lighter areas, not so often, leaving more clean spaces on the white paper. Because they are small enough, the eye integrates adjacent dots and perceives the printout as more or less solid fields of various shades of gray.

The same principle is used in color printers, with the exception that we mix not only black dots and white spaces, but dots of different hues. This makes it possible to create various shades of several basic colors. Dye sublimation printers, however, are different; they apply mixable paints onto the same point on the paper, so the colors are mixed on-the-spot.

Later in the chapter, we'll talk about monochrome printers (as the most common ones), bearing in mind that all the 'shading' techniques can be applied to color mixing nearly as well.

Processing an Image for Printing

Imagine, we have a colored picture on the screen, drawn by hand, scanned, or somehow otherwise software generated. It's ripe and ready, but our troubles aren't over yet. The long road to producing a hard copy is only just beginning. We will need the advice of our Graphics Guru many times throughout this journey.

Setting out on the errand, we first convert the whole color spectrum of our bitmap into 256 shades of gray. But you shouldn't expect the same color resolution from a hard copy as on the screen. You may ask, why we retained 256 shades of gray, when we converted a color picture to monochrome. We'll pass this question over to the Graphics Guru.

Never be in a hurry to make errors. Somebody else will make them for you.

So we try to retain the original color resolution as long as possible before we get to the printing itself. 256 shades seem reasonable for it still gives enough accuracy and, at the same time, it's a convenient byte-per-pixel representation. The brightness of each pixel is calculated by the obvious formula (see Chapter 4, Palettes and Colors):

Brightness = 0.299R + 0.587G + 0.114B

The picture on the screen looks brighter for two reasons: one, the monitor itself is a source of light and two, a screen picture normally has a black background, not white like paper. This is why we must increase the picture's brightness (see Chapter 11, Digital Image Processing).

We also have to raise the contrast of the image, otherwise some details that were quite distinct on the screen may eventually merge into one color with adjacent parts of the picture, because printing techniques normally have less color resolution, as you have learnt.

So far, so good. Now, having transformed our image as required, we should probably get the full WYSIWYG?

 To those of you, seeking WYSIWYG, I shall speak! You will never find it on the road to a hard copy. I've been shown at least See-What-You-Can-Get, when a picture was previewed in poorer quality to give an idea of how it would look printed...

So where do we go from here, O Graphics Guru?

 I see two ways before you.

The first one is the way of the sinner; print the gray picture as it is, without a minute's work, and you won't recognize it.

The second is the way of prudence; carefully choose your methods, depending on each specific picture, printer, paper, aura of the room and you'll get, although not quite WYSIWYG, a decent and recognizable printout...

So all the pre-processing is up to you. From now on, we'll assume that the task of printing a bitmap of 256 shades of gray with all the image processing has already been done.

The following figure shows what else happens to the picture's data before it is transferred to the printer.

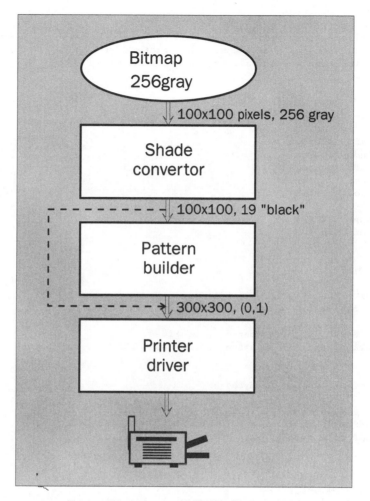

From Bitmap to Printer Codes

In the code on the next page, we have defined the classes for all these functional blocks as well as **print_manager** which manages the whole process. It will give you an idea of how all the program blocks work together and help you understand the next sections:

```
/*
This file contains all classes that operate on different stages of
printing process: shadow_convertor, pattern_builder,
and print_manager, and abstract class printer_driver.
*/

#ifndef PRINT_H
#define PRINT_H

#include <stdio.h>
#include "common.h"
#include "graph.h"
#include "mapper.h"
#include "resize.h"

#define  MAXCELL  6
typedef struct
{
   pointtype a, b;
} RECT;

/* GRAD, the structure to initialize Shade Convertor */
typedef struct
{
   BYTE num;       //number of gradations
   BYTE g[256];    //relative blacknesses, starts from 0, ends with max.
} GRAD;

typedef BYTE *rows_array[64];


typedef BYTE halftone_matrix[MAXCELL][MAXCELL];
typedef BYTE quadred_matr[4][MAXCELL][MAXCELL];


/* shadow_converter is derived from more general purpose class
   color_mapper_gray.
   It actually performs color mapping (see chapter 7)
   (from 256 gray shades to less),
   using Floyd-Steinberg dithering (see below)
   the only difference is that input data for the constructor
   is structure GRAD
*/
class shadow_converter:public color_mapper_gray
{
public:
   shadow_converter(int dots, GRAD &black);
// Convert one row of image
   virtual void one_row(BYTE *source, BYTE *out_line);
};
```

```
class pattern_builder
{
public:
   GRAD shadow_grad;
   int size_x, size_y; // Pattern dimensions
   int passes;
   pattern_builder(int x_size, int y_size);
   void set_shadow_grad(GRAD &shadow);
   virtual void calc_shadow_grad();

// Convert a row of pixels (row_size bytes long) into size_y rows of dots.
// Length of a dot row  is size_x times row_size.
   virtual void one_row(BYTE *row_in, int row_size, BOOL odd_row,
                        BYTE **rows_out) = 0;
};

// Non-abstract descendant from pattern_builder, implementing dithering
class pattern_dither : public pattern_builder
{
   quadred_matr *matrixes;
public:
   pattern_dither(int x_size, int y_size, quadred_matr *matr);
   virtual void one_row(BYTE *row_in, int row_size, BOOL odd_row,
                        BYTE **rows_out);
};

// Non-abstract descendant from pattern_builder, implementing halftone
class pattern_halftone : public pattern_builder
{
   halftone_matrix *matrix;
   void make_matrix(int matr_size);
   public:
   pattern_halftone(int matr_size);
   virtual void one_row(BYTE *row_in, int row_size, BOOL odd_row,
                        BYTE **rows_out);
   virtual void calc_shadow_grad();
   virtual ~pattern_halftone();
};

/* Abstract */
class printer_driver
{
public:
   FILE *out_file;
   int dpi_x, dpi_y, dots_x, dots_y;
   BOOL file_ok;
   int print_x0;  // Left offset in internal units

   printer_driver();
```

```
    BOOL open_file(char *name);

// How many dot rows are printed at a time
    virtual int buffer_rows();

// Form feed, reset printer, close file, or the like
    virtual void finish_print();

// Set left and upper offset in millimeters and initialize printer
    virtual BOOL init_printer(int printX0, int printY0);

// Pass buffer_rows onto printer (rows containing 0,1, and possibly 2).
// Then feed paper to be ready for next portion
    virtual void print(rows_array &rows);
};

class print_manager
{
public:
    shadow_converter *shadow; //initialized and disposed by manager
    pattern_builder *dither;  //disposed along with manager
    printer_driver *driver;   //disposed along with manager
    rows_array buffer;
    BYTE *tmp,*tmp1;

// Input_resizer is an object that converts the input image to the size
// it will be printed of. Preview_resizer resizes printer_driver's input
// to look properly on the screen.
    serial_resize *input_resizer, *preview_resizer;

    int pixels_x, pixels_y,    // after input resize!
        row_n,                 // the row currently being printed
        buf_row_n,             // buffer has buf_row_n filled rows
        buf_rows, buf_length;  // buffer dimensions

    BOOL no_print,
        one_to_one, // no dithering or halftoning
        odd_row;

    RECT pw;   //preview window

    int max_color,act_wid, act_hei;
    BOOL preview,
        order_inverted, // inverse pixel order in row
        top_to_bottom;
    BYTE *color_table;
    int shown_rows;   // number of rows already shown in preview

// use dither_ gradations, if dither_ != NULL otherwise use black
```

```
        print_manager(pattern_builder *dither_, printer_driver *driver_,
                   int pixels_x_, int pixels_y_, GRAD &black);
        virtual ~print_manager();
        void set_preview(RECT preview_window, BOOL order_inverted_,
                     BOOL top_to_bottom_, BYTE *color_table_);

  // Flush buffer, call driver->finish_print()
     virtual void finish_print();

  // Process one row of image and place it into buffer.
     void one_row(BYTE *row);
  private:
  // Pass buffer_rows onto printer.
     virtual void print_bunch();
     void show_on_screen(int row_num);
  };

  #endif
```

The image is passed to **print_manager** row by row. Each row goes through the chain of classes. This makes the whole program independent from the image source, which may reside in the system memory, on the screen, on disk, on a remote drive or even elsewhere.

shadow_converter recalculates 256 shades to a lower color resolution, while at the same time inverting the values so that a pixel with maximum brightness has the value 0. We call this 'gradations of blackness' as opposed to 'shades of gray'. The next program block, **pattern_builder**, converts each pixel into a sequence of 0's and 1's (and possibly 2's): 1 means 'put dot', 0 means 'don't', and 2 means 'put dot twice' - you may think of it as commands for an abstract printer. Some drivers, such as those for matrix printers, can print only a certain number of rows at a time, no more and no less. Print Manager asks the driver for the right number, and gathers rows in batches before passing them to **printer_driver**, which forms the appropriate commands for the specific type of device before finally, sending them to the printer.

Polymorphism of drivers allows the whole program to work the same way regardless of the destination of the printout. It may be anything you can program or think of, like any type of printer, or even a display which is useful if you want to have a preview option.

293

Dithering

Well, ignoring all the perils, you've stepped onto the slippery path of image printing. So what shall we try first? How about good old dithering. We spent plenty of pages in Chapter 4 trying to explain how it works, so we won't bother with all the details here.

However, dithering for printing has its own features. The most general one is this; usually a printer has more spatial resolution and less shades than a screen. Certainly there are color printers and special video systems which provide extra-high resolution, but in everyday life this statement is true. This means that you can accomplish your print dithering in a straight-forward way.

You should simply create a set of dither cells with smoothly increasing density (2×2, 2×3 or even 4×4) and substitute each pixel of the image with a corresponding cell when printing. We will have as many shades of gray as the number of dots in a cell plus one for an empty cell.

When choosing the cell configuration, avoid plain horizontal or vertical patterns, as shown below. The problem is that, even at the limit of its spatial resolution, the human eye easily distinguishes longer horizontal or vertical structures.

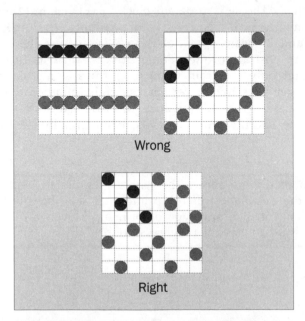

Right and Wrong Cells for Dithering

We implemented another trick to 'de-struct' repeating patterns. For each cell density, or gradation of blackness, we create not one cell, but four cell configurations (generated by rotation and mirroring).

Each pixel of a certain blackness turns into one of these four cells, depending on whether it is in an odd or even row, and an odd or even column.

The class **pattern_dither** is a descendant from abstract class **pattern_builder**. In the following implementation of the one_row method, we've dropped the details and just given you the most essential procedure.

```
void pattern_dither::one_row(BYTE *row_in, int row_size, BOOL odd_row,
                             BYTE **rows_out)
{
   int x, y, i, left_i, matr;
   BYTE val, *row;

   left_i = 0;
   matr =   odd_row;        // Selects one of 4 matrixes
   for (i = 0; i < row_size; i++)
   {
      val = row_in[i];
      matr = ++matr & 3;       // mod 4
      for (y = 0; y < size_y; y++)
         memmove(&rows_out[y][left_i], matrixes[val][matr][y], size_x);
      left_i += size_x;
   }
}
```

Artless but powerful just about sums up pattern dithering. Your firm's annual pie-chart will look fine. But you'd better refrain from printing your wife's portrait using such a technique, for it may cause problems!

Halftoning

Equip yourself with a magnifying glass and take a look at the illustrations or better still, photos in yesterday's paper. You will see diagonal rows of quite distinct black and white dots, just like the tiles on a chessboard. The dots you see are twice as big (or more) as those your favorite LaserJet 4 produces. 'Why?', you exclaim, and, 'How do they manage to produce better results when printing real pictures, using a much lower resolution, and, by the way, why don't they use our beloved pattern dithering?'

We are ready with the answers without even having to bother the Graphics Guru:

▲ The technology used when printing newspapers doesn't provide strong spatial resolution but it does allow the size of the black dot to vary.

▲ It seems that varying the dot size is a more powerful method of handling gray scale and, the biased structure of a picture printed in this way is more pleasant to the eye.

We're sure you won't mind one more magic scroll on printing, so here it is.

It is generally regarded that the fundamentals of offset printing were established in 1880 by Steven Hagen (it seems he managed without any computer assistance). Since then it has been widely used in the printing trade. It's implementation differs slightly from the actual polygraphic method, because it's been adapted for printers, but the results you can achieve are still similar.

The method is a sort of dithering (taking into account the formal definition given in Chapter 4), but we will call it halftoning so as not to confuse it with pattern dithering.

So what's the general idea behind the method? For each pixel in the image, we print a cell with what we call black or white priority. The cells are arranged just like the tiles of a chessboard. For black gradations from 0 to 50%, cells with white priority remain absolutely white (empty), and cells with black priority increase their density from 0 (empty) to 100% (full). For black gradations from 50% to 100%, white priority cells begin to fill up from empty to full, and black priority cells remain full black, as shown in the figure below. Note that the number of gray shades is twice the number of dots in the cell, plus one.

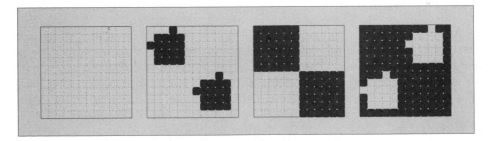

Halftoning Matrices

There is only one requirement for cell matrices, which is black (filled) areas should be solid, and not made up of a speckled pattern as when dithering. When building these matrices, we prefer to simply add dot by dot as black gradation increases, starting from the upper-left corner. Would it be any better, if we tried to reproduce typographic printing fully with round dots?

 In the days of my youth I tried to increase the black area from the center of the cell, and to make the area as round as possible, but it made no improvement to the printout.

pattern_halftone is again descended from abstract class **pattern_builder** and for comparison with the dithering case, we have shown the **one_row** method:

```
void pattern_halftone::one_row(BYTE *row_in, int row_size, BOOL odd_row,
                               BYTE **rows_out)
{
    int x, y, i, left_i;
    int val, val_, what_set, gray50;
    BOOL inverted;

    gray50 = size_x * size_y;

    left_i = 0;
    inverted = odd_row;
    for (i = 0; i < row_size; i++)
    {
        val = row_in[i];
        inverted = !inverted;
        if (inverted)
        {
            if (val > gray50)
                val_ = val - gray50;
            else
                val_ = 0;
        }
        else
        {
            if (val > gray50)
                val_ = gray50;
            else
                val_ = val;
        }

        for (y = 0; y < size_y; y++)
            memmove(&rows_out[y][left_i], matrix[val_][y], size_x);
        left_i += size_x;
    }
}
```

Shade Conversion

So, when using either dithering or halftoning, we can print, say 16 shades of gray. We have to recalculate the initial 256 shades to these 16. Unfortunately, however, these 16 shades may not correspond to equal degrees of color intensity, which is why the proper recalculation is not merely division by 16.

In Chapter 7 on Graphic File Formats, we described quantization, which is the conversion of an image to a lower color resolution. The class **shadow_converter** is derived from the more general-purpose quantizer, the class **color_mapper_gray**. The only difference is that the input data for the constructor is a structure with the type **GRAD**.

GRAD knows the number of shades and the relative blackness of each shade (the larger the value, the darker the shade). You can estimate these relative values by looking at a printout of some test image (it may be fields of different gray shades). For instance, if we take 5 shades, a **GRAD** structure may look like this:

```
GRAD sample_grad = {5,                        // Number of shades
                     {0,25,60,80,100}  // Relative blackness
                    }
```

As you can see, we define blackness here in relative units. The first value, 0 corresponds to shade value 255 in the image (white), the last value, 100 corresponds to shade 0 in the image (black). Value 25 corresponds to 191:

191 = 255 - (25 * 255 / 100)

Repeating this calculation for the other values, we get the corresponding set of gray shades.

Gradation	Blackness	Initial gray shade
0	0	255
1	25	191
2	60	102
3	80	51
4	100	0

Relative Blackness and Gray Shade

In Chapter 7, when discussing color mapping and quantization, we mentioned the Floyd-Steinberg Algorithm. We didn't go into detail about it there, but where printing is concerned, this algorithm becomes far more important.

Floyd-Steinberg Algorithm for Spatial Gray Scale

Let's look once again at the problem of printing multiple shades of gray on a strictly black-and-white device. We can print areas of different darkness by varying the concentration of black dots through an area. Dithering and halftoning do it by substituting each separate pixel with a pattern of dots, thus decreasing spatial resolution. Moreover, they have to reduce the number of gray shades, which creates rough borders where originally we had a smooth change of color.

Additionally, what if we don't have extra spatial resolution? Luckily there are solutions even in this case; what a surprise it was to see an agreeable picture coming out of our good old matrix printer with 72 dpi!

So what are these techniques which can print pixel-to-dot?

The Random Scatter Method

The first of these techniques that we want to mention is the random scattering method. The essence of this method is that a random value from -127 to +127 (we talk about 256 shades of gray) is added to the pixel value. If the result happens to be greater than 128, the dot is white (not printed), otherwise, it is black (printed).

The F-S Adaptive Method

Another is the Floyd-Steinberg adaptive method. In its simplest form, a pixel is rounded to 0 or 255, and the error is transferred to the adjacent pixels, in the proportion shown in the following figure:

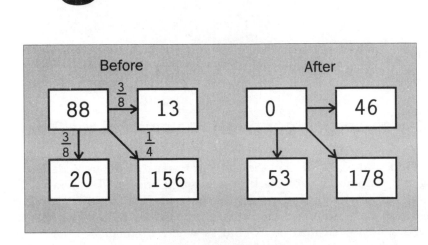

Error Transfer

The fact that the error is transferred to the right and down, not to the left and up, simplifies programming, because we can scan through the image in the normal order, without tracing it backwards.

However, if you use this algorithm you'll notice diagonal structures of dots in areas of plain color. Enhanced up-to-date methods implement improved proportions for error transfer and bi-directional processing of the rows of the image, odd rows - left to right, even rows - right to left, or vice versa.

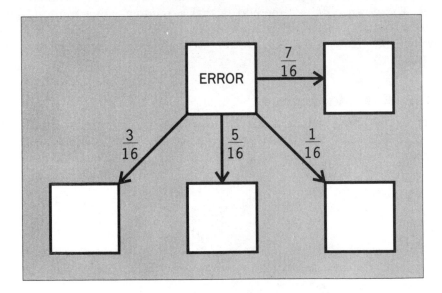

Improved Proportions for Error Transfer

If we have enough spatial resolution, we can apply the above algorithms to more than two black gradations. We have implemented the Floyd-Steinberg method in **shadow_convertor**, so it can be combined with dithering or halftoning.

The code below implements the simplest form of the Floyd-Steinberg algorithm:

```
// error_row      - integer array of errors for currently processing row
// new_error_row  - integer array of errors for next row
// coding_table   - coversion table to transform pixel's gray shade
//                  value (col) to number of printable gradation (val)
// value_table    - actual shade value for val

void shadow_converter::one_row(BYTE *row_in, BYTE *row_out)
{
   int i, col, val, err;
   long l;

   memset(new_error_row, 0, dots_x * sizeof(int));

   for (i = 0; i < dots_x; i++)
   {
      col = row_in[i] + (error_row[i] >> 3); // error is scaled by 8
      if (col < 0) col = 0;
      else if (col > 255) col = 255;
      val = coding_table[col];
      row_out[i] = val;
      err = col - value_table[val];

//erorr transfer
      new_error_row[i+1] += err << 1; // 2/8 = 1/4
      err += err << 1;    // 3/8
      error_row[i+1] += err;
      new_error_row[i] += err;
   }

// prepare for next row processing
   memmove(error_row, new_error_row, dots_x * sizeof(int));
}
```

You can find the code for the enhanced form of the algorithm on the accompanying CD-ROM.

The Optimal Choice

Choosing optimal image processing and printing methods every time is entirely a matter of experimenting and experience, so it's always good to have all your weapons at hand. Unfortunately, as far as we know, none of the commonly used Image Processors implement all these methods, but what they do have should definitely be made more operable.

However, you should bear the following quasi-rules in mind:

- If you print some relatively simple image (like business graphs or scientific illustrations) you'd be better off using dithering with a 4×4 matrix. The printout will look more natural than with halftoning, which is best applied to scanned photos.

- For both dithering and halftoning, it's no use expanding the matrix beyond 5×5 dots. It won't give you more color resolution but will certainly decrease spatial resolution, exceeding the limits of the human eye's integrating capability. On the other hand, a matrix smaller than 3×2 makes no sense, either. The optimum lies between these two.

- If you want to stretch or squeeze a picture, don't change the resolution of the source image, change the size of the matrix.

- When printing at the highest resolution, use halftoning not dithering. Due to step and point size irregularity, printers tend to fuse adjacent dots.

- The Floyd-Steinberg algorithm gives the best spatial resolution, therefore small details appear very realistic. It also has something that we would call a psycho-visual effect, something that may appeal to one person but may leave someone else unimpressed. The points in this case have a special texture, stochastic or photo grid like. It sometimes makes a printout look even more attractive than a photo (you see, vision is a deception of the mind).

This is the best choice for printing portraits, and by the way, we provide the means for doing this on the CD-ROM.

Hints and Tricks for Writing Drivers

Dot Matrix Printer

There are some technical tips about matrix printers that you should bear in mind if you use the code we provide in your own applications.

The key difficulty when using matrix printers for graphics is their habit of printing a band of rows (say 8 dots wide) instead of a one-dot row. It makes you gather an appropriate amount of dot-rows and print them at once. That's why our **print_manager** lets you gather dot-rows in a buffer.

1 **Double strike mode**. In certain cases, such as a well-worn ribbon, double strike mode actually provides one more shadow of black. However, you'd be better using it as a method of increasing the dot size.

2 **Extra high vertical resolution**. It's a common misconception that vertical resolution of matrix printers is limited by the distance between the pins (1/72"). Nevertheless, a printer is able to shift the head vertically by as little as 1/216". There's actually no point shifting it by 1/216" (this is only a little wider than a razor's edge), but 1/108" you may find useful (at least this possibility is implemented in the code).

3 **Difference between pins**. As far as printing graphics is concerned, the pins of a matrix printer head aren't identical. The four middle pins usually produce lighter dots than the rest. Why is this so? Your may choose any explanation you like, such as: it's because the middle pins are more often engaged in text printing, and so wear a lot quicker. But it's a fact and if you don't take it into account, you'll more than likely get a striped printout.

The following is the programming sequence to print on an Epson-compatible dot matrix printer.

a) Feed paper to desired line from current position. Command:

*<Esc>*J*{distance}*

where *{distance}* (1 byte) is the paper shift measured in 1/216". Repeat the command as many times as you need if the desired distance is more than one inch.

303

b) Set any font pitch, which also defines the step of horizontal tabulation. Command to set pica pitch and cancel condensed printing:

*<Esc>*P<^R>

c) Set the vertical spacing, so that we can use the line feed command, using the command:

*<Esc>*3*{spacing}*

where *{spacing}* (1 byte) is the desired line spacing in 1/216" units.

We then transfer the graphics data band by band, repeating steps d-g. A band may consist of 1-8 rows.

d) Return to left margin:

<CR>

e) Move to the beginning of the picture area, using relative tabulation:

<Esc>*#LSB#MSB*

where *#LSB* and *#MSB* are the least significant and most significant bytes of the number of tab units (1/120 inch) respectively.

f) Send the band's data:

<Esc>*3*#LSB#MSB{Data...}*

where **3** means 240 dpi, *#LSB* and *#MSB* are the least significant and most significant bytes of the number of horizontal dots (equal to the number of bytes in the data), and *{Data...}* is a binary raster. Each byte is a vertical column of 8 dots (high-order bits above low-order).

g) Feed one line:

<LF>

The following code implements a dot matrix printer driver (**classepson_drv**):

```
/* Epson driver implementation */
#include <mem.h>
#include "epson.h"

//////////////////////

  char *EpsonReset = "\x1b@",
       *EpsonGraph60 = "\x1b*\x0",
       *EpsonGraph72 = "\x1b*\x5",
       *EpsonGraph80 = "\x1b*\x4",
       *EpsonGraph120 = "\x1b*\x1",
       *EpsonGraph240 = "\x1b*\x3",

       *EpsonLineSpacing = "\x1b""3", //Set line spacing in 1/216 inch
       *EpsonPaperFeed = "\x1bJ",      //one-time paper feed for n/216 inch
       *EpsonMoveRight = "\x1b\\",     //move print head from current pos
       *EpsonElite = "\x1bM",
       *EpsonPica = "\x1bP",
       *EpsonCondensed = "\x0f",
       LF = '\x0a',
       CR = '\x0d';

epson_drv::epson_drv(int dpix_, int dpiy_,
                     int wid, int hei,  // millimetres
                     int actual_pins_, int start_pin_, int pass)
{
   dpi_y = dpiy_;
   dpi_x = dpix_;
   actual_pins = actual_pins_;
   start_pin = start_pin_;
   passes = max(1, min(pass, 2));

   if (dpi_y < 90)
      dpi_y = 72;
   else if (dpi_y < 160)
      dpi_y = 108;
   else
      dpi_y = 216;

   if (dpi_x < 66)
   {
```

```
      dpi_x = 60;
      graph_init = EpsonGraph60;
   }
   else if (dpi_x < 76)
   {
      dpi_x = 72;
      graph_init = EpsonGraph72;
   }
   else if (dpi_x < 100)
   {
      dpi_x = 80;
      graph_init = EpsonGraph80;
   }
   else if (dpi_x < 180)
   {
      dpi_x = 120;
      graph_init =  EpsonGraph120;
   }
   else
   {
      dpi_x = 240;
      graph_init = EpsonGraph240;
   }

   dots_x = wid/25.2 * dpi_x + 0.5;
   dots_y = hei/25.2 * dpi_y + 0.5;
}

BOOL epson_drv::init_printer(int printX0, int printY0)
{
   int y_skip;
   if (!file_ok)
      return FALSE;
   fprintf(out_file, EpsonReset);
// feed paper to picture start
   y_skip = 2160L * printY0 / 254; //y0 in 1/216 inch
   while (y_skip > 216)
   {
      fprintf(out_file,"%s%c", EpsonPaperFeed, 216);
      y_skip -= 216;
   }
   fprintf(out_file,"%s%c", EpsonPaperFeed, y_skip);

   print_x0 = 1200L * printX0 / 254; //x0 in 1/120 inch
   switch (dpi_y) // see print member to understand it
   {
      case 72:
         y_skip = actual_pins * 3 - (passes - 1);
         break;
      case 216:
         y_skip = actual_pins * 3 - 3;
```

```
            break;
        case 108:
            y_skip = ((actual_pins + 1) / 2) * 6 - 6;
    }

//to provide proper LF
    fprintf(out_file, "%s%c", EpsonLineSpacing, y_skip);
//for future tabulation 1/120
    fprintf(out_file, "%s", EpsonPica);
    return TRUE;
}

void epson_drv::finish_print()
{
    if (file_ok)
        fprintf(out_file, "%s", EpsonReset);
}


int epson_drv::buffer_rows()
{
    switch(dpi_y)
    {
        case 72:
            return actual_pins;
        case 216:
            return 3 * actual_pins;
        case 108:
            return ((actual_pins + 1) / 2) * 3;
        default:
            return actual_pins;
    }
}

void epson_drv::print(rows_array &rows)
{
    int i, j, k;
    rows_array rows2, *prows;
    int buf_rows;
    BYTE *zero_row;

    if (!file_ok)
        return;

    switch (dpi_y)
    {
    case 72:
        one_pass(rows, 1); //1st pass
        if (passes == 2)
        {
//move head slightly down
```

```
            fprintf(out_file, "%s%c", EpsonPaperFeed, 1);
//second pass - very BLACK dots
            one_pass(rows, 2);
        }
        fprintf(out_file, "%c", LF);
        break;
    case 108:
        zero_row = new BYTE[dots_x];
        memset(zero_row, 0, dots_x);
        for (k = 0; k <= 2; k++)
        {
            for (i = 0; i < actual_pins; i++) //for rows in buffer
                if (i & 1)
                    rows2[i] = zero_row;
                else
                    rows2[i] = rows[3*(i/2)+k];
            one_pass(rows2, 1);
            if (passes > 1)
                one_pass(rows2, 2);
            fprintf(out_file, "%s%c", EpsonPaperFeed, 2);
        }
        fprintf(out_file, "%c", LF);
        delete zero_row;
        break;

    case 216:
        for (k = 0; k <= 2; k++)
        {
            for (i = 0; i < actual_pins; i++)
                rows2[i] = rows[i*3+k];
            one_pass(rows2, 1); //1st pass
            fprintf(out_file, "%s%c", EpsonPaperFeed, 1);
        }
        fprintf(out_file, "%c", LF);
    }
    file_ok = TRUE;
}

void epson_drv::one_pass(rows_array &rows, int pass)
{
    BYTE b1, b2;
    BOOL first_index_set;
    int xspace, i, j, index, first_index, last_index;
    BYTE *tmp;

    tmp = new BYTE[dots_x];
    index = 0;
    last_index = -1;
    first_index_set = FALSE;
```

```
     for (j = 0; j < dots_x; j++)
     {
        b1 = 0;

// Make column byte.
        for (i = 0; i < actual_pins; i++)
        {
           if (rows[i][j] >= pass)
               b1 = (b1 << 1) | 1;
           else
               b1 = (b1 << 1) & 0xFE;
        }
        b1 <<= 8 - start_pin - actual_pins;
        tmp[index] = b1;

// Find leading and trailing blanks
        if (b1 > 0)
        {
           if (!first_index_set)
           {
              first_index = index;
              first_index_set = TRUE;
           }
           last_index = index;
        }
        index++; // Column byte is made
     }
     if (last_index >= 0)
     {
// Go to where graphics starts (skip left margin and leading blanks)
        first_index -= first_index & 1;
        xspace = print_x0 + (120L * first_index + dpi_x / 2) / dpi_x;
        fprintf(out_file, "%c%s%c%c", CR, EpsonMoveRight, lo(xspace),
                hi(xspace));

// graphics begins
        index = last_index - first_index + 1;
        fprintf(out_file,"%s%c%c",graph_init,lo(index),hi(index));
        fwrite(tmp + first_index, 1, index, out_file);
     }
     delete tmp;
}

print_manager *init_epson_printing(
     int pixels_x, int pixels_y, // picture dimensions
     int wid, int hei,  // millimetres on paper
     int print_x0, int print_y0, // Start position on paper, mm

     char *file_name, BOOL no_print,
     int dpi_x, int dpi_y,
```

```
          int start_pin, int actual_pins, int passes,
          pattern_builder *pb,
          GRAD &black // but uses  dither_ gradations, if dither_ != NULL
       ) // returns NULL if error
{
   epson_drv *drv;
   print_manager *manager;

   if (pb != NULL)
      passes = pb->passes;

   drv = new epson_drv(dpi_x, dpi_y, wid, hei, actual_pins, start_pin,
                       passes);

   if (!no_print)
   {
      if (!drv->open_file(file_name))
      {
         delete drv;
         return NULL;
      }
      drv->init_printer(print_x0, print_y0);
   }

   manager = new print_manager(pb, drv, pixels_x, pixels_y, black);
   manager->no_print = no_print;
   return manager;
}
```

Laser Printer

A driver for laser printers is very straight-forward. We can send data to the printer row by row, forming a byte for every 8 sequential dots in a row.

The following is the programming sequence to print on a laser printer:

a) Set raster resolution:

<Esc>*t75R

Instead of ASCII '75' you can put 100, 150, or 300, the resolution in dpi.

b) Set printer cursor into desired position relative to upper-left corner of the page:

<Esc>***p#Y** for vertical,
<Esc>***p#X** for horizontal position.

Instead of **#** you should put the actual number of dots, say '320'. If you include a plus or minus sign, such as '+20' or '-100', these co-ordinates are relative to the current position, not the start of the page.

> There is a mysterious tradition among programmers of positioning the cursor first to 0,0 (page start), then making a relative shift down and right. When we tried ignoring that rule, the effects were bizarre.

c) Set pure (unencoded) raster type:

<Esc>***b0M**

d) Start raster graphics at current cursor position:

<Esc>***r1A**

e) Transfer raster data row by row. The command for each row is:

<Esc>***b#W** *{Data...}*

where **#** is ASCII string with number of bytes in the row and *{Data...}* is binary raster.

f) End raster graphics:

<Esc>***rB**

> Note that the cursor position remains unchanged, although rows are printed one after another. So, if you don't send the end-of-page command or reposition the cursor, the next picture will overlap the one just printed.

The code following implements a laser printer driver (**class pcl5_drv**), based on the PCL-5 command language:

```c
/* Laser printer driver implementation */
#include "laser.h"

char
   *Pcl5SetRaster = "\x1b*b0M",
   *Pcl5TransferRaster = "\x1b*b",
   *Pcl5TransferRasterTail = "W",

   *Pcl5CursorBy = "\x1b*p",
   *Pcl5VertJump = "Y",
   *Pcl5HorJump = "X",
   *Pcl5StartGraphFromCursor = "\x1b*r1A",
   *Pcl5LineBack = "\x1b&a-1R",
   *Pcl5PushCursorPos = "\x1b&f0S",
   *Pcl5PopCursorPos = "\x1b&f1S",
   *Pcl5EndRasterGraph = "\x1b*rB";

pcl5_drv::pcl5_drv(int dpi, int wid, int hei)
{
   if (dpi < 80)
   {
      dpi_x = 75; dpi_y = 75;
      graph_resolution = "\x1b*t75R";
   }
   else if (dpi < 125)
   {
      dpi_x = 100; dpi_y = 100;
      graph_resolution = "\x1b*t100R";
   }
   else if (dpi < 225)
   {
      dpi_x = 150; dpi_y = 150;
      graph_resolution = "\x1b*t150R";
   }
   else
   {
      dpi_x = 300; dpi_y = 300;
      graph_resolution = "\x1b*t300R";
   }
   dots_x = wid/25.2 * dpi_x + 0.5;
   dots_y = hei/25.2 * dpi_y + 0.5;
}


BOOL pcl5_drv::init_printer(int printX0, int printY0)
{
   int x_skip, y_skip;
   fprintf(out_file, "%s", graph_resolution); // set resolution
```

```
// cursor to 0,0 - mystic dance
   fprintf(out_file, "%s0%s", Pcl5CursorBy, Pcl5VertJump);
   fprintf(out_file, "%s0%s", Pcl5CursorBy, Pcl5HorJump);

// cursor to start position
   y_skip = (long)printY0 * dpi_y / 254;
   fprintf(out_file, "%s+%d%s", Pcl5CursorBy, y_skip, Pcl5VertJump);
   x_skip = (long)printX0 * dpi_x / 254;
   fprintf(out_file, "%s%d%s", Pcl5CursorBy, x_skip, Pcl5HorJump);
   fprintf(out_file, "%s%s", Pcl5SetRaster, Pcl5StartGraphFromCursor);

   line_count = 0;
   return(TRUE);
}

void pcl5_drv::finish_print()
{
   fprintf(out_file, "%s", Pcl5EndRasterGraph);

// move cursor to the end of picture area
   fprintf(out_file, "%s+%d%s", Pcl5CursorBy, line_count, Pcl5VertJump);
   fprintf(out_file, "%s0%s\x0C", Pcl5CursorBy, Pcl5HorJump);
}

void pcl5_drv::print(rows_array &rows)
{
   int i, j, index,bytes_no;
   BYTE b,*line,*tmp;
   bytes_no = (dots_x+7) / 8;
   tmp = new BYTE[bytes_no];
   line = rows[0];

   index = 0; //pack 8 dots in byte
   for (i = 0; i < bytes_no-1 ; i++)
   {
      b = 0;
      for (j = 0; j < 8; j++)
         b = (b << 1) + line[index++];
      tmp[i] = b;
   }

   b = 0; //last byte
   for (j = 0; j < 8; j++)
   {
      b = b << 1;
      if (index < dots_x)
         b += line[index++];
   }
   tmp[bytes_no-1] = b;
   fprintf(out_file, "%s%d%s", Pcl5TransferRaster, bytes_no,
           Pcl5TransferRasterTail);
   fwrite(tmp, 1, bytes_no, out_file);
```

```
      delete(tmp);
      file_ok = TRUE;
   }

print_manager *init_laser_printing(
      int pixels_x, int pixels_y, // picture dimensions
      int wid, int hei,  // millimetres on paper
      int print_x0, int print_y0, // Start position on paper, mm
      char *file_name, BOOL no_print,
      int dpi,
      pattern_builder *pb, GRAD &black
   )
{
   pcl5_drv *prn_drv;
   print_manager *pm;
   int size_x, size_y;

   prn_drv = new pcl5_drv(dpi,wid, hei);
   if (!no_print)
   {
      if (!prn_drv->open_file(file_name))
      {
         delete prn_drv;
         return NULL;
      }
      prn_drv->init_printer(print_x0,  print_y0);
   }
   if (black.num > 2)
   {
      black.num = 2;
      black.g[1] = 100;
   }
   pm = new print_manager(pb, prn_drv, pixels_x, pixels_y, black);
   pm->no_print = no_print;
   return pm;
}
```

Summary

We've tried our best to bring you up-to-date with efficient printing techniques. Did we succeed? On the one hand, yes; we've provided a bunch of unique routines that work, which make printing photos worth trying and the printout worth looking at, together with a set of hints, tricks and recommendations, some leading to optimal quality and some leading you astray.

On the other hand?.. Technology changes the state of the art, and while someone is talking about a paperless office, others are inventing printing machinery of a new generation. In a second edition of this book (or even 1.5), we'd like to write (and print) in the same depth on inkjet printers (256 colors at 600 dpi). But you can be absolutely sure that such a future edition will be much easier to write and read; one day HP will be able to implant enough Artificial Intelligence into its Ink JET 2000 and all you'll need to do will be to train its camera to read your lips.

CHAPTER 10

Fractals

In this chapter, we'll discuss fractals, a very fashionable field of contemporary physics and mathematics, as well as computer graphics. Fractals offer the computer graphics programmer a method of compression which will probably never be improved upon.

Chapter Contents

In this chapter, we will cover:

▲ Fractal Geometry

▲ Fractal Dimension

▲ Drawing Fractal Curves with L-systems

▲ Mandelbrot and Julia Sets

▲ Fractals in Physics - DLA

▲ Fractal Landscapes

▲ Clouds - True 2-3D Fractal Generation

Fractal Geometry

Mandelbrot, the father of fractals, said that just as the shapes of traditional geometry are the natural way of representing man-made objects, such as squares, circles, and triangles, fractal curves are the natural way of representing objects of nature. And even when a fractal object isn't modeling a phenomenon of the real world, it's still usually impressive.

From a programmer's point of view, coding fractal algorithms is normally not too tedious and usually gives quick results, thus making it worth the trouble. The cost is low, the gain is high. If programming excites you, then fractals is definitely the sport for you.

We'll provide you with a collection of techniques for generating different types of fractal image. And as usual, we won't delve too deeply into the scientific aspects, but it would be impossible in this particular chapter to get away without at least a brief discussion of theory.

You may find some sections too short. That's because we wanted to show you a wide range of fractal techniques, the comprehensive explanations of which would expand to a whole book or two.

What are Fractals?

We could hypocritically come out with the classical Mandelbrot definition, 'A fractal is a set whose Hausdorff-Besicovitch dimension is strictly greater than its topological dimension...'

These words are no shorter and no less beautiful than Alice's 'longitudes' and 'latitudes', but this formal definition helps us understand the subject no more than longitudes and latitudes helped Alice get around in the rabbit hole. We'll try to introduce you to 'fractal dimension' - it will be an interesting topic for those of you fond of mathematics. You'll find the explanation of it at the end of this section.

However, you can be a programming expert without any knowledge of high-level mathematics. Luckily, Mandelbrot himself bothered to give us another, non-scientific definition:

'A fractal is any structure, parts of which are in some sense similar to the whole'.

Self-Similarity

Try to guess what the following things of seemingly different nature have in common: a river and its tributaries, a mountain ridge, branches and roots of a tree, clouds in the sky, a von Koch curve, and a Sierpinski gasket.

Von Koch Curve

Sierpinski Gasket

One thing can be said about all these objects - their smaller parts look very much like the whole. Mandelbrot introduced a term for this: **self-similarity**.

Many things other than those we listed above, are self-similar. If you take a closer look at things, a grain of sand may look like a stone, a stone like a rock, and a rock like a whole mountain.

A Quick History of Fractals

When Benoit Mandelbrot first started to publish his works on fractals, we, the authors of this book, were just babes happily playing by the river side, and certainly not thinking about self-similarity. So we can't swear by Almighty God that fractals existed before they were discovered by Mandelbrot, although common sense says that they did.

The term fractal turned up in the world of mathematics about a century ago, when mathematicians such as Cantor, Peano, and von Koch started drawing strange, alien curves. What was so strange about them was that they led somewhere beyond the limits of normal mathematics. For example, the Peano curve could fill space; another one, although continuous, didn't have derivative at any of its points, and so the list continues. They were like infinity served on a plate, because any finite piece of these curves could be stretched to infinity.

Although the ideas associated with these curves were acknowledged, they remained an assorted collection of curious phenomena, something like a mathematical zoo. They were not regarded as a separate theory, nor were they intensely studied. This can be mostly put down to the lack of computer assistance. Iterative methods, which build fractal objects, are not easily implemented on paper, and it's no surprise that nobody could imagine that these 'mathematical monsters' would be used to describe objects of the real world.

But this world is made in such a way, that whatever mathematicians think of, it is sooner or later found in nature. In the 60s, H.E. Hurst, analyzing the annual deviation of the water level in the Nile, discovered (or rather, noticed) a consistency characterizing many natural phenomena. If something is increasing, it will increase further. If something is decreasing, it will decrease further. The diagrams of these processes were explicitly fractal, but his work didn't create much noise, either.

It was in the 70s that Mandelbrot started the fractal revolution. He did the same thing with the ideas of Cantor and Peano, that Lenin did with the ideas of Marx and Engels - he popularized them. But seriously, he was the first to use a computer to explore fractals and turn public interest to fractals in nature.

What are Fractals for?

For us (and we hope, for you) fractals are mainly interesting from the æsthetic point of view. Even when they are just pictures of abstract processes, they have a flavor of alien realism about them.

Fractal mountains touching fractal clouds... fractal trees glimmering in the fractal light of the fractal moon... and fractal snowflakes fractally falling onto the fractal ground.

However, they have both scientific and practical applications. In theoretical physics they are closely associated with chaos and pre-chaotic conditions. Chaos in physics is not the grandfather of Zeus, but the irregular, unpredictable behavior of a dynamic system. Fractals are studied in practically every science: physics, mathematics, chemistry, biology, even in social sciences (as we prove to be fractal, too).

The mystic nature of fractals makes us think that they can be used for many other, still unknown purposes. Barnsley successfully applied them to image compression. Maybe, you'll invent something else.

Fractal Dimension

Dimension has many definitions (or, should we say, there are many types of dimensions). One of the simplest ones is the **box dimension**. A warning though, don't take the following text as a strict mathematical explanation.

Imagine a flat curve, for example a circle with a diameter of 1. We'll cover it with squares with sides of a certain length L and count how many squares (N) we'll need to cover the circle completely. At first N will grow faster than $1/L$. When L=1, N=1, when L=0.5, N=4.

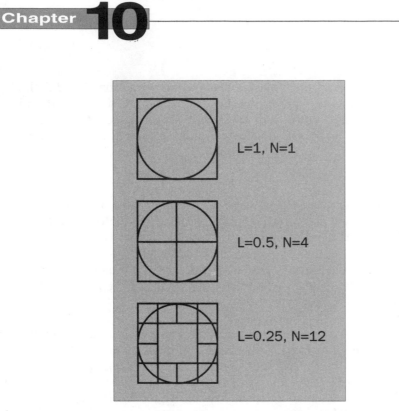

Covering a Circumference of a Circle with Squares

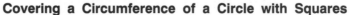

But as L becomes smaller (approaches zero), we'll notice that:

$$N(L) = \frac{Pi}{L}$$

which means that every square covers 1/L of the curve's length.

If we cover the area of a circle in the same way, we'll have

$$N(L) = \frac{Pi}{4L^2}$$

squares of L × L

And to fill the sphere we'll need

$$N(L) = \frac{Pi}{6L^3}$$

cubes of L × L × L.

The power D in every formula $N(L) = a\ L^{-D}$ is a box dimension. As you've already probably guessed, D is 1 for a curve, 2 for a flat figure, and 3 for a spatial figure.

We can drop mathematics for a moment and use some examples from real life. Don't worry, we aren't going to suggest you measure an aquarium with a matchbox. We'll turn to traveling instead. Traveling on highways, you can always see the distance you have to drive on the map. However, when you walk along forest paths, even if you measure them on the map with the greatest of accuracy, the actual distance you walk will be greater because of the twists and turns in the path. And if you row up a small river you can wind through its turns all day long and still see the same oak only a stone's throw from you.

Also there are purely abstract curves that show even more surprising effects. We'll take the von Koch curve as an example. It's constructed in the following way: you take a line, divide it into 3 sections of equal length, and replace the middle section with 2 lines of the same size, see below. Now we have a broken line consisting of 4 lines of the same length, which is 4/3 times longer than the original line. We apply the same routine to each section of the broken line over and over again, infinitely.

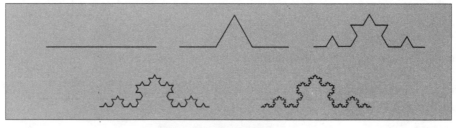

Von Koch Curve

You can see that the length of the curve grows at each iteration step (i)

$$Lc(i) = (4/3)^i$$

which means that it doesn't reach a definite value as i grows! If we start covering the curve with squares (with the sides equal to the length of a segment at iteration i, say $(1/3)^i$), then we'll need a square for each segment, and the total number of squares, N, will be 4^i.

Now we can estimate the dimension of the von Koch curve. As the size of a square, L, is $(1/3)^i$, then

$$i = \frac{\ln(L)}{\ln(1/3)} = \frac{-\ln(L)}{\ln(3)}$$

Therefore,

$$N(L) = 4^{\frac{-\ln(L)}{\ln(3)}} = \exp\left(-\ln(4) * \frac{\ln(L)}{\ln(3)}\right)$$

The dimension D is ln4/ln3 = 1.26. You see, it's a *fractional* number, not an integer.

The box dimension can be used for objects of a self-similar nature, as well as for purely abstract objects, but not in the strict mathematical sense. For figures like the von Koch curve there is a more convenient **similarity** dimension.

We can split a self-similar object into N parts similar to the whole, so that the linear size of each part is R times less than the size of the original object. For a 1-dimensional object N=R. For a 2-dimensional object $N=R^2$, as a square R×R contains R^2 squares 1×1. It is the power of R that is the fractal dimension. As we can split the von Koch curve into 4 segments which are 3 times shorter, then

$$4 = 3^D$$

and so D = ln 4 / ln 3, the same as the box dimension.

Fractal objects with dimensions between 1 and 2 can be built not only by replicating a curve, but also by taking a solid figure apart.

The Sierpinski gasket, which illustrates this point and is shown opposite, can be built like this:

1 Divide each side of a triangle in the middle and connect the division points, thus creating a smaller triangle inside the original one.

2 Take away the inner triangle, leaving a hole.

3 Repeat steps 1 and 2 with the three remaining triangles, and so on.

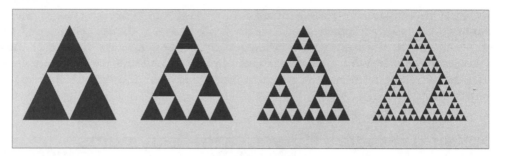

Sierpinski Gasket

You can see that the Sierpinski triangle consists of three similar triangles, the length of whose sides is half that of the original triangle. This makes its dimension:

$$D = \ln 3 \ / \ \ln 2 = 1.58$$

Similarly, the Sierpinski carpet has a dimension of $\ln 8 \ / \ \ln 3 = 1.89$, as shown in the figure below:

Sierpinski Carpet

If you compare the von Koch curve and Sierpinski carpet you'll see that, while the first looks linear, the latter appears more like a solid figure. This intuitive sensation demonstrates the difference in their fractal dimensions - the first has a fractal dimension of 1.26 (closer to 1), the latter 1.89 (closer to 2). Fractals with a dimension of 2 tend to cover all points throughout the area they occupy, as we'll see in a bit.

We won't investigate the fractal dimension of every object we discuss in this chapter. After all, mathematicians have to write books, too. We just wanted to introduce you to the beauty of non-integer dimensions, and we hope that those of you not familiar with logarithms have already turned the page. Take solace from the fact that from now on, we'll proceed with just the beauty of fractal images.

Drawing Fractal Curves with L-systems

There are many other fractal curves that can be constructed that are similar to the classical von Koch curve - one segment of a curve is substituted with a structure of a more complex shape, and this process is repeated infinitely. It would be boring to write a program for each new type of curve, as the algorithms are so much alike. Fortunately, there is a general method for creating such curves, called **L-systems**.

L-systems make up a formal language to describe transformations of expanding structures. They were introduced by Aristid Lindenmayer in 1968 to model the growth of plants. The core of the L-system language consists of only a few symbols, such as 'F', '+', and '-'. The initial shape of a system (the **seed**) is specified by a string, such as:

F++F++F

At each iteration (**generation of growth**), the current string grows according to the following simple rule: all pluses and minuses remain unchanged and all Fs are substituted by a particular replacement string. If we assume that the replacement string is

F-F++F-F

then at the first iteration, our seed will turn into

F-F++F-F++F-F++F-F++F-F++F-F

and so on. So, by specifying the seed and the replacement string, we define the growth of all future generations.

Now, we'll turn to the graphical interpretation of L-systems. A string in L-system language is interpreted as a sequence of commands to an imaginary plotting device, where F means 'draw a line forwards', minus means 'turn clockwise by a particular angle', and plus means 'turn anti-clockwise by the same angle'.

The above example defines the von Koch snowflake, with the assumption that the angle is 60 degrees. The following figure shows the seed and the first three generations:

...och Snowflake

These are L............sic form. In many cases you'll need some extensions.............. being **branching**. Imagine we are modeling a tree. At so.............. trunk we create a branch, and then carry on with the trunk. If ....closed line, the replacing string would have to contain the algorithm to ....s back to the trunk. And that would cause many problems (extra drawing and a paracetamol required!).

This is solved by adding another element to the L-system language. The opening bracket '[' means 'remember the current point and direction', the closing bracket ']' means 'return to the last ['.

We boldly added a few other extensions just for fun. While drawing various fractals, we sometimes found it convenient to add a command or two to our L-system language to make life simpler. Most of them are trivial, so we will only mention what we call variant substitution. We use three symbols 'F', 'G', and 'H', as opposed to just 'F', each of which is substituted in its own way (with a different replacing string). However, all three are drawn the same way in the last generation.

The program includes the code that interprets and draws L-systems. When we started writing the program we thought of two possible ways of organizing it.

The first was to expand the seed to the required generation, and then draw the result. But the last generation can be pretty big, so we decided not to bother with long data strings and so we used a recursive algorithm instead:

```
/*
This program implements an extended version of L-systems.
A particular L-system is defined in a configuration file, which must
be specified on the command line.
The configuration file structure is:

11 1 45 1                               ; max_level line_len angle size_coeff
10.0 10.0 0.0                           ; x0 y0 angle0
-F++G-                                  ; substitutor for F
+F--G+                                  ; substitutor for G
[F]G                                    ; substitutor for H
R6(cc[R8(cH)]--R45(J)++)                ; the seed


X0, Y0, and Angle0 are initial coordinates and direction.
Any text from semicolon till the end of a line is treated as a comment
(sorry for explaining obvious things).
*/

#include <graphics.h>
#include <math.h>
#include <conio.h>
#include <string.h>
#include "common.h"

int max_level = 12;
float line_len = 2;
float size_coef = 2;

// Extended L-system command set:

// '+'  add angle; '-'  sub angle
// 'F,G,H' to be substituted
// '[' - save the current state of drawing (push it on the stack)
// ']' - pop the saved state from stack
// 'C' - inc color
// 'c' - dec color
// 'S' - increse segment size (multiply on coeff.)
// 's' - decrease segment size (divide on coeff.)
// 'J' - jump one step w/o drawing
// 'Rxxx(<text>)' - repeat <text> text xxx times,
//    where <text> is any sequence of the commands

// 4 segment von Koch curve (snowflake)
int angle = 60;
char replacing_string[3][80] = {"F+F--F+F", "", ""};
char init_seed[120] = "F--F--F";
```

```
int current_angle = 0;
float current_x = 320; // Although lines are drawn between integer points,
float current_y = 240; // we need more precision for X and Y.
float current_size = 1;
BYTE current_color = 2;

// Structure to save and restore the current state of drawing
typedef struct save_state {
    float x, y, size;
    int a;
    BYTE c;
    struct save_state *prev;
} save_state;

float sinus[360];
float cosinus[360];

float new_x, new_y;

save_state *saved = 0; // stack top pointer

// The recursive function for drawing and generation.
// It executes all commands except F, G, and H.
// When F, G, or H are encountered, draw() calls itself,
// passing the appropriate replacing string and the decreased level.
// Initial level equals the number of generations.
// The actual drawing is performed only at level 0.
// Draw() returns the index of last processed symbol in the string
// (this is used only to parce repeats).
int draw(char *seed, BYTE level)
{
    int i,j,k, len, r;
    save_state *pss;
    char s[40];

    if (kbhit()) return(0); // stop drawing
    len = strlen(seed);
    for (i = 0; i < len; i++)
    {
        switch(seed[i])
        {
            case 'F':   // Draw a line at level 0 or
            case 'G':   // substitue symbol
            case 'H':   // with the replacing string.
                if (level) draw(replacing_string[seed[i]-'F'], level-1);
                else
                {
                    new_x = current_x + current_size * cosinus[current_angle];
                    new_y = current_y - current_size * sinus[current_angle];
                    line(current_x, current_y, new_x, new_y);
                    current_x = new_x;
```

```
               current_y = new_y;
        }
        break;
   case'J':  // jump, no drawing
        new_x = current_x + cosinus[current_angle];
        new_y = current_y - sinus[current_angle];
        current_x = new_x;
        current_y = new_y;
        break;
   case '+':
        current_angle = (current_angle + angle) % 360;
        break;
   case '-':
        current_angle = (current_angle - angle + 360) % 360;
        break;
   case '[':
        pss = new save_state;
        pss->x = current_x;
        pss->y = current_y;
        pss->a = current_angle;
        pss->c = current_color;
        pss->size = current_size;
        pss->prev = saved;
        saved = pss;
        break;
   case ']':
        if (saved)
        {
           pss = saved;
           saved = saved->prev;
           current_x = pss->x;
           current_y = pss->y;
           current_angle = pss->a;
           current_color = pss->c;
           current_size = pss->size;
           delete pss;
           setcolor(current_color);
        }
        break;
   case 'C':
        setcolor(++current_color);
        break;
   case 'c':
        setcolor(--current_color);
        break;
   case 'S':
        current_size *= size_coef;
        break;
   case 's':
        current_size /= size_coef;
        break;
```

```
        case 'R':
            r = 0;
            i++;
            for (;seed[i] > '0' && seed[i] <'9' && i <= len; i++)
                r = r * 10 + (seed[i] - '0'); // count repeats
            if (seed[i] != '(') return(i); //error
            strcpy(s,&seed[i+1]);
            for (j = 0; j < r; j++) // processes text in ()
                k = draw(s,level);
            i += k+1;
            break;
        case ')': return(i);
    }
}
return(i);
}

void main(int argc, char **argv)
{
    int i, gd = VGA, gm = VGAHI;
    FILE *f;
    char *s;

    if (argc > 1) // configuration file
    {
        f = fopen(argv[1], "rt");
        if (f == NULL)
            printf("Something wrong with file %s",argv[1]);
        else
        {
            sscanf(next_string(f),"%d %f %d %f",
                    &max_level,&line_len,&angle, &size_coef);
            sscanf(next_string(f),"%f %f %d",
                    &current_x,&current_y,&current_angle);
            for (i = 0; i < 3; i++)
                sscanf(next_string(f),"%80s", replacing_string[i]);
            sscanf(next_string(f),"%100s", init_seed);
            fclose(f);
        }
    }

    //prepare sin and cos tables
    for (i = 0; i <= 90; i++)
        sinus[i] = line_len * sin(i*M_PI/180.0);
    for (i = 90; i <= 180; i++)
        sinus[i] = sinus[180-i];
    for (i = 0; i <= 90; i++)
        cosinus[i] = sinus[90-i];
    for (i = 90; i <= 180; i++)
        cosinus[i] = -cosinus[180-i];
    for (i = 181; i < 360; i++)
```

```
    {
        cosinus[i] = -cosinus[i-180];
        sinus[i] = -sinus[i-180];
    }

    initgraph(&gd, &gm, "");

    setcolor(current_color);

    while (kbhit()) i = getch(); // clear keybord buffer

    draw(init_seed, max_level);

    getch();
    closegraph();
}
```

The following example illustrates how to use this L-system tool to draw a particular fractal. Now that we are armed with the necessary fractal alchemy, let's create the Harter-Heightway dragon, as it is shown below. If you haven't yet figured out the algorithm by which the dragon is made, here you are:

▲ Every segment is substituted by two equal segments separated by a right-angle, at 45°.

▲ To make a proper dragon, you have to put replacing pairs of segments alternately to the right and to the left from replaced segments, as shown below

▲ Don't forget to keep a .PCX with a St. George icon in your directory.

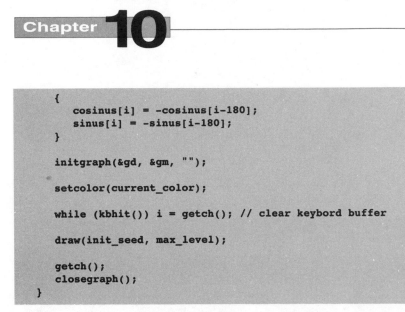

Creating the Harter-Heightway Dragon

We feel that we must mention a rule specific to drawing fractals using L-systems at this point. The replacing segment must leave the L-system in exactly the same state as the replaced one, so that they come to the same point with the same direction. This means that the total of pluses and minuses must equal 0.

In the case of our dragon, we could code the left replacing string as '-F++F-', and the right one as '+F--F+', assuming the angle is 45 degrees. But how do we get the alternating replacement? All we have to do is code the segment as 'F' if it will be substituted with a left-oriented pair, and 'G' if it will be substituted with a right-oriented one. The replacing strings for 'F' and 'G' will be '-F++G-' and '+F--G+' respectively. Now you can see that starting with the seed 'F', we will get the proper sequence of Fs and Gs.

We have included a concise library of famous fractal L-systems on the CD-ROM (config files for the program above, actually). Have a play with them and try writing your own as well.

Mandelbrot and Julia Sets

We mentioned in the introduction that fractals are closely associated with chaos. This topic is too vast to be covered within the confines of this chapter, so we'll make do with just one example of how a rather simple formula can behave unpredictably and how Mandelbrot managed to visualize this and achieve worldwide fame and glory.

The reason for discussing such a purely mathematical subject in this book is that these kind of functions have extremely gorgeous visual interpretations. We've taken a wide variety of pictures and animated them using `ColorWheel` (see Chapter 8 on animation), and we believe that for this kind of result, it is worth reading half a page of mathematics.

We'll take an iterated function $z(n)$

$$Z_{n+1} = Z_n^2 + C$$

where both z and c are complex numbers.

A complex number is a strange beast if you have never seen one before. Without going into too much detail imagine that all numbers lie on a line starting at -infinity and going to infinity. These are the real numbers that you are familiar with. Complex numbers are numbers that **don't** lie on this line! A complex number is made of two parts: a real part that lines on the line, and an imaginary part which is at right-angles to this line. Complex numbers can be thought of as a graph, where the x axis is the real component, and the y axis the imaginary. All normal numbers then lie on the x axis ($y = 0$).

Complex numbers are expressed as:

complex = real + imaginary

Mathematicians differentiate between the real and imaginary part by putting a i after the number (3 + 2i). One of the special features of imaginary numbers is that if you multiply two positive imaginary numbers, you get a negative real number. For example:

$3i \times 2i = -6$

> All these imaginary numbers stem from the solution to a problem that mathematicians faced many years ago when they tried to solve certain quadratic equations. In certain cases, the solutions to these equations resulted in the mathematicians attempting to square root a negative number. As you all know, this is not possible, but still the problem existed. To 'solve' it, they 'invented' a new rule of mathematics that said that $I^2 = -1$, thus allowing them to solve their equations. A new level of mathematics was born, and complex numbers came into the world for the first time.

Going back to our equation for the fractal, if we say that a is the real part and b the imaginary part of z, cr the real part of c and ci the imaginary, then:

$a_{n+1} = a_n^2 - b_n^2 + cr$
$b_{n+1} = 2a_nb_n + ci$

You can see that with a relatively large z_0, the function quickly approaches infinity. It was actually proved that the function approaches infinity if the magnitude of z_n becomes greater than 2. But we can find combinations of c and z_0, such as $|a| < 0.25$, $|b| < 0.25$, $|Re(c)| < 0.25$, $|Im(c)| < 0.25$, that will guarantee $|z_n| < 0.5$ and so will never grow to infinity.

> Note that the notation $|a|$ means 'the size or magnitude of a', therefore $|-3| = 3$ and $|4| = 4$.

It's not easy to predict the function's behavior between these two sets of conditions. The only reasonable way is to calculate a certain number of iterations, and so Julia sets were not studied until digital computers came into use.

Mandelbrot explored a particular situation with $z_0 = 0$ and suggested regarding c as a co-ordinate on the complex plane (or x=cr and y=ci) as 2-D coordinates. For every point in a set, he computed how many iterations it took $|z|$ to grow over 2, and marked each point with the corresponding color.

In terms of programming, to calculate a picture, we have to choose the ranges of x and y, and the width and height of the picture, by which we mean the number of pixel columns and rows. For every point on the screen we find its x and y values, and repeat iterative calculations of z until it becomes greater than 2.

> We set a limit of something like 150 iterations to avoid those instances where it never gets to 2.

Then we put a pixel on the screen. However, color selection is not so evident and deserves a special explanation, but in the meantime, take a look at the actual code.

The classes for Mandelbrot and Julia Sets are:

```
#ifndef MANDSET_H
#define MANDSET_H
typedef struct {
    int iterations;
    float mod;
} SET_POINT;

enum COLOR_SCHEME  {DETAILS, LINEAR, LOG, NONE};

//basic class for all classes, and mandelbrot set itself
class mandelbrot_set
{
public:
    double x_min,x_max,y_min,y_max,dx;
    int   screen_x,screen_y;
    int   max_it;
    SET_POINT *row;

// use colors from _col1 to _col2
    int order_col1, order_col2, order_scheme;

// to show respective part of set
    int chaos_col1, chaos_col2, chaos_scheme;
    BYTE *order_color_map; // size max_it
    BYTE chaos_color_map[256];
```

```
      mandelbrot_set(int max_it_, int screen_x_, int screen_y_,
                     float x_min_, float x_max_, float y_min_, float y_max_);
      virtual ~mandelbrot_set();
      virtual void calc_one_row(double y);
      void set_coloring(int chaos_coll_,int chaos_col2_,int chaos_scheme_,
                        int order_coll_,int order_col2_,int order_scheme_);
      void show_row(int iy);
      void calculate_set();
};

//mandelbrot set with integer arithmetic
mandelbrot_int: public mandelbrot_set
{
public:
      mandelbrot_int(int max_it_, int screen_x_, int screen_y_,
                     float x_min_, float x_max_, float y_min_, float y_max_);
      virtual void calc_one_row(double y);
};

class julia_set: public mandelbrot_set
{
public:
      float c_real,c_image;
      julia_set(int max_it_, int screen_x_, int screen_y_,
                float c_re, float c_im, float x_min_, float x_max_,
                float y_min_, float y_max_);
      virtual void calc_one_row(double y);
};

class julia_int: public julia_set
{
public:
      long c_real_long,c_image_long;
      julia_int(int max_it_, int screen_x_, int screen_y_,
                float c_re, float c_im, float x_min_, float x_max_,
                float y_min_, float y_max_);
      virtual void calc_one_row(double y);
};
#endif
```

A Mandelbrot and Julia Sets implementation:

```
#include <graphics.h>
#include <math.h>
#include <conio.h>
#include <string.h>

#include "common.h"
#include "mand_set.h"
```

```
mandelbrot_set::mandelbrot_set(int max_it_, int screen_x_, int screen_y_,
                               float x_min_, float x_max_, float y_min_,
                               float y_max_)
{
   max_it = max_it_;
   screen_x = screen_x_;
   screen_y = screen_y_;
   x_min = x_min_;
   x_max = x_max_;
   y_min = y_min_;
   y_max = y_max_;
   row = new SET_POINT[screen_x];
   order_color_map = NULL;
   set_coloring(0,0, NONE, 1,getmaxcolor(), DETAILS);
}

mandelbrot_set::~mandelbrot_set()
{
   free(row);
   if (order_color_map != NULL) free(order_color_map);
}

void mandelbrot_set::calc_one_row(double y)
{
   int iter_no,ix;
   double im, re, im_sq, re_sq, x;

   x = x_min;
   for (ix = 0; ix < screen_x; ix++,x += dx)
   {
      iter_no = 0;
      im = re = im_sq = re_sq = 0.0;
      while (im_sq + re_sq < 4.0 && iter_no++ < max_it)
      {
         im =  2*re*im + y;
         re =  re_sq - im_sq + x;
         re_sq = re*re;
         im_sq = im*im;              .
      }

      row[ix].iterations = --iter_no;
      row[ix].mod = im_sq + re_sq;
   }
}

void mandelbrot_set::set_coloring(int chaos_col1_, int chaos_col2_,
                                  int chaos_scheme_, int order_col1_,
                                  int order_col2_, int order_scheme_)
{
   int i, d;
   float f;
```

```
        chaos_col1 = chaos_col1_;
        chaos_col2 = chaos_col2_;
        chaos_scheme = chaos_scheme_;

        order_col1 =  order_col1_;
        order_col2 = order_col2_;
        order_scheme = order_scheme_;

        if (order_color_map == NULL)
            order_color_map = new BYTE[max_it];



        switch(order_scheme)
        {
           case DETAILS:
              d = order_col2-order_col1+1;
              for (i = 0; i < max_it; i++)
                 order_color_map[i] = order_col1 + i % d;
              break;

           case LINEAR:
              f = (max_it-1.0) / (order_col2-order_col1);
              for (i = 0; i < max_it; i++)
                 order_color_map[i] = order_col1 + i / f;
              break;

           case LOG:
              f = log(max_it-1)/ (order_col2-order_col1);
              for (i = 0; i < max_it; i++)
                 order_color_map[i] = order_col1 + log(i)/f;
              break;
           case NONE:
              for (i = 0; i < max_it; i++)
                 order_color_map[i] = order_col1;
        }

        switch(chaos_scheme)
        {
           case DETAILS:
              d = chaos_col2-chaos_col1+1;
              for (i = 0; i < 256; i++)
                 chaos_color_map[i] = chaos_col1 + i % d;
              break;

           case LINEAR:
              f = 255.0 / (chaos_col2-chaos_col1);
              for (i = 0; i < 256; i++)
                 chaos_color_map[i] = chaos_col1 + i / f;
              break;
```

```
        case LOG:
            f = log(255)/ (chaos_col2-chaos_col1);
            for (i = 0; i < 256; i++)
                chaos_color_map[i] = chaos_col1 + log(i+1)/f;
            break;
        case NONE:
            for (i = 0; i < 256; i++)
                chaos_color_map[i] = chaos_col1;
    }
}

void mandelbrot_set::calculate_set()
{
    int iy;
    double dy,y;

    dy = (y_max - y_min) / screen_y;
    dx = (x_max - x_min) / screen_x;

    for (iy = 0, y = y_min; iy < screen_y; iy++, y += dy)
    {
        if (kbhit()) return;
        calc_one_row(y);
        show_row(iy);
    }
}

void mandelbrot_set::show_row(int iy)
{
    int ix,col;
    for (ix = 0; ix < screen_x; ix++)
    {
        if (row[ix].iterations < max_it)
            col = order_color_map[row[ix].iterations];
        else
            col = chaos_color_map[row[ix].mod * 64];
        putpixel(ix,iy,col);
    }
}

mandelbrot_int::mandelbrot_int(int max_it_, int screen_x_, int screen_y_,
                               float x_min_, float x_max_, float y_min_,
                               float y_max_):
            mandelbrot_set(max_it_, screen_x_,  screen_y_,
                           x_min_, x_max_,  y_min_,  y_max_)
{}

void mandelbrot_int::calc_one_row(double y)
{
```

```
    int iter_no,ix;
    double x;
    long im, re, im_sq, re_sq, xl, yl;

    yl = y*0x4000000 +0x1000;
    x = x_min;

    for (ix = 0; ix < screen_x; ix++,x += dx)
    {
       xl = x * 0x4000000 + 0x1000;

       iter_no = 0;
       im = re = im_sq = re_sq = 0;
       while (im_sq + re_sq < 0x10000000 && iter_no++ < max_it)
       {
          im =  (2*re*im + yl) >> 13;        // 0x2000;
          re =  (re_sq - im_sq + xl) >> 13; // 0x2000;
          re_sq = re*re;
          im_sq = im*im;
       }
       if (iter_no >= max_it)
           iter_no = iter_no;

       row[ix].iterations = --iter_no;
       row[ix].mod = (float)(im_sq + re_sq) / 0x4000000;
    }
}

julia_set::julia_set(int max_it_, int screen_x_, int screen_y_,
                    float c_re, float c_im, float x_min_, float x_max_,
                    float y_min_, float y_max_):
         mandelbrot_set(max_it_, screen_x_,  screen_y_, x_min_, x_max_,
                         y_min_,  y_max_)
{
   c_real = c_re;
   c_image = c_im;
}

void julia_set::calc_one_row(double y)
{
   int iter_no,ix;
   double im, re, im_sq, re_sq, x;

   x = x_min;
   for (ix = 0; ix < screen_x; ix++,x += dx)
   {
      iter_no = 0;
      im = y; re = x; im_sq = im*im; re_sq = re*re;
      while (im_sq + re_sq < 4.0 && iter_no++ < max_it)
      {
          im =  2*re*im + c_real;
```

```
                re =  re_sq - im_sq + c_image;
                re_sq = re*re;
                im_sq = im*im;
            }

            row[ix].iterations = --iter_no;
            row[ix].mod = im_sq + re_sq;
    }
}


julia_int::julia_int(int max_it_, int screen_x_, int screen_y_,
                    float c_re, float c_im, float x_min_, float x_max_,
                    float y_min_, float y_max_):
            julia_set(max_it_, screen_x_,  screen_y_, c_re, c_im,
                    x_min_, x_max_,  y_min_,  y_max_)
{
    c_real_long = c_real*0x4000000 + 0x1000;
    c_image_long = c_image*0x4000000 + 0x1000;
}

void julia_int::calc_one_row(double y)
{
    int iter_no,ix;
    double x;
    long im, re, im_sq, re_sq, xl, yl;

    yl = y*0x2000+0.5;
    x = x_min;

    for (ix = 0; ix < screen_x; ix++,x += dx)
    {
        xl = x*0x2000+0.5;

        iter_no = 0;
        im = yl; re = xl;
        re_sq = re*re; im_sq = im*im;

        while (im_sq + re_sq < 0x10000000 && iter_no++ < max_it)
        {
            im =  (2*re*im + c_image_long) >> 13;      // 0x2000;
            re =  (re_sq - im_sq + c_real_long) >> 13; // 0x2000;
            re_sq = re*re;
            im_sq = im*im;

        }
        if (iter_no >= max_it)
            iter_no = iter_no;

        row[ix].iterations = --iter_no;
        row[ix].mod = (float)(im_sq + re_sq)/ 0x4000000;
    }
}
```

Precision is a very crucial aspect of iterative algorithms. The error accumulates with every step. If you want high precision calculating Mandelbrot sets, then you should use the type **long double** and increase the maximum number of iterations to 512 or more. We can't promise that it'll make the pictures better, but the program will work much slower, that's for sure. Also remember, if the number of iterations is too high it can produce the opposite effect - by striving for greater precision, you lose it due to excessive error.

But there's also an argument for using integers since, if the function actually approaches some finite value, or indeed infinity, a minor arithmetical error won't really make any difference. The error only becomes crucial near the edge of the infinity area. We tried it both ways, and it seems that if your main goal is images, then you can forget about mathematical purity. Use integer arithmetic and an iteration limit of less than 200, and you'll get good quality images. We've included two versions of the program: one with **long** and one with **double** data types. If your PC isn't equipped with a math coprocessor, then you'd better try the integer version.

Assigning colors is also a matter of choice. Mandelbrot sets look OK in 16-color video mode if you simply assign the number of iterations to the color.

> In fact, iterations 1 and 65 will give the same blue, as only 4 low-order bits of a color are used, so the picture may look like a parakeet.

Obviously, if you modify the display palette, the same picture will look different, but we normally adjust the palette to give a smooth transition from shade to shade of 7 main colors. But we still have complete freedom in the coloring, because we can always choose how to assign color numbers to pixels.

We recommend the following guidelines for selecting colors:

- The whole area is divided into two main parts: the first is where you've reached the iteration limit and the second is where the function exceeds 2.

- Sometimes you can just fill one of the parts with the background color.

- For the first part you can choose the color according to the function value at the last iteration. For the second part, you can use the number of iterations.

In both cases we see three different ways of assigning colors to numbers:

1   Detail emphasis - successive sub-ranges are assigned contrasting colors.

2   Linear coloring, where the color gradually changes in direct proportion to the increasing value.

3   The color number is proportional to the logarithm of the value.

You can magnify a fragment of a Mandelbrot set by recalculating the image for a small sub-range of x and y and see that it's not just like zooming in on a bitmap, where every pixel becomes a larger rectangle. As always with fractals, a close-up shot will reveal new elements with a similar structure. This means that you can explore deeper and deeper into the set.

But again, you have to deal with the problem of precision. Starting with a relatively small area, adjacent points are coded with the same number. If you work with type integer, this situation occurs sooner on larger area sizes, than if you work with type double. In either case this error results in a kind of pixelation effect by which we mean that distinct squares become visible, and the picture loses its fractal qualities.

If the Mandelbrot set is the mapping of the equation:

$$Z_{n+1}^2 = Z_n^2 + c$$

with the assumption that $z_0 = 0$, then a Julia set is a more general case. We fix a certain value of c and analyze the function behavior at different values of z_0. You can use the Mandelbrot set as Captain Flint's map to seek for a Julia set's treasure troves. From the visual point of view, the richest places are at the border of two areas, one where the function approaches infinity, and the other where we hit the iteration limit. Note that, whereas in the Mandelbrot set the first kind of areas are more interesting, in Julia sets we look for the latter.

And now yet another set for your collection - the Dragon set. It's the mapping of the equation:

$$Z_{n+1} = c * Z_n (1-Z_n)$$

This looks exactly like the well-known population growth equation, with the exception that in this case c and z are complex numbers.

But please don't hurry to write another fractal program, here comes a mathematical trick. Assume:

$$X' = -c * (Z - 1/2)$$

$$b = \frac{(2-c) * c}{4}$$

Now putting x as z and b as c into the Mandelbrot set equation:

$$X_{n+1} = X_n^2 + b$$

and having done all the obvious transformations we'll have the Dragon set equation:

$$Z_{n+1} = c * Z_n (1 - Z_n)$$

So you can explore the Dragon set with the same program we use for Mandelbrot and Julia sets. If you want to see the function behavior at a certain point defined by z_0 and c, you have to analyze the behavior of the Mandelbrot set equation:

$$X_{n+1} = X_n^2 + b$$

with

$$X_0 = -c * (Z_0 - 1/2)$$

$$b = \frac{(2-c) * c}{4}$$

It's not that we're too lazy to write another program (which of course we are). In fact, the program that iterates the Dragon set equation directly, works slower than the Mandelbrot one, because the expression on the innermost loop level is longer.

Fractals in Physics - DLA

The fractal boom began in the 1980s. Physicists chased fractals as keenly as entomologists chase new bugs. Fractal models were found in practically every field of physics. We bet that if you search through any recent issue of a journal on general physics, you'll find an article with the word 'fractal' in the title. Was this revolution in physics inevitable? Or was the new generation attracted by the psychedelic pictures? Or, maybe, the contemporary scientist is more familiar with computers than with mathematical analysis. It's too late to guess now - in theoretical physics, fractals are here to stay.

Here we'll discuss just one model in its simplest form - Diffusion Limited Aggregation (DLA). DLA is probably the best-known model of fractal growth. Imagine the molecules of a substance floating freely in a solution. Somewhere in the solution, the dissolved substance begins to come together in a cluster. When free molecules run into the cluster, they cling to it and become part of it, so it grows.

A formal model, more suited to programming, would look something like this: the growing clusters are placed over a square lattice, each molecule sitting on a node, taking a two-dimensional model to make life simpler. A free particle wanders randomly from node to node until it gets to a node connected to the cluster, where it gets caught. The model then sets off a new roaming particle.

In our example program, we discarded the random wandering because it takes too long for the particles to stick to the cluster, especially in its 'baby' phase. We replaced it with 'random rain' - a new particle is started at a random speed and bounces off the borders of the model space until it sticks to the cluster. We have also assumed that the cluster begins to grow from one whole row of cells, and not one single cell, again for illustrative purposes:

```
/* This program demonstrates model of diffusion limited aggregation */

#include <conio.h>
#include <values.h>
#include <stdlib.h>
#include <math.h>
#include <graphics.h>
#include "common.h"

const int max_x = 300; // area width
const int max_y = 450; // area height

int min_neighby = max_y; // the first empty row above the cluster

BOOL *neighb[max_y+2]; // working area : x - 1..max_x; y - 1..max_y
                       // indexes 0,max+1 - dummy

// This procedure models the behaviour of a particle
void one_particle(int &x, int &y)
{
    float vx, vy, // velocity components
          tx, ty, // time in which the particle gets to
                  // the adjacent cell
          t,      // min of tx and ty
```

```
            angle,  // at which a particle begins its movement
            fx, fy; // precise coordinates
    int  i, j,
         inc_x; // horizontal direction (-1 or +1)

    angle =  (random(359)/2+0.25) * (M_PI/180.0);
// angle ranges from 0 to pi (excluding the limits), but can't be pi/2
// (just to avoid division by zero)

    vx = cos(angle);
    vy = sin(angle);

    x = random(max_x-2)+1; // initial coordinates
    fx = x;

// we start the particle from the first empty row
    y = min_neighby-1; fy = y;

    inc_x = (vx > 0) ? 1 : -1;

    while(!neighb[y][x]) // while cluster not found
    {
       if (inc_x > 0)
          tx = (x+1-fx) / vx;
       else
          tx = -(fx - x) / vx;
       ty = (y+1-fy) / vy;

       if (tx > ty)
       {
          y++;
          t = ty;
       }
       else
       {
          x += inc_x;
          t = tx;
       }

// We can't simply write x = fx, or x = round(fx),
// so we increment (x,y) and (fx,fy) independent.

       fy += t*vy;
       fx += t*vx;

       if (x < 1) //fx = 1; bounce from the left border
       {
          vx = - vx;
          inc_x = 1;
          x = 1;
       }
```

```
            else if (x > max_x) // fx = max_x+1 bounce from the right border
            {
                vx = - vx;
                inc_x = - 1;
                x = max_x;
            }
        }

    // particle is just near the cluster
    // add it to the cluster and mark its neighbours
        for (i = -1; i <= 1; i++)
            for (j = -1; j <= 1; j++)
                neighb[y+i][x+j] = TRUE;

        if (y-1 < min_neighby)
            min_neighby = y - 1;
    // we've reserved dummy columns 0 and max_x+1, so now bravely fill
    // array elements not checking index range
    }

void main()
{
    int gd, gm;
    int i, x, y;
    long count;
    struct palettetype pal;

    gd = VGA;
    gm = VGAHI;
    initgraph(&gd, &gm, "c:\bcpp\bgi");

    randomize();
    for (i = 0; i < max_y+2; i++)
    {
        neighb[i] = new BOOL[max_x+2];
        if (neighb[i]==NULL)  return;
        if (i < max_y)
            memset(neighb[i], 0, max_x+2);
        else
            memset(neighb[i], 0xFF, max_x+2);
    }

    getpalette(&pal);
    setrgbpalette(pal.colors[0], 0, 30, 50); //water
    for (i=1;  i<7;  i++)
        setrgbpalette(pal.colors[i], 63, (7-i)*5, (7-i)*5);
    for (i=7; i<16; i++)
        setrgbpalette(pal.colors[i], 63, (i-7)*5, (i-7)*5);

    do
    {
```

```
        one_particle(x,y);
        count++;
        putpixel(100+x, y, (count / max_y) % 15+1);
    } while (min_neighby >= 2);
    getch();
    closegraph;
}
```

This code needs some explanation. For the lattice we declared a two-dimensional binary array called **neighb**, the elements of which have the value 1 if any of the adjacent cells belong to the growing cluster, and the value 0 if they don't. When the particle sticks to the cluster, we assign 1 to all the cells in the neighborhood, so we don't have to check all the neighbors while the particle moves.

To move the particle to every next cell, we estimate whether it will reach the horizontal or vertical neighbor first. Then we move it to the point on the border of this neighbor, and appropriately increment precise co-ordinates **fx** and **fy**, which have type float. We also increment **x** and **y**, which are indexes in the array **neighb**.

When the particle gets to a border of the area, we change the x-component of velocity to the opposite:

```
vx = -vx
```

With these basic rules, you can see what we can grow in the following figure. Isn't it just like a coral?

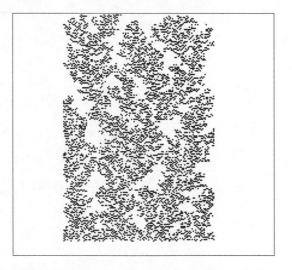

Diffusion Limited Aggregation Grows Corals

348

We've also included a version with integer arithmetic on the accompanying CD-ROM, which works faster than the floating-point version, even if you have a coprocessor. However, the algorithm for tracing the grid nodes is more complex, so what we've provided here is just the illustrative floating-point version.

Fractal Landscapes

In the introduction to this chapter we told you that fractals can be found everywhere in nature, and yet the pictures we've drawn so far, although maybe curious and attractive, haven't had a thing to do with the real world. In this section, we'll describe some techniques which can be used to create realistic scenes or landscapes.

Midpoint Displacement

Midpoint displacement, an efficient and simple method of generating fractal landscapes, was developed and popularized at the beginning of the 1980s by Fournier, Fussell, and Carpenter. The essence of this method can be explained as follows:

You take a triangle and shift the middle points of each side horizontally and vertically a short, random distance, proportional to the size of the side. This gives you four triangles, to which you apply the same procedure.

In this case, we can't get away with a simple recursive routine, because, as you can see in the figure, some sides belong to two triangles and must be distorted accordingly.

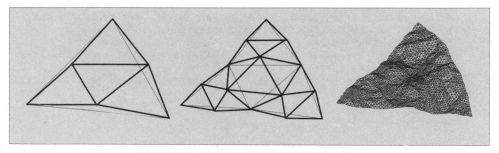

Midpoint Displacement Method

The code for drawing a mountain by midpoint displacement is as follows:

```c
/*
This procedure draws the outline of a mountain using
the midpoint displacement method.
*/
#include "common.h"
#include <stdlib.h>
#include <graphics.h>


const WORD powers2[16] = {1, 2, 4, 8, 16, 32, 64, 128, 256, 512,
                          1024, 2048, 4096, 8192, 16384, 32768};

const BYTE start_level = 6;
float along_displacement = 0.12; // Along the line
float perp_displacement = 0.12;  // Perpendicular to the line

POINT point_, p1, p2;
int dx, dy;
long ad, pd, //along_displacement  and perp_displacement scaled by 256
     rn;

// This procedure splits a line in two and calls itself twice passing
// the coordinates of each segment. The coordinates of the line are
// points[start] and points[finish].
// On exit from the procedure all points[] between start and finish
// will be filled with coordinates of ends of the intermediate segments.
void divide_line(BYTE level, POINT* points, int start, int finish)
{
   int pos;

   p1 = points[start];
   p2 = points[finish];

   dx = p2.x - p1.x;
   dy = p2.y - p1.y;

// We'll use integer arithmetics. ad,pd, and rn are scaled by 256 and
// so result is divided by 256*256 via shift right.
   rn = random(256) - 128;
   point_.x = p1.x + (dx+1)/2 + (rn * (ad*abs(dx) + pd*abs(dy)) >> 16);
   rn = random(256) - 128;
   point_.y = p1.y + (dy+1)/2 + (rn * (ad*abs(dy) + pd*abs(dx)) >> 16);

   pos = (start + finish) / 2;
   points[pos] = point_;

   if (level > 1) // go deeper
   {
```

```
        divide_line(level-1, points, start, pos);
        divide_line(level-1, points, pos, finish);
   }
}


POINT pp1, pp2, pp3;

// Given the coordinates of a triangle apexes pp1, pp2, and pp3,
// this routine distorts its sides and draws the resulting broken
// lines on the screen. This is merely a service procedure and
// doesn't help understanding the algorithm.
void make_sides(BYTE level, int slen, POINT* &s1, POINT* &s2, POINT* &s3)
{
   int i;
   s1 = new POINT[slen+1];
   s2 = new POINT[slen+1];
   s3 = new POINT[slen+1];

   s1[0] = pp1;    s1[slen] = pp3;
   s2[0] = pp3;    s2[slen] = pp2;
   s3[0] = pp2;    s3[slen] = pp1;

   if (level > 1)
   {
      divide_line(level-1, s1, 0, slen);
      divide_line(level-1, s2, 0, slen);
      divide_line(level-1, s3, 0, slen);
   }
   drawpoly(slen+1, (int  *)s1);
   drawpoly(slen+1, (int  *)s2);
   drawpoly(slen+1, (int  *)s3);
}

// This is the main routine that performs the midpoint displacement.
// It accepts three sides of a triangle, creates arrays for three sides
// of the inner triangle and calls itself to process the four created
// triangles.
void triangle(BYTE level, POINT* side1, POINT* side2, POINT* side3)
{
   POINT *s1, *s2, *s3;
   int slen;

   slen = powers2[level-1];
   pp1 = side1[slen];
   pp2 = side2[slen];
   pp3 = side3[slen];


   make_sides(level, slen, s1, s2, s3); // allocates s1, s2, and s3
                                        //do not forget to kill
```

```
    if (level > 1)
    {
        triangle(level-1, side1+slen, side2, s3);
        triangle(level-1, side2+slen, side3, s2);
        triangle(level-1, side1, s1, side3+slen);
        triangle(level-1, s1, s2, s3);   //internal triangle
    }

    delete s1;
    delete s2;
    delete s3;
}

int gd, gm;

void main()
{
    POINT *s1, *s2, *s3;
    int len;

    gd = VGA;
    gm = VGAHI;
    initgraph(&gd, &gm, "c:\bcpp\bgi");

    randomize();
    ad = 0.5 + along_displacement * 256;
    pd = 0.5 + perp_displacement * 256;

    pp1.x = 50; pp1.y = 400;
    pp3.x = 350; pp3.y = 100;
    pp2.x = 550; pp2.y = 450;

    len = powers2[start_level];

    make_sides(start_level+1, len, s1, s2, s3);
    triangle(start_level, s1, s2, s3); //internal

    delete s1;
    delete s2;
    delete s3;
}
```

As you can see from the program, we solve the problem in a sort of straight-forward way. When a new line appears, we distort it repeatedly, down to the specified recursion level, and remember all the endpoints of the segments. The procedure **triangle()** accepts these distorted sides and doesn't change them. In this way, the common sides of adjacent triangles are distorted differently. The segment co-ordinate arrays are kept in the memory only as long as they are needed, so the program doesn't eat up too much of the system's resources: about $3*2^{N+2}$ points, where N is the number of recursion levels.

On the CD-ROM, we've included a more complex program which draws a colored mountain. Maybe it's even too complicated, but we tried to make our model realistic.

We've distinguished 6 types of landscape elements: rock, ice, snow, stones, grass, and forest, each of which has its own color gamut or rather the probability of meeting a particular color. At a certain level of detail, a triangle is randomly assigned one of these six types, the probability depending on the triangle height from the foot of the mountain. Later, when the triangle is divided, they can change their type, but normally they keep the type inherited from the parent triangle. This means that relatively large areas contain something specific (e.g. rocks or grass), but they can also include small pieces of different types, just like the real thing! We select the colors of the elementary triangles from a color set corresponding to each type using a random function.

Clouds - True 2-3D Fractal Generation

Midpoint displacement produces landscapes that could be described as the 'poor man's' alternative. They look agreeable and are generated quite fast, but that's about all. The picture remains flat. We can't change the light source or fly around a rock. A real landscape is not a picture on the screen, but a function of two variables. It has a dimension slightly greater than 2.

All the methods of generating fractals with dimensions between 2 and 3, or in other words, landscapes, as well as those with dimensions between 3 and 4, such as the distribution of water vapor, are based on works by Mandelbrot and Richard F. Voss. Here we'll show you one of the algorithms, a simple but powerful one called **successive random additions**.

Imagine we have a square area, on which we calculate the function $z(x,y)$. Initially z is only defined in the corners. We add a normal Gaussian random number with mean square variation v, initially equaling 1, to these four values at the corners of the square. The four endpoints are then considered as nodes of the calculation grid. At every iteration, we divide the grid step by 2, or in other words, we find the midpoint between each pair of nodes. Then we apply the function $z(x,y)$ to these new points before dividing v by 2^H and the process is repeated, using all nodes of the grid, both old and new, until we reach the required resolution.

Here H is the control parameter, ranging from 0 to 1, that determines what kind of picture you'll get. The fractal dimension is:

3 - H

so with H close to 1 you'll get a smooth surface, while H being closer to 0 produces a good simulation of a city after a massive bomb attack. Try experimenting with the following program to produce these effects:

```
#define  MAXSIDE  1024

float hurst  = 0.7; // The control parameter H
                    // named so in the honor of H.E. Hurst

int current_side = 256; // Array size

float *map[MAXSIDE+1];

// The essential routine that performs successive random additions.
void  div_map()
{
    double sigma_coef;
    BOOL odd_line;
    int x,y,side,side2,points;
    float *up_row,*down_row,*cur_row;
    float sigma;

    sigma_coef = exp(hurst*log(0.5 ));

    side = current_side;
    sigma = 1;

    do
    {
// add randoms to all existed points
        for (y = 0; y <= current_side; y += side)
        {
            cur_row = map[y];
            for (x = 0; x <= current_side; x += side)
                cur_row[x] +=  norm_random(sigma);
        }

        side2 = side/2;

        // calculate new values for square's centers
        for (y = side2; y <= current_side; y += side)
        {
```

```
        cur_row = map[y];
        up_row = map[y-side2];
        down_row = map[y+side2];
        for (x = side2; x <= current_side; x += side)
            cur_row[x] = 0.25*(up_row[x-side2] + up_row[x+side2] +
                          down_row[x-side2] + down_row[x+side2]);
    }


    //calculate middles of rect. sides

    for (y = 0, odd_line = FALSE; y <= current_side;
         y += side2, odd_line = !odd_line)
    {
      cur_row = map[y];
      if (y == 0)
        up_row = map[side2];
      else
        up_row = map[y-side2];

      if (y == current_side)
        down_row = map[current_side-side2];
      else
        down_row = map[y+side2];

      if (odd_line)
      {
        cur_row[0] = 0.25*(up_row[0] + down_row[0]+ cur_row[side2]*2);
        cur_row[current_side] = 0.25*(up_row[current_side]
                                + down_row[current_side]
                                + cur_row[current_side-side2]*2);
        x = side;
      }
      else
        x = side2;


      while (x < current_side)
      {
        cur_row[x] = 0.25*(up_row[x] + down_row[x]
                      + cur_row[x+side2] + cur_row[x-side2]);
        x += side;
      }
    }

  side = side2;
  sigma *= sigma_coef;
}
while (side > 1);
```

```
    //last time add randoms
    for (y = 0; y <= current_side; y+= side)
    {
        cur_row = map[y];
        for (x = 0; x <= current_side; x+= side)
            cur_row[x] +=  norm_random(sigma);
    }
}
```

By trying different values of **Hurst**, you can vary the character of the images. Another advantage of this method is that you can start the process from a certain grid resolution by specifying initial values for more than 4 points in the area. For example, fractalize an image, generated by a 3-D function of traditional mathematics, or make a rough draft of a relief and let SRA fill in the details.

However, this method has one disadvantage, in that we can't make it a recursive procedure, and so have to keep a big array of all the points in the memory.

Anyway, a function isn't a landscape yet. The problem now is to show what we have computed. In the demo program **CLOUDS.CPP**, included on the CD-ROM, we just show the resulting values as corresponding color. The technique works all right for clouds, but never for landscapes. In Chapter 14, we'll discuss the creation of 3-D images.

Summary

As Mandelbrot wrote, "clouds are not spheres, mountains are not cones, coastlines are not circles, and bark is not smooth, nor does lightening travel in a straight line". We must add that merely stochastic isn't yet realistic; a single repeated note is not always music, though it is hardly ever just noise. Fractals are able to reach this fine balance between the dull monotonous shapes of Euclidean geometry and absolute chaos, the balance inherent in real nature and appealing art.

In this chapter we took a ride through various realms of the dreamy world of fractals, picking up magic devices along the way, which we hope you will enjoy long after you're back from the trip.

Digital Image Processing

When we planned this book, we wanted to avoid the pitfall of covering a very large subject in a few pages. We feel that we have achieved this in all the chapters until now. Image processing is a huge subject area, which some universities spend three years teaching, just to cover the basics. However, we feel that any book on bitmapped graphics, would be incomplete without some kind of treatment of this subject.

We should give you one word of warning. Digital image processing (DIP) has its feet firmly entrenched in the world of mathematics, and not always simple maths at that. But we'll do our best to protect you as much as possible...

Chapter Contents

In this chapter, we will cover:

- DIP, What Is It? and Do We Need It?
- Point Operations
- Window Operations
- Noise Reduction, Smoothing and Low-Pass Filtering
- Edge Detection, Contrasting and High-Pass Filtering
- Band-Pass Filtering
- Some DIP Techniques, Just For Fun

DIP, What Is It? and Do We Need It?

Where might you meet DIP techniques and why would you use them? Does it ever take place in real life? The fact is, image processing takes place:

▲ When you use your camera or when a Photo CD is prepared for you.

▲ When you are seen through an X-ray tomograph or when data is obtained from a satellite for the weather forecast.

▲ When the illustrations for this book were prepared.

All of these involve some sort of image processing, and as you can see, it happens rather often.

Moreover, image processing is not a one-step procedure. We can easily distinguish several stages that are usually performed in an established sequence, and so we can draw up a kind of flowchart to point out the different image processing techniques:

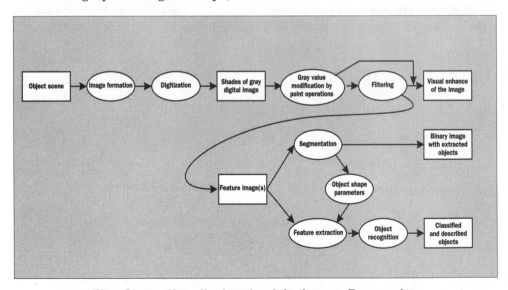

The Steps Usually Involved in Image Processing

As you can see the whole process can be quite long, so what is the point of image processing? You can use DIP techniques to:

▲ Enhance (adapt) an image for human vision. By the way, it often happens that making the image look better involves some loss of information.

▲ Identify objects, trace their motion or reconstruct a 3D scene, for further computer aided analysis.

▲ Prepare images for another type of medium, say for printing.

Maybe we had better arrange this chapter according to the reasons DIP techniques are used, and call the subsections something like - 'DIP for Humans', 'DIP for Machines', 'DIP for Media...'. However, very similar techniques can be used successfully both for enhancing the contrast of an X-ray image for further visual diagnostics, and for binarization in OCR (Optical Character Recognition) systems. That's why we have to look for a more creative classification.

First we are going to distinguish the DIP techniques which work with each separate pixel. Then we'll consider the ones that look at the whole neighborhood. Finally, we'll end up with a kind of tree of knowledge, showing the hierarchical structure of DIP technology, as shown below. Together we'll climb this tree as high as we can. We'll give a brief overview of the branches we don't reach in the summary.

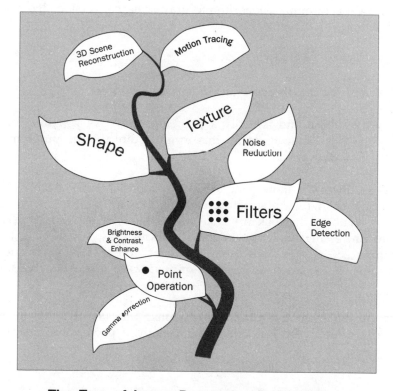

The Tree of Image Processing Technology

Point Operations

An image is composed of pixels, each holding an amount of information, and in some cases this information can be processed separately. We'll call this category of DIP techniques **Point Operations**. This term generally means that none of the adjacent pixels are involved in calculations. This is what we mentioned in the previous chapter as changing pixel colors according to the 'global rule'. So the question is, what is the rule and how does it work?

Counting Pixels - Histogram

You can create the rule as a mathematical formula. Here is an example of such a formula. In previous chapters we mentioned the term **gamma correction** which deals with the logarithmic characteristic of human visual perception. Suppose you scan a picture with a device based on the CCD (charge coupled device) sensor. You can think of it as if each element of the sensor counts the photons falling on it. So the output should be linear, as the more photons are absorbed, the higher the charge. Suppose you'd like to adapt this image for your eyes by performing a logarithmic gray scale conversion. It's easy, and it looks something like this:

$$I_{new} = 25.5 \times Log(I_{old} + 1)$$

where I_{new} and I_{old} are the new and old pixel color value.

This is pretty simple and is really a point operation, as you treat each pixel separately. If you decide to apply this formula directly, the program will work slowly, but it will work.

Nevertheless, there's a more general way to represent this global rule for the point operations. It uses a structure called a look-up table. You can pass a pixel color value to the look up table and obtain the new color value at once. If you are processing an image in 256 shades of gray, you need a look up table of only 256 entries. Sometimes, however, you may need a much larger look up table, if for instance, pixel co-ordinates are taken into consideration as well.

The look up table can make point operations quite fast, but the next question is how do we make the look up table? Usually, a pixel value distribution, in the form of a **histogram**, is used as the informational basis for point operation. We've already met histograms, so we'll omit the details.

Although it's hardly ever directly mentioned, most of the traditional DIP techniques rely on the image being represented in shades of gray. For some DIP algorithms, adding color just means three passes instead of one. There are, however, some tasks that become fundamentally more complicated for color images (remember quantization?). The formation and estimation of the histogram belong to this class. Anyway, we're not going to start a detailed discussion of colored DIP - there's enough to do even without colors. After all, in most cases it's possible to use the same techniques by processing each color component separately.

Brightness and Contrast

Brightness and contrast enhancement are the most frequently used point operations. They adapt images for our eyes, so you may think it's just a question of comfort, and indeed it is. However, these things are essential in helping you recognize and identify objects. That's why each and every DIP software package provides facilities for manually controlling the brightness and contrast.

Brightness is controlled in the simplest way you can think of - just by increasing or decreasing the color value of every pixel by a constant value. You can let the user specify a particular level or calculate it yourself, the task doesn't become more complicated.

In contrast, contrast improvement (sorry, got a bit carried away with our contrasts there) seems to be the subject of infinite studies by DIP researchers, and you'll meet it on several occasions throughout this chapter. However, in this section, we'll just show you the techniques which belong to the class of point operations.

There are various methods based on histogram modification. The following code fragment implements the three point technique, which is often used for manual contrast control. The following diagram shows the result of applying the method to the histogram of an image to increase the contrast. As you can see, the histogram gets spread out, and at the same time the peaks of brightness are reduced and so the total brightness of the image as a whole is unchanged.

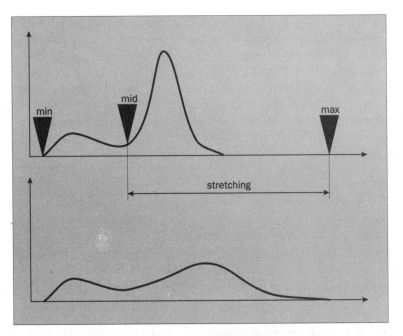

Three Point Manual Contrast Control

```
// calculate the Look Up Table for manual contrast control

void contrast(BYTE *table, int min, int mid, int max, int newmin,
              int newmax)
{
    int i,v;
    for (i = 0; i < min; i++)
        table[i] = max(0,newmin);
    for (i = 0; i < mid-min; i++)
    {
        v = newmin + ((mid - newmin)*(long)i) / (mid - min);
        table[i+min] = max(0,v);
    }
    for (i = 0; i < max-mid; i++)
    {
        v = mid + ((newmax - mid)*(long)i) / (max - mid);
        table[i+mid] = min(255,v);
    }
    for (i = max; i < 256; i++)
        table[i] = min(255,newmax);
}
```

Equalization

Equalization of a histogram seems a more consistent and theoretically grounded way to enhance contrast. What do we mean by that? The problem of poor image contrast can be formulated as the uneven density of pixels on different quantization levels. You can remap the levels so that they hold approximately the same number of pixels. This operation will almost certainly improve the contrast. Sounds pretty easy, but there is a pitfall.

Remapping simply means that you 'glue' some poorly inhabited levels into one. However, you can't divide an 'overcrowded' level into two, so the total number of levels decreases. Certainly if you initially had, say, a 10-bit image (1024 levels) and you squeezed it by equalization into 255 shades of gray, the result would be fine. If, however, you start with 255 levels, you may end up with 50-70 equalized ones, and the results of such a contrast enhancement can sometimes look disappointing. See the figure below for details.

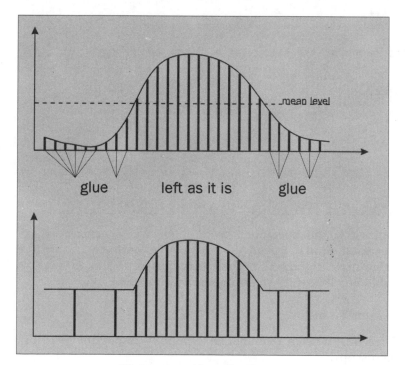

Histogram Equalization

The following code fragment squeezes the set of quantization levels called **input_levels** into **output_levels** by equalization. If it can't find output levels, it sets them uniformly within **output_levels** space:

```
void optimal_contrast(long hist[], int input_levels, BYTE table[],
                      int output_levels)
{
   int i,
       j, // current cell
       k; // count of skipped  places in output range

   long sum = 0,   // sum of all cells of histogram
        sum2 = 0; // sum of currently re-defined cells

   for (i = 0; i < input_levels; i++)
      sum += hist[i];
   j = 0;   k = 0;
   for (i = 0; i < output_levels; i++)
   {
      k++;
      while (sum2 < sum*(i+1)/output_levels)
      {
// try to shift into the center of "free space"
         if (j > 0)
             table[j-1] += (k+1) >> 1;

         table[j] = i;
         sum2 += hist[j++];
         k = 0;
      }
   }
}
```

Correction of Irregular Illumination

The examples of point operations given above were **homogeneous,** or in other words, the result didn't depend on the pixel co-ordinates. Sometimes, however, a pixel value must change according to its position. This means, by the way, a look-up table equal to the whole image.

Real life examples include:

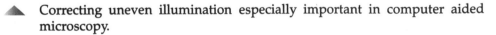 Correcting uneven illumination especially important in computer aided microscopy.

Suppression of optical path induced noise (dust on the sensor's glass window or uneven sensitivity of sensor elements).

You can treat both problems at the same time if you can obtain a **background image** (the picture without any object). Then the recipe is simple: you should apply the following formula to each pixel in your image:

$$I_{cor} = \frac{I_{ini}}{I_{back}}$$

where I_{cor}, I_{ini}, I_{back} are pixel values in the corrected, initial and background images respectively.

Window Operations

Now we are going to go further in our exploration of DIP techniques. In this section, we'll show you the next phase of the DIP sequence in all its complexity. We'll call it **window operations**. The difference between these and point operations is that when you process a pixel by a window operation, you always take into account the neighborhood, or in other words, the values of adjacent pixels. Is this really important? It seems that it is. After all, what you see on the PC screen is not the color value of individual pixels but rather the spatial relationship between pixels.

There are many window operations, and in fact, most DIP techniques use the window representation. Different window operations differ in the dimensions of the neighborhood and the particular way the pixels are processed within it. There are two completely different approaches:

▲ Digital Convolutions

▲ Rank Sequences

Convolution

Suppose you have an odd-sized filter mask, say a 2n+1 × 2n+1 matrix. Digital convolutions is a simple mathematical operation to calculate the value of a pixel:

$$I_{i,j}^{new} = \sum_{k=-n,m=-n}^{n,n} (F_{k,m} \times I_{i+k,j+m}^{old})$$

where $F_{k,m}$ are the components of the filter mask.

So to get each pixel value you simply place the filter mask on a pixel, multiply the values of all covered pixels by the corresponding weight in the mask and sum the multiplications.

> The mask does not have to be square, in fact, it can even be unidimensional, or in other words, just one row or one column.

This operation is performed for every pixel of an image. There is a problem with the pixels near to the image borders, because for those pixels, some part of the window falls outside the image. In practice, the problem is solved by adding as many duplicates of the border rows and columns as is needed to fit the mask size.

Another thing to note is that you can't perform convolution 'in place' by which we mean writing the results of the calculations directly to the image. The reason is obvious - the pixels from, for example row n, are required for the calculation of row n+1. That's why you have to preserve a part of the image in a special buffer. However, there is a class of filters called recursive, that are based on using the values of already processed pixels in the calculations.

Rank Sequences

The idea behind rank sequences is different. It works like this: instead of calculating something, you construct, for each current pixel, a sorted sequence of the pixel values within the window. The current pixel value is estimated according to this sequence.

What are window operations usually used for? The two most frequent applications are:

 Noise reduction (the images always have some noise, either "white" or Gaussian).

 Edge detection (on the one hand, it's a kind of contrast enhancing technique, on the other, the first step in image segmentation, which, in its turn, precedes the object identification).

> The **edges** are the narrow areas in the picture where brightness changes rapidly.

Noise reduction may also be referred to as **low-pass** filtering, and edge detection as **high-pass** filtering. In this subsection we'll construct something similar to the graphic equalizer you see on your stereo set - but for pictures, not for sound. Isn't the analogy great? It may seem so, but it's not really that analogous.

Certainly high-, low-, and even the term filtering are inherited from radio engineering. However, there is a difference. Sound is composed of real waves which have frequencies. But there are no high or low 'spatial waves' in your images, unless of course, you have a photo of the ocean.

Nevertheless, the temptation to exploit this poor analogy was too great. The exploration, consideration and comparison of different filtering techniques will be easier to understand in terms of frequencies. I hope you remember the description of JPEG and DCT. The main idea remains the same (as for JPEG); you can easily see what's happening with your image by only considering frequency co-ordinates. In other words, it lets you treat spatial modes with different frequencies separately. These mysterious spatial modes are simply the patterns with a characteristic size.

In this section we will use the term 'frequencies'. High frequencies stand for edges and noise. 2D Fourier transformation is a great DIP tool. For example, you can predict how the filter will transform your whole image by studying how it affects different spatial frequencies. However, the mathematical basis, although not too complicated, is beyond this book.

At this point, we face quite a dilemma, so let's make a deal. We'll try to explain everything in words and if you feel a need for mathematical exactness, you'll have to find it in special literature. We suggest 'Digital Image Processing' by Dr. Bernd Jahne.

Later in this section, we'll show you some traditional filtering techniques and also provide a short overview of some recent research in this field, together with some sample images. But first some details of implementation.

OOPed Implementation of the Filters

This subsection is only the implementation vocabulary, so it'll only be useful if you decide to use our sources for image filtering in your applications. Otherwise, just have a look at the figure below as it gives you an idea of the window operations in their most compact form, and skip the details.

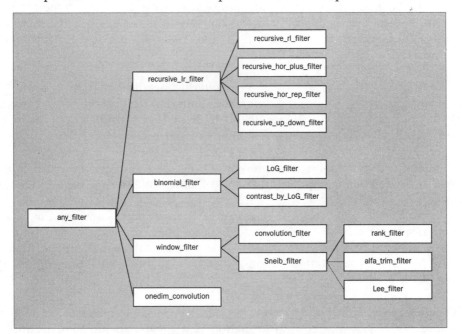

The Hierarchy of the Filter Objects

```
class any_filter
{
public:
   int width, height;
   int in_line_num, out_line_num;

   any_filter(int width_,int height_);
   virtual ~any_filter() {};

// returns TRUE if output_line was constructed,
// if FALSE then output_line is undefined
   virtual BOOL one_row(BYTE *input_line, BYTE *output_line)
   {
      return TRUE;
   }
};
```

```
// left to right
class recursive_lr_filter : public any_filter
{
protected:
   int p_shift, p1, p2;
// p = 2 power p_shift,  and p1 = p-1, p2 = p/2
public:
   recursive_lr_filter(int width_,int power);
   virtual BOOL one_row(BYTE *input_line, BYTE *output_line);
};

//... Here should have been several incarnations of recursive
// filters, not too different in nature, so I omit them ...

// left to right plus right to left (add transition functions)
class recursive_hor_plus_filter : public recursive_lr_filter
{
public:
   recursive_hor_plus_filter(int width_,int power):
      recursive_lr_filter(width_,power) {};
   virtual BOOL one_row(BYTE *input_line, BYTE *output_line);
};

class window_filter : public any_filter
{
protected:
   BYTE **  buffer;
   int line_len;
   int filter_square;
   void accept_line(BYTE *input_line);
// formal
   virtual void process_line(BYTE *output_line) {};
public:
   int filter_wid,filter_hei;

   window_filter(int width_,int height_, int half_wid_, int half_hei_);
   virtual ~window_filter();
   virtual BOOL one_row(BYTE *input_line, BYTE *output_line);
// shows line from buffer
   BYTE *input_line(int line_no);
};

#define tmptype long

// use long if filter coefficients are large enough
// You MUST use long if you use binomial filters with size more
// than 7

// If you manage to decompose your 2-D convolution mask in two
// 1-D (horizontal and vertical), it'll work much faster
```

369

```
// (2*N + 1 instead N*N, where N is the dimension of filter
// mask).
// If so happens you may find the following object useful.

class onedim_convolution : public any_filter
{
protected:
   int filter_wid;
   int *filter;
   BYTE *tmp;
// filter elements are scaled by it
   int scale_factor;
// scale_factor/2 + background*scale
   int s0;
public:
// background - useful for edge detecting filters
   onedim_convolution(int width_,int half_filter_size_, int *filter_,
                    tmptype scale_factor_,int  background);
   virtual ~onedim_convolution();
// returns true always
   virtual BOOL one_row(BYTE *input_line, BYTE *output_line);
};

class convolution_filter: public window_filter
{
protected:
// it's actually a matrix [filter_size , filter_size]
   int *filter;
// filter elements are scaled by it
   tmptype scale_factor;
// scale_factor/2 + background*scale
   tmptype s0;
   virtual void process_line(BYTE *output_line);
public:
// background - useful for edge detecting filters
   convolution_filter(int width_,int height_, int half_filter_wid_,
                    int half_filter_hei_, int *filter_,
                    tmptype scale_factor_, int background);
   virtual ~convolution_filter();
};

class binomial_filter: public any_filter
{
protected:
   convolution_filter *vertical;
   onedim_convolution *horizontal;
   BYTE *tmp;
public:
   binomial_filter(int width_, int height_, int half_size);
```

```
    virtual ~binomial_filter();
    virtual BOOL one_row(BYTE *input_line, BYTE *output_line);
};

class LoG_filter : public binomial_filter
{
protected:
    int background, shift;
public:
    LoG_filter(int width_, int height_, int half_size,
               int background_, int shift_);
    virtual BOOL one_row(BYTE *input_line, BYTE *output_line);
};

class contrast_by_LoG_filter : public binomial_filter
{
    int beta;
public:
    contrast_by_LoG_filter(int width_, int height_, int half_size,
         int beta_): binomial_filter(width_, height_, half_size)
    {
       beta = beta_;
    };
    virtual BOOL one_row(BYTE *input_line, BYTE *output_line);
};


/////////////// Rank Filters ///////////////////////////

class Sneib_filter: public window_filter
{
protected:
    BYTE *Sneib,              // pixel's S neighborhood
         *neib_last_line,     // pointer to new subcolumn added to
                              // neighborhood
         *neib_first_line,    // pointer to first subcolumn of current
                              // neighborhood
         *current;            // pointer to current point

    int *sorted,  // pixel's sorted S neighborhood
        *mediana; // array [filter_hei+1][filter_wid], lines are subcolumns
                  // of input array

// calculate one value by S and, possibly, some values of previous points
    virtual void process_line(BYTE *output_line);
// here median filter implemented
    virtual int process_pixel()
    {
```

```
          return(*mediana);
       }
// calculate one value by S
    virtual int first_pixel()
    {
          return(*mediana);
    }
public:
    BOOL needsort;
    Sneib_filter(int width_, int height_, int half_filter_size_,
                  BOOL sort);
    virtual ~Sneib_filter();
};
```

Note the simple but powerful feature of the **Sneib_filter** implementation. When you move the filter across the image, after each step, there are pixels which enter the **s**-neighborhood and those that leave it. If you manage to implement **process_** procedures so that they don't need to recalculate anything for the pixels that remain within the **s**-neighborhood, the filter will work much faster, 2*N + 1 instead of N*N, where N is the size of the filter mask.

```
class rank_filter: public Sneib_filter
{
    int hist[256];
    virtual int process_pixel();
    virtual int first_pixel();
public:
    rank_filter(int width_, int height_, int half_filter_size_);
};

class Alpha_trim_filter: public Sneib_filter
{
    int skip_points, use_points;
    int s0;     // use_points/2
    virtual int process_pixel();
    virtual int first_pixel() {return process_pixel();};
public:
    Alpha_trim_filter(int width_, int height_, int half_filter_size_,
                      float Alpha);
};

// The following filtering techniques,
// usually called Lee's local statistics, is just a bonus.
// It's a smoothing filter based on the estimation of
// statistical properties of noise.

class Lee_filter: public Sneib_filter
{
    int noise, scale;
```

```
    // sum of the squares of pixels values
       long sum,sq_sum;
    // calculates one value by S, sum and sq_sum
       virtual int process_pixel();
    // calculates one value by S
       virtual int first_pixel();

    public:
       Lee_filter(int width_,int height_,int half_filter_size_,int noise_);
    };
```

We've given this whole structure because we think it will help you understand the following subsections on the one hand, and on the other hand because we like its logic. We're sure there must be something similar to this somewhere, but we've yet to see it.

Noise Reduction, Smoothing and Low-Pass Filtering

One of the most useful filters you can apply to an image is a low-pass filter. This reduces the higher frequencies in the image, or in other words, smoothes the edges in the image. If you recall back in Chapter 5, we discussed anti-aliasing primitives to alleviate the problem of pixelation. One way to do this, is to use a low-pass filter on the image.

Another popular use for a low-pass filter is to remove the problem of noise in the image.

White Noise Reduction, Median Filter

First, what is 'white' noise? It's when the values of some pixels are wrong and don't correlate with the image, in fact they don't correlate with anything at all. White noise has a uniform frequency spectrum, or in other words, all frequencies are present in it, just as they are present in white light. The origin of such noise can be, for instance, imperfect equipment as it's very difficult to produce an image sensor without a bad element, or transmission errors.

A median filter is the classical application of the rank sequence approach and it suppresses white noise excellently. The idea is pretty simple: if an image is smooth enough, as real images usually are, you can use the value from the middle of the rank sequence as the pixel value. The values of 'bad' pixels will most probably lie near the top or the bottom of the sequence, as shown below:

An Image with 'White' Noise (Artificial) and the Result of Median Filtering

As you can see, median filtering also affects the edges and makes the picture look slightly blurred. This is because an image isn't smooth near the edges of objects. However, the median filter makes it smooth. This blurring may be almost unnoticeable on real life images, but if you look at the figure below - median filtering can distort some images drastically, killing almost every thin line.

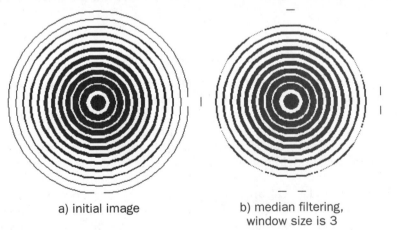

a) initial image

b) median filtering,
window size is 3

Median Filtering of Artificial Images with Thin Lines

Continued

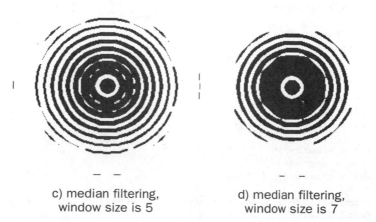

c) median filtering,
window size is 5

d) median filtering,
window size is 7

Median Filtering of Artificial Images with Thin Lines

The following code fragment is just a single method of the **Sneib_filter** object, which is the origin of all filters using the rank sequence approach. This method does the following:

▲ Builds the rank sequence

▲ Sorts it if necessary

▲ Supports the 'balance' technique, by which we mean after each step it removes the column which exits the filtering window from the rank sequence, and adds the one that enters the window.

When this is complete, different rank filters select a different point in the filtered sequence:

```
void Sneib_filter::process_line(BYTE *output_line)
{
   register int val;
   register int *srtd;
   register BYTE *neib;
   BYTE **bf;
   BYTE *line;
   int j,col,row,col_cnt,rez,size2, size21;

// fill neighborhood for the first time
   for (row = 0; row < filter_hei; row++)
   {
      neib = neib_first_line + row;
      line = buffer[row];
      for (col = filter_wid; col > 0; col--, neib += filter_hei)
```

```c
        *neib = *(line++);
}
size2 = filter_square;
size21 = size2+1;

if (needsort)
{
   neib = neib_first_line;
   sorted[0] = 256;
   for (j = size2; j > 0; j--)
   {
      val = *(neib++);
      srtd = sorted;
      while (*(srtd++) < val);
      srtd--;
      memmove(srtd+1, srtd, sizeof(int) * (size21-srtd+sorted));
      *srtd = val;
   }
}

rez = first_pixel();
*(output_line++) = int_in_byte(rez);

col = filter_wid;
for (col_cnt = width-1; col_cnt > 0; col_cnt--, col++)
{
   memmove(Sneib,neib_first_line,size2);
   bf = buffer;
   neib = neib_last_line;
   for (row = filter_hei; row > 0; row--)
      *(neib++) = (*(bf++))[col];

   if (needsort)
   {
      neib = Sneib; // delete subcolumn
      for (j = filter_wid; j > 0; j--)
      {
         val = *(neib++);
         srtd = sorted;
         while (*(srtd++) < val);
         memmove(srtd-1, srtd, sizeof(int) * (size21-srtd+sorted));
      }

      neib = neib_last_line; // add subcolumn
      for (j = filter_wid; j > 0; j--)
      {
         val = *(neib++);
         srtd = sorted;
         while (*(srtd++) < val);
         srtd--;
```

```
            memmove(srtd+1, srtd, sizeof(int) * (size21-srtd+sorted));
            *srtd = val;
        }
    }
    rez = process_pixel();
    *(output_line++) = int_in_byte(rez);
  }
}
```

Gaussian Noise Reduction - Convolution Filters

Gaussian noise, in contrast to white noise, as you can tell from the name, has an unequal frequency distribution. That's why we can construct a filter which will suppress a particular range of frequencies and so reduce the noise.

Now is the right time to have a more detailed look at the convolution based filters, and so here is a code fragment for the abstract implementation of digital convolution:

```
void convolution_filter::process_line(BYTE *output_line)
{
    int col, row;
    register tmptype s;
    register int j;
    register BYTE *in;
    register int *flt;
    BYTE **bf;
    int scale = scale_factor;

    for (col = 0; col < width; col++)
    {
        bf = buffer;
        flt = filter;
        s = s0;
        for (row = filter_hei; row > 0; row--, bf++)
        {
            in = &(*bf)[col];
            for (j = filter_wid; j > 0; j--)
                s += (tmptype)*(flt++) * *(in++);
        }
        s /= scale;
        *(output_line++) = int_in_byte(s);
    }
}
```

Quite easy then - just some multiplication, summing and a kind of normalization. What makes it work in so many different circumstances are the numbers in the convolution mask.

377

Box Filter

The easiest one. The convolution mask looks like this:

$$\frac{1}{9} \times \begin{bmatrix} 1 & 1 & 1 \\ 1 & 1 & 1 \\ 1 & 1 & 1 \end{bmatrix} \quad \text{or} \quad \frac{1}{25} \times \begin{bmatrix} 1 & 1 & 1 & 1 & 1 \\ 1 & 1 & 1 & 1 & 1 \\ 1 & 1 & 1 & 1 & 1 \\ 1 & 1 & 1 & 1 & 1 \\ 1 & 1 & 1 & 1 & 1 \end{bmatrix}$$

Box filtering is nothing more than calculating the mean value of the neighborhood. It may seem that the box filter will act like a heavy smoothing iron on your image. This isn't quite so. Generally speaking, the box filter is a rather poor low-pass filter. You can experiment yourselves or take it for granted. The main disadvantage of the box filter is that it doesn't take into account the following: in real images, the closer together the pixels are, the more their values correlate.

Binomial Filter

Binomial filters are much better low-pass filters. What's more, they illustrate the idea of constructing complex filters from simple 'building blocks'.

Consider the simplest 1D convolution mask - just the mean value of two adjacent pixels:

$$B^1 = 1/2 \times [1\ 1]$$

Suppose we apply it repeatedly. The resulting, multiplied filter mask will look like this:

$$B^2 = 1/4 \quad \times \quad [1\ 2\ 1]$$

$$B^3 = 1/8 \quad \times \quad [1\ 3\ 3\ 1]$$

$$B^4 = 1/16 \quad \times \quad [1\ 4\ 6\ 4\ 1]$$

These masks contain **binomial coefficients**. You'll obtain the same figures if you expand $(a+b)^n$ for different n:

$$(a+b)^2 = \mathbf{1} \times a^2 + \mathbf{2} \times ab + \mathbf{1} \times b^2$$

$$(a+b)^3 = \mathbf{1} \times a^3 + \mathbf{3} \times a^2b + \mathbf{3} \times ab^2 + \mathbf{1} \times b^3, \text{ and so on.}$$

The algorithm for the recursive computation of the binomial coefficients is known as Pascal's triangle.

```
void pascal_triangle(int coefficients[], int power)
{
    int *coef;
    int i;
    coefficients[0] = 1;
    if (power == 0)
        return;
    coefficients[power] = 1;

    coef = new int[power];
    pascal_triangle(coef,power-1);
    for (i = 1; i < power; i++)
        coefficients[i] = coef[i]+coef[i-1];
    delete coef;
}
```

We can obtain a 2D binomial filter mask simply by combining the horizontal and vertical 1D masks.

$$B^2 = B_h^2 \times B_v^2 = \frac{1}{4} \times [1\ 2\ 1] \times \frac{1}{4} \times \begin{bmatrix} 1 \\ 2 \\ 1 \end{bmatrix} = \frac{1}{16} \times \begin{bmatrix} 1 & 2 & 1 \\ 2 & 4 & 2 \\ 1 & 2 & 1 \end{bmatrix}$$

Filter Decomposition

You've probably realized that the binomial filter is a combination of simpler filters. This idea is fairly important for filter design. And on the other side of the coin, we should consider the possibility of the decomposition of complicated filters, as it may significantly improve the performance.

Digital convolution is a rather computationally expensive technique. Generally speaking, you need N*N multiplications and N*N - 1 additions for each pixel, plus some time to support nested loops. Of course, with your new Pentium processor the multiplication costs you almost nothing, however, the task of performance optimization still remains.

You may remember the 'balance' approach which was used for the **median** filter. It lets you perform 2*N operations instead of N*N. Decomposition of the 2D convolution mask into two 1D masks works in the same way (2*N instead of N*N). It may be shown that decomposition into a series of simpler symmetrical masks is possible for any convolution matrix. Unfortunately, this

doesn't suggest a general, all purpose method to do it, but at least you know the recipe for the binomial filter.

Recursive Filter

The last group of low-pass techniques we'd like to illustrate is the recursive filter. Suppose we start with the same simple averaging mask we used for the binomial filter, but apply it so that already-processed pixels take part in the computation. The formula we'll use is as follows:

$$I_{m,n+1}^{new} = \frac{1}{p} \times ((p-1) \times I_{m,n}^{new} + I_{m,n}^{new})$$

Recursive filters are rather powerful low-pass filters. However, they have one shortcoming (at least): they must be applied in different directions to the same picture, otherwise your picture will almost certainly be distorted. Usual practice means that the filter is applied from left to right and back, then from the top to the bottom and back.

Some tips for computational efficiency: if you make parameter **p** a power of 2, then a recursive filter can be implemented using only the addition and shift operations. And this is how it's implemented in our system. Remember, all sources can be found on the accompanying CD-ROM.

The following figure shows the result of applying the three filters we have discussed to an image:

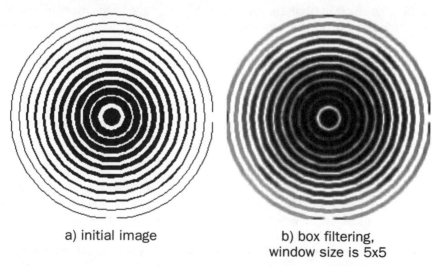

a) initial image

b) box filtering,
window size is 5x5

Low-pass Filtering of an Artificial Image

Continued

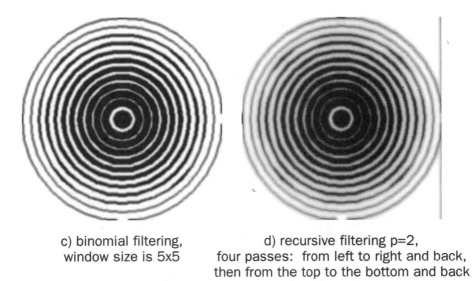

c) binomial filtering,
window size is 5x5

d) recursive filtering p=2,
four passes: from left to right and back,
then from the top to the bottom and back

Low-pass Filtering of an Artificial Image

Alpha-Trim Filter

In 1990, in the journal CG&A, there was an article in which we met the idea of Alpha-trim filters for the first time. It seemed pretty easy and we gathered it was just another filtering scheme. However, we'd like to describe it here because it provides a simple and easy method (and the only one we know, by the way) of combining both neighborhood approaches: convolution and rank sequence. What's more, you can do it in a controlled manner, by which we mean that there is a numerical parameter which you can vary to make your filter act either as an actual **median** filter or as a **box** filter, and all the intermediate states in between.

Why is this important? If you have any experience with different filters you may quite possibly have found that neither rank nor convolution filters can provide perfect noise reduction. Each of these techniques has its own shortcomings. Hopefully, when the two approaches are combined, we will also combine the advantage of both techniques, leaving the shortcomings behind.

How does it work? We do exactly the same as we did for median filtering - construct a rank sequence. But then instead of getting the median, we trim the 'tails' of the sequence and find the mean value of those pixels which remain. Let **Alpha** be the trimming parameter between 0 and 0.5, the fraction of the rank sequence to be trimmed.

When **Alpha** is 0, no values are trimmed and so it's simply a box filter. When **Alpha** is 0.5, then none of the rank sequence elements participate in averaging, so we have a pure median filter. Look at following figure which clearly illustrates the Alpha-trim technique:

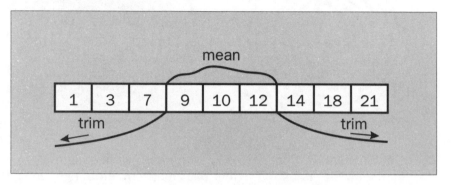

Alpha-trim Filtering Scheme

In some cases, it will be useful to apply the Alpha-trim technique iteratively, so that each pass over the image works on the output of the previous filter. In this case, different settings of mask size and **Alpha** can be used to select the best effects of Alpha-trim filtering. The following figure shows the results of the Alpha-trim filtering of an artificially generated sample image, where the convolution mask is 5×5:

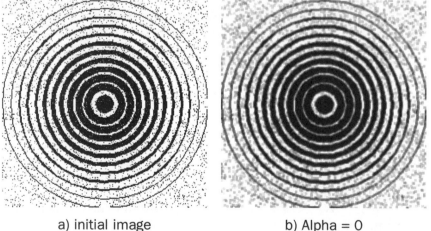

a) initial image

b) Alpha = 0
- pure box filtering

Alpha-trim Filtering of an Artificial Image

Continued

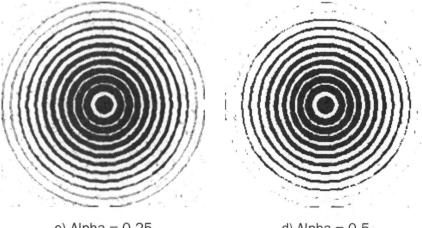

c) Alpha = 0.25
- intermediate

d) Alpha = 0.5
- pure median filtering

Alpha-trim Filtering of an Artificial Image

Edge Detection, Contrasting and High-Pass Filtering

This is just the opposite of what we have discussed above, so what is our purpose? The main reasons for using high-pass filters is for edge detection as well as for sharpening the image, as you will see.

First and Second Order Derivative Filters

The low-pass filters discussed above, suppressed structures with high spatial frequencies and so such techniques are used for noise reduction and smoothing. However, there is the need for the opposite task - emphasizing edges, or structures which correspond to these high frequencies.

Firstly, accentuating the edges of an image gives more contrast, and secondly, you can filter an image so that only the edges will remain and perform **binarization**, which is the conversion of the image to black-and-white. An image transformed in this way is sometimes much easier to recognize and so identify. This is how the OCR systems prepare documents for recognition.

The basic technique remains the same - digital convolution. Only the filtering masks are changed. Digital approximations of derivative operators of the first and second order are usually used for the purposes of edge detection. This is because the derivative is high when the function (and so the image brightness) changes rapidly and low within the areas where the function changes slightly.

'Digital approximation of derivative' sounds very scientific, but it simply means that you subtract the value of the previous pixel from the current one. According to the formal definition, we should also divide the difference by the co-ordinate step, but we can think of it as 1 and forget about it. The simplest convolution mask is:

$$D_x^- = [-1 \ 1] \text{ from left to right}$$

$$D_x^+ = [1 \ -1] \text{ from right to left}$$

$$D_x^s = \frac{1}{2} \times [1 \ 0 \ -1] \text{ symmetrical form for } \mathbf{x} \text{ direction}$$

$$D_y^s = \frac{1}{2} \times \begin{bmatrix} 1 \\ 0 \\ -1 \end{bmatrix} \text{ symmetrical form for } \mathbf{y} \text{ direction}$$

You can apply these masks using the **onedim_convolution** object to emphasize horizontal or vertical edges. Contrasting the edges of an arbitrary orientation is a bit more complicated. You can do it by combining D_x and D_y to get the value of gradient. The **gradient** is the vector sum, which means that it has a direction (it points in the direction of the most rapid brightness change) and value. We need this value so the resulting formula can be written like this:

$$|\text{Grad(I)}| = (D_x^2 + D_y^2)^{1/2}$$

Strictly speaking, such notation isn't mathematically correct but it gives us the basis for our calculations. We should execute the following steps:

1 Independently apply D_x^s and to D_y^s to the image.

2 Square the value of each pixel of both filtered images.

3 Add them and calculate the square root of the sum. If we follow this exact method, then edge detection will work extremely slowly. Therefore, a rougher approximation is often used:

$$|\text{Grad(I)}| = |D_x| + |D_y|$$

Laplace Filter

The second order derivative can be used for edge detection, too. The 1D mask can be derived simply by applying the first order mask twice:

$$D_x^2 = [1\ \text{-}2\ 1]$$

If we combine them the same way we did for the binomial mask, we'll get the smallest filter mask that approximates to the Laplacian operator:

$$L = \begin{bmatrix} 0 & 1 & 0 \\ 1 & -4 & 1 \\ 0 & 1 & 0 \end{bmatrix}$$

Approximation can also be performed with either Difference of Gaussian or Laplacian of Gaussian contrast enhancement (see subsection Band-Pass Filtering). In digital image processing, it is thought that the subtraction of the image's Laplacian from the image itself can give a filtering technique similar to a human's ability to detect movement.

The idea is rather straightforward. We can think of the initial image as the sum of low and high frequencies. If we apply a low-pass filter (say, binomial) to an image and subtract the result from the initial image, we'll remove the low frequencies from the sum and so get a high-pass filtering technique, as shown below:

The Results of Laplacian of Gaussian Contrast Enhancement

The following code fragment shows the implementation of this technique:

```
BOOL contrast_by_LoG_filter::one_row(BYTE *input_line, BYTE *output_line)
{
   BYTE * out,*in;
   int j,val;
   int c1,c2;

   if (binomial_filter::one_row(input_line, output_line))
   {
      out = output_line;
      in = vertical->input_line(out_line_num);
      c2 = beta; c1 = 64 + c2;
      for (j = width; j > 0; j --)
      {
         val = (c1 * (*(in++)) - c2 * (*output_line) + 32)  >> 6;
         *(output_line++) = int_in_byte(val);
      }
      return (TRUE);
   }
   else
      return (FALSE);
}
```

Local Adaptive Contrast Enhancement

Here we want to risk providing a very short review of the article 'Investigations Of Image Contrast Space Defined by Variations on Histogram Equalization' by John M. Gauch published in GVGIP in July 1992. The main idea is to create a technique of contrast enhancement, which lets you emphasize details of different characteristic sizes.

Since we can vary the characteristic size, we can think of a number of interactive image exploration techniques. Whole images can be displayed with a user-defined contrast size. Alternatively, the image can be examined with a magic window which magnifies the contrast of selected areas in the image.

Adaptive Histogram Equalization

There were six different algorithms proposed in the original paper. We chose to implement the simplest and by coincidence, the fastest one. It works like this: within some local neighborhood we construct a histogram of pixel values. The value of a processed pixel is selected as being optimal according to this local histogram. The good old rank sequence is constructed, and the index of a processed pixel value within the sequence becomes the new value for this pixel, after the necessary normalization.

The neighborhood is square. More than that, we don't use any kind of weights for different positions within the window. It works well enough this way and we can use the `Sneib_filter` object to implement it. The figure below shows an example of this filter application:

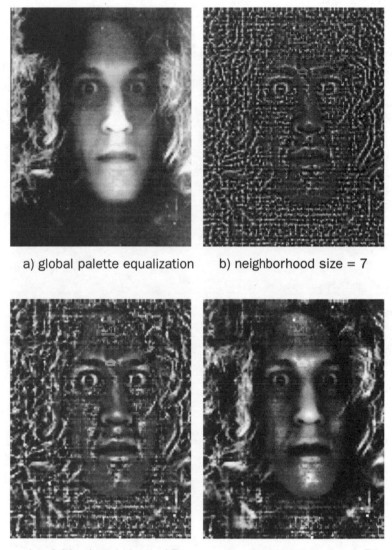

a) global palette equalization   b) neighborhood size = 7

c) neighborhood size = 15   d) neighborhood size = 51

**Local Adaptive Contrast Enhancing Technique
Applied to a Poor Quality Photo**

The implementation looks like this:

```
int rank_filter::first_pixel()
{
   register int j,s;
   register int  *h;
   BYTE *w;
   int fs;

   memset(hist, 0, 256*sizeof(int));
   fs  = filter_square;
   h = hist; w =  neib_first_line;

// accumulate histogram
   for (j = fs; j > 0; j--)
      h[*(w++)]++;

   j = *current;        // calculate rank of current pixel:
   s = hist[j] >> 1;    // half of the [?]equal
   j--;                 // plus sum of those less than
   h = hist+j;
   for (;j > 0; j--)
     s += *(h--);
   return (((long)s << 8) - s + (fs >> 1)) / fs;
   //normalize to 0..255
};

int rank_filter::process_pixel()
{
   register int j,s;
   register int *h;
   BYTE *w;
   int fs;
// recalc histogram
   h = hist;
// delete left edge of window
   for (j = filter_hei, w = Sneib; j > 0; j--)
      h[*(w++)]--;
// add right edge of window
   for (j = filter_hei, w = neib_last_line; j > 0; j--)
      h[*(w++)]++;
   j = *current;        // calculate rank of current pixel
   s = hist[j] >> 1;    // half of equal
   j--;                 // and sum of less then it
   h = hist+j;
   for (;j > 0; j--)
      s += *(h--);

   fs  = filter_square;
   return (((long)s << 8) - s + (fs >> 1)) / fs;
   //normalize to 0..255
};
```

Band-Pass Filtering

Well, now we know how to low-pass and high-pass filter our image. One question still remains. Can we perform **band-pass** filtering, or in other words, suppress both high and low spatial frequencies with controllable cut-off levels? Easy! We take two low-pass filters with different cut-off levels (for instance, two binomial filters with different mask sizes), apply them to the same image and subtract the results.

This operation will emphasize structures, or patterns, of some characteristic size.

The question is what would we use it for? Maybe to emphasize a texture pattern. The figure below shows some results which we find interesting. We took completely random binary sand, by which we mean an image which consists of random black and white pixels, which is a kind of white spatial noise. By definition, such an image contains structures with various spatial frequencies (characteristic sizes). We extracted some of them by band-pass filtering with different cut-off levels, applying two binomial filters with mask N and 2*N to the same image and subtracting the results. Remember, the initial sand image was the same for all the resulting images:

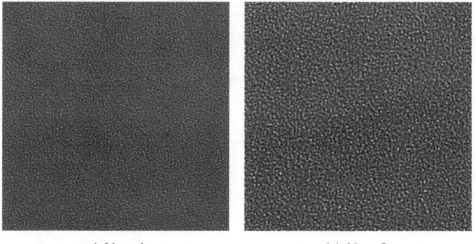

a) N = 1   b) N = 3

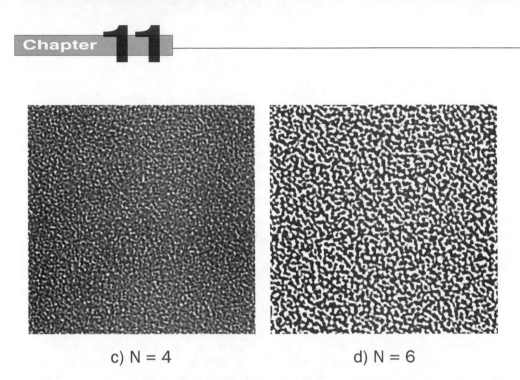

c) N = 4   d) N = 6

Texture Extraction by Band-Pass Filtering

Strictly speaking, this family of filters has its own name: **Difference of Gaussian**. This is because the binomial mask rapidly converges to the Gaussian function.

Some DIP Techniques, Just For Fun

Colorize Palette Technique

You may have seen old black and white film that has had color artificially added by a process known as colorization. A similar trick on the PC is called **colorize palette**. The idea is simple - you have an image in shades of gray and try to display it using the palette of a colored image.

The simplest way to do this is to use the palette of a colored image as it is. Unfortunately, you can't assume that both palettes are sorted. That's why in the following code fragment, we've tried to map the palettes in a one-to-one fashion, choosing the most appropriate shade of gray for each color:

```
void find_nearest_gray(BGRpalette color_pal, BGRpalette gray_pal,
                       BYTE *table)
{
  long *values;
  int i,j;
  register int val,mindiff,minno;

  values = new long[256];
  for (j = 0; j < 256; j++)
     values[j] = (color_pal[j].r * 299L + color_pal[j].g * 587L +
                  color_pal[j].b * 114L + 5) / 10;

  for (i = 0; i < 256; i++)
  {
     val = gray_pal[i].r*100;
     minno = 0;
     mindiff = abs(val - values[0]);
     for (j = 1; j < 256; j++)
        if (abs(val - values[j])  < mindiff)
        {
           minno = j;
           mindiff   = abs(val - values[j]);
        }
     table[i] = minno;
  }
}
```

You can find some samples using false palettes on the accompanying CD-ROM. Sometimes it works surprisingly well. Does this mean that the color values don't mean anything? No it doesn't. However, if you choose the right color prototype (say a seascape for the seascapes) you can be almost sure that the colors in the picture will also be right, or at least realistic. This is because you will hardly ever have two different colors that match the same shade of gray in your relatively small color palette.

False Coloring

A related process is known as false coloring an image. In this process, you change an image's palette, but you don't follow any rules! The idea is to use a palette that enhances the details on the image by using colors which are generally contrasting. For example, if you have a gray scale image where the detail is only one level above the background level, then the detail is indistinguishable from the background. By assigning colors to the grays, it would be possible to pick out the detail.

The easiest way to achieve this is to display an image with just the first eight colors from the standard VGA palette, (ie, black, white, red, blue, green, cyan, purple and yellow) repeatedly with the formula:

```
color = gray_scale % 8;
```

The resulting image looks gaudy, but details become clearer.

Line Pictures

You've probably seen pictures which look like a relief formed from a set of parallel lines. It looks like the kind of engraving sometimes used as the background on some documents. If you've never noticed anything like that, just take a hundred (or a one) dollar bill and look at the President. You'll see thin lines that give his face more contrast. This is what we're talking about.

The following code fragment allows you to draw any picture you like this way. Not for forgery (we hope) but just for fun. Such pictures are easy to show and therefore print, because you don't need any rasterizing. In the figure below you can see a shot of one of the authors (in the days of his youth) transformed by this technique:

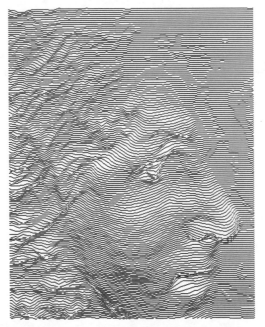

Sample Photo Transformed Into Lines

```
void draw_line(BYTE *liney, int width, int y0, int x0)
{
    int j, x,y, vy, vyold,yold;
    long ylong;

// the ratio of biasing
#define koef 6000L
// the limit of the second order derivative
#define max2deriv 9

    setcolor(0);
    ylong = ((long)y0 << 16) + koef*((int)liney[0] - 128);
    y = (ylong + (1<<15)) >> 16; vy = 0;
    moveto(x0,y);
    for (j = width,x = x0; j > 0; j -= relief_stepx,
         liney += relief_stepx  , x += relief_stepx)
    {
        vyold = vy; yold = y;
        ylong += (long)koef*(liney[relief_stepx] - liney[0]);
        y = (ylong + (1<<15)) >> 16;
        vy = y - yold;
        if  ((vy - vyold) > 0)
            vy = min(vy, vyold + max2deriv);
        else
            vy = max(vy, vyold-max2deriv);
        y = yold+vy;
// lineto(x,y);
        setcolor(0); line(x -  relief_stepx, yold, x, y);
        setcolor(255); line(x -  relief_stepx, yold-1, x, y-1);
    }
}
```

Bais Relief

Bais relief is the technique of producing an image which appears as though it has been embossed on a surface, and then illuminated from a particular direction. This is done by applying a filter which removes all the low frequency components of the image. We know we have done this already, but here we add a twist by taking the mask

D = [1 -1]

and applying it in only one direction.

We'd just like to add a few words about these funny pictures. What you see in the figure can hardly be considered as a bitmap image. The image is represented in the form of a **texture** that makes it almost impossible to restore as a bitmap. However, your eyes can recognize it without any problem. I'm sure some day, there will be a texture-analyzing technique able to do the same.

Summary

So, our short excursion into DIP is over. Here, we'd like to remind you of the most significant terms and ideas. We also want to briefly review some techniques we couldn't cover in the time available.

Images are composed of pixels which is why most low-level image processing routines (and all the simplest ones) are point operations. These DIP techniques treat each pixel separately. The point operations are used in different methods of image rendering, such as gamma correction, and to adapt the digital image for human eyes, by means of brightness and contrast enhancement. The most remarkable implementation idea connected with point operations is the look-up table.

However, the information an image contains isn't only in pixel values. Most of it is in the relationship between adjacent pixels. That's why we have to take into account the neighborhood. Hence window operations.

There are various windows techniques. We divided them into two groups according to the way pixels are combined within the neighborhood. We looked at two of them in detail: rank sequence and digital convolution. We've seen how windows operations are applied for noise reduction, edge detection, image smoothing and contrasting. An implementation idea worth recalling is the decomposition of the convolution mask and balance approach, which helps improve the performance significantly.

The next branch on the tree is named **Texture**. Textures can be as simple as those we picked up from random sand or as complicated as the relief images. Why are textures important? You almost never see a plain color surface in real life. Wooden, brick and marble walls are textured. We need to be able to recognize textures to distinguish objects. The methods used to do this are usually based on searching for some characteristic texture properties.

Reconstruction from projection is an attempt to restore a 3D scene from its 2D image. The most developed method is based on the idea of binocular vision. Two photos of the same scene taken from two distant points are processed. If some point on the first image (say, the corner of a building) is shifted just a little bit on the second image, it means this point is far from the camera, and vice versa, if the shift is big, then the object is close.

The problem of **Motion tracing** is, to some extent, similar to 3D reconstruction, although it seems more complicated. However, it is closely connected to top-secret things such as robot vision, target tracing and fire control, so we thought it best to leave it out.

Now the most developed high-end DIP technique is **image recognition**. This technique is widely used, from OCR systems to medical diagnostics. However, it's still under development. What makes recognition so easy for humans, and so difficult for computers? The main problem is that it's too difficult to compare pictures - to find that one face is similar to another. Various approaches are being tested. Neural networking is possibly the most promising (or at least, the most popular) at present.

One of the more traditional implementations of image recognition is that after edge detection and binarization, the objects on the image are transformed to the contour representation, or in other words, the problem of image comparison is simplified to that of contours. These contours are then extracted and compared with a database of standard contours. The bracketing of contours can be performed either directly or by computing a set of numbers called contour descriptors which, in their turn, are easy to compare.

Image Manipulation Techniques

Imagine that at last you've got enough raw graphical materials: glimmering Julia jewelry, GIFted land-escapes and fairies' photos from the Photo CD library. Let's also assume that you want to compose your on-screen masterpieces from these pieces, just by picking a pattern here, a color spot there. To do this, you'll need the means to manipulate images, and not only to cut-and-paste; what about the tools for image reduction and expansion, rotation and mirroring, the tools for blurring, pixelating, embossing, not to mention the rest of the tribe?

Chapter Contents

In this chapter, we will cover:

- Image Effects - An Attempt to Classify Them
- Picture Format
- General Solution
- Calculating the Coefficients by Three Points
- Special Issues
- Two and Three Step Rotation
- Special Effects
- Effect Algorithm Reverse Engineering
- Nonlinear Transformations

Image Effects - An Attempt to Classify Them

There are many different effects that you can use on an image, so we've introduced a kind of simple classification. It's obvious that reduction and expansion are relatives, and that they differ from emboss and motion blur effects; therefore we'll divide the topic in two and distinguish between:

- spacial pixel transformations, which cover expansion, rotation, and so forth

- pixel color transformation, which cover motion blur, pixelate, and so on

In this chapter, we'll start by introducing you to a kind of general solution for spacial pixel transformations and then we'll provide you with a collection of various effects based on pixel color transformation.

Spacial Pixel Transformations

Are there any problems with moving pixels around? Yes, as some of them could get lost. This seems a bit vague? Let us explain. Your PC screen, as you know, is an array of raster pixels that have discrete locations. So if you move them according to precise transformation rules, you can't be sure that each one will fall within the grid. In other words, when transforming the image, we can't simply move the corresponding color values from one raster pixel to another, we have to use an **interpolation** method. Therefore, the key issue of spacial transformations is the interpolation of pixel colors.

Interpolation

For each pixel in the source image, calculate the corresponding point within the target area, then find the nearest raster pixel and add the value of the initial pixel into the target pixel's color value. However, this straightforward method has one problem. For instance, if an image is reduced or expanded, some of the target image pixels may accumulate several values while others may be missed.

The problem becomes easier if we attack the problem by adopting the reverse approach - for each pixel of the target image we find the corresponding point within the source image, find the nearest raster pixel of the original image and get its color value. This approach sets the corresponding color value from the source for each pixel of the target image. It's true that some source image pixels will be chosen over and over again while others will never be used, and strictly speaking this isn't interpolation at all. However, this method works and what's more, we regard 'the nearest neighbor' approach as the most suitable in certain instances, such as with paletted files.

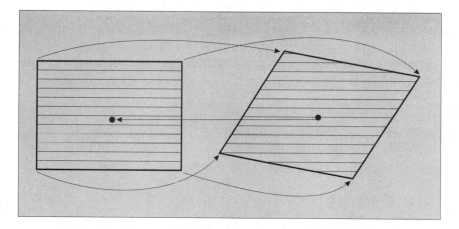

Spacial Image Transformations, the Origin of Interpolation

We can easily enhance the suggested approach by using a more sophisticated technique to interpolate the color value of a target pixel, in accordance with four (or even more) neighbors rather than just the nearest one. Here, we consider just the linear interpolation method as it's easy to implement and works well. But there's plenty of room for experimentation; you could choose something like a four-point cubic spline, eight-point cubic spline, or B-splines, to name but a few.

The quality you get depends on the particular interpolation method you choose. That's why we've isolated the interpolation procedure within the main routine - to mark the right place for you to plug in your own interpolation method. However, this organization will test your patience as the transformations become slower as you proceed.

We should stress that the routines we've chosen here were designed to make the explanation clearer, rather than speed up the computations. However, we will be telling you how you can optimize these routines.

For each of the spacial transformations there are some special cases. When dealing with them you'll find the complexity of the general routine useless and sometimes harmful. Horizontal and vertical mirroring, rotation by 0, 90, 180, 270 and 360 degrees and expansion by an integer factor should therefore be treated specifically.

Pixel Color Transformations

As opposed to the spacial transformations described above, the following color ones are rather a matter of craftsmanship and fortune. Each time you meet something pretty or weird manipulating the pictures, you can simply add it to your own 'Album of Effects'.

 Most of the Pixel Color Transformations can be formulated as specific matrix operations applied to the source image. This has been described in Chapter 11, 'Digital Image Processing'.

Picture Format

Before we proceed further, let's have a bit of a break and discuss what kind of image format may be chosen for internal use in our routine. The simplest representation is to keep the image in the memory as an array of horizontal lines. For the original image, all lines have equal x co-ordinates and sizes, so the area of this image can be characterized by column and row numbers. For the transformed image, we need to know the x co-ordinate and the size of each separate line, because the transformed image will have a more complex representation than the original, and the calculation of a template for such an image can cause problems.

The following class defines initial image representation:

```
class real_picture
{
public:
    int row_number, column_number, left_x, top_y;
    // left_x, top_y are screen coordinates of
    // the first pixel in the top line of the image.
    BYTE max_plan;
    // max_plan is number of color components
    // 1 - shades of gray, 256 colors
```

```
    // 3 - TrueColor, 3 bytes for pixel
    PICTURE_ROWS pict[4];
    // pict is the array of color component matrix
    int nt;
    // nt is the number of transformed images
    trans_picture *pp[MAX_TRANSFORM];
    // pp is the array of pointers to transformed images
    real_picture(int row_number_, int column_number_,
                 int left_x_, int top_y_, BYTE max_plan_);
    ~real_picture();
    void interpolate(float x, float y, byte4 &color);
    // x,y id point inside this image
    // color is interpolated color for this point
    void create_trans_picture(float coef1, float coef2,
                              float coef3, float coef4, TRANSFORMATIONS t);
    void show();
    real_picture *duplicate();
};
```

The following code represents the transformed image:

```
class trans_picture
{
public:
    int row_number, left_x, top_y;
    float a, b, c, d, dx, dy;
    // coefficients of the transformations Real -> Transformed
    real_picture *rp;
    // rp is the pointer to the source image
    BYTE max_plan;
    PICTURE_ROWS pict[4];
    int *row_shift, *row_size;
    // row_shift is the shift of each row relative to left_x
    // row_size is the size of a row
    trans_picture(real_picture *rp_, BYTE max_plan_,
                  float  dx_, float dy_, float a_, float b_, float c_,
                  float d_);
    ~trans_picture();
    void show();
    void calc_line(int from_line, int to_line, float &shift_x,
                   float &right_x, float &incr_x, float &incr_r);
    // this procedure is for internal use only
};
```

Both the original and transformed images are displayed pixel by pixel:

```
void real_picture::show()
{
    int i, j;
    switch (max_plan)
```

```
    {
        case 1 :
            for (i = 1; i <= row_number; i++)
                for (j = 1 ; j <= row_size[i]; j++)
                    putpixel(left_x + row_shift[i] +j-1, top_y + i-1,
    pict[0][i][j]);
            break;
        case 3 : // If you can work with
            // TrueColor you should add
            // putRGBpixel(), where parameters
            // pict[0][i][j], pict[1][i][j], pict[2][i][j]
            // are color components
            // for (i = 1; i <= row_number; i++)
            // for (j = 1 ; j <= column_number; j++)
            //  putRGBpixel(left_x + j-1, top_y + i-1,
            //  pict[0][i][j], pict[1][i][j], pict[2][i][j]);
            break;
    }
}

void trans_picture::show()
{
    int i, j;
    switch (max_plan)
    {
        case 1 :
            for (i = 1; i <= row_number; i++)
                for (j = 1 ; j <= row_size[i]; j++)
                    putpixel(left_x + row_shift[i] +j-1, top_y + i-1,
    pict[0][i][j]);
            break;
        case 3 :
            break;
    }
}
```

If the image is represented in shades of gray, then **max_plan** = 1. For TrueColor images, **max_plan** = 3 and the components of RGB are kept in separate matrices.

General Solution

One of the problems with transformed images is that they can't be restored to their initial state by reversed transformation. To avoid this problem, your program must keep track of all transforming operations, so when you add a new one, the whole combination of them is applied to the original image. This way you don't need to keep any intermediate images, and can easily undo an unwanted step.

The general approach is to describe all the transformations in a similar way, by co-ordinate reorganization:

$$Xnew = A*X + B*Y + dX$$

$$Ynew = C*X + D*Y + dY$$

where dX, dY are the values of the co-ordinate shifts, and A, B, C, and D are coefficients of the transformation matrix. All our transformations, as well as their results, have their own co-ordinate shifts and matrix coefficients. To apply a new conversion to the transformed image, new parameters must be calculated from the image and the new transformation. The resulting image will then remember these parameters.

We'll write the equations for each case separately and explain all the constants, as they appear:

For the scrolling transformation:

$$Xnew = 0*X + 0*Y + dX$$

$$Ynew = 0*X + 0*Y + dY$$

where dX, dY are values of shifts along the x and y axes respectively.

For the reduction or expansion transformation:

$$Xnew = ax*X + 0*Y + (1-ax)*Xo$$

$$Ynew = 0*X + ay*Y + (1-ay)*Yo$$

where Xo, Yo are the co-ordinates of the pixel that doesn't change after the transformation; ax is the reduction (ax < 1) or expansion (ax > 1) factor along the x-axis and ay is the same along the y-axis. We can perform these conversions as x-reduction with y-expansion or vice versa, at the same time.

For the rotating transformation:

$$Xnew = cos(p)*X + sin(p)*Y + [Xo*(1-cos(p))-Yo*sin(p)]$$

$$Ynew = -sin(p)*X + cos(p)*Y + [Xo*sin(p)+Yo*(1-cos(p))]$$

where Xo, Yo are the co-ordinates of the rotation center, and p is the rotation angle (positive p means anti-clockwise).

For the mirroring transformation:

$$Xnew = -(a^2-b^2)/(a^2+b^2)*X - 2*a*b/(a^2+b^2)*Y - 2*a*c/(a^2+b^2)$$

$$Ynew = -2*a*b/(a^2+b^2)*X + (a^2-b^2)/(a^2+b^2)*Y - 2*b*c/(a^2+b^2)$$

where a, b, c are coefficients of the line equation $a*X+b*Y+c=0$. This line is known as the mirror line.

For the shearing transformation:

$$Xnew = 1*X + ax*Y - ax*Yo$$

$$Ynew = ay*X + 1*Y - ay*Xo$$

where Xo, Yo are co-ordinates of the pixel that doesn't change after transformation, ax is the shearing coefficient along the x-axis, and ay along the y-axis. We can perform shearing in an arbitrary direction.

The following figure gives examples of these transformations:

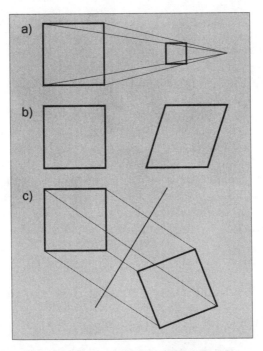

Examples of Transformations

Parameter Recalculation

Let's suppose that the last transformed image has parameters A, B, C, D, dX and dY. The new transformation that is to be applied is characterized by the parameters Anew, Bnew, Cnew, Dnew, dXnew and dYnew. We can calculate the combined parameters Asum, Bsum, Csum, Dsum, dXsum and dYsum (after this new conversion) using the following formulae:

$$dXsum = Anew*dX + Bnew*dY + dXnew$$

$$dYsum = Cnew*dX + Dnew*dY + dYnew$$

$$Asum = A*Anew + C*Bnew$$

$$Bsum = B*Anew + D*Bnew$$

$$Csum = A*Cnew + C*Dnew$$

$$Dsum = B*Cnew + D*Dnew$$

Four Points and Template

The next question to be answered is which raster pixels will belong to a new transformed image. We know that this image will be obtained from the original one, by conversion with a group of coefficients A, B, C, D, dX and dY. There is also the matrix of the original raster pixels. The initial rectangle, containing original raster points, is converted to a parallelogram containing raster points of the new image, so the first task is to transform four pixels - the corners of the rectangle. If the co-ordinates of the corners are (1,1), (ColumnNumber, 1), (1, RowNumber) and (ColumnNumber, RowNumber), then the co-ordinates of the parallelogram corners are:

$$X1 = A*1 + B*1 + dX$$

$$Y1 = C*1 + D*1 + dY$$

$$X2 = A*ColumnNumber + B*1 + dX$$

$$Y2 = C*ColumnNumber + D*1 + dY$$

$$X3 = A*1 + B*RowNumber + dX$$

Y3 = C*1 + D*RowNumber + dY

X4 = A*ColumnNumber + B*RowNumber + dX

Y4 = C*ColumnNumber + D*RowNumber + dY

All the raster pixels that are located inside the parallelogram that has these vertices are attached to the new transformed image.

The next task is to construct a template to hold all the data, or in other words, to create empty arrays to be filled with pixel color components. We must find the first row, the number of rows and, for each row, the start position and size. We sort the parallelogram vertices so that Y1 <= Y2 <= Y3 <= Y4 and if Y(i) = Y(i+1) then X(i) < X(i+1). The various spacial configurations of these sorted vertices are shown below. Note the incorrect case when lines which connect vertices intersect. This happens because of rounding errors. Special treatment is given to these cases in our routine.

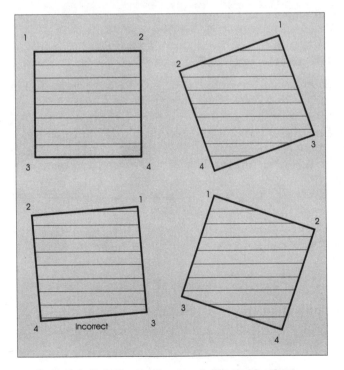

Spacial Configurations of Four Vertices

The rows that belong to the transformed image lie between Ceiling(Y1) and Floor(Y4), where the Ceiling function returns an integer number greater than or equal to Y1, and the Floor function returns an integer less than or equal to Y4. The start and end positions of the first row can be calculated as follows:

$$StartX = X1 + (Ceiling(Y1) - Y1)*IncrX$$

$$FinishX = X1 + (Ceiling(Y1) - Y1)*IncrR$$

where IncrX, IncrR are increments of corresponding values that were allowed when the row number increased by 1. These increments remain constant until the row number is less than or equal to the Y co-ordinate for the next vertex. The initial values can be obtained by the following formulae:

$$Incr1 = (X2 - X1) / (Y2 - Y1)$$

$$Incr2 = (X3 - X1) / (Y3 - Y1)$$

$$IncrX = min(Incr1, Incr2)$$

$$IncrR = max(Incr1, Incr2)$$

because the increment of the right end of each line must be greater then the increment of its left end.

The transition through the next vertex demands greater care because, in general, the co-ordinates of vertices aren't integer numbers. Only one of the pair (IncrX, IncrR) changes during one transition. For example, if IncrX changes as it passes through the vertex with co-ordinate Y2, then we must recalculate not only IncrX but also StartX values (IncrR and FinishX retain their previous values):

$$StartX = StartX+(NewIncr - IncrX)*(Floor(Y2) + 1 - Y2)$$

The shift and size of each row can be obtained as follows:

$$RowShift = Ceiling(StartX)$$

$$RowSize = Floor(FinishX) - Ceiling(StartX) + 1$$

When Floor(Y1) = Floor(Y2) and Floor(Y3) = Floor(Y4), the case is simpler, as you can see in the routine below:

```cpp
void trans_picture::calc_line(int from_line, int to_line, float  &shift_x,
                              float &right_x, float &incr_x, float &incr_r)
{
    int i, pl;
    for (i = from_line + 1; i <= to_line + 1; i++, shift_x += incr_x,
        right_x += incr_r)
    {
        row_shift[i] = ceil(shift_x);
        row_size[i] = floor(right_x) - ceil(shift_x) + 1;
        for (pl = 0; pl < max_plan; pl++ )
            pict[pl][i] = new BYTE[row_size[i] + 1];
    }
}

trans_picture::trans_picture(real_picture *rp_, BYTE max_plan_, float dx_,
                             float dy_, float a_, float b_, float c_,
                             float d_)
{
    int n, i, size, pl;
    SINGLE_POINT v[4], vo;
    float shift_x, right_x, incr_x, incr_r, new_incr;

    rp = rp_;
    max_plan = max_plan_;
    dx = dx_;
    dy = dy_;
    a = asp_ratio * a_;
    b = asp_ratio * b_;
    c = c_;
    d = d_;

    //transformation of vertexes
    v[0].x = a * 1 + b * 1 + dx;
    v[0].y = c * 1 + d * 1 + dy;
    v[1].x = a * rp->column_number + b * 1 + dx;
    v[1].y = c * rp->column_number + d * 1 + dy;
    v[2].x = a * 1 + b * rp->row_number + dx;
    v[2].y = c * 1 + d * rp->row_number + dy;
    v[3].x = a * rp->column_number + b * rp->row_number + dx;
    v[3].y = c * rp->column_number + d * rp->row_number + dy;

    //sorting of transformed vertexes
    for (n = 0; n < 3; n++)
        for (i = 0; i < 3; i++)
            if ((floor(v[i].y) > floor(v[i+1].y) ||
                ((floor(v[i].y) == floor(v[i+1].y)) &&
                (floor(v[i].x) > floor(v[i+1].x)))))
```

```
            {
               vo = v[i];
               v[i] = v[i+1];
               v[i+1] = vo;
            }

   left_x = rp->left_x;
   top_y = rp->top_y + ceil(v[0].y) - 1;
   row_number = floor(v[3].y) - ceil(v[0].y) + 1;

   for (pl = 0; pl < max_plan; pl++ )
      pict[pl] = new BYTE*[row_number+1];
   row_shift = new int[row_number+1];
   row_size = new int[row_number+1];
   memset(row_shift, 0, (row_number+1) * sizeof(int));
   memset(row_size, 0, (row_number+1) * sizeof(int));

   if (round(v[0].y) == round(v[1].y))
   {
      // image staies a rectangle
      if (v[0].x > v[1].x)
      {
         vo = v[0];
         v[0] = v[1];
         v[1] = vo;
      }
      // to avoid rounding errors we must check :
      if (v[2].x > v[3].x)
      {
         vo = v[2];
         v[2] = v[3];
         v[3] = vo;
      }
      size = floor(v[1].x) - ceil(v[0].x) + 1;
      // each row has equal size
      incr_x = (v[2].x - v[0].x) / (v[2].y - v[0].y);
      shift_x = v[0].x;
      for (i = 1; i<=row_number; i++, shift_x += incr_x)
      {
         for (pl = 0; pl < max_plan; pl++)
            pict[pl][i] = new BYTE[size+1];
         row_shift[i] = ceil(shift_x);
         row_size[i] = size;
      }
   }
   else
   {
      // image doesn't remain rectangular
      incr_x = (v[1].x - v[0].x) / (v[1].y - v[0].y);
      incr_r = (v[2].x - v[0].x) / (v[2].y - v[0].y);
      if (incr_x > incr_r)
```

```
          {
              new_incr = incr_x;
              incr_x = incr_r;
              incr_r = new_incr;
          }
          shift_x = v[0].x + (ceil(v[0].y) - v[0].y) * incr_x;
          right_x = v[0].x + (ceil(v[0].y) - v[0].y) * incr_r;
          calc_line(0,floor(v[1].y) - ceil(v[0].y),
                    shift_x, right_x, incr_x, incr_r);
          // when new line passes through a vertex
          // we need to recalculate some increments
          new_incr = (v[3].x - v[1].x) / (v[3].y - v[1].y);
          if ((new_incr - incr_x) > (incr_r - new_incr))
          {
              shift_x += (new_incr - incr_x) * (floor(v[1].y) + 1 - v[1].y);
              incr_x = new_incr;
          }
          else
          {
              right_x += (new_incr - incr_r) * (floor(v[1].y) + 1 - v[1].y);
              incr_r = new_incr;
          }
          calc_line(floor(v[1].y) - ceil(v[0].y) + 1,
                    floor(v[2].y) - ceil(v[0].y),
                    shift_x, right_x, incr_x, incr_r);
          new_incr = (v[3].x - v[2].x) / (v[3].y - v[2].y);
          if ((new_incr - incr_x) > (incr_r - new_incr))
          {
              shift_x += (new_incr - incr_x) * (floor(v[2].y) + 1 - v[2].y);
              incr_x = new_incr;
          }
          else
          {
              right_x += (new_incr - incr_r) * (floor(v[2].y) + 1 - v[2].y);
              incr_r = new_incr;
          }
          calc_line(floor(v[2].y) - ceil(v[0].y) + 1,
                    floor(v[3].y) - ceil(v[0].y),
                    shift_x, right_x, incr_x, incr_r);
      }
  }
```

Interpolation

So, to get pixel values in the new image we must perform a sort of interpolation. In our routine we use a kind of linear interpolation. To explain it, we'll take all raster pixels, not as dots, but as rectangles and call them 'large' pixels. After transformation, one original 'large' pixel overlaps one, two, or four new 'large' pixels and makes certain contributions to their color values. If we add all the contributions (with weighted coefficients) from all the participating original 'large' pixels, we'll obtain color values for the new (transformed) 'large' pixels. This is explained in more detail in the figure below, where V1, V2, V3, and V4 are pixels in the original image, S1, S2, S3, and S4 are squares from the corresponding rectangles, the big dot is a reverse transformed raster pixel from the new image, and R, G and B are values of its color components.

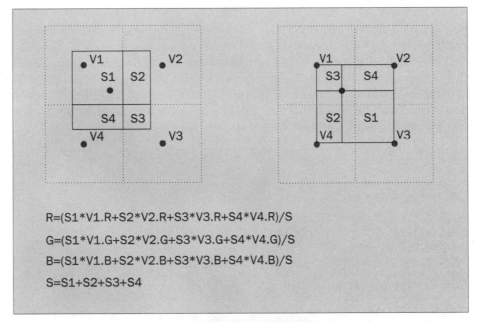

R=(S1*V1.R+S2*V2.R+S3*V3.R+S4*V4.R)/S

G=(S1*V1.G+S2*V2.G+S3*V3.G+S4*V4.G)/S

B=(S1*V1.B+S2*V2.B+S3*V3.B+S4*V4.B)/S

S=S1+S2+S3+S4

Linear Interpolation

The next task is the interpolation procedure, namely, a reverse transformation of pixels. When we know the coefficients A, B, C, D, dX and dY for the transformed image, we can perform the direct transformation. To execute the reverse transformation, we have to calculate other coefficients - Arev, Brev, Crev, Drev:

$$Det = A*D - B*C$$

$$Arev = D \ / \ Det$$

$$Brev = -B \ / \ Det$$

$$Crev = -C \ / \ Det$$

$$Drev = A \ / \ Det$$

411

Using these coefficients we can obtain the (Xold, Yold) co-ordinates of the point in the original image which corresponds to the pixel (X,Y) in the transformed image.

$$Xold = Arev*(X - dX) + Brev*(Y - dY)$$

$$Yold = Crev*(X - dX) + Drev*(Y - dY)$$

Because Xold and Yold are generally non-integer numbers, interpolation is required and it must be done using the nearest four raster points. The routine given below illustrates this technique for linear interpolation. Note that the interpolation for each color component is carried out separately. You should bear in mind that boundary points have less than four neighbors. If you don't want to check for this condition, you have to increase the image in memory by duplicating the first and last row and column.

```
void real_picture::interpolate(float x, float y, byte4 &color)
{
    int row, column, pl;
    float delta_x, delta_y, aa, bb, cc, dd;

    row = y;
    column = x;
    delta_y = y - row;
    delta_x = x - column;
    aa = delta_x * delta_y;
    bb = delta_y - aa;
    cc = delta_x - aa;
    dd = 1 - delta_y - cc;
    for (pl = 0; pl < max_plan; pl++ )
        color[pl] = 0.5 + aa * pict[pl][row+1][column+1] +
                    bb * pict[pl][row+1][column] +
                    cc * pict[pl][row][column+1] +
                    dd * pict[pl][row][column];
}
```

It is easier to explain the linear interpolation method using the idea of a 'large' point. In this case, the initial image is split into identical rectangles, in the centers of which lie raster pixels. The purpose of interpolation is to determine the RGB components for a new point, which is not a raster pixel. This point can be placed in the center of a rectangle, the same size as the raster pixel rectangles. The new rectangle overlaps between one and four initial ones. The overlapping portion of each initial rectangle can be chosen as weighting factors for estimating the contributions made by the raster pixels to the RGB components of the new point. If the new point falls on one raster pixel, the weighting factor for the given raster pixel is 1, and for all others raster pixels it is 0. If the new point falls in a section connecting two pixels, only these pixels have weighting factors different from 0, and the interpolation becomes a usual linear interpolation between two points.

Calculating the Coefficients by Three Points

We'll now discuss how to organize the user-interface for transformations such as scrolling, reduction and expansion, rotation and shearing. The first step is to let the user choose the transformation type. Suppose a transformation has been chosen and now, using the mouse, we point out what we want to be done. Using the mouse, we define the corners of an arbitrary parallelogram. We pick up a vertex by clicking the mouse, and point this vertex to a new position. The vertex opposite the chosen one, will be the fixed point whose co-ordinates will not change during the transformation. The set of possible new positions is determined by the transformation type.

This procedure has given us the co-ordinates of three points: the stable point (Xo,Yo), the transition point (X,Y), and the new point $(Xnew,Ynew)$. Transformation parameters can then be calculated using this collection of points. These are the formulae for each conversion type.

For scrolling:

$$dX = Xnew - X$$

$$dY = Ynew - Y$$

For reduction and expanding:

$$ax = (Xnew - Xo) / (X - Xo),$$

$$ay = (Ynew - Yo) / (Y - Yo).$$

For rotating:

$$\cos(p) = ((Xnew-Xo)*(X-Xo) + (Ynew-Yo)*(Y-Yo)) / ((X-Xo)^2 + (Y-Yo)^2)$$

$$\sin(p) = ((Xnew-Xo) - (X-Xo)*\cos(p))/(Y-Yo),\ if\ Y <> Yo,$$

$$\sin(p) = ((Ynew-Yo) - (Y-Yo)*\cos(p))/(Xo-X),\ if\ X <> Xo.$$

413

For shearing:

$$ax = (Xnew - Xo) / (Y - Yo)$$

$$ay = (Ynew - Yo) / (X - Xo)$$

However, mirroring is different, and so is its procedure. Instead of choosing a parallelogram vertex we choose two arbitrary points (X1,Y1) and (X2,Y2). The line connecting these points is the mirroring line with the parameters:

a = Y2 - Y1
b = X1 - X2
c = X2*Y1 - X1*Y2

Special Issues

Simple Cases

For each of these transformations, we can set apart the cases when the converted image can be obtained by simpler means: horizontal and vertical shearing, horizontal and vertical mirroring, rotation by 0, 90, 180, 270 and 360 degrees, and expansion with integer coefficients. You may be able to think of other special cases, but for now we'll show you how to perform these transformations.

If expansion coefficients are just integer, we can simply duplicate every row and/or column of pixels. The only unpleasantness is that the pixelization effect is immediately noticeable.

As we decided that internal image representation is the array of pointers to rows, the implementation of horizontal shearing is much easier than vertical shearing. To perform horizontal shearing we can simply shift each row to the new starting position. To perform vertical shearing we not only have to repack the existing rows, but create new ones. If we had decided that the internal representation was the array of pointers to columns, the situation would have been reversed.

Horizontal and vertical mirroring can be performed very easily. Vertical mirroring just requires the pointer array to be sorted in reverse order, and horizontal mirroring requires a similar sorting of pixels in each row.

Rotation by 0 or 360 degrees is meaningless. Rotation by 180 degrees is a combination of vertical and horizontal mirroring. To rotate by 90 or 270 degrees, we have to convert rows into columns.

We've selected these cases and called them 'simple' because they require no interpolation. These transformations can be performed much quicker than the others.

Aspect Ratio

Aspect ratio is a feature of raster displays that you may never think of, even if you program graphics. Yes, a pixel is a point, but not in the strict mathematical sense. It's a dot, which also has a shape.

Depending on the selected video mode, a monitor screen has vertical and horizontal sizes in pixels: MaxX and MaxY. For example, MaxX is 640 and MaxY is 480 under 640×480. This means that the screen has 480 rows and 640 columns and 640×480 raster pixels. If the ratio (3*MaxX) / (4*MaxY) equals 1, then your screen has **rectangular pixels**. A problem arises when this ratio is not 1. Suppose that an image is a rectangular area of 100×100 pixels and the video mode is 320×200 (with the ratio (3*320)/(4*200) > 1). After rotation by 45 degrees the image appears non-rectangular, which is very frustrating. Therefore, we have included a variable AspR in the routines for direct and reverse transformations to correct aspect ratio effects.

Two and Three Step Rotation

Here we'll discuss rotation in more detail. This transformation is considered a basic operation in image manipulation, but we don't know why, and so it's widely discussed. Various rotation methods were invented. The one we've shown above is referred to as direct, or one-step rotation. There are, however, methods performed in more than one step.

These specific methods usually require less computer memory (which could be valuable if you're working with large images) and may also work faster. These methods differ quite significantly from one-step rotation, because interpolation is applied after every step and, what's more, to the previous step image, not the original one.

The two-step algorithm was proposed for computer graphics applications by Catmull and Smith and independently for image processing by Friedman. We assume a point (Xo,Yo) as the rotation center and p as the rotation angle. After the first step, a pixel (X,Y) passes to the point (X1,Y1) and after the second step it passes to the point (X2,Y2). For the interpolation, we have to write the reverse transformations for each step.

The first step gives the following expressions:

$$X = X1$$

$$Y = (X1-Xo)*(-tan(p)) + (Y1-Yo)/cos(p)$$

which show that there are no changes in the x-direction and that there is shearing and reduction in the y-direction.

For the second step:

$$X1 = (X2-Xo)*cos(p) + (Y2-Yo)*sin(p) + Xo$$

$$Y1 = Y2$$

Unlike the first step, there is shearing and expansion in the x-direction and no changes in the y-direction. If we combine both steps into one then we obviously obtain the old formula for rotation.

Friedman observed a serious imperfection in this algorithm. The intermediate image, after the first step, can't retain all the high-frequency components of the original image. The rotation angle p causes compression with cos(p) in the vertical dimension. The data compression is obvious since the area of the intermediate image is smaller than that of the original image. To avoid the loss of information, Friedman resamples and expands the original image in the horizontal direction. The expansion factor should be 1/cos(p) which means that we actually have a three-step procedure: (X,Y) to (X1,Y1) to (X2,Y2) before finally moving to (X3,Y3).

The first step is expansion in the x-direction:

$$X = (X1-Xo)*cos(p) + Xo$$

$$Y = Y1$$

The second step is shearing and reduction in the y-direction:

$$X1 = X2$$

$$Y1 = (X2-Xo)*(-\sin(p)) + (Y2-Yo)/\cos(p) + Yo$$

The third step is shearing in the x-direction:

$$X2 = X3 + (Y3-Yo)*\tan(p)$$

$$Y2 = Y3$$

This rotation method requires less computations than one-step rotation. An additional advantage is that all operations are one-dimensional interpolations and data moves. Only one row or column at a time is to be available for fast access and processing.

The final algorithm covers three-step rotation, where all three steps are shearing transformations. This method was discovered independently by several authors. As in the previous case, we'll write each step for reverse transformation:

The first step is shearing in the y-direction:

$$X = X1$$

$$Y = (X1-Xo)*(-\tan(p/2)) + Y1$$

The second step is shearing in the x-direction:

$$X1 = X2 + (Y2-Yo)*\sin(p)$$

$$Y1 = Y2$$

The third step is just another shearing in the y-direction:

$$X2 = X3$$

$$Y2 = (X3-Xo)*(-\tan(p/2)) + Y3$$

The virtue of this decomposition, compared to the two-step algorithm, is that it consists of three shearing transformations, by which we mean movements by only one co-ordinate, and that all these shearings can be performed as a kind of parallel shift, row by row and column by column, as shown in the following figure.

Sometimes it's impossible to keep large images in high-speed RAM during processing. In this case, the two-step and three-step algorithms have a definite advantage since memory requirements can be limited to the size of a single row or column. Since the two-step algorithm enlarges the images at the first extra step, this algorithm takes more total memory than the other two.

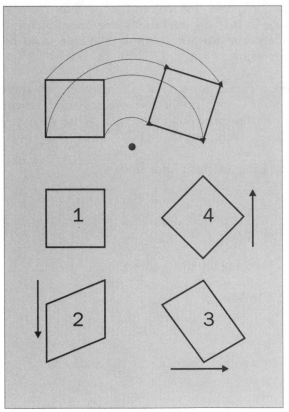

Rotation and its Representation as Three Shearings

Using the Routine

Here we'll explain which parameters to use for each transformation. After the graphics system is initialized, we need to read a `.BMP` file from a disk and then possibly display it. We don't have to read the entire image. The part which lies inside the rectangle with (x1, y1), the top-left corner, and (x2, y2), the bottom-right corner will be enough. The variable `rpp` is a pointer to the image read.

```
rpp = read_bmp_file_to_real_picture ( file_name, x1,y1, x2,y2 );
rpp->show ( );
```

To scroll the image we need to set shift length dx and dy.

```
rpp-> create_trans_picture ( dx, dy, 0, 0, SHIFT );
```

The same effect can be obtained without making a new image, but by carrying out the following operations on the initial image:

```
rpp->left_x += dx;
rpp->top_y += dy;
```

For the mirror transformation we need to set line factors a*x+b*y+c=0, depending on the mirror orientation.

```
rpp-> create_trans_picture ( a, b, c, 0, MIRROR );
```

The factors a, b, c can be replaced with the co-ordinates of two points (xx1, yy1) and (xx2, yy2), which are the points the given line goes through:

```
rpp-> create_trans_picture ( yy2-yy1, xx1-xx2, yy1*xx2 - xx1*yy2, 0, MIRROR);
```

For rotation we need to set the co-ordinates of the center (xc, yc), and the angle.

```
rpp-> create_trans_picture ( xc, yc, angle, 0, ROTATE );
```

For shearing and zooming, we have to set the co-ordinates of the transformation center (xc, yc) and the shearing or zooming power along the x and y axes, ax and ay respectively.

```
rpp-> create_trans_picture ( xc, yc, ax, ay, SHEAR );
rpp-> create_trans_picture ( xc, yc, ax, ay, ZOOM );
```

After a transformation the obtained image can be shown by the following:

```
rpp->pp[rpp->nt-1]-> show( );
```

Special Effects

We'll now show you some pictures from our 'album of effects'.

Twist

We divide the whole image into squares of a specified size and rotate each of these squares by 90, 180, or 270 degrees. The effect looks more attractive if the rotation angle for each square is randomly chosen from these three:

```
real_picture *twist( real_picture *po,   // pointer to the image
                     BYTE twist_type,    // angle:   0 - 90,
                                         //          1 - 180,
                                         //          2 - 270,
                                         //          any other - random
                     BYTE  n )           // rotated box dimension (n x n)
{
   int i, j, io, jo, pl;
   real_picture *p;
   BYTE tt;

   p = po->duplicate();
   i = 0;
   while ( i <= p->row_number - n )
   {
      j = 0;
      while ( j <= p->column_number - n )
      {
         for ( io = 1; io <= n; io++ )
            for ( jo = 1; jo <= n; jo++ )
            {
               if ( twist_type > 2 )
                  tt = random(3);
               else
                  tt = twist_type;
               switch (tt)
               {
                  case 0 :
                     for (pl = 0; pl < p->max_plan; pl++)
// Note that for this effect the loop
// for color components must be inside
// the loops for coordinates,
// because we must move each pixel as a whole
```

```
                        p->pict[pl][i+io][j+jo] =
                            po->pict[pl][i+n-jo+1][j+io];
                    break;
                case 1 :
                    for (pl = 0; pl < p->max_plan; pl++)
                        p->pict[pl][i+io][j+jo] =
                            po->pict[pl][i+n-io+1][j+n-jo+1];
                    break;
                case 2 :
                    for (pl = 0; pl < p->max_plan; pl++)
                        p->pict[pl][i+io][j+jo] =
                            po->pict[pl][i+jo][j+n-io+1];
                    break;
                }
            }
            j+=n;
        }
        i+=n;
    }
    return p;
}
```

Texture

This effect combines two images in such a way that an image is imposed on the original image as a texture. A factor Alpha (from 0 to 100) is chosen, which indicates how much the texture affects the original image. If you want to invert the image, the factor should be negative. Then it's divided by 80. For each RGB component of each pixel in the image, the following operation is executed:

NewColor = OldColor + Alpha * (TextureColor - 128)

If the texture image is smaller than the original image, it is applied repeatedly. But in this case you'll usually see distortion lines appear on the borders:

```
real_picture *texture( real_picture *po, // pointer to the image
                       real_picture *tp, // pointer to the texture image
                       BOOL invert, BYTE alpha )
{
    int i, j, coef, b, io, pl;
    real_picture *p;

    if (po->max_plan > tp->max_plan)
        return NULL;
```

```
      coef = 5*alpha;
      if (invert)
         coef = - coef;
      p = po->duplicate();
      for (pl = 0; pl < p->max_plan; pl++)
         for ( i = 1; i <= p->row_number; i++ )
         {
            io = (i-1) % tp->row_number + 1;
            for ( j = 1; j <= p->column_number; j++ )
            {
               b = po->pict[pl][i][j] + ( coef*((long) tp->pict[pl][io][(j-1)
                  % (tp->column_number + 1)] - 128 ) ) / 400;
               setbyte;
// setbyte is a macro :
// #define setbyte
//    if ( b < 0 )
//       p->pict[pl][i][j] = 0;
//    else if ( b > 255 )
//       p->pict[pl][i][j] = 255;
//    else
//       p->pict[pl][i][j] = b;
            }
         }
      return p;
}
```

Mosaic

The implementation of this effect is similar to the previous one. The only difference is that instead of a file, the size of the mosaic tile is chosen. Each tile's size corresponds to some default texture image which consists of rectangles of different sizes. Each rectangle has illuminated sides and shadows which gives a sort of 3D look to the resulting image. What's more, opposite borders of the texture image have the same configuration so the obtained image has no distortion on the borders.

The key operation for each RGB component of each pixel is:

NewColor = OldColor + (128 - MosaicColor).

Pixelate

The image is divided into rectangles of a specified size, then the average value of each RGB component is found for all the pixels inside each rectangle. The average color is attributed to all pixels of a rectangle. As a result, the image consists of rectangular areas of uniform color:

```
real_picture *pixelate(real_picture *po,        // pointer to the image
                       BYTE n, BYTE m )         // box size
{
    int i, j, io, jo, pl;
    real_picture *p;
    int s;
    BYTE q;

    p = po->duplicate();
    for (pl = 0; pl < p->max_plan; pl++)
    {
        i = 0;
        while ( i <= p->row_number - n )
        {
            j = 0;
            while ( j <= p->column_number - m )
            {
                s = 0;
                for ( io = 1; io <= n; io++ )
                    for ( jo = 1; jo <= m; jo++ )
                        s += p->pict[pl][i+io][j+jo];
                q = s / (n*m);
                for (io = 1; io <= n; io++)
                    for (jo = 1; jo <= m; jo++)
                        p->pict[pl][i+io][j+jo] = q;
                j += m;
            }
            i += n;;
        }
    }
    return p;
}
```

Facet

This effect is a simple implementation of the method known as 'median filtering'. A rectangle of a specified size is taken around each pixel of the original image. For each RGB component, an array is made of the colors of all the pixels inside the rectangle. Then each array is sorted. Instead of the average color value, the median array value is attributed to the chosen pixel. The procedure is repeated for every pixel in the original image:

```
real_picture *facet(real_picture *po, // the pointer to the image
                    int n, int m )
{
    int i, j, io, jo, k, di1, di2, dj1, dj2, pl;
```

```
    real_picture *p;
    BYTE rarr[100];
    BYTE b;

    p = po->duplicate();
    di1 = n / 2;
    di2 = n - di1 - 1;
    dj1 = m / 2;
    dj2 = m - dj1 - 1;
    for (pl = 0; pl < p->max_plan; pl++)
       for ( i = di1 + 1;  i <= p->row_number - di2; i++ )
          for ( j = dj1 + 1; j <= p->column_number - dj2; j++ )
          {
             k = 0;
             for ( io = -di1; io <= dj2; io++ )
                for ( jo = -dj1; jo <= dj2; jo++, k++ )
                   rarr[k] = po->pict[pl][i+io][j+jo];
// sort ---------------------------------------
             for ( io = 0; io < k-1; io++ )
                for ( jo = io+1; jo < k; jo++ )
                   if ( rarr[io] > rarr[jo] )
                   {
                      b = rarr[io];
                      rarr[io] = rarr[jo];
                      rarr[jo] = b;
                   }
// --------------------------------------------
             p->pict[pl][i][j] = rarr[ k / 2 ];
          }
    return p;
}
```

Crystallize

This effect accentuates similar colors to create an 'impressionist' picture, and this is the most time consuming effect described here. Again, a rectangle is taken around a pixel. Then we make arrays of the RGB components for all the pixels inside the rectangle, a separate array for each RGB component. Each array is sorted and the pair of colors with the nearest values is found. The smaller of the two is attributed to the given pixel. If the difference between these two nearest values is 0, or in other words, they have the same component values in the array, then the value which occurs more frequently is taken as the attribute color.

```
real_picture *crystallize(real_picture *po, //the pointer to the image
                          int n, int m) // height and width
{
   int i, j, io, jo, k, ir, ig, ib;
   int i1, i2, j1, j2, di1, di2, dj1, dj2;
```

```
    real_picture *p;
    int rarr[100];
    int rmin, b, pl;
    BYTE nr;

    memset( rarr, 0, sizeof(rarr) );
    p = po->duplicate();
    di1 = n / 2;
    di2 = n - di1 - 1;
    dj1 = m / 2;
    dj2 = m - dj1 - 1;
    for (pl = 0; pl < p->max_plan; pl++)
       for ( i = 1; i <= p->row_number; i++ )
       {
          if ( i - di1 >= 1 )
             i1 = i - di1;
          else
             i1 = 1;
          if ( i + di2 <= p->row_number )
             i2 = i + di2;
          else
             i2 = p->row_number;
          // these two "IFs" help avoid boundaries errors
          for ( j = 1; j <= p->column_number; j++ )
          {
             if ( j - dj1 >= 1 )
                j1 = j - dj1;
             else
                j1 = 1;
             if ( j + dj2 <= p->column_number )
                j2 = j + dj2;
             else
                j2 = p->column_number;
             k = 0;
             for ( io = i1; io <= i2; io++ )
                for ( jo = j1; jo <= j2; jo++, k++ )
                   rarr[k] = po->pict[pl][io][jo];
// sort ----------------------------------------
             for ( io = 0; io < k-1; io++ )
                for ( jo = io+1; jo < k; jo++ )
                   if ( rarr[io] > rarr[jo] )
                   {
                      b = rarr[io];
                      rarr[io] = rarr[jo];
                      rarr[jo] = b;
                   }
// --------------------------------------------
             rmin = 255;
             nr = ir = 0;
             for ( io = 0; io < k-1; io++ )
                if ( rarr[io+1] == rarr[io] )
```

425

```
                {
                    jo = 1;
                    while ((rarr[io+jo+1] == rarr[io]) && (io+jo+1 <= k-1))
                        jo++;
                    if ( jo > nr )
                    {
                        rmin = 0;
                        nr = jo;
                        ir = io;
                    }
                    else
                        if ( rarr[io+1] - rarr[io] < rmin )
                        {
                            rmin = rarr[io+1] - rarr[io];
                            ir = io;
                        }
                }
                p->pict[pl][i][j] = rarr[ir];
            }
        }
    return p;
}
```

Emboss

This effect simulates the embossing of an image on a piece of metal. The edges of the image are emphasized and shadows are simulated along these edges. We choose one of the eight directions of 'light' which are up, down, left, right, or one of the four diagonals, and a background color. The original image is duplicated and the duplicate is slightly shifted sideways from the original in the indicated direction usually by two or three pixels. Then the two images are put together. For each RGB component of every pixel of the image the following operation is executed:

NewColor = OldColor - ShiftColor + Background

```
    real_picture *emboss(real_picture *po,     // the pointer to the image
                         int vert,             // -1 (up), 0, or 1 (down)
                         int hor,              // -1 (left), 0, or 1 (right)
                         BYTE back)            // background
    {
        int i, j, b, pl;
        real_picture *p;

        p = po->duplicate();
```

```
    for (pl = 0; pl < p->max_plan; pl++)
    {
      if ( vert > 0 )
      {
         p->pict[pl][0] = p->pict[pl][ p->row_number ];
         memmove( &p->pict[pl][2], &p->pict[pl][0],
                  p->row_number*sizeof(void *) );
         p->pict[pl][1] = p->pict[pl][ p->row_number + 1 ];
         memmove(&p->pict[pl][1][1],&p->pict[pl][3][1],p->column_number );
         memmove(&p->pict[pl][2][1],&p->pict[pl][3][1],p->column_number );
      }
      if ( vert < 0 )
      {
         p->pict[pl][ p->row_number + 1 ] = p->pict[pl][1];
         memmove( &p->pict[pl][0], &p->pict[pl][2],
                  p->row_number*sizeof(void *) );
         p->pict[pl][ p->row_number ] = p->pict[pl][0];
         memmove( &p->pict[pl][p->row_number-1][1],
                  &p->pict[pl][p->row_number-2][1],
                  p->column_number );
         memmove( &p->pict[pl][p->row_number][1],
                  &p->pict[pl][p->row_number - 2][1],
                  p->column_number );
      }
      p->pict[pl][0] = p->pict[pl][1];
      p->pict[pl][ p->row_number + 1 ] = p->pict[pl][p->row_number];

      if ( hor != 0 )
         for ( i = 1; i <= p->row_number; i++ )
         {
            memmove( &p->pict[pl][i][1+hor], &p->pict[pl][i][1],
                     p->column_number );
            memmove( &p->pict[pl][i][1+hor], &p->pict[pl][i][1],
                     p->column_number );
         }
      for ( i = 1; i <= p->row_number; i++ )
      {
         for ( j = 1; j <= p->column_number; j++ )
         {
            b = p->pict[pl][i][j] - po->pict[pl][i][j] + back;
            setbyte;
         }
      }
    }
    return p;
}
```

Blur

This effect differs from Pixelate only in that the color components averaged among all the pixels inside the rectangle are attributed to one central pixel, not to all of them. As a result the image becomes smoother and blurred.

Motion Blur

This effect creates the illusion of movement within your image.

The weighted averaging of an array of pixels in a given direction is used. The length of this array and/or weights depend on the motion speed:

```
real_picture *motion_blur(real_picture *po,     // the pointer to the image
                          int vert,             // -1 (up), 0, or 1 (down)
                          int hor,              // -1 (left), 0, or 1 (right)
                          BYTE v )              // "velocity"
{
   int i, j, jo, n, pl;
   real_picture *p;
   long b;

   if ( vert*hor == 1 )
      v = v*10 / 14;
   p = po->duplicate();
   for (pl = 0; pl < p->max_plan; pl++)
      for ( i = 1; i <= p->row_number; i++ )
         for ( j = 1; j <= p->column_number; j++ )
         {
            b = 0;
            n = v;
            for ( jo = 0; jo < v; jo++ )
            {
               if ( ( i+vert*jo >= 1 ) && ( i+vert*jo <= p->row_number ) &&
                  ( j+hor*jo >= 1 ) && ( j+hor*jo <= p->column_number ) )
               {

                  b += n*p->pict[pl][i+vert*jo][j+hor*jo];
                  // b is a weighed sum
                  n--;
               }
            }
            b = b / ((v-n+1)*(v+n) / 2);
            setbyte;
         }
   return p;
}
```

Maximum

This effect differs from Facet only in that the maximum component value is taken instead of the median values. This brightens and blurs the image.

Minimum

The effect is the same as the Maximum effect, but uses the minimum component values. This darkens and blurs the image.

Diffuse

For a given rectangle, the color of the central pixel is replaced with the color of a pixel randomly picked out from the rectangle, so the colors run. The procedure should be applied separately to each component if you also want to shift colors:

```
real_picture *diffuse(real_picture *po,    // the pointer to the image
                      int n, int m,        // height and width
                      BOOL allow_color_shift )
{
    int i, j, io, jo, pl;
    int i1, i2, j1, j2, di1, di2, dj1, dj2;
    real_picture *p;

    p = po->duplicate();
    di1 = n / 2;
    di2 = n - di1 - 1;
    dj1 = m / 2;
    dj2 = m - dj1 - 1;
    for ( i = 1; i <= p->row_number; i++ )
    {
        if ( i - di1 >= 1 )
            i1 = i - di1;
        else
            i1 = 1;
        if ( i + di2 <= p->row_number )
            i2 = i + di2;
        else
            i2 = p->row_number;
        for ( j = 1; j <= p->column_number; j++ )
        {
            if ( j - dj1 >= 1 )
                j1 = j - dj1;
            else
                j1 = 1;
```

```
            if ( j + dj2 <= p->column_number )
               j2 = j + dj2;
            else
               j2 = p->column_number;
            if (allow_color_shift && (p->max_plan == 3))
            {
               io = i1 + random( i2 - i1 + 1 );
               jo = j1 + random( j2 - j1 + 1 );
               p->pict[0][i][j] = po->pict[0][io][jo];
               io = i1 + random( i2 - i1 + 1 );
               jo = j1 + random( j2 - j1 + 1 );
               p->pict[1][i][j] = po->pict[1][io][jo];
               io = i1 + random( i2 - i1 + 1 );
               jo = j1 + random( j2 - j1 + 1 );
               p->pict[2][i][j] = po->pict[2][io][jo];
            }
            else
            {
               io = i1 + random( i2 - i1 + 1 );
               jo = j1 + random( j2 - j1 + 1 );
               for (pl = 0; pl < p->max_plan; pl++)
                  p->pict[pl][i][j] = po->pict[pl][io][jo];
            }
         }
      }
   }
   return p;
}
```

Add Noise

For this effect, you have to specify the color components that will be
changed and the range of changes (from 0 up to 255). A random variable
which assumes (with equal probability) values from 0 up to the maximum is
added to or subtracted from the components being changed:

```
real_picture *add_noise(real_picture *po,   // the pointer to the image
                        BOOL rb, BOOL gb, BOOL bb,
                        int value)           // 0..255
{
   int i, j, b, pl;
   real_picture *p;
   BOOL arr[3];

   p = po->duplicate();
   arr[0] = rb;
   arr[1] = gb;
   arr[2] = bb;
   for (pl = 0; pl < p->max_plan; pl++)
      if (arr[pl])
```

```
        for ( i = 1; i <= p->row_number; i++ )
           for ( j = 1; j <= p->column_number; j++ )
           {
              b = p->pict[pl][i][j] + (1 - 2*random(2))*random(value+1);
              setbyte;
           }
     return p;
}
```

Blend

This effect implements weighted averaging for each pixel's color component among its five or, if the **WideApperture** is chosen, nine neighbors. You also have to specify the total weighting of the neighbors:

```
real_picture *blend(real_picture *po,    // the pointer to the image
                    BOOL wide_apperture,
                    int percent)         // 0..100
{
   int i, j, io, jo, pl;
   int i1, i2, j1, j2, di1, di2, dj1, dj2;
   real_picture *p;

   p = po->duplicate();
   for (pl = 0; pl < p->max_plan; pl++)
      for ( i = 1; i <= p->row_number; i++ )
         for ( j = 1; j <= p->column_number; j++ )
            if (wide_apperture)
               p->pict[pl][i][j]=((100 - percent)*
                                 (long) po->pict[pl][i][j] +
                                 percent*((long) po->pict[pl][i-1][j-1] +
                                 (long) po->pict[pl][i-1][j] +
                                 (long) po->pict[pl][i-1][j+1] +
                                 (long) po->pict[pl][i][j-1] +
                                 (long) po->pict[pl][i][j+1] +
                                 (long) po->pict[pl][i+1][j-1] +
                                 (long) po->pict[pl][i+1][j] +
                                 (long) po->pict[pl][i+1][j+1]) / 8) / 100;
            else
               p->pict[pl][i][j] = ( ( 100 - percent )*
                                   (long) po->pict[pl][i][j] +
                                   percent*( (long) po->pict[pl][i-1][j] +
                                   (long) po->pict[pl][i][j-1] +
                                   (long) po->pict[pl][i][j+1] +
                                   (long) po->pict[pl][i+1][j]) / 4) / 100;
   return p;
}
```

Edge Detection

This effect can be achieved in various ways, for example, by transforming color components as follows:

```
real_picture *edge_detection( real_picture *po)
{
   int i, j, b, pl;
   real_picture *p;

   p = po->duplicate();
   for (pl = 0; pl < p->max_plan; pl++)
      for ( i = 1; i <= p->row_number; i++ )
         for ( j = 1; j <= p->column_number; j++ )
         {
            b = 2*abs( (int) po->pict[pl][i][j] -
               (int) po->pict[pl][i+1][j+1] ) +
               2*abs( (int) po->pict[pl][i][j+1] -
               (int) po->pict[pl][i+1][j] );
            setbyte;
         }
   return p;
}
```

Ripples

This effect simply shifts each pixel to a new position determined by some wavy function - Sin() or Cos() are good examples:

```
real_picture *ripples(real_picture *po)     // the pointer to the image
{
   int i, j, pl;
   real_picture *p;

   p = po->duplicate();
   for (pl = 0; pl < p->max_plan; pl++)
      for ( i = 1; i <= p->row_number; i++ )
         for ( j = 1; j <= p->column_number; j++ )
            p->pict[pl][i][j] = po->pict[pl][i+1.5*sin(1.5*(i+j))][j];
   return p;
}
```

Effect Algorithm Reverse Engineering

Suppose you get your new image processing system and find the effect you've dreamed of for so long. You think it's a really brilliant effect and decide to suss out its algorithm. If this is you, then you may find this subsection useful.

The task of cracking the image effect algorithm is not so easy, but in many cases it can be solved quite successfully. So take a look at the following recipes, based on our own experience.

First you should carefully analyze the list of parameters which need to be set before invoking the effect. If the system asks you to select a file, it means that some kind of combination of two images will be done. In this case, it's often enough to find out the way RGB components of two corresponding pixels are mixed together.

If the system doesn't prompt you to choose a file, it doesn't necessarily mean that the second image will not be engaged. For example, after asking the user about the mosaic size (small, average or large), the effect 'Mosaic' in PhotoFinish by ZSoft uses one of the three default files: **MOSAIC1.PCX**, **MOSAIC2.PCX**, or **MOSAIC3.PCX**. While reverse engineering this effect, the best choice is to substitute the images stored in these files with something simpler.

Then it's necessary to find out whether pixels are affected by their neighbors. Usually, if you're prompted to specify 'the cell size', that means they are affected. You should start by choosing the minimum possible size. Then it is necessary to create a test image composed of separately located small groups of gray pixels on a white background (a separate pixel, two horizontal or vertical pixels or something like that). Then you should analyze how the effect influences your resulting image. So you need to find out:

▲ whether the pixels change their locations

▲ whether their quantity is changed

▲ whether their colors are transformed

If you find spacial displacement of pixels, you can try to connect the displacement size with the pixel co-ordinates. If the colors are changed, you have to determine whether the adjacent pixels count. Again you have to change the target pixel colors in order to find out the precise relationship. The constants you'll find should be connected with those that have been set before the effect was invoked.

You should always remember that some randomness may be hidden in the effect. This fact is easy to uncover. Prepare two absolutely identical images and apply the effect to both of them with the same set of constants. If you obtain two different results, this means there is some randomness. If this happens, you'll have to rely on your intuition and experience to go further.

When, at last, you've managed to write your own algorithm that produces the same visual result, you don't have to bother asking yourself, "Have I really managed to recreate that algorithm?". Well, if you've cracked the visual effect, you don't need the exact algorithm - your version works!

Nonlinear Transformations

All of the described transformations have a pleasant common feature: they are implemented using only linear co-ordinate operations. This makes it possible to calculate the reverse transformations very easily. Moreover, the sum of several effects has the same properties and can be calculated as a single transformation. However, non-linear transformations promise to be much more impressive. It seems they'd produce something similar to 'stretching morphing'.

A number of difficulties arise when we introduce non-linearity. Reverse transformations can't be calculated so easily. Template calculations for a transformed image are essentially complicated because borders don't remain straight lines, and even elementary functions used as the basis for the transformation slow the calculations down. But to show you that something interesting can still be made and that there's nothing to fear, we're going to offer you an example of such a transformation.

To avoid complications, or at least to reduce their number, we've chosen the transformation of a lens with a very short focal length, commonly called a fish-eye lens. In this case, the borders of the image are changed just a bit. All the points of the image are displaced from the center of the lens and the displacement length depends on the distance to the center. The degree of distortion is set by parameter **alpha0**. If **alpha0** > 0, then the distortion is away from the center, otherwise it is towards the center:

```
real_picture *nonlinear_example( real_picture *po, float alpha0 )
{
    int i, j, pl, xc, yc;
    real_picture *p;
    float alpha;
    byte4 color;

    p = po->duplicate();
    xc = p->column_number / 2;
```

```
    yc = p->row_number / 2;
    for (pl = 0; pl < p->max_plan; pl++)
       for ( i = 1; i <= p->row_number; i++ )
          for ( j = 1; j <= p->column_number; j++ )
          {
             alpha = exp( alpha0*log( ( (i-yc+0.3)*(i-yc+0.3) +
                         (j-xc+0.3)*(j-xc+0.3) ) / ( xc*xc + yc*yc ) ) );
             po->interpolate( xc+alpha*(j-xc), yc+alpha*(i-yc), color );
             p->pict[pl][i][j] = color[pl];
          }
    return p;
}
```

Summary

Well, that's about it. By now you probably understand the details of image manipulation better than we do! However, before we part with this attractive theme, we'd like to give you a short résumé.

We can logically distinguish three different groups of image manipulation and processing techniques:

▲ 'Transformation' in its literal meaning is when pixels change their locations. There are linear and nonlinear variations. We described the linear techniques thoroughly in this chapter. The nonlinear ones we only touched on slightly, because they are very akin to stretching morphing (see Chapter 13 'Morphing' for details).

▲ Image 'effects'. The color values of pixels are changed in accordance with some 'local' rule. With your 'album of effects' plus some recipes for effect algorithm reverse engineering, we think you are now quite well equipped.

▲ Whole image color spacial transformation. The color values of pixels are changed according to some 'global' rule. Brightness and contrast corrections, color-gray mapping, and those tricks with the color histogram all belong to this third group.

It may seem that now you've got almost everything to do with image processing and manipulation techniques, however, there are still problems to be solved.

All three groups of image manipulation techniques suffer from palette color representation. When interpolating the color value you can't be sure that the value you obtain belongs to the current image palette. Therefore, you either have to perform posterior quantization (see Chapter 7 and the discussion in Chapter 4) or interpolate to the nearest color from the current palette; both ways can cause computational overheating. However, you can use something like 'the nearest neighbor' approach in order to stay within the source image palette. But anyway, as you know, TrueColor and 256 shades of gray never cause such problems. I suggest that you should use these representations in order to avoid these obstacles.

CHAPTER

13

Morphing

With the celebrated success of 'liquid-metal' robots in movies such as 'Terminator 2', the name of this particular computer graphics technique has become a widely used term. We planned the morphing chapter in this book with a degree of hesitation. We hadn't any morphing experience to speak of, so we had to start exploring this mysterious area from the very beginning. However, we (like all children) were all pretty experienced in the art of Plasticine modeling, and so with GG's blessing, we plunged into this fascinating world. We added a bit of creative mathematics and came up with what we think is a miraculous morphing tool.

Chapter Contents

In this chapter, we will cover:

- The Types of Morphing
- The Morphing Points
- Manual Triangulation
- How to Map a Triangle into a Triangle
- Distortion Morphing
- Transition Morphing
- How to Improve the Results

The Types of Morphing

Before we can get onto the programming aspects of this technique, we require a definition of the term 'morphing'. You could say, 'Morphing is a method of transforming an image or a sequence of images from one state to another'. Well, it's a solid, philosophically correct definition, but it doesn't help us at all. Once again we have to disturb our respectable GG, simply to get something with which to start.

Yes, transformation, is usually mentioned whenever morphing is concerned. However, the principle question is, 'Why do we distort or mix images?' Morphing can be used either as a method of keyframing (remember this animation term?) to produce a specific set of intermediate frames, or as a powerful image manipulation technique.

Morphing is mostly famous for its application in animation, but nevertheless it may be applied as an image editing tool as well. But you've seen many techniques for keyframing and image manipulation in this book. Is this one really worth a separate chapter?

Morphing is a much more complex technique than these other more traditional tools. As you may have seen in the infamous helicopter scene in T2, if it's properly applied, the results can be unbelievable. Anyway, perhaps morphing is in fashion at the moment, because it realizes man's subconscious ambition to transform into something else. Because of these reasons, we're going to investigate morphing, and to start, as usual, we'll draw up a simple kind of classification.

GG has already mentioned one distinctive feature - its field of application. Regardless of what you use it for, there are really two different types of morphing today: two dimensional and three dimensional. Although the logic of the morphing process is very similar, 3D morphing involves, as you would expect, some additional steps.

3D Morphing

3D morphing usually means that the computer models an object, or at least its surface, and then transforms the model. That's why at present 3D morphing almost always works with mathematically defined or computer generated objects. In most 3D morphing systems, the emphasis is put on transforming 3D models or some kind of surface approximations, such as a triangular mesh. Surface reconstruction, rendering, and texture mapping are those additional steps which have to be performed afterwards.

2D Morphing

2D morphing gives the visual effect of a 3D change of shape by warping a 2D image. By means of digital warping algorithms, the source image is deformed to fit into the shape of the target one. At the same time, the texture of the initial image is conveyed to that of the target bit by bit.

A detailed account of implementing 3D morphing is beyond the scope of this chapter. 'Is this because of its complexity?' you ask. Not entirely. We agree that playing with 3D morphing almost always involves a lot of computations. However, the basic idea looks even clearer without these details.

Generally speaking, the triangular representation we use, makes both types of morphing very similar, at least while the topology of a 3D surface remains the same. What actually makes the difference are the 'color calculations':

▲   A kind of interpolation in 2D.

▲   Rendering, texture mapping, and so on in 3D.

3D rendering is itself complicated enough to be worth a separate chapter (the next one, by the way) with or without morphing. You may try to build a 3D morphing system yourself, if you dare, and it doesn't seem to be too hard, but for this chapter, we'll assume morphing to be mostly two dimensional.

On that note, you should be aware that there are two types of 2D morphing - distortion and transition.

Distortion Morphing

Distortion morphing is a fairly easy process. It operates on a single image and performs a **local warp** upon it. By using distortion morphs, you can bring to life practically any image. You wouldn't believe what you can do, until you see an example, so...

The Sequence of Frames Showing Distortion Morphing

A possible application for distortion morphing is to change someone's expression on a photograph, or use a continuous sequence of these altered photographs to give the impression of someone talking.

Transition Morphing

Transition morphing is a more complicated technique. It operates on two images at a time, fading smoothly from one to the other. But we have already had some fading techniques in the animation chapter, so what's the difference? Those simple image-changing effects will never create the illusion of morphing, because they just mix some pixels from one image and some from another, and put the resulting ones into exactly the same positions. That's why if you change a human face for another one and the two images don't coincide, you'll get something with four eyes on your tweens.

So, transition morphing is smooth fading together with a simultaneous distortion morph. Squeezing together the source and destination images helps make the sequence look perfectly real. The figure below shows the intermediate frames of one transformation. To be quite honest, none of us could expect it to look like this.

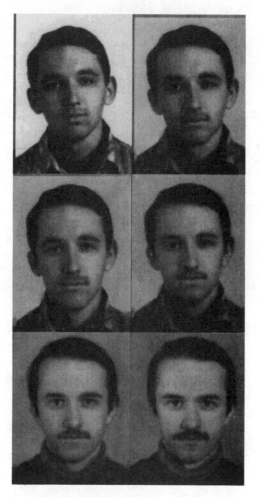

The Sequence of Frames Showing Transition Morphing

 Transition morphing becomes a matter of art only if each of the intermediate frames looks intuitively (virtually) real. For instance, if you transform one human face to another, each of the tweens should look like a real face as well.

At last, the final definition. Morphing is an image manipulation or keyframing technique that involves:

 local deformation of a 2D image or a 3D object, mostly on its surface, in combination with **color calculation**.

For 2D morphing, this calculation is usually a relatively simple interpolation, while for 3D, it involves some additional, rather complicated steps, such as rendering, texture mapping, and so on.

The Morphing Points

OK, it seems we can define morphing, but the question is how do we do it. As we've established above, one of the most important features of morphing is its **locality**. This means that you normally have to manually specify the areas you want to be morphed.

Usually these areas are marked by setting **morphing points** - the anchor points of the morphing transformation. You can think of them as pairs of corresponding points, one on the source image and one on the target image. During a morphing transformation each morphing point of the source image is transferred to the corresponding point of the target.

Only the morphing points themselves are transformed precisely as you specify. The area adjacent to the morphing point is mapped to the corresponding area of the target image. The actual definition of this area and the mapping rule can vary from one morphing system to another. However, morphing points remain as the way to specify the local transformation, especially if you use or are building an interactive morphing system.

It is generally thought that the more morphing points that are set, the smoother the transformation looks. We would agree with this, however, the problem is to achieve good results without too much work with the morphing points. If you were to specify each pixel of the target image as a morphing point, the result would be great, as would the amount of hard work. Still, the efficiency of a morphing system depends on how local areas are defined.

Tessellation

The name given to the method of dividing the image into small areas is **tessellation**. Tessellation varies between different morphing systems. The most commonly used tessellation is triangular tessellation, otherwise known as **triangulation**. There are many reasons for using this particular representation, some of which we give below.

However, it should be mentioned that morphing isn't always done with triangular patches. Some morphing systems use different kinds of splines defined on the morphing points, implemented with a continuous mapping function; cubic splines are the usual choice. Triangular pieces have to be small enough and well chosen to give an equally smooth result, but they are much simpler to operate with.

Why did we choose triangulation? Before we answer this question we should define exactly what triangulation is:

▲ It is a way to divide a surface into triangular parts or an attempt to cover a surface with a triangular mesh.

There are several reasons why triangulation is used, not only for morphing, but also for motion planning, object reconstruction, digital terrain modeling, and so on:

▲ It's relatively easy to triangulate a plane - just drop some points and connect them with lines

▲ It's almost as easy to approximate a surface with a triangular mesh, and this approximation is excellently adapted to variable density of data points

▲ Using a simple iterative routine, we can make triangulation more detailed by adding points one by one. The idea being to place a point, find the triangle it's in and divide it into three parts.

There is, however, a matter for careful consideration. For a given set of points you can build many different variations of triangulation. Some of them are better than others as the figure below illustrates:

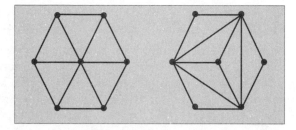

Two Versions of Triangulation on the Same Set of Points.

Fortunately, there are mathematical criteria to estimate the 'quality' of triangulation, and here is the one we'll use:

 The triangulation of an area is said to be optimal if it has the smallest overall edge length or if the minimum angle of its triangles is the largest among all possible triangulations, or in other words, we use equilateral triangles, or as close approximations to them, to cover the area.

Delaunay triangulation is the most attractive from this point of view, as it seems to fit both conditions. A triangular tessellation is called **Delaunay**, if for each adjacent pair of triangles, **flipping** their mutual edge (if it's possible) only decreases the minimum angle of the two triangles. By the way, flipping the edge is one of the commonest procedures in triangulation, and it is illustrated below:

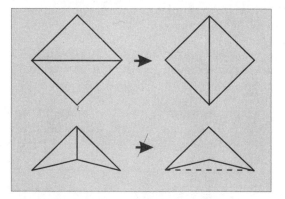

Flipping the Mutual Edge of Two Triangles

It's obvious why Delaunay triangulation seems to be the best for morphing purposes. The triangles are transformed independently, and the mapping function is not smooth on their edges, which causes an error along the edges. Therefore, the shorter the overall length of the edges, the smoother the picture.

Delaunay triangulation looks fine and seems smart enough for morphing. Nevertheless, purely automatic Delaunay triangulation has one shortcoming. Each time we add a new morphing point the algorithm rearranges the triangulation in the adjacent area (by flipping) and it may erase some important lines, such as those that bind distinct characteristic parts of the image. The key areas on the image must be separated to stop them from dissolving during morphing.

So it would be useful to mark solid lines that aren't affected by flipping. Triangulation of this kind is usually referred to as **Constrained Delaunay Triangulation** (CDT).

Our aim was to develop an interactive algorithm that would allow us to add new points and edges incrementally. This problem can be split into the three following subproblems:

 How do you compute the initial triangulation of the domain?

How do you add a point?

How do you add an edge?

To be able to use CDT in the interactive morphing system we had to add three more facilities to:

 Delete a point

Move a point

Perform a manual flip

We implemented all six facilities. However, practical usage showed that the first one (initial Delaunay triangulation of the domain) was almost useless. So, we decided to implement completely manual triangulation. This is why the morphing code on the CD-ROM doesn't contain the actual implementation of Delaunay triangulation on a set of points. If, for some reason you still feel you need it, you'll have to contact us.

Manual Triangulation

A manual triangulation program must include at least the following features:

 Add point

 Edge flipping

This set lets you manually construct any triangulation you like. In addition, to providing the user with an 'Undo' option we have to add one more operation:

 Delete point

For transition morphing these three would be enough, but for distortion morphing, the ability to move a point is also a requirement. You could do it by successive deleting and adding, but it would be much more civilized to be able to move a point, and so we added this feature as well:

 Move point

We've decided how to operate the system, and now we need to invent the necessary data structures, or in other words, what to operate on. One thing to note before we begin is that each morphing point you specify can be the vertex of at least three triangles (or even more) and therefore it'd be more convenient to keep all the points in one data structure or array.

Moreover, with transition morphing, we have two different sets of morphing points (one for each image) with one triangular tessellation. So the particular points array that the vertices use is dependent on which image is treated.

Each vertex, in its turn, is represented by the following structure (see the accompanying figure for details):

```
typedef struct
{
    int no;       // point No within pp[] array of triangle_system
    triangle* pb;    // pointer to the neighboring triangle
    edge_status sb;
    BYTE nb;
} onevertex;
```

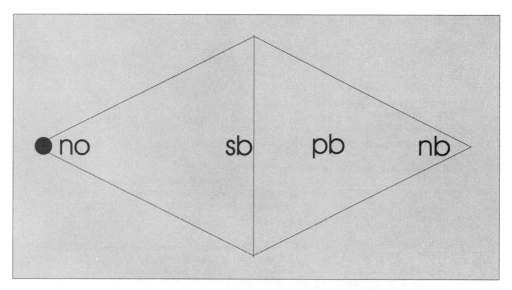

What is What in the Vertex Data Structure

Three vertices make a triangle.

```
class triangle
{
public :
    int t;      // index of this triangle in tp array
    onevertex vertex[N];
    triangle( int a_, int b_, int c_ ,
              edge_status sa_, edge_status sb_, edge_status sc_,
              triangle* pa_,triangle* pb_, triangle* pc_ ,
              BYTE na_, BYTE nb_, BYTE nc_,int t_);
    BOOL my_point( int x0, int y0,long double &adir,
                long double &bdir, long double &cdir, BYTE &in3,
                triangle* &p );
/* (adir,bdir,cdir) - search direction;
   in3 - is the additional point to points
   between which the direction line enters this triangle;
   after exit In3 is the same for the next triangle,
   if the target point (X,Y) doesn't belong to this triangle;
   P is pointer to the next triangle */

    BOOL is_boundary( BYTE &in3, triangle* &p);
    void draw_triangle( BYTE color );
    void my_line( int n1, int n2, BYTE colour);
};
```

Triangulation involves a set of triangles. Here is its structure:

```
class triangle_system
{
public :
    triangle_array* tp;
    record_for_flip* false_flip;
    int dt[100];
    int num_triangles, max_num_triangles, ndt;
    int false_flip_number, max_false_flip_number;

    triangle_system(int max_num_triangles_,
                    int max_false_flip_number_,int x0, int y0, int x1,
                    int y1, int x2, int y2, int x3, int y3, int x0_,
                    int y0_, int x1_, int y1_, int x2_, int y2_,
                    int x3_, int y3_);

    void one_flip( int t1, BYTE i3, BOOL obligatory, int deleted_point);
    void find_triangle( int x0, int y0, triangle* &p );
    void divide_triangle_to_three(int x0, int y0,triangle *p);
    void add_for_flip( int tx, BYTE nx );
    void delete_from_flip( int tx );
    void add_point( int x0, int y0 );
    void send_neighbour( triangle *p, BYTE nx );
    void delete_point( long int x0, long int y0 );
    void manual_flip( int x0, int y0 );
    void new_point( long int xn, long int yn );
    ~triangle_system();
};
```

So much for the headers, now for the actual implementation of the basic routines.

Point Adding

To add a point as a vertex of triangulation, we have to:

▲ Search for the triangle to which the point belongs.

▲ Divide the triangle into three triangular parts by connecting the new point with its vertices.

The search can be performed simply by testing each triangle for whether the new point belongs to it or not. This method would be effective enough as the number of triangles for 2D morphing would be unlikely to exceed 1000, and so the process wouldn't take long. However, in the case of 3D morphing our limit of 1000 can easily be surpassed and so, not to limit the further development of the system, we decided to implement the search along the beam. This helps decrease the number of triangles to be checked.

When the triangle has been found, it isn't a problem to split it into three parts.

 As you can see, the incremental building of triangular tessellation doesn't appear so difficult to implement. But what if you have to construct triangulation upon previously set points? This problem is much more complicated.

Target Triangle Search

Now we'll show the search in detail. First, we take one of the boundary triangles, by which we mean that some of its edges lie on the boundary of the image. We choose the middle of a boundary edge as the starting point for the beam, and it is this end of the beam that we search for.

The search may now be performed by checking the triangles one by one. Each check involves the following steps:

▲ Does the target point belong to the current triangle? If it does, then we've found the triangle we were looking for. If it doesn't then go to the next step.

▲ Which triangle do we go to next? To find out, we see which edge the beam passes through when it exits the triangle. The adjacent triangle bordering on this edge is the next to be checked. It may happen that the beam passes through a vertex. If so, we can go to either of the two triangles that share this vertex. We only have to define the new beam, using the middle of this edge as the new starting point.

The following sample code implements the search algorithm:

```
void triangle_system::find_triangle( int x0, int y0, triangle* &p )
{
    BYTE in1, in2, in3;
    int i;
    long double adir, bdir, cdir;
    BOOL triangle_found;

    for ( i = 0; (!(tp[i]->is_boundary(in3, p)) && (i < num_triangles)); i++
);
```

```
      if ( i >= num_triangles )
         stop();
      in1 = ( in3 + 1 ) % N;
      in2 = ( in3 + 2 ) % N;
      calc_line( pp[p->vertex[in1].no].x + pp[p->vertex[in2].no].x,
                 pp[p->vertex[in1].no].y + pp[p->vertex[in2].no].y,
                 2*x0, 2*y0, 2, adir, bdir, cdir );

      do
         triangle_found = p->my_point( x0, y0, adir, bdir, cdir, in3, p );
      while (( !triangle_found ) && ( p != NULL ) );
      if ( p == NULL )
         return; // p is triangle pointer
}

BOOL triangle::is_boundary( BYTE &in3, triangle* &p )
{
   int i;

   for ( i = 0; i < N; i++ )
      if ( vertex[i].pb == NULL )
      {
         in3 = i;
         p = this;
         return TRUE;
      }
   return FALSE;
}


BOOL triangle::my_point( int x0, int y0, long double &adir,
                         long double &bdir, long double &cdir,
                         BYTE &in3, triangle* &p )
{
   int p1, p2, p3;
   long double a13, b13, c13, a23, b23, c23;
   long double dev1_23, dev2_13, dev0_23, dev0_13;
   BOOL first, second;
   BYTE in1, in2;

   in1 = ( in3 + 1 ) % N;
   in2 = ( in3 + 2 ) % N;

   p1 = vertex[ in1 ].no;
   p2 = vertex[ in2 ].no;
   p3 = vertex[ in3 ].no;

   calc_line( pp[ p1 ].x, pp[ p1 ].y, pp[ p3 ].x, pp[ p3 ].y, 1,
              a13, b13, c13 );
   calc_line( pp[ p2 ].x, pp[ p2 ].y, pp[ p3 ].x, pp[ p3 ].y, 1,
              a23, b23, c23 );
```

```
     dev0_13 = a13*x0 + b13*y0 + c13;
     dev0_23 = a23*x0 + b23*y0 + c23;
     dev2_13 = a13*pp[p2].x + b13*pp[p2].y + c13;
     dev1_23 = a23*pp[p1].x + b23*pp[p1].y + c23;

     if ( ( ( dev0_13*dev2_13 > 0 ) && ( dev0_23*dev1_23 >= 0 ) ) ||
          ( ( dev0_13*dev2_13 >= 0 ) && ( dev0_23*dev1_23 > 0 ) ) )
        return TRUE;
     first = ( ( adir*pp[ p1 ].x + bdir*pp[ p1 ].y + cdir )*
               ( adir*pp[ p3 ].x + bdir*pp[ p3 ].y + cdir ) ) < 0;
     second = ( ( adir*pp[ p2 ].x + bdir*pp[ p2 ].y + cdir )*
                ( adir*pp[ p3 ].x + bdir*pp[ p3 ].y + cdir ) ) < 0;
     if ( ( first && second ) || (!first && !second ) )
     { //we'll do so that first becomes TRUE and second becomes FALSE
       //recalculation of adir, bdir, cdir
       calc_line( pp[p1].x + pp[p3].x, pp[p1].y + pp[p3].y,
                  2*x0, 2*y0, 2, adir, bdir, cdir );

       first = TRUE;
     }
     if (first)
     {
        in3 = vertex[ in2 ].nb;
        p = vertex[ in2 ].pb;
     }
     else
     {
        in3 = vertex[ in1 ].nb;
        p = vertex[ in1 ].pb;
     }
     return FALSE;
}
```

Point Deleting

The problem of deleting a triangulation vertex is a bit more complicated. The fact is that each vertex is shared by 3 or more triangles. The polygonal area they cover may be triangular, but not as a general rule. That's why each time we delete a vertex, we have to perform a triangulation of this polygonal area. This may not seem so difficult, but remember that the triangulation algorithm we use is incremental, or in other words, it can't triangulate an arbitrary polygonal area. We have to invent something more creative.

And this is the idea, pretty and simple. We'll flip the edges of the triangles that contain our 'sentenced' vertex until the area they cover becomes a true triangle. Each flip turns a pair of adjacent triangles into a single triangle.

Although we can't flip every pair, we can always get our triangle by cyclically checking all the pairs. When we've made the area triangular, the deletion is simple - instead of the three triangles, we leave the covering one, as shown below:

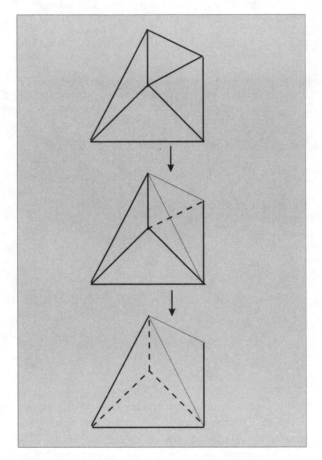

Deleting a Vertex of Triangular Tessellation

Certainly, before we start to 'triangularize' the area, we have to make a list of the triangles containing the vertex. To do this we first find any one of them (just like we do when we add a point) and then cyclically go around the vertex and add to the list.

It works like this:

```cpp
void triangle_system::delete_point( long int x0, long int y0 )
{
    triangle *p, *newp;
    BYTE i, j, k, i0, i1, i2, newi1, newi2;
    long int d, min_d;
    int deleted_point, start_t;
    int tt[4], ni[4], sum[4];
    BYTE ii[4];

    find_triangle( x0, y0, p );
    if ( p == NULL )
        return;
    min_d = 64000*32000;
    for ( i = 0; i < N; i++ )
    {
        d = (pp[p->vertex[i].no].x-x0)*(pp[p->vertex[i].no].x-x0) +
            (pp[p->vertex[i].no].y-y0)*(pp[p->vertex[i].no].y-y0);
        if ( d < min_d )
        {
            min_d = d;
            i0 = i;
        }
    }

    i1 = ( i0 + 1 ) % N;
    i2 = ( i0 + 2 ) % N;
    deleted_point = p->vertex[i0].no;
    if ( deleted_point < 4 )
    {
        printf("\a");
        return;
    }
    start_t = p->t;

//at beginning we must group all triangles with deleted point in flip array

    false_flip = new record_for_flip[max_false_flip_number];
    memset(false_flip, 0, max_false_flip_number*sizeof( record_for_flip ));
    false_flip_number = ndt = 0;
    do
    {
        add_for_flip( p->t, i1 );
        add_for_flip( p->t, i2 );
        dt[ ++ndt ] = p->t;
        newp  = p->vertex[i1].pb;
        newi2 = p->vertex[i1].nb;
        newi1 = ( newi2 + 1 ) % N;
        if ( newp->vertex[newi1].no == deleted_point )
```

```
            newi1 = ( newi2 + 2 ) % N;
      p   = newp;
      i1 = newi1;
      i2 = newi2;
   } while ( p->t != start_t );

   tr_for_del = false_flip_number / 2;
   while ( (false_flip_number > 0) && (tr_for_del>3) )
   {
      false_flip_number--;
      one_flip( false_flip[ false_flip_number ].tf,
               false_flip[ false_flip_number ].nf, TRUE, deleted_point );
   }

   delete false_flip;
   false_flip = NULL;
   false_flip_number = 0;

   k = 0;
   for ( i = 1; i<= ndt; i++ )
      for ( j = 0; j < N; j++ )
         if ( tp[dt[i]]->vertex[j].no == deleted_point )
         {
            ii[++k] = j;
            tt[k]   = dt[i];
            sum[k] = tp[dt[i]]->vertex[(j+1) % N].no +
                     tp[dt[i]]->vertex[(j+2) % N].no;
         }

   ni[1] = ( sum[1] - sum[2] + sum[3] ) / 2;
   ni[2] = sum[1] - ni[1];
   ni[3] = sum[2] - ni[2];

   if ( k != 3 )
      stop();

newp = new triangle(ni[1], ni[2], ni[3], tp[tt[2]]->vertex[ii[2]].sb,
                    tp[tt[3]]->vertex[ii[3]].sb,
                    tp[tt[1]]->vertex[ii[1]].sb,
                    tp[tt[2]]->vertex[ii[2]].pb,tp[tt[3]]->vertex[ii[3]].pb,
                    tp[tt[1]]->vertex[ii[1]].pb,
                    tp[tt[2]]->vertex[ii[2]].nb,
                    tp[tt[3]]->vertex[ii[3]].nb,
                    tp[tt[1]]->vertex[ii[1]].nb,tt[1] );

   send_neighbour( newp, 0 );
   send_neighbour( newp, 1 );
   send_neighbour( newp, 2 );
```

```
        delete tp[tt[1]];
        delete tp[tt[2]];
        delete tp[tt[3]];

        tp[tt[1]] = newp;

    //arrange in increase order

        if ( tt[2] > tt[3] )
        {
            i = tt[2];
            tt[2] = tt[3];
            tt[3] = i;
        }
        if ( tt[3] != num_triangles - 1 )
        {
            tp[tt[3]] = tp[ num_triangles - 1 ];
            tp[tt[3]]->t = tt[3];
        }
        if ( tt[2] != num_triangles - 2 )
        {
            tp[tt[2]] = tp[ num_triangles - 2 ];
            tp[tt[2]]->t = tt[2];
        }
        num_triangles -= 2;

        if ( deleted_point != num_points - 1 )
            for ( i = 0; i < num_triangles; i++ )
                for ( j = 0; j < N; j++ )
                    if ( tp[i]->vertex[j].no == num_points - 1 )
                        tp[i]->vertex[j].no = deleted_point;

        pp[ deleted_point ] = pp[ num_points - 1 ];
        if (transition)
            pp2[ deleted_point ] = pp2[ num_points - 1 ];
        num_points--;
    }
```

Point Moving

Moving a vertex isn't complicated at all, because it doesn't change the topology
of triangulation. We meet just one problem - not every move is allowed. A
vertex can't leave the area covered by its triangles, and under certain
circumstances, the allowed area is even smaller than the triangles.

```
    void triangle_system::new_point( long int xn, long int yn )
    {
        triangle *p, *newp;
        BYTE i, j, i0, i1, i2, newi1, newi2;
```

```
      long int d, min_d;
      int shiftpoint, start_t;
      long double adir, bdir, cdir;

      find_triangle( xn, yn, p );
      if ( p == NULL )
         return;

      min_d = 64000*32000;
      for ( i = 0; i < N; i++ )
      {
         d = (pp[p->vertex[i].no].x-xn)*(pp[p->vertex[i].no].x-xn) +
             (pp[p->vertex[i].no].y-yn)*(pp[p->vertex[i].no].y-yn);
         if (d < min_d)
         {
            min_d = d;
            i0 = i;
         }
      }
      i1 = ( i0 + 1 ) % N;
      i2 = ( i0 + 2 ) % N;
      shiftpoint = p->vertex[i0].no;
      if ( shiftpoint < 4 )
      {
         printf("\a");
         return;
      }
      start_t = p->t;

   // at the beginning we must group all triangles with the deleted
   // point in flip array
      ndt = 0;
      do
      {
         calc_line( pp[p->vertex[i1].no].x, pp[p->vertex[i1].no].y,
                    pp[p->vertex[i2].no].x, pp[p->vertex[i2].no].y,
                    1, adir, bdir, cdir );
         if ( ( adir*pp[ shiftpoint ].x + bdir*pp[ shiftpoint ].y + cdir )*
              ( adir*xn + bdir*yn + cdir ) <= 0 )
         {
            printf("\a");
            return;
         }
         dt[ ++ndt ] = p->t;
         newp  = p->vertex[i1].pb;
         newi2 = p->vertex[i1].nb;
         newi1 = ( newi2 + 1 ) % N;
         if ( newp->vertex[newi1].no == shiftpoint )
            newi1 = ( newi2 + 2 ) % N;
         p  = newp;
         i1 = newi1;
```

```
        i2 = newi2;
    } while ( p->t != start_t );

    hide_mouse();
    for ( j = 1; j <= ndt; j++ )
        for ( i = 0; i < N; i++ )
            if ( tp[dt[j]]->vertex[i].no != shiftpoint )
            {
                setcolor( del_color );
                line( pp[tp[dt[j]]->vertex[i].no].x,
                      pp[tp[dt[j]]->vertex[i].no].y,
                      pp[shiftpoint].x, pp[shiftpoint].y );
                setcolor( draw_color );
                line( pp[tp[dt[j]]->vertex[i].no].x,
                      pp[tp[dt[j]]->vertex[i].no].y, xn, yn );
            }
    show_mouse();

    pp[ shiftpoint ].x = xn;
    pp[ shiftpoint ].y = yn;
}
```

Flipping

As we mentioned above, flipping the common edge of two adjacent triangles is one of the basic operations in triangulation. The following routines show how it's performed:

```
void triangle_system::manual_flip( int x0, int y0 )
// x0, y0 are the screen coordinates of the point in which you
// call the flip. In order to find out which particular edge
// you mean we first get the triangle you've pointed out and
// then the edge nearest to (x0,y0).
{
    triangle *p;
    BYTE i, i0;
    long double adir, bdir, cdir, d, min_d;

    find_triangle( x0, y0, p );
    if ( p == NULL )
        return;
    min_d = 64000*32000;
    for ( i = 0; i < N; i++ )
    {
        calc_line( pp[p->vertex[(i+1) % N].no].x,
                   pp[p->vertex[(i+1) % N].no].y,
                   pp[p->vertex[(i+2) % N].no].x,
                   pp[p->vertex[(i+2) % N].no].y,
```

```
                        1, adir, bdir, cdir );
      d = abs( adir*x0 + bdir*y0 + cdir ) / sqrt( adir*adir + bdir*bdir );
      if ( d < min_d )
      {
         min_d = d;
         i0 = i;
      }
   }
   one_flip( p->t, i0, FALSE, p->vertex[( i0 + 1 ) % N].no );
}

void triangle_system::one_flip( int t1, BYTE i3, BOOL obligatory,
                                int deleted_point )
{
   BYTE i, i1, i2, j1, j2, j3;
   triangle *p1, *p2, *pnew1, *pnew2;
   int t2;
   long double d1, d2, adir, bdir, cdir;
   BOOL add_t1_in_false;

   p1 = tp[t1];
   if ( p1->vertex[i3].sb == HARD )
      return;
   p2 = p1->vertex[i3].pb;
   j3 = p1->vertex[i3].nb;

   t2 = p2->t;
   i1 = ( i3 + 1 ) % N;
   i2 = ( i3 + 2 ) % N;
   j1 = ( j3 + 1 ) % N;
   j2 = ( j3 + 2 ) % N;
   if ( p1->vertex[i1].no != p2->vertex[j1].no )
   {
      i = j1;
      j1 = j2;
      j2 = i;
   }

// check if flip is possible
   calc_line( pp[p1->vertex[i3].no].x, pp[p1->vertex[i3].no].y,
              pp[p2->vertex[j3].no].x, pp[p2->vertex[j3].no].y,
              1, adir, bdir, cdir );
   d1 = adir*pp[p1->vertex[i1].no].x + bdir*pp[p1->vertex[i1].no].y
        + cdir;
   d2 = adir*pp[p1->vertex[i2].no].x + bdir*pp[p1->vertex[i2].no].y
        + cdir;
   if ( d1*d2 > 0 )
      return;
   if ( ( d1*d2 == 0 ) && !obligatory )
      return;
```

```
    if (transition)
    {
        calc_line( pp2[p1->vertex[i3].no].x, pp2[p1->vertex[i3].no].y,
                   pp2[p2->vertex[j3].no].x, pp2[p2->vertex[j3].no].y,
                   1, adir, bdir, cdir );
        d1 = adir*pp2[p1->vertex[i1].no].x + bdir*pp2[p1->vertex[i1].no].y
             + cdir;
        d2 = adir*pp2[p1->vertex[i2].no].x + bdir*pp2[p1->vertex[i2].no].y
             + cdir;
        if ( ( d1*d2 == 0 ) && !obligatory )
           return;
    }

    p1->my_line( i1, i2, del_color );

    if (obligatory)
    {
        delete_from_flip( t1 );
        delete_from_flip( t2 );
    }

// the flip itself
    pnew1 = new triangle( p1->vertex[i1].no, p1->vertex[i3].no,
                          p2->vertex[j3].no,
                          FREE, p2->vertex[j2].sb, p1->vertex[i2].sb,
                          NULL, p2->vertex[j2].pb, p1->vertex[i2].pb,
                          0, p2->vertex[j2].nb, p1->vertex[i2].nb, t1 );
    tp[ t1 ] = pnew1;

    pnew2 = new triangle( p1->vertex[i2].no, p1->vertex[i3].no,
                          p2->vertex[j3].no,
                          FREE, p2->vertex[j1].sb, p1->vertex[i1].sb,
                          pnew1, p2->vertex[j1].pb, p1->vertex[i1].pb,
                          0, p2->vertex[j1].nb, p1->vertex[i1].nb, t2 );
    pnew1->vertex[0].pb = pnew2;
    tp[ t2 ] = pnew2;

    send_neighbour( pnew1, 1 );
    send_neighbour( pnew1, 2 );
    send_neighbour( pnew2, 1 );
    send_neighbour( pnew2, 2 );

    if ( ( pnew1->t != t1 ) || ( pnew2->t != t2 ) )
       stop;

    delete p1;
    delete p2;

    if ( !obligatory )
       return;
```

```
    tr_for_del--;
    if ( ( pnew1->vertex[0].no != deleted_point ) &&
         ( pnew2->vertex[0].no != deleted_point ) )
       stop;
    if ( pnew1->vertex[0].no == deleted_point )
    {
       add_for_flip( t1, 1 );
       add_for_flip( t1, 2 );
    }
    else
    {
       add_for_flip( t2, 1 );
       add_for_flip( t2, 2 );
    }
}
```

Store and Load

Triangulation is done manually, and is certainly the most time consuming part of the morphing process. Therefore, it would be useful to have some kind of load and store capabilities. The simplest way to implement this is as a macro that contains all the operations performed (add point, delete point or edge flipping) and the screen co-ordinates where the actions took place. This is the way we have decided to go, thus giving a facility that lets you get the desired results in an iterative fashion.

How to Map a Triangle into a Triangle

The actual process of morphing is the distortion of the triangles from the initial tessellation to the final tessellation, regardless of whether we use one or two images. We therefore need to discuss how to map the internal points of one triangle to another. The most natural co-ordinate system when dealing with triangles is the barycentric one. The barycentric co-ordinates (a_1, a_2, a_3) of a point (x,y) within a triangle satisfy the following conditions:

$$x = a_1{}^*x_1 + a_2{}^*x_2 + a_3{}^*x_3$$

$$y = a_1{}^*y_1 + a_2{}^*y_2 + a_3{}^*y_3$$

$$a_1 + a_2 + a_3 = 1.$$

where (x_1,y_1), (x_2,y_2), (x_3,y_3) are the triangle vertices, $a_{(1..3)}$ is a linear function $F(x,y)$, and is the scaled distance between the point and the corresponding edge, varying between 0 and 1.

Two different triangles can be mapped by mapping the points with the same barycentric co-ordinates. Assume that we have a triangle with vertices $(x1_1,y1_1)$, $(x1_2,y1_2)$, $(x1_3,y1_3)$ and a point inside, say (x,y). Then we find the corresponding point (X,Y) lying inside the second triangle with vertices $(x2_1,y2_1)$, $(x2_2,y2_2)$, $(x2_3,y2_3)$. We can do this in two steps:

1 Calculate the barycentric co-ordinates of point (x,y) in the first triangle:

$$a_1 = ((x-x1_2)(y-y1_3) - (x-x1_3)(y-y1_2))/((x1_1-x1_2)(y1_1-y1_3) - (x1_1-x1_3)(y1_1-y1_2));$$

$$a_2 = ((x-x1_3)(y-y1_1) - (x-x1_1)(y-y1_3))/((x1_2-x1_3)(y1_2-y1_1) - (x1_2-x1_1)(y1_2-y1_3));$$

$$a_3 = ((x-x1_1)(y-y1_2) - (x-x1_2)(y-y1_1))/((x1_3-x1_1)(y1_3-y1_2) - (x1_3-x1_2)(y1_3-y1_1)).$$

2 Find the corresponding point (X,Y) in the second triangle as a point with the same barycentric co-ordinates:

$$X = a_1{}^*x2_1 + a_2{}^*x2_2 + a_3{}^*x2_3;$$

$$Y = a_1{}^*y2_1 + a_2{}^*y2_2 + a_3{}^*y2_3.$$

The order of the triangle vertices is important.

> Barycentric co-ordinates map **any triangle** to the same unit cube 1×1×1 in the (a_1,a_2,a_3) space.

So, we've established the correspondence between the points of the source and target images. Now we have nothing left but the color calculation. But before we go any further, we'll just review the logic of the whole process.

1 We start by setting the morphing points and defining the triangular tessellation. For each morphing point of the source image there is a corresponding one in the target image. Therefore, for each 'source triangle', there is a corresponding target one.

2 During transformation morphing, points are transferred to their counterparts, while matching triangles are mapped into each other using barycentric co-ordinates. The mapping may be performed either at the time or dichotomized into a sequence of steps for further animation.

3 For each mapping step we interpolate the colors of pixels exactly the way we did before, for rotation, shearing, and so on.

Distortion Morphing

First you choose the image you'd like to warp. It's initially subdivided into two triangles. Then you can add morphing points, delete them and flip edges until you get the appropriate tessellation. You'll begin to get a feel for what is 'appropriate' after some practice of your own.

The next step is distortion morphing itself. You do this by moving some of the morphing points, the vertices of the triangles, to other positions. Note that only those triangles that have the point you move as the vertex will be transformed. So only those parts of the image they cover will be warped. It should be mentioned that the new position of a morphing point lies within the affected triangles. However, it may happen that the allowed area is smaller than the triangles.

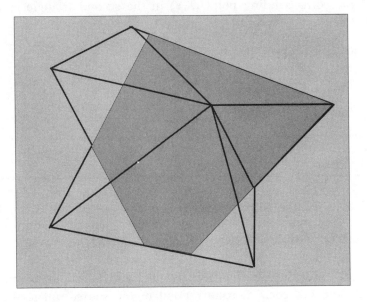

The Area Allowed for Moving a Morphing Point

When the new position of the morphing point is specified, we have to modify the affected part of the image. We do this in the following way:

- For each pixel covered by the transformed triangle, we find the corresponding point (with the same barycentric co-ordinates) of the initial triangle.

- Then we interpolate the color, just like we did in Chapter 12 Image Manipulation.

Such a technique has one important feature: the result you get depends only on the initial and final triangulation, so it doesn't matter how many times you tried new locations for a point. The figure below shows the triangulation for the distortion morphing example shown in the first section of the chapter.

Sample Triangulation for Distortion Morphing

Transition Morphing

For transition morphing you only need two images. As for distortion morphing, you have to construct a triangular tessellation. This time, however, you have to operate on two pictures simultaneously. And this makes the following difference:

- ▲ When you add a morphing point to the first image you have to add a corresponding one to exactly the corresponding triangle on the second image.

- ▲ If you delete a point on the first image, the corresponding point must be erased from the second one.

▲   The same applies to edge flipping, but with one restriction - each particular flip must be allowed for both triangulations.

Warning! As you will remember, morphing points mark corresponding features of two images. But it may happen that a corresponding detail you'd like to mark on the second image lies outside the allowed triangle. If this happens, you have to change the triangulation of this particular local area, so that the corresponding details reside in the corresponding triangles.

The figure below shows the triangulation that was used for the transition morphing example shown in the first section of the chapter.

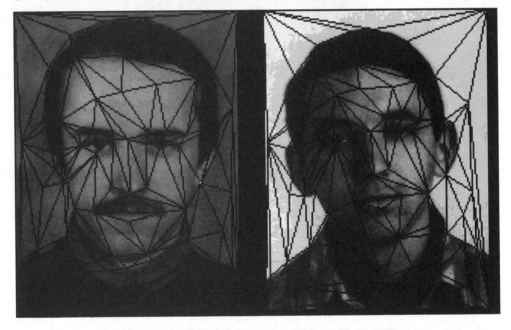

Sample Triangulation for Transition Morphing

We're sure that after a few goes, you'll manage the triangulation step of the process. When the tessellation is ready, you have to specify the percentage constant (we'll call it beta) of each image in the result. After this you have to do the following:

1   Calculate two spatial coefficients to account for the possible difference in the dimensions of the images:

$$\text{coef\_x} = (\text{width}_{result} - 1)/(\text{beta}*\text{width}_1 + (1\text{-beta})*\text{width}_2 - 1);$$

$$\text{coef\_y} = (\text{height}_{result} - 1)/(\text{beta}*\text{height}_1 + (1\text{-beta})*\text{height}_2 - 1);$$

2 Determine the positions of morphing points for the resulting image:

$$x = (\text{beta}*x_1 + (1\text{-beta})*x_2 - 1)*\text{coef\_x} + 1;$$

$$y = (\text{beta}*y_1 + (1\text{-beta})*y_2 - 1)*\text{coef\_y} + 1;$$

3 For each pixel of the resulting image we get two colors - one from each of the images, just the way we did for distortion morphing.

4 And finally we interpolate the colors:

$$\text{color} = \text{beta}*\text{color}_1 + (1\text{-beta})*\text{color}_2,$$

This particular formula works for an image in shades of gray. You have to apply it three times for each of the primary colors when working with TrueColor images.

These calculations are performed for each of the tweens. If you intend to generate only a single intermediate frame, just set the beta factor you prefer and calculate. If your aim is to create a sequence of frames for animation, consider beta as 'time', increment it the way you like and calculate as many tweens as you need.

How to Improve the Results

Morphing software won't ever produce perfect results on its own. The user must work hard to make morphing smooth and believable. In this section, we'll give you some recipes that may help you in practice. Some of them have been obtained from morphing literature, while others (the smaller part) are based on our own experience.

The easiest way to make morphing results look smoother is to define a larger number of morphing points.

Probably the most crucial step for successful morphing is making sure the start and end frames have similar features. For instance, it is impossible (at least with the representation we use), to get a realistic morphing between an image

of someone facing left and someone facing straight-on. In addition, you should choose subjects that are positioned similarly to morph together. This isn't a strict rule but it may considerably simplify your work.

The same is true for the lighting conditions of the image - they should be similar. If you want to morph two images with different lighting conditions, you can always use an image editing program to adjust the light.

You should also pay particular attention to the characteristic features of the image (eyes, nose and mouth if working with faces).

You may want to morph different parts of an image at different times. To do this, you have to specify the speed at which each triangle is to be transformed. (We haven't implemented this facility, but you can easily do it yourselves). This trick distracts the viewer's attention and might make your animation more convincing.

Morphing is a very manual process. The results depend heavily on the experience of the operator. As morphing software becomes more popular and available, especially on the PC, these extra artistic features will help distinguish quality morphing from amateurish attempts.

Summary

We aimed to demystify morphing for you in this chapter, and we hope we've succeeded. Of course, we could have written it as a piece of fiction such as 'Load the Morphing program by clicking on its icon..'. However, the idea of implementing morphing by ourselves and describing it in detail was an irresistible temptation. So there we are.

As a result, the chapter is a bit overloaded with mathematics (though fairly simple) and computational geometry (rather complicated). Indeed it should be, because after all, isn't morphing a kind of computer aided magic? We think it is. So we give you both the scroll of spells (this chapter) and the wand (the program). You may either read the scroll or just use the wand. You can also do both, which is the way we particularly enjoy and the way that provides the best results. At least now, you have the source code of a morphing system that works.

CHAPTER 14

3D Graphics

A chapter on 3D graphics is of course obligatory of this type of book. Indeed, what else do you need bitmap graphics for, if not for a realistic rendering of 3D scenes? Therefore in this chapter we'll attempt to give you at least the basics required to start you down the road into the three dimensional world.

Chapter Contents

In this chapter, we will cover:

- ▲ Origins
- ▲ 3D World On A 2D Screen
- ▲ Mathematical Bedrock
- ▲ Implementation Of The Projecting System
- ▲ Eliminating The Invisible
- ▲ 3D Rendering
- ▲ Ray Tracing
- ▲ 3D Texture Mapping

Origins

There is no doubt that such marvelous things as realistic 3D objects on a flat computer screen were first born in R & D. It seems that 3D graphics were first used for scientific and engineering visualization. Yes, it may be useful to display a function of two variables (say, position and time) as a colored surface. Of course, it is useful to show the picture of a new space shuttle flying vividly, especially when struggling for funds for its development.

So 3D rendering had been just another tool of computer graphics until it was used for special effects in the film industry. Recently Industrial Light and Magic showed everyone how powerful it could be when they used it in Terminator 2 - Judgment Day and Jurassic Park. They let everyone look at what was even difficult to imagine. Then this became the main idea, to see something unimaginable, real or unreal, but not available.

What we are going to build will be a project of a full-featured 3D graphics framework. We don't intend to make it ready to use in Terminator 3, but you should have some useful experience and fun nonetheless.

Once again, the starting sections may seem pretty boring to those who have experience with 3D, and, at the same time, too concise for neophytes. That can't be helped, but at least we give working code, and some short explanations - that should be enough for you to start with.

You may think that this chapter is the focus of the book and that would be quite right. We'll draw from techniques that are scattered across the book - from the fast drawing routines of Chapter 5 to the image-mapping techniques of Chapter 10, as well as OOP.

Why are 3D graphics so tempting? We asked GG:

The ability to artificially produce a photo-realistic image of an object gives the illusion of understanding the object in detail.

3D World On The 2D Screen

Following on from Michael Abrash, we'd like to point out that 3D graphics is rather more a matter of fooling the eye and the mind than of mathematically exact modeling. To make this magic work, we must provide cues for the eye not only to pick out boundaries, but also detect depth, orientation and motion. This involves the projecting, shading and proper handling of hidden surfaces.

Each step inside the perfect physics of your 3D graphics model costs you, in time and effort, as much as all the steps in the previous chapters together, and gives you less than half of the 'realistic features'. So the question is, 'Is the very first step necessary?'. Unfortunately it is, but it requires only a school level physics, some geometrical optics and a bit of vector algebra.

We'll quickly go over some facts and formulae before we start with our 3D graphics.

Light Sources

All that we see is either emitted or reflected light. So, first we should understand what a light source is. There are hundreds of different light sources ranging from the sun to a flame. However, they have one thing in common, too much energy. For instance, when electrons excite the molecules of the CRT phosphors, the latter can't hold onto the extra energy, and the molecules radiate it as light, which we see.

The intensity and spectrum of emitted radiation varies and sometimes falls into the range which we call visible light, approximately 350 - 750 nanometers. When this is the case, we can see the light source. If the spectrum distribution isn't uniform the light looks colored (see Chapter 4 'Palettes and Colors' for details). Most of the real light sources, both natural and artificial have radial distribution, that is, they emit light in all directions equally. This means that the brightness of the light falling on a surface is dependent on the distance from the light source - the further the surface from the source, the dimmer the illumination. To understand this, imagine the light source in the middle of a sphere. The amount of light falling on the whole inner surface of the sphere is always the same, no matter how big the sphere is. But as the radius of the sphere increases, the surface area of the sphere increases as a square of the

radius, so the light is spread thinner. If we take a little square of this sphere, then rotate it away from the light source, then the brightness gets even less because the light source 'sees' even less area. We can write this down as a simple equation:

$$I = I0 * \cos(\theta) \ / \ 4 * R^2$$

where I is illuminance, I0 is the intensity of the light source, R is the distance from the light source to the object and θ is the angle of the surface to the light source. This is illustrated in the figure below. This type of light source is known as a point source, because the source is thought of as having no size. Also, it is generally accepted that this equation is used for sources that are close to the object.

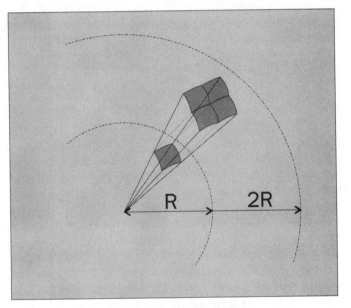

The Point Light Source

If we imagine the sun to be our light source, then using the equation, R is 1.495985×10^{11} meters, and therefore if we move away from the sun by a meter, the illuminance doesn't really change (it actually changes by a factor of 4×10^{-22} to be pedantic). In other words, we can say that the rays of light are parallel. Another sort of light which follows this rule is a laser. We'll call these types of light sources spotlights. We can simplify the above equation for spotlights to:

$$I = I0 * \cos(\theta)$$

Again, I is the illuminance, I0 the intensity, and θ is the angle the surface makes to the light.

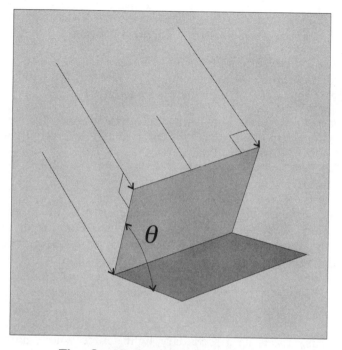

The Spotlight Light Source

You can think of more sophisticated sources yourselves. For instance, you can make the radial distribution uneven or you could make the intensity time dependent. In both cases you should use a look-up table approach, because calculation of the illuminance is one of the most computationally expensive procedures in 3D rendering.

Surfaces and Reflection

Well, we've made it clear how the light is emitted. Now, what about reflection and scattering? The physics of these phenomena seems more sophisticated. The theory of these "simple" things is overloaded with plenty of specific cases. The spectral and angular distribution of light, the type of illuminated material and smoothness of its surface - everything counts. We can hardly believe that accurate accounting of all this really improves 3D rendering. After all, even the Siggraph guys don't consider, say, polarization in rendering (or at least we

believe they don't). Here again we should remind you that 3D graphics is just a deception of the mind.

Because, in our 3D graphics framework, we rely on simple rules of geometrical optics, we'll describe surfaces in the following terms:

▲ diffuse reflection which means that the light is scattered in all directions. These surfaces tend to be colored, by which we mean they only reflect light of particular wavelengths

▲ specular reflection, from shiny or mirrored surfaces, for example, which for simplicity, don't affect the color of the reflected light

▲ transparency, again colored, so it only allows light of a particular color through them

Most natural surfaces are opaque, or in other words, they generally diffuse the light. Each element of such a surface scatters the light in all directions equally, as an ideal Lambertian radiator. The following expression gives the intensity of diffused light scattering from an opaque surface, illuminated by a spotlight source:

$$I = Idkd * \cos(\theta)$$

In other words, it acts as a secondary light source whose illuminance depends only on the intensity of the incident light and kd - the coefficient of diffuse scattering.

This formula, however, has two drawbacks:

▲ it produces zero illuminance for overshadowed surfaces, which cannot be true because of the ambient light

▲ it assumes that the illuminance doesn't depend on the distance. That means you can't distinguish a close object from a distant one if they are equally illuminated

It's become a kind of tradition to implement the following empirical improvements:

$$I = Iaka + Idkd * \cos(\theta)/(D+R)$$

where Ia and ka are respectively the intensity and coefficient for the ambient component, Id and kd are the same as before, R is the distance to the object, and D is a constant, present just to prevent division by zero.

Now it's time to add some terms for shiny surfaces, such as mirrors or the surface of a lake. Speaking the language of geometrical optics, mirror reflection differs from the diffuse form in one respect: its intensity very much depends on the angle of view. Most people know that the angle of reflection equals the angle of incidence. So, if the light from a laser falls on a mirror at an angle of 30º, you can only see the laser from the opposite side at an angle of 30º. If you look from a slightly different angle you'll see nothing. Fortunately real materials aren't so rigorous, and you'll see a patch of light. However, its brightness will decrease quickly with increasing angle. There are several models of mirror reflectivity, which are more or less empirical. Here we have given the traditional one, introduced by B.P. Phong:

$$I = Iaka + (kdiff * \cos(\theta) + kmirr * \cos(\alpha)^n) * Id/(D+R)$$

where $\cos(\alpha)^n$ is the model function for the intensity of a mirror reflection which depends on the angle of slope. The constant value n usually varies from 1 to 50. The larger n is, the smaller the amount of diffuse reflection, or glimmer. See the following figure for details of Phong's model. This expression will serve as a kind of 'optical basis' for 3D shadowing.

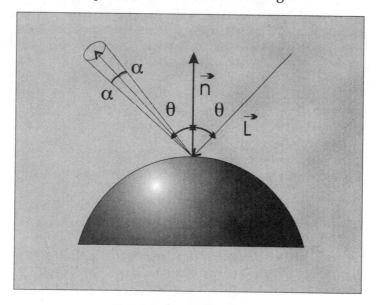

The Mirror Reflection

Unfortunately, we can't take transparency into account in the same easy way; we can't just add a refraction member to the formula. This is because the contribution due to refraction very much depends on the form of the object. Therefore we must postpone any consideration of refraction until we come to ray tracing.

Scene and Co-ordinate Systems

Well, we have the light to illuminate our space and the objects (or surfaces) to reflect it. Now it's time to create the world.

The World and Camera Co-ordinates

The position of an object can be defined in two different co-ordinate systems. We can use the one related to the scene (world co-ordinates) or we can use the 'camera-centric' system. We'll denote the first as $Xw(X,Y,Z)$ and the second as $Xc(x,y,z)$. It's useful to direct the z axis of the camera co-ordinate system along the optical axis of the camera. Being so orientated, the z co-ordinate gives the distance to the object.

Because of this, it's clear that camera co-ordinates are better for imaging. However, we can't expect that each and every scene description will be given in a way that is particularly convenient for us. That's why we have to consider the scene described in world co-ordinates. After all there can be several cameras, each with its own co-ordinate system. So there is one thing that we must demand from a co-ordinate system - we must be able to transform one system to another.

Transition from one co-ordinate system to another (say from the world to the camera system) can be performed as a sequence of translations (of the center) and rotations (of the axes). The following figure illustrates these points. In other words, to find the camera co-ordinates of an object defined in the world co-ordinate system you have to perform the following mathematical transformation:

$$Xc = R(Xw-T)$$

where the vector T defines the translation of the co-ordinate system center, and the matrix R defines the rotation of the axes.

R may look something like this:

$$\begin{bmatrix} \cos(\theta) & \sin(\theta) & 0 \\ -\sin(\theta) & \cos(\theta) & 0 \\ 0 & 0 & 1 \end{bmatrix}$$ rotation about x axis by angle θ.

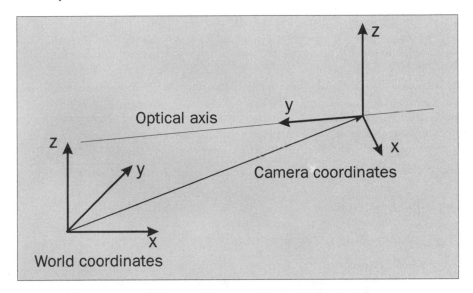

The World and Camera Co-ordinate Systems

> We are going to use a right-handed co-ordinate system. Right-handed means that if you hold your right hand with fingers clenched and the thumb sticking out, the thumb points along the z axis and the fingers point in the direction of rotation from the x axis to the y axis. Rotations about an axis are anti-clockwise, as viewed looking down the axis toward the origin.

The choice of a right-handed system is just one of convention and is generically used for object and world space. However, a left-handed one would do equally well.

Cameras and Projections

Before we can view the world, we must consider the camera with which we will view it. The first and simplest type is the pinhole camera. The optics of this imaging device aren't too complicated, it's just a very small hole:

 Every imaging technique essentially means that the 3D world is projected to the flat 2D screen, or in other words, each point of the scene has a corresponding point in the image. However, this correspondence isn't one-to-one. This means that several different points of the scene can be projected to a single point in the image. Actually, 3D - 2D = 1D, so one dimension, along with the information contained in it, is lost. What kind of information is it? It's the distance to, and the size of, an object. That's why we can hardly distinguish something small and near from something large and distant by means of a 2D image.

Now about the projection and how it's related to the pinhole camera.

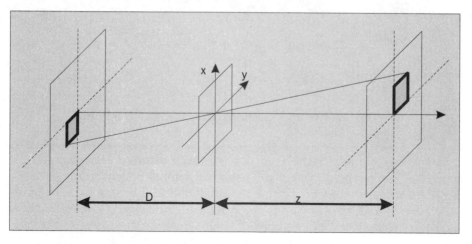

Imaging with the Pinhole Camera, Perspective Projection

Look at the figure and imagine that every dot of the scene is a point light source, which shouldn't be to difficult as it's not so far from reality. Only one ray from the total number emitted by each dot can pass through the hole and so contribute to the image. Of course, this is if a dot is visible, or in other words, if it's not overshadowed by another object in the scene. Now it's clear why the hole must be small. What we see on the screen is an image of the hole, produced by the light from the dot. If the hole is too big, we get a circular image, and so the image gets blurred.

 A pinhole camera can be considered as a perfect optical scheme, because it has infinite focal depth and doesn't cause any distortions. It has only one drawback, albeit a very serious one, in that the brightness of the image is proportional to the square of the radius of the hole, which is why, for the pinhole camera, it always will be extremely low.

The following expressions give the screen co-ordinates of a dot as a result of pinhole imaging (perspective projection):

$$xi = -D * X/Z, \quad yi = -D * Y/Z$$

where D is the distance between the hole (the center of projection) and the screen.

Pretty simple, isn't it? Just a proportion. But don't forget we must consider the scene in the camera co-ordinate system. If our world co-ordinates aren't the same as the camera co-ordinates, then we must do a transformation before we can get an image.

Notice that there is a minus sign in both these equations. This means that the image we get has been rotated through 180°. All our pictures would be up-side-down! However, we can fix this by placing the screen before the pinhole. This changes the sign of D, and so cures the problem. You can't build a pinhole camera like this, but we are using a computer, where almost anything is possible.

So you see, getting a 2D image of a 3D scene is not too complicated a task. You only have to make a sequence of co-ordinate transformations. There is, however, some mathematical magic, which helps to perform them all at once. We're speaking about the homogeneous co-ordinates representation. Widely used wherever projections are applied, this description is the foundation for 3D computer graphics. Next, we'll look at the mechanism of transformations.

Mathematical Bedrock

And so, homogeneous coordinates of a point are a four component vector:

Xh=(X*t,Y*t,Z*t,t)

where X,Y,Z are ordinary 3D co-ordinates, and t is merely a formality. An arbitrary transformation of a 3D co-ordinate system can be performed by multiplying the vector Xh by a special 4×4 matrix, say M. Fortunately, the multiplication of matrices is associative and it allows us to represent any kind of transformation as a combination of elementary ones:

- translation
- rotation
- scaling
- projecting

You can obtain the matrix of the combined transformation simply by multiplying all the elementary ones.

Matrices

If you are a little rusty on matrix maths, here are the three basic rules. All the rules are based on generic matrices such as:

$$\begin{bmatrix} a & b \\ c & d \end{bmatrix} \quad \text{and} \quad \begin{bmatrix} e & f \\ g & h \end{bmatrix}$$

Matrix Addition

You can add to matrices together using the following rule:

$$\begin{bmatrix} a & b \\ c & d \end{bmatrix} + \begin{bmatrix} e & f \\ g & h \end{bmatrix} = \begin{bmatrix} a+e & b+f \\ c+g & d+h \end{bmatrix}$$

Matrix Scaling

You can multiply a matrix by a scalar using the following rule:

$$z \begin{bmatrix} a & b \\ c & d \end{bmatrix} = \begin{bmatrix} za & zb \\ zc & zd \end{bmatrix}$$

Matrix Multiplication

You can multiply two matrices together using the following rule:

$$\begin{bmatrix} a & b \\ c & d \end{bmatrix} \begin{bmatrix} e & f \\ g & h \end{bmatrix} = \begin{bmatrix} ae+bg & af+bh \\ ce+dg & cf+dh \end{bmatrix}$$

Note that you can only add matrices with the same dimension, or in other words, the same shape; you can apply a scalar multiplier to any matrix, and with matrix multiplication, the number of elements in the rows of the first matrix must be the same as the elements in the first column of the second matrix, and so on.

Translation

Translation is as simple as it looks - nothing more than an addition of X, Y, and Z offsets. Translation is used to move something linearly through the space, or in other words to move the object around in space. A translation matrix looks like this:

$$T = \begin{bmatrix} 1 & 0 & 0 & 0 \\ 0 & 1 & 0 & 0 \\ 0 & 0 & 1 & 0 \\ x & y & z & 1 \end{bmatrix} \quad \text{Translation by (x,y,z)}$$

To apply the transformation, simply apply this matrix to your original point using matrix maths.

Rotation

A 3×3 rotation matrix of the ordinary 3D space becomes the upper-left portion of 4×4 rotation matrices in homogeneous co-ordinates that also perform translation, scaling and projecting.

$$Rx = \begin{bmatrix} \cos(\theta) & \sin(\theta) & 0 & 0 \\ -\sin(\theta) & \cos(\theta) & 0 & 0 \\ 0 & 0 & 1 & 0 \\ 0 & 0 & 0 & 1 \end{bmatrix} \quad \text{Rotation about X axis by } \theta;$$

$$Ry = \begin{bmatrix} \cos(\theta) & 0 & \sin(\theta) & 0 \\ 0 & 1 & 0 & 0 \\ \sin(\theta) & 0 & \cos(\theta) & 0 \\ 0 & 0 & 0 & 1 \end{bmatrix} \quad \text{Rotation about Y axis by } \theta;$$

$$Rz = \begin{bmatrix} 1 & 0 & 0 & 0 \\ 0 & \cos(\theta) & \sin(\theta) & 0 \\ 0 & -\sin(\theta) & \cos(\theta) & 0 \\ 0 & 0 & 0 & 1 \end{bmatrix} \quad \text{Rotation about Z axis by } \theta;$$

Projection

Perspective projection can also be performed as multiplication by the following matrix:

$$P = \begin{bmatrix} 1 & 0 & 0 & 0 \\ 0 & 1 & 0 & 0 \\ 0 & 0 & 1 & -1/D \\ 0 & 0 & 0 & 1 \end{bmatrix} \quad \text{Perspective projection}$$

However, it's formulated in a slightly different way than the one given in the previous section. Multiplication of vectors:

$$X_h = (X^*t, Y^*t, Z^*t, t)$$

by P yields:

$$X_h = (X^*t, Y^*t, Z^*t, t^* (D-Z)/D)$$

and finally, after division by the fourth co-ordinate, we have:

$$X_i = X * D/(D-Z), \quad Y_i = Y * D/(D-Z)$$

where the screen is positioned in Z=0 and the center of projection is moved to (0,0, -D).

Scaling

Scaling is as simple as translation, as all you need to do is multiply each co-ordinate by the scaling factor. Anyway, this transformation can be performed in the same 'matrix multiplication pipeline', so why leave it separate?

$$S = \begin{bmatrix} Sx & 0 & 0 & 0 \\ 0 & Sy & 0 & 0 \\ 0 & 0 & Sz & 0 \\ 0 & 0 & 0 & 1 \end{bmatrix} \qquad \text{Scaling by the scaling factors Sx,Sy,Sz.}$$

And so, the overall transformation from the world co-ordinates to the image ones will look like this:

$$M = TRxRyRzPS$$

At the end of this 'mathematical' section, we'd like GG to explain the point of using this 'four-dimensional space'.

The reasons behind the use of a four dimensional space are easy to understand. You need to combine both translations and rotations in a single matrix multiplication. However, you have to add to translate and multiply to rotate. These two operations cannot be united, unless you add one more dimension, the fourth row in the matrix, devoted to addition.

Implementation Of The Projecting System

You may think that our 3D drawing framework consists of two nearly equal (as far as the implementation is concerned) parts. The first one describes the 3D world with all the light sources, objects, materials, textures... and the second is the projecting system. The latter isn't too complicated in terms of the algorithms, but the overall performance heavily depends on the efficiency of its coding:

```
// necessary definition for homogeneous coordinates domain
typedef float vector[4];
typedef float matrix[4][4];

typedef struct
{
    float x, y, z;
} point3d;

typedef struct
{
    point3d a0, direction;
    // start point and normalized vector for direction
} ray;

// Some useful vector "arithmetic".
// scalar (point) product of two vectors (point3d)
#define s_prod(a,b) (a.x*b.x + a.y*b.y + a.z*b.z)

/* vector (cross) product of two vectors usually defined as a following
determinant:

          i  j  k
  UxV =  Vx Vy Vz     i,j,k are the unit vector in direction of
         Ux Uy Uz     the axes x,y,z


the resulting vector is normal to both U and V and, consequently, to the
plane they define
*/
#define v_prod(c,a,b) {c.x = a.y*b.z-a.z*b.y;
                       c.y = a.z*b.x-a.x*b.z;
                       c.z = a.x*b.y-a.y*b.x;}

// length of vector
#define v_len(a) sqrt(a.x*a.x + a.y*a.y + a.z*a.z)
```

```
// sub vectors c = a-b
#define v_sub(c,a,b) {c.x = a.x-b.x; c.y = a.y-b.y; c.z = a.z-b.z;}

// add vectors c = a+b
#define v_add(c,a,b) {c.x = a.x+b.x; c.y = a.y+b.y; c.z = a.z+b.z;}


class projection
{
protected:
    vector VRP;    // View Reference Point. Last 1 - always!
    vector VPN;    // View Plane Normal
    vector VUP;    // View Plane vertical
          // Define u-v coord system

    matrix view;
    // translate, rotate, and scale coordinate system

    vector scaler;
     // (adjust axes, and scale volume to unit cube)
    matrix mnorm;

    float back_dist;
    // borders of visible volume  ( world coords )
    float front_dist;    // MEMO : F<=B! , Back is ahead VPN


    float dx,dy;    // View window on screen
    float xcenter,ycenter;
    float umin,umax,vmin,vmax;
    // View plane window dimensions ( world coords )

     void make_rotation_matrix(matrix &R);
    virtual void calc_matrix() {};

public:
    projection();
    // adjust View Plane position
    void adjust_VP(point3d  VRP_,    // Reference Point
                   point3d  VPN_,    // Plane Normal (2nd point)
                   point3d  VUP_);   // Vertical Axe V (2nd point)

    // adjust View Volume, view coordinates
    void adjust_VPV(float umin_,float umax_,
                    float vmin_,float vmax_,
                    float front_dist_,float back_dist_);

    void set_view_window(int dx_,int dy_);
```

```
    // world to screen coordinates
    virtual void convert(matrix m, point3d p,float &xp, float &yp) {};
    void get_conv_matrix(matrix &mconv_) {};
     ~projection() {};

    virtual void convert_point(point3d &p);
    // according to mnorm matrix !
    virtual void convert_screen(point3d p, int &xp,int &yp) {};
    virtual void convert_screen(point3d p, float &xp, float &yp) {};
    // perspective and scaling calculations,
    // point is already in view coordintes
    virtual void ray_for_xy(int &xp,int &yp, ray &b) {};
};
```

Two types of projection are implemented:

- central (perspective) as mentioned before

- parallel, which you can consider as the central projection with an infinitely distant center

```
class parallel_projection : public projection
{
protected:
    vector DOP; // Direction of projection, for non-ortho
    virtual void calc_matrix();
public:
    parallel_projection();
    virtual void get_conv_matrix(matrix &mconv_);
    virtual void convert(matrix m, point3d p,int &xp,int &yp);
    virtual void convert(matrix m, point3d p,float &xp, float &yp);

    virtual void convert_screen(point3d p, int &xp,int &yp);
    virtual void convert_screen(point3d p, float &xp,float &yp);
    // just scaling calculations,
    // point is  already in view coordintes
    virtual void ray_for_xy(int &xp,int &yp,ray &b);
    //in view coordinates!
};

class central_projection : public projection
{
    vector COP;    // Center of Projection (world coordinates)
    matrix mpersp;
    float Zvmin;   // position of the intersection with the
                   // foreground plane
    float Zview;   // View plane z-coordinate after transform
    virtual void calc_matrix();
    float  kz1,kz2; // coefficients for convert_screen method
```

```
public:
   central_projection();
   void set_COP(point3d COP);
    virtual void get_conv_matrix(matrix &mconv_);
   virtual void convert(matrix m, point3d p,int &xp,int &yp);
   virtual void convert(matrix m, point3d p,float &xp,float &yp);

   virtual void convert_screen(point3d p, int &xp,int &yp);
   virtual void convert_screen(point3d p, float &xp,float &yp);
   // scaling calculations,
   // point is already in view coordintes
   virtual void ray_for_xy(int &xp,int &yp,ray &b);
   //in view coordinates!
};


extern "C" void mult_matrix(matrix &matr1,matrix &matr2,matrix
&res_matr);
```

This routine is used to compose the matrix for the overall transformation. Usually it isn't too crucial as far as performance is concerned, unless you want to implement fast movement of the view point. It doesn't matter to us, as the following short assembly routine works at least five times faster than the C variant. By the way, in the source code on the accompanying CD-ROM you can find optimized routines for projecting a point, routines that are performance-critical, even with the Pentium-aware versions of the code. We don't give them here because of their size.

```
/* the result is a 4x4 matrix, as follows:
   --      --    --       --     --       --
   |        |    |         |     |         |
   |  4x4   |  X |   4x4   |  =  |   4x4   |
   |        |    |         |     |         |
   --      --    --       --     --       -- */
.model large
.386             ; Pay attention to these lines.
.387             ; Only for 386+387 !!!
 public _mult_matrix

M1           EQU dword ptr [bp+6]
M2           EQU dword ptr [bp+10]
OffsetM2     EQU word ptr [bp+10]
Mres         EQU dword ptr [bp+14]

_mult_matrix    proc far
   push  bp
   mov   bp,sp
```

```
        push  ds
        push  si
        push  di

        les   di,M1
        lds   si,M2
        lgs   bx,Mres

        mov   al,4
    next_row:
        mov   si,OffsetM2
        mov   ah,4
    next_item:
        fld   dword ptr es:[di]
        fmul  dword ptr [si]
        fld   dword ptr es:[di+4]
        fmul  dword ptr [si+4*4]
        fld   dword ptr es:[di+2*4]
        fmul  dword ptr [si+8*4]
        fld   dword ptr es:[di+3*4]
        fmul  dword ptr [si+12*4]
        faddp st(1),st
        faddp st(1),st
        faddp st(1),st

        fstp  dword ptr gs:[bx]    ; result(i,j)
        add   bx,4

        add   si,4
        dec   ah
        jnz   next_item
        add   di,16
        dec   al
        jnz   next_row

        pop   di
        pop   si
        pop   ds
        pop   bp
        ret
    _mult_matrix    endp
    end
```

Once upon a time, it was in fashion to use the fixed-point 32-bit representation in such routines. Now machines without a numeric coprocessor (oh, sorry, without FPU) are rather rarely seen, so the floating-point implementation seems reasonable (especially on Pentium with its floating-point hardware multiplier). By the way on a 486 DX2-66 **_mult_matrix** performs matrix multiplication up to 33000 times per second.

3D Graphics Framework

Now we are ready to proceed to our most complete, OOPed, 3D drawing framework, or more precisely, the results of this framework - our world. First let's count all the entities we are going to address:

- light sources
- 3D objects
- scene
- camera - just a plug for projecting system

Additionally, we should mention some things to make abstract 3D objects look more realistic:

- material (the optical model of the surface),
- texture.

Now we can look at the headers of the 3D framework classes. By the way, you shouldn't consider them only as sample code. This is simply the most compact way to represent the idea of a particular object. Actual code can be found on the accompanying CD-ROM, and it contains some minor details which we omit here:

```
typedef struct
{
   point3d center; float r;
} sphere;// for circumscribed sphere

typedef struct
{
   point3d a, b, c, d;
} box;   // for circumscribed box

typedef struct
{
   point3d a0, direction;
   // starting point and normalized vector for direction

   matrix *transf;
} ray_to_trace;

typedef struct
{
```

```
      float r, g, b;
} ray_intensity;

class created_image: public image_keeper
{
public:
   void set_point(int x, int y, colortype color, float z = 0) {}
   //z   for z-buffer implementation
   void set_row(int x0, int width, int y,
              BYTE *r,BYTE *g,BYTE *b, float *z = NULL){}
};

// abstract 3d object to be rendered
class abstact3d : public  Sortable
{
protected:
   point3d anchor_point, orientation1, orientation2;

/* orientations define rotation of object around anchor_point.
They are the second points of normalized vectors (first point is
anchor_point). All our transformations don't change the length of vectors,
so vectors remain normalized.
*/
   float minz,maxz;
public:
   /* methods to sort objects */
   virtual int isLessThan(const abstact3d& testObject) const;
   virtual int isEqual(const abstact3d& testObject) const;
   virtual void  camera_changed(projection &proj);

   /* pure virtual methods to satisfy C++ compiler */
   virtual hashValueType hashValue() const {return 0;}
   virtual classType isA() const {return 0;}
   virtual char _FAR *nameOf() const {return "object 3d";}
   virtual void printOn(ostream& outputStream) const {;}

   abstact3d(point3d position, point3d  direct1,point3d direct2);
// normalize directions
   abstact3d();
};

class object3d:  public abstact3d  // visible object in scene
{
protected:
   sphere sphere_check; // circumscribed sphere
   box box_check;       // circumscribed box both will be used in ray
                        // tracing technique for the ray-intersection check

   BOOL usebox;         // whether a box or a sphere is used

   int material_index;  // refer to global list of materials
```

```
    SortedArray *subordinated_objects;
    //objects are sorted by z
public:
    object3d();            // constructor
    virtual ~object3d(); // destructor

    // provide methods for transformations (rotation,
    // translation,.. etc.)
    virtual void camera_changed(projection &proj);
    // recalculate all coordinates
    // resort subordinated_objects
    virtual int shadowing(projection &proj, created_image &img)
    {
        return 0;
    }
    virtual int ray_sphere_check(ray &the_ray);
    virtual int ray_box_check(ray_to_trace &the_ray)
    {
        return 0;
    }
    // returns 0 if doesn't intersect

    virtual int ray_section(ray_to_trace &the_ray,
                            ray_intensity &diffuse_intensity,
                            ray &mirror_ray,
                            ray_intensity &mirror_intensity,
    // start point - point of the_ray and object section
                            ray &refracted_ray, ray_intensity &refracted)
    {
        return 0;
    }
    // returns 0 if doesn't intersect
    virtual int ray_section(ray_to_trace &the_ray,
                            ray_intensity &diffuse_intensity,
                            ray &mirror_ray,
                            ray_intensity &mirror_intensity)
    // start point of mirror_ray - point of the_ray and object section
    {
        return 0;
    }
};

class camera: public abstact3d
{
protected:
    float COPdist;
    central_projection *proj;
public :
    camera(point3d position, point3d direction, point3d  Vdirection,
           float COPdist_, float du,float dv);
    virtual ~camera();
```

```
    virtual void switch_on_me(int dx, int dy);
// initialize projection, we assume that there can be several
// cameras
};

class light_source: public abstact3d
{
protected:
   ray_intensity intensity;
public :
   light_source(point3d position, point3d orientation,
               ray_intensity intensity_) :
               abstact3d(position, orientation, orientation)
   {
      intensity = intensity_;
   }
   virtual BOOL is_plain()
   {
      return TRUE;
   }
   virtual void point_intensity(point3d &anchor_point, ray_intensity
&intens)
   {
      intens = intensity;
   }
};

class EasyObject: public Object
{
/* pure virtual methods to satisfy C++ compiler */
/* never mind */
public:
   virtual hashValueType hashValue() const
   {
      return 0;
   }
   virtual classType isA() const
   {
      return 0;
   }
   virtual char _FAR *nameOf() const
   {
      return "object 3d";
   }
   virtual void printOn(ostream& outputStream) const {}
};


class material: public EasyObject
{
protected:
```

```
      // Phong reflection model is used (cos(a)) , max = 1!
      float mincos,step; float *refl_function;
      // provide one extra point in array refl_function
      // with the same value as for 1.0
      float refl_by_cos(float cosa);
public:
   BOOL mirror, transparent;
   ray_intensity diffuse;

   // mirroring:
   ray_intensity reflected_fraction;
   // {a, a, a} for non-metal
   // a <= 1,  reflected fraction of light

   // refraction:
   float   optical_density;
   ray_intensity refracted_fraction;

   material(float r, float g, float b);
   void set_mirroring(float mincos_,float step_,
                      float *reflected_, ray_intensity intensity);
   void set_refraction(float optical_density,
                      float refracted_part) {}

   // for  ray_direction below : assumed that
   // ray vector is directed from surface point to light
   // source
   // diffuse reflected light

   virtual void point_intensity(ray_intensity ray_int,
                                point3d ray_direction, // normalized!!!
                                point3d normal,        // normalized!!!
                                ray_intensity &point_int);

   // diffuse and mirror reflected light
   virtual void point_intensity(ray_intensity ray_int,
                                point3d ray_direction,
                                point3d normal,
                                point3d view_direction,
                                ray_intensity &point_int);
};


class texture: public EasyObject
{
protected:
   image_keeper *bitmap;
   float minvalue, // for zero
         coef; // coef = (maxvalue - minvalue)/255
   int repeater_x, repeater_y;
   virtual void mapping(float a,float b, float &x, float &y);
```

```
      // bitmap coordinates by abstract
   public:
      texture(image_keeper *bitmap_,
               float size_x, float size_y,  // size of mapping surface
               float pixel_x, float pixel_y); // size of pixel
      virtual ~texture();
      virtual void rgb(float a,float b, ray_intensity &point);
      // return r, g and b by two abstract coordinates
      // (e.g. altitude and magnitude for sphere)
      virtual void displacement(float a, float b, point3d &point);
      // displacement of normal to surface
      // calculated as gradient of bitmap brightness
   };

   class scene:  public EasyObject
   {
   protected:
      SortedArray *objects; // objects are sorted by z
      Array *cameras;
      Array *materials;
      Array *light_sources;

      int screen_dx,screen_dy;
      int current_camera;
   public:
      scene();
      virtual ~scene();
      // if a material is new, add it to materials, set material # for obj
      void add_object(object3d *obj, material *material);

      int add_camera(camera *obj); // sets dx,dy
      int add_light_source(light_source *obj);

      void ray_tracing(created_image &image,BOOL mirrors, BOOL transparency);
      void shading(created_image &image,BOOL shadows);
      void set_camera(int i);
   };

   ////////////////////////////////////////////////////////////////////
   class sphere_object:  public object3d  // visible object in scene
   {
      sphere_object(float x,float y,float z, float r);
      virtual int ray_section(ray_to_trace &the_ray,
                              ray_intensity &diffuse_intensity,
                              ray &mirror_ray, ray_intensity
   &mirror_intensity);
   };
```

We'll use this first real **sphere_object** to illustrate different 3D rendering techniques. We should point out that it is a true sphere, and not a 72-facet polyhedron.

3D Primitives

Let's stop for a moment and discuss possible methods of 3D object organization. Basically, two slightly different approaches are feasible. The first is based on a kind of universal representation of 3D surface, polygonal meshes. Each 3D object of that type is built from polygons that approximate the surface of the object. Every object consists of a list of vertices and a list of faces, with the vertices of each face defined by pointers to the vertex list; this allows each vertex to be transformed exactly once, even though several faces may share one vertex.

Polygonal meshes have one great advantage - applying projecting transformation to each of the polygon vertices is equivalent to transforming the polygon. In other words it is not necessary to transform every point in a polygon, just the vertices. Likewise, transformation of all the polygon vertices in an object fully transforms that object.

More than that, it's possible to make polygonal representation more mathematically consistent by using triangulation. It's important, because a polygon having more vertices than a triangle isn't necessarily flat in 3D space. Polygons that aren't flat may cause serious errors in rendering. That's why you have to check each polygon for 'flatness', especially in interactive systems.

It seems that the polygonal model is closely related to computer aided design systems where it's the basic representation. It relies on accompanying software tools for creating 3D shapes. Of course, it would be excellent to have an interactive 3D object generator, such as 3D Shaper, with resource editing, and perhaps we'll write our own... one day.

However, there is a problem with the polygonal model. The computational cost of most rendering procedures increases, at least linearly, with the number of polygons, and this number must be great to produce a smooth picture. Consider this - you have to solve a simple equation to find out where a ray intersects a sphere, and you have to perform even more complex calculations for each polygon of the model. Moreover, handmade polygonal models can hardly be used for natural scenes, such as landscapes, because too many polygons are needed for a realistic appearance.

Taking into account all the pros and cons, we decided to organize our 3D framework in a slightly different way. The system provides a kind of abstract, virtual programmers interface. All that it requires from an object is answers to a set of predefined questions and the fulfillment of a set of predefined actions. It supports radically different sorts of graphical objects with unique methods of drawing, shading, or texture mapping.

Eliminating the Invisible

In this section, rather than giving a detailed discussion on particular polygonal models of 3D surfaces, we will describe a specific example. We'll consider one traditional method of scientific visualization called **grid graphics**. What does the term mean? Suppose you have a function F(x,y), defined in the box Xmin < x < Xmax and Ymin < y < Ymax and you want to see it as a surface in 3D.

In most cases, the function F(x,y) is tabulated so it's simply a big matrix. One interesting association is that you can use any of your bitmap images as F (row, column) and see it as a relief. Suppose you make a quadrangular mesh, so that the vertices of a polygon (i,j) are:

```
(xi,yj,    F(xi,yj))        (xi+1,yj,    F(xi+1,yj))
(xi,yj+1,  F(x,yj+1))       (xi+1,yj+1,  F(xi+1,yj+1))
```

Sample Grid Surface Drawn by Lines

If you draw this mesh with the **draw_poly** routine you'll get something like the previous figure. Yes, this representation appears more visual than a table, but still it can, and should, be enhanced. Why? It's simply because some unnecessary faces have been drawn:

- ▲ hidden surfaces - the polygons that are screened by the others;

- ▲ back surfaces - each polygon has two visible sides, say upper and lower, which should be distinguishable;

Hidden Surfaces

There are various methods for treating hidden surfaces. The best, and the slowest without special hardware support, is z-buffering, where each pixel is checked as it's drawn to see whether it's the foremost at those co-ordinates. The simplest (and sometimes the fastest) technique relies on that obvious fact that if objects are drawn in reverse order, the nearer ones are drawn on top.

This technique is known as the painter's algorithm. Look at the figure below, the painter's algorithm works well for functions displayed as grids. Moreover, in this particular case, you don't even have to sort anything. You only have to find the most distant corner of the (Xmin < x < Xmax, Ymin < y < Ymax) box and start drawing from there.

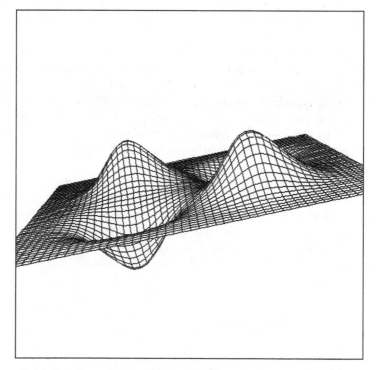

Grid Surface Drawn Using the Painter's Algorithm

Sorting by depth is fast, but it has at least two serious shortcomings:

-  it relies on accurate drawing of nonconvex objects, so if you draw a sphere with a hole, the area of the screen covered by the hole must remain unchanged

- what point of the object should be used when sorting? The nearest? The anchor? Or the farthest one? No matter which point you prefer, some overlap cases won't be handled properly anyway.

One- and Two-sided Polygons: Backface Detection

The problem of backfaces sounds different for closed polygonal objects (polyhedrons) and for 'open' surfaces. The difference is obvious - you can see the back side of an open surface and you can't see the inner side of a closed polyhedron. So for open surfaces, you should only decorate backfaces (by color or something else), while for closed objects they must be removed.

Anyway it would be useful to have some 'spell' for quick detection of whether the inside or outside face of each polygon is facing us. This is especially important for closed objects, say in the case of a single convex polyhedron, where removal of the backfaces will also solve the problem of hidden surfaces.

Sure you can easily invent several backface checks of your own. However, if you try to, you'll find it rather difficult to make them work quickly. Fortunately, there is a trick that can help you with this problem. You may remember the operation of vector cross-product, which we defined in the vector arithmetic part of the projecting system. The result of cross-product is perpendicular to the plane in which the two original vectors lie. That's why, when normalized, it gives the unit normal to the plane.

So the recipe is simple. You take the cross-product of the vectors that form two edges of a polygon, the result being a vector perpendicular to the polygon; then, you mark the polygon as a backface if the cross-product vector points away from the viewer. Generally speaking, you don't even need the entire cross-product vector, but only its Z component (in the camera co-ordinate system), negative Z means a backface. The Z component can be calculated very efficiently, just by two multiplications and a subtraction.

However, we need one more thing to make it work. The cross-product can actually point either way, depending on the order in which we evaluate the edges of a polygon, so we have to establish a convention, say the first and the last edge in a clockwise direction.

 At the risk of disappointing you, I still have to mention that cross-product as a backface indicator works correctly only for flat polygons.

By the way, on the accompanying CD-ROM, you can find a demo program called **GRIDTEST**, which views any tabulated function as a surface, changing the view point on the fly.

3D Rendering

Shading

Now, how about adding more realistic colors to our surfaces? In the real world (or at least in our model of it), the intensity of color on a surface varies depending on how brightly it is illuminated. The possibility of simulating the illumination of a surface would contribute greatly to our system.

As we've established, the overall shading of a surface is the superimposition of several shading components. Let's recall the last formula for illuminance:

$$I = I_a k_a + (k_{diff} * \cos(\theta) + k_{mirr} * \cos^n(\alpha)) * I_r / (D + R)$$

where Ia and ka are the intensity and coefficient for the ambient component, Ir, kdiff, and kmirr. So for the diffuse and mirror ones, R is the distance to the object, D is the add-in constant, θ is the angle between the direction of light and surface normal, $\cos^n(\alpha)$ is the model function for intensity of mirror reflection which depends on the slope angle.

The following is clear: we have to calculate the illuminance for every point of the surface and assign the corresponding color to it. The ambient component is background light, all surfaces are equally illuminated by it, regardless of anything. Add it and forget it!

The diffuse component depends on the direction of light and the surface normal, and therefore has to be calculated, or at least approximated, for every point on the surface. Let's look into this taking a sphere as our surface. It's clear why we prefer them - because of the surface normal. For a point on a

unit sphere, the normal vector is just the vector to this point, due to the fact that we consider the center of the coordinate system to be the center of our sphere. Now about the direction of light, it's also a vector. Therefore we only need to find the cosine of the angle between these two vectors. Fortunately, this is pretty easy to do - just normalize the scalar (point) product (see vector arithmetic of the projecting system and also look at the figure below):

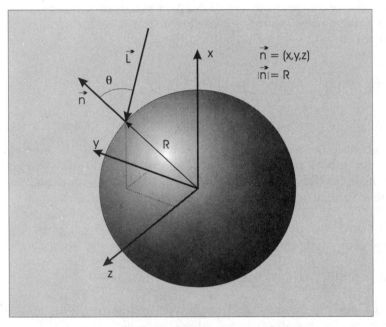

Diffuse Shading of a Sphere

That's easy enough to calculate, but for each point it seems slow. By the way, what points do we mean? If it's the points on the sphere, then it's bad news as there are so many of them. We'd better do the following: consider a circle on the screen which is the projection of the sphere. For each point (pixel) of this circle it's easy to calculate the corresponding point on the sphere, and therefore the desired normal vector, cosine, and at last the intensity of diffuse components. The only trick we have, is that the direction of the light vector must be reversed, just to get the cosine positive. Consider the code of the **make_sphere_brightness** routine at the end of this section and the demo program **SPHERE** amongst the sources for this chapter on the CD-ROM. This demo creates a flock of colored 3D spheres, flies them, and lets you interactively change all the parameters affecting the shading.

Shading is one of those rare techniques where you have to perform gamma correction yourself.

Thanks for mentioning this, GG. A possible implementation of gamma correction applied to shading may look like this:

```
int gamma_cor(int i,      // the level to correct
              int Imax,   // maximum intensity
              int Nmax,   // maximum number of levels
              float gamma)
{
   return round(Nmax * pow((double)i/Imax, 1.0/gamma));
}
```

Mirror Shading

It may sound like a joke, but it's possible to take the mirror component of the brightness into account in a similar way. The only difference is in the cosines, and unfortunately, they are a bit more complicated:

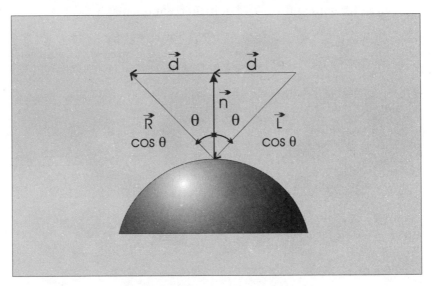

Mirror Shading of the Sphere

The plan is this. First, we have to obtain the vector of the reflected ray, and then find the cosine $\cos^n(\alpha)$ as a point product of the vector and the direction to the viewer V (0,0,1). If we make the size of the vector L, which is the direction of the light, equal to $|N / \cos(\theta)|$, where N is the normal to the point on the sphere, we'll be able to write the following two vector equivalencies:

$$d = L + N \quad \text{and} \quad d = R - N$$

where R is the reflected ray vector, $|N / \cos(\theta)|$ in size. Hence,

$$R = L - 2^* N * \cos(\theta)$$

and finally we have:

$$\cos(\alpha) = (L - 2 * N * \cos(\theta)) * V / |L - 2 * N * \cos(\theta)|$$

Additionally, we have to raise $\cos(\alpha)$ to the power of n, the Phong coefficient. Consider the following code fragment. It calculates the shading map for a sphere, considering both diffuse and mirror components:

```
void make_sphere_brightness(float lx, float ly, float lz,
                            float K_diff,float K_mirror, int n_Phong,
                            int r, BYTE map[])
{
   int r, lr, x, y, xk, yk;
   float lx_, ly_, lz_,
         yq, r_1, rq_1, l_norm, rq, z,
         dx, dy, dz,
         coef, delta,cos0, cosD,   bri;

   memset(map, 0, r * r * 4);
   r_1 = 1/r;
   l_norm = 1/sqrt (lx*lx + ly*ly + lz*lz);
   lx_ = lx * r_1* l_norm;
   ly_ = ly * r_1* l_norm;
   lz_ = lz * r_1* l_norm;

   rq = r * r;
   rq_1= 1/rq;
   for(y = -r; y < r; y++)
```

```
    {
      yq = y*y;
      lr= round(sqrt(rq-yq));
      for(x = -lr; x < lr; x++)
      {
        z = sqrt( abs(rq-x*x - yq));
        cosO = - ( lx*x + ly*y + lz*z );
// diffuse component is ready
// minus for light direction reverse
// now mirroring
        if (cosO>0)
        {
          coef = 2*cosO*rq_1;
          dx = lx + x*coef;
          dy = ly + y*coef;
          dz = lz + z*coef;
// the components of the auxiliary vector d (see Figure 13.#)

          cosD = dz / sqrt( dx*dx + dy*dy + dz*dz );
          delta = pow(cosD,2*n_Phong);
          bri = max( max_brightness * (K_diff*cosO + K_mirror*delta),
                     min_brightness ); // min_brightness for ambient
        }
        else
          bri = min_brightness;

        map[(map_dy-y)*map_dx + x+r] = min( max(min_brightness, round(bri) ),
                                            max_brightness);
      }
    }
  }
```

Traditional Polygonal Shading Techniques

For these techniques, we simply compute the brightness for each screen pixel of the object's projection.

The polygonal models are usually calculated from objects (not from their projections), which means that for each visible polygon, you have to find it's projection on the screen, the normal, and then the brightness of its pixels. Generally speaking all pixels of one polygon should have the same color. Nevertheless, interpolation is often used here to make the resulting image smoother.

You may meet the three following terms:

- ▲ flat shading - no interpolation,

- ▲ Gouraud shading - the color is interpolated,

- ▲ Phong shading - direction of the surface normal is interpolated.

The latter technique provides the best results. You can implement it yourself, but keep in mind that if you have too few polygons in your model, then no amount of shading will help you to make it smooth. On the other hand, if you have a lot of polygons in your model, their projections on the screen may be 3-5 pixels in size, which means that interpolation is hardly necessary.

Ray Tracing

Well, the shading technique can produce realistic 3D images of separate objects. Accurate calculation of the illumination gives you specular reflections on mirrored surfaces and even refraction. But as soon as you try to perform precise rendering of the whole scene which contains several objects and (but not 'or') light sources, simple shading fails, due to shadows. In other words, in order to calculate the brightness of a point, you have to check each light source for overshadowing and each object for specular reflection visible from this point. The magic that helps you do it is called ray tracing.

The key idea is pretty simple. First, you work with pixels of the actual screen. For each pixel you trace the ray, starting in the viewer's eye and passing through this particular pixel, until it meets an object of the scene. At this point, which we'll call a node point, you calculate the direction of the reflected and maybe refracted ray and trace them both further to the next reflection. The process goes on until each of the generated rays leaves the scene or enters a light source. When, you've traced a ray using this technique, you can trace it back calculating the illuminance of each node point, taking into account the ambient and diffuse components as well as the contribution of the oncoming reflected and refracted rays.

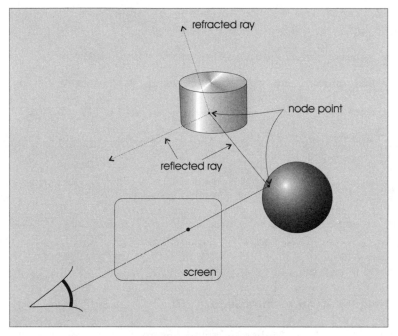

Ray Tracing Algorithm

 In other words, for each pixel, you gather the intensity of the through-passing light, contributed to by all the secondary sources in accordance with the rules of reflection and refraction.

There's a great deal written about this ray tracing technique, so we won't go too deeply into the details; code for the method **ray_tracing** of the class **scene** can be found on the accompanying CD-ROM). So here are some important tips:

Each new 'generation' may contain twice as many rays, so you should support a 'tree' of rays, because on some materials, rays can both reflect and refract. You should also note that if you give up support of transparent materials, you'll always have only one ray, but - alas! - no refraction.

Each new 3D object you add to the framework must have the following members if you plan it for ray trace rendering:

- **ray_sphere_check** - intersection check using the circumscribed sphere

- **ray_box_check** - intersection check using the circumscribed box

- **ray_section** - returns information about illuminance of the node point.

When you calculate the diffuse component of the illuminance at a node point, you should consider the preceding node merely as another light source.

The computational cost of ray tracing increases by at least:

(No. of objects) * (No. of sources) * (No. of reflections)

so don't forget to add a progress indicator into your ray tracer, or the user may get a bit annoyed. You can speed your ray tracing routine by putting a lower limit of illuminance, by which we mean that you neglect dimmer rays, without any great harm to the realism.

Note that if you set the number of reflections to 1, you'll see no reflections, but this will give you a tool for calculating and projecting shadows.

 Ray tracing is indeed a powerful technique. But actually, it's brilliant only for a precise generation of the mirror reflections, and it also manages shadows excellently. Ray tracing is usually regarded as a technique one level more complex than shading. But consider this, the shading you saw in the previous section is just simplified ray tracing.

Voxels

Opaque surfaces, mirror and textured faces are enough indeed to create a realistic natural scene. However, scientific visualization is once again pushing progress forward. Those greedy scientists now wish to see three-dimensional data. What kind of data? Well, consider a field of current or the propagation of gravitational waves.

In contrast to surface rendering, this class of computer visualization techniques is called volume rendering. The governing approach is, however, the most straight-forward. Assume that you have divided the volume in which your data is defined, into small, cubic pieces, which we are going to call voxels. Then you 'illuminate' or should we say 'irradiate', this volume and calculate the scattering and absorption.

Yes, some results of volume rendering look marvelous, and it's a practical way to see the unimaginable. We don't support volume rendering in our 3D framework because of its limited appeal. If you really feel the lack of voxel rendering on the PC, let us know.

3D Texture Mapping

Although we can already perform a kind of 3D rendering for various objects, we are still far from reality. That's because we have used an extremely simple model of the surface, which only describes perfectly polished or specially etched metals and plastics, some kinds of painted surfaces and, maybe even glass.

If you look around, you'll certainly notice that almost every surface has a kind of pattern on it. These patterns are called textures. Texture mapping is the term for techniques that provide such an appearance. It should be mentioned that the textures contribute a lot to a realistic 3D feel to the image. It's not easy to persuade a disbeliever that your image is in fact a wooden table, if you don't apply a wooden texture to it!

How can such mappings be performed? We have the image with a texture and set a correspondence between the elements on a 3D surface and the pixels of the image. Then we either:

▲ use a pixel value as the color of the corresponding surface element (paint the surface with the texture)

▲ 'modulate' the coefficient of diffuse reflection for each of R, G, and B

Now, how to set this correspondence. The most OOPed approach provides a kind of virtual solution - each object knows how to map its own personal texture. There are, however, some general techniques, two of which we'll illustrate here:

 flat mapping (usually for faces of polygonal models)

 spherical mapping: an approach that can work with an almost arbitrary object

Flat mapping is the easiest of the two. Generally speaking, it's just the same thing we've used in the image manipulation chapter for the rotation and scaling of a picture, so we won't go into any details. There is only one drawback. Everything goes fine while you use separate patterns for different polygonal faces, or a kind of local texture (like the binary sand we've used in the image processing chapter), but as soon as you want the pattern to continue beyond going from polygon to polygon, you hit a problem which, it seems, you can only solve interactively, if at all.

Spherical mapping is more sophisticated. Assume that we managed (somehow) to map the desired texture on a circumscribed sphere. If so, the problem of correspondence is immediately solved - we simply trace a ray from the center of the sphere, through the given point on the object, until it intersects with the sphere. The point on the sphere holds the texture information we need, and so we can start practising spherical mapping on the sphere itself.

Imagine the unit sphere defined in spherical co-ordinates. In the plane of angular co-ordinates (say, phi and theta) it looks like the rectangle 2pi×2pi. That's why, if we manage to find the angular components of spherical co-ordinates, it would reduce the problem to one of flat mapping. The following fragment of our routine calculates phi and theta (it goes into the routine **make_sphere_brightness** described in the previous sections):

```
...
if (Texture)
    {
    phi = acos((float)y/r);
    if (x<0) thetta=pi; else thetta=pi/2;
    if (x != 0) {
        buff = x/(r*sin(phi));
        if ((coef > -0.99) && (coef < 0.99))
        thetta = acos(buff);
        }
...
```

As you may remember, **x** and **y** are point co-ordinates, and **r** is the radius of the sphere.

The next function returns the texture coefficient, which is a floating-point value from 0.01 to 1.0, used to modulate Kdiff. Texture and diffuse reflections are considered achromatic for simplicity:

```
float spherical_texture(float phi, float thetta)
{
    int x,y;
    x = round(thetta/pi* (real_picture_pointer->column_number-1)+1);
    y = round(phi/pi*(real_picture_pointer->row_number-1)+1);
    return 0.99*(real_picture_pointer->pict[0][y][x] /255.0)+ 0.01;
}
```

Instead of the simple 'nearest neighbor' approach, you can use the interpolation technique introduced in the image manipulation chapter.

Finally the brightness of the point (diffuse component):

```
bri  =  max(max_brightness*(K_diff*spherical_texture(phi,theta)  *
                  cos0),  min_brightness);
```

where **cos0** is the cosine of the angle between the surface normal and the direction to the light source.

Bump Texture Mapping

Bump mapping was introduced by Jim Blinn in 1978 for more realistic shading of relief surfaces. The idea is pretty simple. Blinn considers a relief as a small displacement of the surface in the direction of its normal. The effect of a bumpy appearance occurs because of highlights on hills and shading in valleys. This representation is much simpler than realistic modeling of bumpy surfaces, say by means of the polygonal mesh.

More than that, Blinn managed to get the approximate formula for the normal of such a 'disturbed' surface in terms of the initial surface description, the displacement function, and their derivatives. Since then some simpler variants of the final formula were derived. It seems that the simplest one was proposed by K. Perlin:

$$Nd = (N +h)/|N+h|$$

where Nd and N are the unit normal vector for the disturbed and initial surfaces, and h is the gradient of the displacement function.

Bump Texture Mapping

If you like this image you can look for details of bump mapping implementation on the accompanying CD-ROM. Remember that for the displacement function h, defined as h(x,y), the gradient looks like this:

h= (dh(x,y)/dx, dh(x,y)/dy, -1)

If you'd like more information about this technique, look through the article by Nelson L. Max in the July (1994) issue of Computer Graphics and follow up the references given there.

Summary

This chapter has touched on most of the important topics connected with 3D graphics. It sometimes seems very strange that people are interested in 3D modeling on the PC, but the results are often encouraging and it is worth waiting hours for a hard-working Pentium machine. Anyway, we've given you an OOPed framework which allows you to go further and invent your own objects and models and textures, and even your own optical laws (well why not?).

Chapter 14

APPENDIX A

VESA BIOS Extension

As promised, we'll now have a look at the VESA BIOS extension (Versions 1.0 and 1.1). The VESA extension defined 8 calls at INT 10h function 4Fh. At the time of writing, most manufacturers have included the VESA Extension into the ROM BIOS or helped their devices along with VESA counterparts.

Appendix Contents

In this appendix, we will cover:

Adapter Compatibility

VESA extensions help to solve the problem of adapter incompatibility, so making SVGA programming much simpler. The main advantages that VESA provides are:

 A standard way to get all the information on supported SVGA modes necessary for programming.

▲ A standard table of SVGA modes. You can skip the manufacturer's unique modes, but these are accessible too.

▲ A standard solution for bank switching.

We'll divide the 8 VESA calls into two parts: information service functions and actions, and we'll start with information.

VESA BIOS Functions

Each function reports Status in AX. The meanings are as follows:

AL = 4Fh   Function supported.
AL != 4Fh   Function not supported.
AH = 00h   OK.
AH = 01h   The call fails.

Function 00h Return SVGA Information
Description
Used to confirm the VESA compatibility of the adapter and also to get vendor-specific information about the hardware.

A 256-byte buffer should be reserved to hold the returned information.

Input
    AX   Set to 4f00h
    ES:DI far pointer to the 256 byte buffer.

Output

AX   Status

The table now located in **ES:DI** has the following structure:

Name	Offset	Size (bytes)	Description
VESASignature	0	4	Signature usually ('VESA')
VESAVersion	4	2	VESA version number
OEMStringPtr	6	4	Far pointer to OEM string
Capabilities	10	4	Capabilities (currently undefined)
VideoModePtr	14	4	Far pointer to the mode table
MemoryAmount (version 1.1)	18	2	64K memory blocks installed

The higher byte of the VESA version field specifies the major version number and the lower one the minor version number. All future revisions will be compatible with version 1.0.

The OEMStringPtr field is a far pointer to a null terminated OEM-defined string, which may be used to identify the video chip, adapter configuration and so on. There are no standards as to what you will find here, but you will probably find the manufacturer's name and adapter type.

The Capabilities field is currently reserved. In a future version, it may specify general features of the adapter.

The mode table is simply a list of the supported mode numbers, terminated by 0FFFFh. Each mode number is a 16-bit word defining either a VESA standard SVGA or a manufacture-specific mode. Standard VESA modes begin with 100h. Vendor-specific modes cover the range 14h-7Fh with the exception of 6Ah which is the original VESA scout.

The MemoryAmount field contains video memory size in 64K blocks. For example, an adapter with 1M would return 10h.

Function 01h Return SVGA Mode Information

Description

Used to get information about a particular SVGA mode.

A 256-byte buffer should be reserved to hold the return information.

Input

AX	Set to 4f01h
ES:DI	far pointer to the 256 byte buffer.

Output

AX	Status

The table now located in **ES:DI** has the following structure:

Name	Offset	Size (bytes)	Description
ModeAttributes	0	2	Mode attributes
WinAAttributes	2	1	Window A attributes
WinBAttributes	3	1	Window B attributes
WinGranularity	4	2	Window granularity
WinSize	6	2	Window size
WinASegment	8	2	Segment address of Window A
WinBSegment	10	2	Segment address of Window B
WinFuncPtr	12	4	Address of the Window Function Call
BytesPerScnLine	16	2	Bytes per scan line

Continued

XResolution	18	2	Horizontal resolution
YResolution	20	2	Vertical resolution
XCharSize	22	1	Character cell width
YCharSize	23	1	Character cell height
NumberOfPlanes	24	1	Number of bit planes
BitsPerPixel	25	1	Total number of bits per pixel
NumberOfBanks	26	1	Number of memory banks
MemoryModel	27	1	Memory model type
BankSize	28	1	Size of memory bank in Kb
NumberOfPages	29	1	Number of display pages available
	30	1	Reserved.

For version 1.2, the SVGA Mode Information Block contains 6 or 7 more fields. We can easily guess what these fields mean - they deal with RGB components in HighColor and TrueColor modes. Nevertheless, we've omitted that specific information here, you'll have to find the description of the standard elsewhere.

Fields with offsets 0 - 16 are obligatory, 18 and above are optional. The optional part of the Mode Information Block is mostly used for manufacture-specific modes. If this information is available, bit 1 of the mode attributes will be set.

Mode attribute bit meanings:

Bit	Description
0	Set to 1 if the hardware configuration supports this mode
1	Set to 1 if the optional mode information is available
2	Set to 1 if the BIOS functions (PutPixel,..) support this mode

Continued

Bit	Description
3	Set to 1 if the mode is color (register and memory configuration not the monitor type)
4	Set to 1 if the mode is a graphics one
5-15	Reserved

When programming in SVGA modes (both VESA standard and vendor-specific) using BIOS functions, you should remember that some functions are not supported - just the most useful, such as PutPixel, or write string. The presence or absence of such support can be determined through this function call (bit 2).

The function 01h also returns information on the mode's windowing method. You can get it by reading the status bits of the WinA(B)Attributes field.

Bit	Description
0	Set to 1 if particular window exists
1	Set to 1 if the window is readable
2	Set to 1 if the window is writable
3-7	Reserved

Window Granularity is the smallest step allowed when the addressing Window is moved, or switched, within the video memory.

WinSize is usually 64K or 32K. WinA(B)Segment is simply the CPU segment address for the window.

WinFuncPtr is the address of the routine that changes the starting offset of a Window, such as when it executes a bank switch. A far call to this address is much faster than using the BIOS call (4F05h). Unlike the BIOS call, registers are not preserved by the direct call, and **AX** will not contain any return information.

The optional X and Y resolution information will be in either character cell units (for text modes) or pixel (for graphics modes). XCharSize and YCharSize are character cell sizes, measured in pixels. NumberOfPlanes usually 4 for 16 color modes and 1 for 256 and higher modes. The BitsPerPixel field determines the number of colors available.

The MemoryModel is defined like this:

Value	Memory Model
0	Text Mode
1	CGA Graphics
2	Hercules Graphics
3	4-plane planar
4	Packed pixel
5	Non-chain 4, 256-color
6	HighColor & TrueColor modes (Version 1.2)
7-0fh	Reserved by VESA
10h-0ffh	Vendor defined

Version 1.1 adds a new field The NumberOfPages which returns the maximum number of screen buffers available for page switching (like the standard BIOS display pages).

Function 02h Set SVGA Mode

Description

Used to set a SVGA mode instead of call 0h (standard video BIOS Set Mode). Bit 15 works like bit 7 of the standard VGA Set Mode. If the call fails, the mode doesn't change and the old environment remains.

Not all VESA adapters will support every mode. You should use functions 4f00h and 4f01h to determine which modes are available. Manufacturer-specific modes may also be set by this function call.

Input

AX   Set to 4F02h
BX   SVGA mode number

Output

AX   Status

Function 03h Return SVGA Mode

Description

Obtains the current SVGA Mode. This call should be used instead of call 0Fh (standard video BIOS Current VideoState). All modes including standard VGA, VESA, and vendor specific may be determined through this call.

Input

AX   set to 4F03h

Output

AX   Status
BX   Mode Number

Function 04h Save/Restore SVGA Video State

Description

This function contains three subfunctions which save and restore SVGA state information and report the required buffer size in 64 byte blocks. This function is analogous to the standard BIOS function 1Ch (Save/Restore Video State). Unlike the standard function, the structure of the memory blocks is unique and contains additional SVGA information.

Input

AX   set to 4f04h
CX   Selected States

Four possible 'states' may be saved in various combinations depending on the **CX** value:

CX's Bit	Description
0	Video Hardware state (registers)
1	BIOS Data state
2	DAC state
3	SVGA state

Output

Which particular subfunction will be called depends on the value of the **DL** register:

Subfunction	DL	Output	
Get Buffer Size	0	**AX**	Status
		BX	Buffer Size Required (in 64 byte blocks)
Save state	1	**AX**	Status
Restore state	2	**AX**	Status

Function 05h Video Memory Window Control
Description

This function contains two subfunctions which are used to set or get the position of a specified window in the video memory. You can control both windows A and B. Function 05h is used to perform bank switching by means of VESA BIOS. The offset is specified in the units of Window Granularity (see function 4F01h field WinGranularity).

The value of Window Granularity may differ for different adapters. For example, the Paradise SVGA (Western Digital) has a 4K Granularity thus possible bank offsets from the beginning of Video memory may be 0, 4K, 8K and so on. As was mentioned above, you may take advantage of direct far calling instead of using this function to improve performance.

Input - Output

AX   set to 4f05h

Which particular subfunction will be called depends on the value of the **BH** register:

Subfunction	BH	Input		Output	
Set Window Position	0	**BL**	Window Number 0=Window A, 1=Window B)	**AX**	Status
		DX	Offset in video memory (in granularity units)		
Get Window Position	1	**BL**	Window Number (0=Window A, 1=Window B)	**AX**	Status
				DX	Offset in video memory (in granularity units)

Example of SwitchBank by means of VESA BIOS Extension and a direct far call. Note that the Granularity is considered to be 64K:

```
SwitchBank   proc    near     ;DX = bank nubmer
    push  bx
    xor   bx,bx              ;BH = 0 (Set Window Position)
                            ;BL = 0 (Window A)
    mov   ax,4f05h          ;Video Memory Control function
    int   10h               ;perform switch bank
    pop   bx
    ret
SwitchBank   endp
```

```
SwitchBank   proc    near     ;DX = bank nubmer
    push  bx
    xor   bx,bx              ;BH = 0 (Set Window Position)
                            ;BL = 0 (Window A)
    call  dword ptr WinFuncPtr  ;perform switch bank
    pop   bx
    ret
SwitchBank   endp
```

Function 06h Get/Set Logical Scan Line Length

(Version 1.1 and later)

Description

This function contains two subfunctions which set and report the BytesPerLine value. Thus it helps you to display something larger than the physical display size, handling the situation when the CRT will show only a portion of the full picture. This is useful for good old tricks such as smooth horizontal scrolling and panning (see also function 4f07h). Additionally, it may be used to pad out the length of the scan line to prevent a scan line from splitting across 64K segments.

> The line lengths are requested in pixels. You may ask for any value you like, but you can hardly predict whether your VESA hardware will consider it valid or not. You should try different settings to obtain the rule your particular adapter obeys. Some of them will round up the value specified to make it 16 (or 8) pixels aligned, some will set only aligned values. The function may or may not work in the True and HighColor modes. Don't worry, VESA is a young standard, and it's certainly worth some patience. The actual value you've set may be checked by the output of Subfunction 1.

Input - Output

AX   set to 4F06h

Which particular subfunction will be called depends on the value of the BL register:

Subfunction	BL	Input		Output	
Set Scan Line Length	0	CX	New scan line length in pixels	AX	Status
				BX	Number of bytes in one scan line
				CX	Number of pixels in one scan line

Continued

Subfunction	BL	Input	Output	
Get Scan Line	1		DX	Maximum number scan lines (virtual vertical resolution)
			AX	Status
			BX	Number of bytes in one scan line
			CX	Number of pixels in one scan line
			DX	Maximum number of scan lines (virtual vertical resolution)

Function 07h Get/Set Start of Display

(Version 1.1 and later)

Description

This function contains one of two subfunctions which is used to set or get the starting address, by which we mean the address of the upper left corner, of the physical CRT image within the virtual one. This makes smooth scrolling possible (see function 4F06h), or switching of display page in multiple pages mode.

The offsets are specified in horizontal and vertical pixels. Again, try this function before relying on it for anything serious.

Input and Output

AX   set to 4f07h

Again, which subfunction will be called depends on the value of the BL register.

Subfuction	BL	Input		Output	
Set Position	0	**BH**	0 (Reserved, must be 0)	**AX**	Status
		CX	Horizontal Pixel Offset		
		DX	Vertical Pixel Offset		
Get Position	1			**AX**	Status
				BH	0 (Reserved, always 0)
				CX	Horizontal Pixel Offset
				DX	Vertical Pixel Offset

INDEX

The Book

The Beginner's Guide To C++

The ideal start for the newcomer to the world of programming languages. This Beginner's Guide contains comprehensive coverage of the language syntax. You will

The Beginner's Guide to C++

master procedural programming in easy stages, and then learn object

Author - O. Yaroshenko

oriented programming - the essential programming methodology of the future.

ISBN - 1-874416-26-5

The Series

BEGINNER'S GUIDE TO ....

These guides are designed for beginners to the particular language or to programming in general. The style is friendly and the emphasis is on learning by doing. The chapters focus on useful examples that illustrate important areas of the language. The wealth of examples and figues help make the transition from beginner to programmer both easy and successful.

The Book

The Revolutionary Guide to OOP

Using C ++   Benefit from the authors' years

of experience using C and C++ in some of the

most complex and demanding programming

environments around today. This book aims to

ease the difficulties in making the transition from

The Revolutionary Guide to OOP Using C++

C to C++, and will show you the power of object-oriented C++.
Authors - V. Olshevsky

A. Ponomarev

ISBN - 1-874416-18-4

The Series

REVOLUTIONARY GUIDE TO .....

Learning the programming techniques

of the industry experts with the

Revolutionary Guides. This series guides you

through the lastest technology to bring your skills

right up to date. Example applications are used to illustrate new

concepts and to give you practical experience in the language.

The Book

C++ is widely taught as a first programming

language because of its power and simplicity.

This book provides wide coverage of the C++

programming language aimed squarely at

the beginner to C++.

Instant C++ Programming
Author: Ian Wilks $19.95
ISBN 1-874416-29-X

INSTANT....................

Designed as a rapid introduction to the

programming language, these books deliver

fundamental essential knowledge in an

entertaining, painless way. These books are

ideal for student looking for a swift grounding,

or indeed for anyone wanting to make a quick

breakthough into programming profficiency

The Series

Assembly Language Master Class

Authors: P. Kalachin, Y. Kiselev and I, Chebotko.

Price: $44.99

ISBN 1-874416-34-6

Assembly Language Master Class covers

the 386, 486 and Pentium processors, this guide

gives aspiring experts a tutorial covering subjects

such asdirect SVGA access, serial communications,

device drivers, protected mode and Windows, and

virus protection secrets.

............*MASTER CLASS*

The aim of this series is to bring together the ideas

of a number of the leading edge experts in one

indispensable book. Each chapter has a defined

objective built around the key application areas of

the language.